THE SINCERE CHRISTIAN: VOLUME I

By

Right Rev. Bishop George Hay

In Five Volumes

VOL. I.

Edited Under the Supervision of the
The Right Rev. Bishop Strain

St Athanasius Press

ISBN: 979-8-9911176-3-0

CONTENTS

A Short Account of the Right Rev. George Hay
By
John Menzies Strain

Memoir

Since the religious revolution of the sixteenth century, to no man has the Catholic Church in Scotland been so much indebted as to Bishop Hay. He is pre-eminently her bishop of the last three hundred years.

He appeared at a time when the prospects of religion in this country were the most gloomy — when Catholic interests and Catholic hopes had sunk to the lowest point. At present it is difficult, if not impossible, fully to realise what was then the position of Catholics in Scotland. The systematic work of depression which had been carried on for years by the grinding operation of the penal laws, seemed to be completed by the disastrous rising in favour of the Stuarts in 1745. With their cause all the Catholic families of wealth and influence in the kingdom had identified themselves, and the result was widespread ruin.

The Catholic body was left crushed and dispirited. Many fled to seek an asylum in foreign countries; and those who still clung to their native land were, with few exceptions, stripped of everything.

In their poverty and sufferings it was difficult for them even to retain their faith. They were without churches, and almost without pastors to minister to their spiritual wants or to impart instruction; and consequently, not only individuals but many entire families fell away from their religion. In this trying crisis, the zeal, energy, and apostolic labours of a single, unpretending, but truly great prelate, contributed materially to the preservation of the faith. Indeed he may be justly said to have gathered together and consolidated the scattered fragments of the ancient Church in Scotland, for much of what she now possesses is the result of his wise and vigorous administration.

The Right Rev. Dr George Hay was born at Edinburgh, August 24, 1729. He was the only son of Mr James Hay, a non-juring Episcopalian, who had been put in irons and sentenced to banishment for his adherence to the Stuarts in 1715. From his mother he received early religious impressions, and by her was taught the practice of night and morning prayer, a circumstance to which he looked back with gratitude in later life. Being destined

5

for the medical profession, in his sixteenth year he entered the Edinburgh University, then rising to the zenith of its fame. There he rapidly distinguished himself in his studies; and some of his fellow-students, themselves eminent, afterwards declared that had he persevered, he would have stood at the head of his profession. But his medical studies were interrupted, and finally abandoned.

The Highland army, under Prince Charles Stuart, entered Edinburgh on the 17th September 1745, and found many of the citizens secretly disposed to favour them. Mr George Lauder, Mr Hay's professor, was an enthusiast in the cause, and many of his pupils were animated by the same spirit. He was appointed chief surgeon to the Prince's army, and, in a few days, was called to attend the wounded on the field of Prestonpans. Mr Hay, who had been educated in the politicfal principles of his family, willingly accompanied his professor, and followed the fortunes of the army in its march into England.

On its retreat, his health being broken by exposure and fatigue, he was unable to proceed beyond Crieff, and therefore returned to Edinburgh in February 1746. As he had served not in a military but purely professional capacity, assisting indiscriminately the sick and wounded of both armies, he hoped he would be put to no trouble. He was soon undeceived, however, for he was first committed to Edinburgh Castle for three months, and thence removed to London along with other prisoners implicated in the same cause. In London his captivity was not a rigorous one, but twelve months elapsed before his liberation under the Habeas Corpus Act in June 1747.

For himself he had no longer any cause of apprehension, but fearing lest he might be cited in evidence against some of the unfortunate adherents of the Stuarts, he retired to the seat of Sir Walter Montgomery, a relative in Ayrshire. As soon as all danger of this seemed past, he returned to Edinburgh and resumed his medical studies. Other important matters, however, now occupied his thoughts. Naturally he was of a serious cast of mind, and this had been strengthened by early training. But that he had no Catholic tendencies is sufficiently evident from the fact, that in the fervour of youth he had bound himself by a double vow to read a portion of the Bible daily, and to do his utmost to extirpate Popery from his native country. In London, however, he had chanced to hear the doctrines of the Catholic Church explained by an English gentleman, in a manner which excited his surprise; and in his retreat in Ayrshire he had fallen upon a well-known little work,

A Papist represented and misrepresented, or a twofold character of Popery. Doubts were excited in his mind, and Air Hay was not of a character to set aside doubts upon an important subject without due investigation.

As the surest means of obtaining correct information regarding the Catholic faith, he resolved to apply to a Catholic priest, and accordingly obtained an introduction to Sir Alexander Seaton, the Jesuit missionary, then resident in Edinburgh. From him he received the information and explanation he desired, and after a lengthened course of instruction was received into the Catholic Church. On the Feast of St Thomas, 21st December 1749, he made his first communion with extraordinary fervour — a fervour in which he happily persevered to the end of his long and useful life.

Mr Hay, in embracing the Catholic faith, had no idea of relinquishing the medical profession. On the contrary, he continued to prosecute his studies with his characteristic vigour, became a member of the Royal Medical Society, and took a lively interest in everything becoming his position. He soon discovered, however, that his prospects of success in life must be materially injured by his change of religion. By the penal laws he was debarred from graduating in the University, and from obtaining the diploma of the Royal College of Surgeons. These restrictions naturally excited a desire of leaving Scotland, and of retiring to some foreign country where he might enjoy liberty of conscience and have the prospect of rising in his profession. With this view he accepted the appointment of surgeon on board a trading-vessel chartered for the Mediterranean.

While in London making the necessary arrangements for his departure, he was introduced to the illustrious Bishop Challoner, who was himself a convert, and could therefore sympathise with the young Scotch surgeon, driven from his home by the intolerant laws of his country. The Bishop soon discovered his genuine worth. He admired his vigorous intellect, sound judgment, and depth of religious feeling, and was probably in no small degree instrumental in leading Mr Hay to devote himself to the service of God and his neighbour in the ecclesiastical state. Certain it is that the acquaintance of these two remarkable men at this time led to their being afterwards united in the bonds of the closest friendship. At a later period they entered into a pious compact, that on the death of either, the survivor should offer up the holy sacrifice three times every week for the repose of his soul; and this engagement Dr Hay fulfilled with scrupulous fidelity for nearly a quarter of a century after the decease of his esteemed friend.

But whatever was the advice given by Dr Challoner at this time, or whatever effect it may have had upon Mr Hay's mind, he was not a person to
decide hastily in such an important matter. He took full time for mature
deliberation, proceeded to the Mediterranean, completed his engagement
there, and it was not till the 10th September 175 1 that he entered the
Scotch College in Rome — nearly two years after he had embraced the
Catholic faith. There he found only nine students, but that little band contained no less than four persons who were afterwards well known by their
services to religion — the Rev. William Guthrie, Bishop Geddes, Bishop
John M Donald, and Cardinal Erskine.

In Rome he spent eight years in the study of philosophy and theology, and
his progress is well attested by the valuable works with which he afterwards
favoured the world. But his chief care during his college life was to sanctify himself, by the exact and fervent discharge of all his religious duties.
Having completed his course of studies in the Scotch College, he was
ordained priest, and immediately set out for the scene of his future labours,
accompanied by the Rev. Messrs John Geddes and William Guthrie. They
travelled through France and embarked at Dunkirk; but knowing that the
greatest vigilance was exercised by the British Government to prevent the
ingress of Catholic priests, they avoided the principal ports, and landed at
Burntisland on the eve of the Assumption, 1759. Next day they presented themselves to Bishop Smith at Edinburgh, and Mr Hay was appointed
to assist Bishop Grant, coadjutor in the important mission of Preshome,
Banffshire. Here he began his missionary career, and laboured for eight
years with untiring zeal in the work of the ministry — preaching, administering the sacraments, and promoting ever}pious practice among the
faithful.

On the death of Bishop Smith, in 1767, Mr Hay was appointed to accompany Bishop Grant, now Vicar Apostolic, to Edinburgh, to arrange the
papers of the deceased prelate. This he executed to the satisfaction of all
concerned, discharging at the same time the duties of procurator of the
mission, and serving the congregation.

Bishop Grant, whose constitution had been shattered by rigorous confinement in the prison of Inverness, soon perceived that his increasing infirmities rendered the nomination of a coadjutor and successor necessary,
and he felt no hesitation in making his selection. The piety, learning, and
ability of Mr Hay recommended him as the person eminently qualified for
the arduous and difficult position. Bishop Grant therefore procured his

appointment, and, assisted by Drs Hugh and John M'Donald, consecrated him Bishop of Daulia (in partibus) at Scalan on Trinity Sunday, the 19th May 1769.

From that day the whole burden of the Vicariate may be said to have devolved on him; for the Vicar Apostolic, no longer able to perform the duties of his office, transferred all his faculties to his coadjutor. Henceforth Bishop Hay becomes more properly a subject of history than of biography, for a full account of his life would necessarily embrace all the important events connected with the Catholic Church in Scotland during his long episcopate.

Bishop Hay was unremitting in his attention to his flock, hearing confessions, visiting the sick, and giving instructions almost continuously. Preaching he regarded as the indispensable duty of every pastor of souls; and he himself was most assiduous in that duty. He spoke in a plain, familiar, and unaffected style; and his discourses, enriched with a variety of texts from Holy Scripture, were admirably calculated to convince the understanding and to gain the heart. His edifying example stimulated the zeal of the clergy under his charge, and his frequent Pastorals enlightened and directed them in the discharge of their duties.

To the general interests of his extensive Vicariate Dr Hay gave the most vigilant attention, visiting the various missions and corresponding frequently with his clergy. But his active charity did not rest there; he published the first English Catholic version of the Holy Scriptures printed in Scotland, and made incredible exertions to supply the faithful with pious and instructive books. He composed several excellent works in defence of religion, and entered with ardour into all the measures, then in agitation, for the repeal of the penal laws against Catholics. To attend to such a multiplicity of affairs must have necessitated a rigorous disposition of time, but the regularity of Dr Hay's life enabled him to utilise every moment. He rose very early, made an hour's meditation, recited Prime, Tierce, Sext, and None; then prepared himself, by long and fervent acts of devotion, for saying Mass; heard another, if possible; and concluded his morning exercises with spiritual reading, from the best ascetic writers. The day he devoted to business, and in the evening recited the Divine Office. At eight o'clock he retired for an hour's contemplation before the blessed Sacrament; and after supper and evening prayers, resumed his studies till midnight, when he usually retired to rest. The life of this holy bishop was a finished model of that humility and self-denial which he so strenuously inculcated in his writings.

Yet Bishop Hay was always cheerful and agreeable. His virtue had nothing in it gloomy or morose, for, though severe to himself, he was ever condescending and tender to others. Conformity to the will of God was his favourite virtue and the subject of his daily meditation. Hence arose that resignation to all the appointments of Divine Providence which no accident seemed capable of disturbing, and that meekness which the most injurious treatment could not arouse to resentment. To aid others in acquiring this virtue of conformity, he made a collection of the different passages of Scripture in which it is enforced; and he used to comment on them with singular delight and devotion. The serenity of his mind was truly marvellous. Once only — on learning that His Holiness, Pius VI., was a prisoner in the hands of the French Revolutionists — was it observed to give way, and then but for a short time. He retired to his orator}-, and there, in presence of the blessed Sacrament, soon regained his usual placid resignation. His peace rested on God, and nothing earthly could permanently disturb it. It may readily be supposed that the claims of the poor were not disregarded by such a man as Bishop Hay. They received due attention at his hands. In the frequent visitation of his Vicariate he distributed liberal alms, and gave medical advice to the sick poor who could not procure a physician.

Not long after his promotion to the episcopate, the Catholics in the island of Uist were subjected to a cruel persecution. One of the principal proprietors of the island, wishing to eradicate the ancient faith, served notice of ejectment upon all the Catholics on his estate, leaving them the choice of apostasy or eviction. The poor people at once adopted the only alternative which conscience allowed, and were ruthlessly driven from their homes. The misery of the persecuted and suffering islanders aroused the active sympathy of Bishop Hay. He made a powerful and successful appeal on their behalf to the charity of the Catholics of Great Britain, and by this means enabled them to cross over to North America. They were accompanied in their forced exile by Mr Macdonald of Glenaladale, who sold his property in Scotland, and generously devoted himself to the protection of his poor countrymen. Thus commenced that system of emigration which eventually depopulated many parts of the Highlands, and laid the foundation of a powerful and prosperous Catholic colony in North America. The brave exiles transmitted their faith to their descendants, and taught them to revere the memory of their benefactor. Bishop Hay.

Bishop Hay first appeared as an author in 1771, in a spirited detection of the errors contained in a sermon published by a celebrated Presbyterian minister of Aberdeen. This was followed by his Letters on Usury and Interest, in which he throws much light on a difficult subject, and reconciles the practice of taking interest with the doctrine of the Scriptures. The dispute upon the subject of miracles between Dr Middleton and his antagonists, induced Bishop Hay to write his Scripture Doctrine of Miracles Displayed, which is, perhaps, the best work that has appeared on that difficult and important subject. Not long after, his Sincere, Devout, and Pious Christian were successively laid before the public, and were received with much favour. The Catholic Bishops of Ireland bestowed on them the highest encomiums, and strongly recommended them to the use of the faithful. The reputation of Dr Hay as an author was now established, and the most distinguished prelates in both kingdoms entered into correspondence with him. The British Government having at length evinced a disposition to repeal some of the most oppressive of the penal laws which had so long been a disgrace to the legislature. Bishop Hay seized the favourable moment to procure some relief for the Catholics of Scotland, who felt even more heavily than their brethren in England and Ireland the iron rod of persecution. The fanatics, all over Scotland, immediately took alarm. Declarations and Resolutions were everywhere published against the mitigation of the penal statutes. The press teemed with misrepresentations and calumnies, the pulpits resounded with furious invectives against Catholics. The popular fury was especially directed against the Bishop, and a day was fixed for burning the chapel and house which he had lately built in Chalmers' Close, High Street. Handbills were distributed inviting all to aid in the good work, as it was impiously termed; and at length, on the 2d of February 1779, the mob assembled, and, with the assistance of five hundred sailors from Leith, proceeded to their work of destruction. Repeated applications were made to the Lord Provost for protection against the rioters, but he was deaf to all entreaties. The Duke of Buccleuch, and some other officers, fired with indignation at such daring excesses, hastened, with a few troops, to the spot, seized the most forward of the incendiaries, and would have dispersed the mob, but the authorities positively refused to allow him to proceed, and the work of destruction went on. The chapel and house were soon reduced to ashes, and the rabble then spread themselves over the city, burning and destroying everything belonging to Catholics which came in their way. At this crisis Bishop Hay arrived from London, and, unaware of the state of matters, proceeded on his way home. The unusual crowd in the street, however, soon attracted his attention, and addressing a woman whom he met near the foot of Blackfriars Wynd, he asked her what it meant. "Oh, sir," she replied, "we are burning the Popish chapel, and we only wish we had the Bishop to throw him into the fire." — (Abbé Macpherson's Hist, of Scott. Missions.) The Bishop prudently turned aside, and found an asylum in the Castle, where a number of his flock had taken refuge.

The next morning the mob plundered the chapel-house in Blackfriars Wynd, and attempted to destroy the residence of Principal Robertson, who had courageously opposed their lawless proceedings on the previous day.

After a few days Bishop Hay returned to London, and, through the interest of Mr Burke and other influential friends in Parliament, succeeded in obtaining some indemnification for the sufferers in the riot. The erection of another chapel and chapel-house in Edinburgh, however, was retarded for many years. Dr Hay deemed it prudent to continue in his humble dwelling in Blackfriars Wynd, and to use the upper floor as a chapel. It was not till 1814 that St Mary's, Broughton Street, was built by his successor, Bishop Cameron.
Upon the death of Bishop Grant in 1778, Bishop Hay became Vicar Apostolic, and selected the Rev. John Geddes, his college companion, a clergyman of distinguished merit, as coadjutor.

The Scotch College at Rome had, for some years, been in a very unsatisfactory state. Those intrusted with the administration of it, after the suppression of the Jesuits, had given occasion to many complaints. Repeated remonstrances proved ineffectual, and at length Bishop Hay resolved to go in person and lay the case before His Holiness. His desire to have the Statuta Missionis approved and printed furnished a pretext for the journey, and he set out for Italy in the summer of 1781. Passing through Germany, he visited the Scotch Benedictine monasteries at Wurtsburg and Ratisbon, and. arrived in Rome about the middle of October. Cardinal Antonelli, Prefect of Propaganda, received him with marked distinction, and soon after he was admitted to a private audience of the Holy Father. His great object was to get national superiors placed in the Scotch College. After repeated conferences on the subject with Albani, Cardinal Protector of Scotland, he obtained his consent to the immediate admission of a member of the Scotch mission, with a promise that in a little time the entire administration should be placed in his hands. Many years elapsed, however, before the desired change was effected.

After a stay of six months at Rome, Bishop Hay returned to Scotland. Soon after his arrival, the illness and subsequent death of the Rev. Andrew Dawson obliged him to remove to Scalan. Here, in addition to the work of the mission, he superintended the cultivation of the farm attached to the Seminary, composed small treatises for the use of the students, and taught them the elements of literature. His leisure moments he devoted to the study of metaphysics, for which he had a special predilection, and made a compendium of Reid's Inquiry into the Human Mind. From this congenial employment he was recalled, by the illness of Bishop Geddes, to resume his former functions in Edinburgh, where affairs of vital importance soon absorbed his whole attention.

By the destruction of the Scotch Missionary Colleges on the Continent, the prospect of future labourers in the ministry was destroyed. This calamity was deeply felt by Bishop Hay, but it did not shake his confidence in God. With his usual energy he applied himself to remedy the evil, and though possessed of very slender means, began to build a new Seminary at Aquhorties. Thither, on its completion in 1799, he removed the students from Scalan, and laid the foundation of an establishment which afterwards supplied Scotland with many distinguished priests.

All hope of the recovery of Bishop Geddes being now at an end, Dr Hay was obliged to nominate another coadjutor, and after mature deliberation he made choice of the Rev. Alexander Cameron. From personal acquaintance with this gentleman, he had formed a high idea of his virtue and talents; and that idea had been confirmed by the ability which Mr Cameron had displayed in the government of the Scotch College in Spain. The appointment gave general satisfaction, and Dr Hay applied to Rome for the Papal Briefs. On the 13th of August 1797 he informed Mr Cameron himself of his promotion, conjuring him to hasten to his assistance, and to relieve him of a burden which he was no longer able to support. The distracted state of the Continent, however, prevented Bishop Cameron, for a considerable time, from undertaking his journey; but at length, tranquillity being restored by the peace of Amiens, he embarked for Scotland.

On the 20th of August 1802, Mr Cameron arrived in Edinburgh; and Bishop Hay, following the example of his predecessor, Bishop Grant, immediately imparted to him complete faculties to govern the Vicariate. It was, indeed, his anxious wish to be entirely freed from the responsibility of his charge; but this being a case specially reserved to the Holy See, he could not resign without the express permission of the Holy Father. Cardinal Antonelli, to whom he had, long before, intimated his desire, positively refused to countenance any application of the kind, and insisted, in the name of the Sacred Congregation, that he should continue to govern the Mission while he had strength to do so. Indeed it was only a few years before his death, when mental and bodily prostration rendered it impossible for him any longer to superintend the affairs of the Vicariate, that His Holiness could be prevailed upon to accept his resignation.

The zeal and prudence of his coadjutor, however, did much to lessen the burden of responsibility on Dr Hay, and to reconcile him to his position. He had unbounded confidence in Dr Cameron, and he, on his part, did nothing without the advice and consent of his superior.

At length he was relieved of his charge, and he retired to the Seminary at Aquhorties to prepare for death. Here he devoted himself to prayer and pious reading until his mental faculties began to give way. The intense study and continual mortification of his long and active life had worn him out, and he sank, literally exhausted by labour, into a second childhood. In this state, rendered still more affecting by the loss of speech from paralysis, he continued for nearly two years, enjoying, in other respects, comparatively good health. At last a severe illness exhausted his remaining strength, and he gradually sank till his death, on the 15th of October 1811, in the eighty-third year of his age, and forty-third of his episcopal dignity.

The influence which Bishop Hay had so long exercised in the cause of religion did not die with him. It has been perpetuated and extended by his writings. Nor is this surprising when we consider their character and spirit. The study of the Holy Scriptures was the comfort and the solace of his life; and his writings show how copiously he drew from that sacred source. Indeed, in perusing them we forget the individual and see before us only a saintly prelate filled with the thought of God and His Divine truth, teaching and exhorting through the Scriptures. The more we examine his works, the more clearly do we see how appropriately they bear their unpretending, but expressive, title — The Sincere, Devout, and Pious Christian, instructed in the faith of Christ from the Written Word.

THE
SINCERE CHRISTIAN
INSTRUCTED IN
THE FAITH OF CHRIST FROM THE
WRITTEN WORD.

INTRODUCTION

JESUS CHRIST, the eternal wisdom of God, who is Himself "the way, the truth, and the life" addressing His heavenly Father, pronounces this sacred oracle: "This is eternal life, that they may know Thee, the only true God, and Jesus Christ, whom Thou has sent," John xvii. 3.

The securing to ourselves eternal life is the great end for which we were created; it is the "one thing necessary" without which we are lost for ever; it is an affair of all others the most important, or rather, it is the only important affair we have to think of: "For what shall it profit a man, if he gain the whole world, and lose his own soul? Or what shall a man give in exchange for his soul?" Mark viii. 36. Seeing, then, that the knowledge of God the Father, and of Jesus Christ, His Son, in such a manner as we are capable of knowing Them in this world, is declared by Christ Himself to be the eternal life of our souls — that is, to be the necessary and undoubted means of acquiring that eternal life, and of bringing us to the full knowledge and possession of God in the world to come — how much ought we to esteem that Divine knowledge! How assiduous and careful ought we to be to get ourselves fully instructed in it!

What will it profit a man to know all things else, if he be ignorant of his God and of his Saviour? What though he understand the motions of the stars, the measure of the earth, and the whole circle of human sciences, if he be ignorant of that important science, the science of the saints, which alone will conduct him to eternal bliss? "If any man consents not," says St Paul, "to the sound words of our Lord Jesus Christ, and to that doctrine which is according to godliness, he is proud, knowing nothing, but sick about questions and strifes of words," I Tim. vi. 3. To promote this heavenly wisdom among men, to instruct the ignorant in the knowledge of the great truths of God and of eternity, has at all times been esteemed by the Christian world as a most sublime employment: and God Himself has promised a most ample reward to those who practise it, saying, by His holy prophet Daniel, "They that are learned shall shine as the brightness of the firmament, and they that instruct many to justice, as stars for all eternity," Dan.

xii. 3. Hence it is, that, in every age, we find men of the greatest genius and learning, who have employed themselves with great zeal in instructing the ignorant in the truths of salvation, both by their apostolical labours during their lifetime, and by the pious monuments of their charity and zeal which they have left behind them in their valuable writings, for the benefit of future ages. ' To contribute my mite towards so laudable a purpose is the design of the present publication; to which I have been induced by several considerations.

I have often thought that the great truths of Christianity, if digested in a regular orderly method, so that the establishing one point should be a prelude and preparation to the next, would show that Divine religion in a more amiable point of view, and be a great ease and help both to those who are to instruct others, and to those who are learners: this idea has been confirmed by frequent experience, and I hope that the method which I have found so useful may prove equally beneficial to others. There are many excellent works published in our language upon different parts of religion; but I am afraid they too often suppose the generality of their readers better instructed in these matters than they commonly are, and are written more for the learned than the ignorant. The view I have had in this present work is to assist the most unlearned, and beginning with the first rudiments of Christianity, to conduct the reader, step by step, through the whole body of the principal truths of revelation, so that the knowledge of one truth may serve as an introduction to those which follow.

The sacred Scriptures are an inexhaustible fountain of heavenly knowl-edge, but are commonly less used than they might be in illustrating and establishing the truths of religion. A text or two hinted at now and then seem lost in the multitude of other reflections and reasons which surround them; but, when the principal stress both of the explanation and proof is laid upon these Divine oracles, and a number of texts are placed in the proper order for illustrating the point in question, they give an incredible force to what is proposed, show that it is God Himself who speaks, and cut off all occasion for human sophistry to enter. This I have had in a particu-lar manner in view in these instructions, and have endeavoured to collect together the several testimonies of the Word of God where the point in question is explained, illustrated, or established; that, showing the constant uniform doctrine of the Holy Scripture, I might bring full and complete conviction to the mind. Some may perhaps think I have crowded too many texts together on some occasions; but I have had in view the benefit of those who are to instruct others, that they may have a proper variety out of which to choose what they may find, by experience, to be most adapted to the various capacities of their pupils.

After this brief explanation of the plan and design of the work, I have only two things to recommend to my readers. The first is, to make themselves masters of one chapter before they proceed to another — to consider it well, to comprehend it, to penetrate the force of the reasons used in it. This will render the understanding of what follows easier, and, at the same time, more satisfactory and convincing. The second thing is, when examining the proofs from Scripture brought for any controverted point, not to consider so much how far the ingenuity of man could wrest the meaning of any particular text to a sense different from what it is brought to prove; but to consider what is the plain, natural, obvious meaning of all the various texts brought together in proof of the point proposed; for this surely must be presumed to be the sense intended by the Holy Ghost.

CHAPTER I.

OF GOD.

Q. I.What is God?

A. God is a Spirit infinitely perfect, the Creator and Sovereign Lord of all things.

Q. 2. What do you mean by a Spirit?

A. An immaterial being, quite distinct from body. Now God is a most pure, uncreated Spirit, without any body; and those expressions of Scripture where mention is made of the hands of God, or His feet, or the like, are only figurative ways of speaking, accommodated to our weak understandings.

Q. 3. What do you mean by infinitely perfect?

A. I mean that all possible perfections essentially belong to God, and are in Him in an infinite degree, without bounds or limitation.

Q. 4. What are the perfections of God?

A. Power, wisdom, goodness, justice, mercy, holiness, truth, beauty, eternity, immensity, and many others, of which we can have no idea. So that God is infinitely powerful, infinitely wise, infinitely good, infinitely just, infinitely merciful, infinitely holy, infinitely true, infinitely beautiful, eternal, immense, and unchangeable.

Q. 5. What do you mean by infinitely powerful?

A. I mean that God can do all things whatsoever He pleases, and in what manner He pleases; so that nothing is impossible or difficult to Him.

Q. 6. How does this appear from Scripture?

A. On this head the Scripture declares (1.) That "with God all things are possible," Mat. xix. 26; and that "no word shall be impossible with God," Luke, i. 37. (2.) That He created this world, and all that it contains, out of nothing, by His word alone; for "in the beginning God created the heavens and the earth," Gen. i. i. "He made the heavens and the earth, the sea and all things that are in them," Ps. cxlv. 6. "In Him were all things created, in heaven and on earth, visible and invisible, whether thrones or dominations, or principalities or powers, all things were created by Him and in Him," Col. i. 16. "He spoke the word, and they were made; He commanded, and they were created," Ps. cxlviii. 5. (3.) That He can do in all creatures whatsoever He pleases; for "whatsoever the Lord pleased He hath done in heaven, in earth, in the sea, and in all the depths," Ps. cxxxiv. 6, (4.) That "all things are in His power, and that there is none that can resist His will," Esther, xiii. 9; for "He alone is mighty, the King of kings, and Lord of lords," i Tim. vi. 15.

Q. 7. What do you mean by infinitely wise?

A. I mean that God knows all things, past, present, and to come, even the most secret thoughts of the heart of man, and all things that possibly can be.

Q. 8. How is this proved?

A. His holy Word declares that "there is no creature invisible in His sight; for all things are naked and open in the eyes of Him with whom we speak," Heb. iv. 13. "The works of all flesh are before Him, and there is nothing hid from his eyes; He sees from eternity to eternity, and there is nothing wonderful before Him," Ecclus. xxxix. 24. "For the eyes of the Lord are far brighter than the sun, beholding round about all the ways of men, and the bottom of the deep, and looking into the hearts of men, into the most secret parts; for all things were known to the Lord God before they were created; so also after they were perfected, He beholdeth all things," Ecclus., xxiii. 28. "The heart is perverse above all things, and unsearchable, who can know it? I am the Lord who search the heart and prove the reins," Jer. xvii. 10.

Q. 9. What do you mean by infinitely good?

A. I mean that as God is infinitely perfect and infinitely happy in Himself, so He has the most earnest desire of communicating Himself and His happiness to His creatures, and, in consequence of this, is continually bestowing good things upon them, according as they are capable of receiving them; for "every good and perfect gift is from above, coming down from the Father of lights," James, i. 17. And God "giveth to all abundantly, and upbraideth not," James, i. 5. All the creatures by whose means we receive any benefit are but the instruments God makes use of to communicate good things to us; for "there is none good but God alone," Luke, xviii. 19.

Q. 10. What do you mean by infinitely just?

A. I mean that God gives to all men the necessary means of saving their souls, and will never require any thing of us above our strength; so that we only are to blame, if we fail in our duty to Him: that, therefore, He will exercise the most impartial justice on all men, according to their deservings, without respect of persons; for, as St Paul assures us, God will "render to every one according to his works; to them indeed who, according to patience in good works, seek glory, and honour, and incorruption, (He will render) eternal life; but to them who are contentious, and obey not the truth, but give credit to iniquity, (He will render) wrath and indignation," Rom. ii. 6. That "He will not judge according to the sight of the eye, nor argue according to the hearing of the ear, but will judge in justice," Isa. xi. 3; and that "He will not accept of any person, nor receive any gift," Deut. X. 17.

Q. 11. What do you mean by infinitely merciful?

A. I mean that God has the most tender compassion for the miseries of His creatures, knowing their frailty and their weaknesses, and is most desirous and ready to deliver them from them; "He wills none to perish, but that all should come to repentance," 2 Pet. iii. 9. "For, as T live, saith the Lord, I will not the death of a sinner; but rather that he should turn and live," Ezek. xxxiii. 11. Hence "the Lord is gracious and merciful, patient and plenteous in mercy: the Lord is sweet to all, and His tender mercies are over all His works," Ps. cxliv. 8; and "His mercy endureth for ever," Ps. cxxxv. Yea, in the midst "of anger He will remember mercy," Hab. iii. 2. For "as a father hath compassion on his children, so hath the Lord compassion on them that fear Him; for He knoweth our frame. He remembereth that we are dust. . . . But the mercy of the Lord is from eternity to eternity, upon them that fear Him," Ps. cii. 13. Hence, "Thou hast mercy upon all, because Thou canst do all things, and overlookest the sins of men for the sake of repentance; for Thou lovest all things that are, and hatest none of the things that Thou hast made; for Thou didst not appoint or make any thing hating it. . . . But Thou sparest all, because they are Thine, O Lord, who lovest souls," Wis. xi. 24.

Q. 12. What do you mean by infinitely holy?

A. I mean that God is holiness itself, infinitely pure, and free from every spot or stain, or shadow of imperfection. Hence He is called in Scripture the Holy of Holies; and the blessed in heaven continually adore Him under this title, saying, "Holy, holy, holy. Lord God of Hosts," Isa. vi. 3.

Q. 13. What do you mean by infinitely true?

A. I mean that God is truth itself; that He never can be deceived Himself, and that it is impossible He should deceive His creatures; for "God is true, but all men are liars," Rom. iii. 4. "God is not like men, that He should lie," Num. xxiii. 19. "God is faithful in all His words," Ps. cxliv. 13. "And heaven and earth shall pass away; but My words," says He, "shall not pass away," Luke, xxi. 33.

Q. 14. What do you mean by infinitely beautiful?

A. I mean that God is beauty itself, infinitely lovely, infinitely excellent; that all the beauty and perfections which we see in creatures are but emanations of His divine beauty; and that, though all the beauties of the whole universe were collected together in one, it would be infinitely less than a spark of fire is to the sun, or a drop of water to the ocean, if compared to the beauty of God. "Let them know how much more the Lord of them is more beautiful than they; for the First Author of beauty made all those things," Wis. xiii. 3. For from the rising of the sun to the going down thereof, out of Sion the loveliness of His beauty," Ps. xlix. i. This Divine beauty is so great that all the blessed saints and angels in heaven are enraptured with inexpressible delight in the contemplation of it, and the enjoyment of it makes God Himself infinitely and essentially happy. Hence the Scripture says: "O taste and see how sweet the Lord is; blessed is the man that hopeth in Him," Ps. lxxxiii. 9. "They shall be inebriated with the plenty of Thy house, and Thou shalt make them drink of the torrent of Thy pleasures; for with Thee is the fountain of life, and in Thy light we shall see light," Ps. xxxv. 9. "O how great is the multitude of Thy sweetness, O Lord, which Thou hast hidden for them that fear Thee! . . . Thou shalt hide them in the secret of Thy face," Ps. xxx. 20, 21.

Q. 15. What do you mean when you say God is eternal?

A. I mean that God had no beginning, and will have no end; that He always was, is, and ever will be; for "thus sayeth the High and the Eminent who inhabiteth eternity," Isa. lvii. 15. "Thou art the same, and Thy years shall not fail," Heb. i. 12. "I am the first and the last, — and behold I live for ever and ever," Rev. i. 17.

Q. 16. Had God no beginning?

A. No; God is a self-existent, necessary Being; from Himself alone, and wholly independent on any other; and therefore never had, nor could have, any beginning, but must have been from all eternity. Hence He says of Himself to Moses, "I am who am; thus shalt thou say to the children of Israel, He who is hath sent me to you," Exod. iii. 14. In order to show that He alone is essentially, and that all things else are a mere nothing in comparison to Him, according to that text, "Behold the nations are as a drop of a bucket, and are counted as the smallest grain of a balance; behold the islands are as a little dust ... all nations are before Him as if they had no being at all, and are counted to him as nothing and vanity," Isa. xl. 15, 17.

Q. 17. What do you mean by the immensity of God?

A. I mean that God filleth all places and all things, and that He is intimately present in all creatures; for "in Him we live, and move, and have our being," Acts, xvii. 28. "He is higher than the heavens, and what wilt thou do? He is deeper than hell, and how wilt thou know? The measure of Him is longer than the earth, and broader than the sea," Job xi. 8. "Am I, think ye, a God at hand, saith the Lord, and not a God afar off? Shall a man be hid in secret places, and I not see him? saith the Lord. Do not I fill the heaven and the earth? saith the Lord," Jer. xxiii. 23, 24. Hence the royal Prophet cries out to God: "If I ascend up to heaven, Thou art there; if I descend into hell. Thou art there; if I take to me the wings of the morning, and dwell in the uttermost parts of the sea, even there also shall Thy hand lead me, and Thy right hand shall hold me,'" Ps. cxxxviii. 8. "O Israel, how great is the house of God, and how vast is the place of His possession! It is great, and hath no end; it is high and immense," Bar. iii. 24.

Q. 18. Is it possible for us to comprehend God?

A. No, no. It is impossible for any creature to comprehend God; for how can finite comprehend what is infinite? how can the creature comprehend the Creator? Hence the Scripture says: "O most mighty, great, and powerful, the Lord of Hosts is Thy name; great in counsel, and incomprehensible in thought," Jer. xxxii. 16. "Behold God is great, exceeding our knowledge; the number of His years is inestimable,'" Job xxxvi. 26. "He dwelleth in light inaccessible, whom no man hath seen, nor can see," i Tim. vi. i6. "The Lord is the everlasting God, who hath created the ends of the earth; He shall not faint nor labour, neither is there any searching out of His wisdom," Jer. xl. 28. "We shall say much, and yet shall want words; but the sum of our words is, He is all. What shall we be able to do to glorify Him? For the Almighty Himself is above all His works. The Lord is terrible, and exceeding great, and His power is admirable. Glorify the Lord as much as ever you can, for He will yet far exceed; and His magnificence is wonderful. Blessing the Lord, exalt Him as much as you can, for He is above all praise. When you exalt Him, put forth all your strength, and be not weary; for you can never go far enough," Ecclus. xliii. 29, &c.

Q. 19. Is God capable of changing?

A. No; God is always the same, and altogether incapable of any manner of change whatever. Thus the Holy Scripture declares, "God is not as man that He should lie, nor as the son of man that He should be changed; "Num. xxiii. 19. And God Himself says, "I am the Lord, and I change not," Mai. iii. 6. Hence the royal Prophet shows this great difference between God and creatures, that "they shall perish," says he to God, "but Thou remainest; and all of them shall grow old like a garment, and as a vesture Thou shalt change them, and they shall be changed; but Thou art always the self-same, and Thy years shall not fail," Ps. ci. 27. And St James declares, that with "God there is no change, nor shadow of alteration," James, i. 17.

Q. 20. Why then is God said to be sorry, to repent, to be angry, or the like?

A. These are only figurative expressions, accommodated to our way of conceiving things, and only mean, that God so acts in His external conduct as if such changes actually happened in Him; but, as "the works of all flesh are before Him, and there is nothing hid from His eyes, and as He sees from eternity to eternity, and there is nothing wonderful before Him" (Ecclus. xxxix. 24), so nothing can be new to Him; past, present, and to come, are all continually present to Him: nothing can happen in time but He sees from eternity; hence nothing can make any new impression in Him, or cause any change to sorrow, anger, or repentance in Him.

CHAPTER II.

Of The Blessed Trinity.

Q. I. What do you understand by the Trinity?

A. I understand that there is but one living and true God, and that in God there are three distinct Persons, called the Father, the Son, and the Holy Ghost.

Q. 2. What do you mean by One God?

A. I mean that the Divine Nature, the Divine Substance, the Divinity, or the Godhead, which all signify the same, is but one - and therefore that God is one; and that there cannot possibly be more than one such divine Nature, nor more than one God, seeing that God is immense and infinite, and filleth all places and all things.

Q. 3. How does the unity of God appear from Scripture?

A. In Scripture it is thus declared: "Hear, O Israel, the Lord thy God is one Lord," Deut. vi. 4 . And all the wonderful things that God did for His people, when He brought them out of the land of Egypt, are declared to have been wrought expressly that "they might know that the Lord He is God, and beside Him there is no other," Deut. iv. 35 . And God Himself, by Moses, says: "See ye that I alone am, and there is no other God besides Me; I will kill, and will make alive; I will strike, and I will heal; and there is none that can deliver out of my hand," Deut. xxxii. 39. And by Isaiah, He says, "I am the first and the last, and besides Me there is no God," Isa. xliv. 6 . Hence He expressly commands us, "Thou shalt have no other God but Me," Exod. xx.

Q. 4. Can it be shown from the Old Testament that there are three Persons in God?

A. Yes, it can; "For God said, Let Us make man to Our image and likeness," Gen. i. 26 , where these words, God said, show the unity of the Godhead; and these other, Let Us make, and to Our image, show the plurality of the Persons. So also, "God said, Lo, Adam is become as one of Us, knowing good and evil," Gen. iii. 22 , where the same truth appears. Again, "The Lord said to my Lord . . . from the womb, before the day-star, I begot Thee,"

Ps. cix. 1 , 3, where God the Father speaks to God the Son as to a distinct person. Also God the Son says, "I am appointed King by Him over Sion, His holy mountain, preaching His commandment: the Lord hath said to Me, Thou art My Son, this day have I begotten Thee," Ps. ii. 6 , 7. Lastly, "By the Word of the Lord the heavens were established, and all the powers of them by the Spirit of His mouth," Ps. xxxii. 6 , where all the three Persons are expressly mentioned, the Lord, who is the Father, the Word of the Lord, who is the Son; and the Spirit of the Lord, who is the Holy Ghost.

Q. 5. How is the Trinity of the Persons shown from the New Testament?

A. This appears from several texts of Scripture; thus, our Saviour says, "I will ask the Father, and He will give you another Comforter, the Spirit of Truth," John, xiv. 16 , where the three persons are clearly pointed out as distinct Persons - to wit, God the Son, who speaks, I will ask; God the Father, of whom He promises to ask; and God the Holy Spirit, who, He promises, shall be given. So also, "There are three who bear testimony in heaven - the Father, the Word, and the Holy Ghost, and these three are One," i John, v. 7 . Here the Trinity of the Persons and the Unity of the Godhead are expressly declared. Hence the Apostles are commanded to baptise "in the name of the Father, and of the Son, and of the Holy Ghost." In the name, and not in the names, to show there is but one God; and "of the Father, and of the Son, and of the Holy Ghost," to show there are three Persons in God.

Q. 6. Are these three Persons really distinct among Themselves?

A. Yes, They are really distinct Persons, as appears from the above sentence, spoken by Jesus Christ, where He says, "I will ask the Father, and He will give you another Comforter . . . the Spirit of Truth," John, xiv. 16 ; for one who asks is evidently a distinct person from the one of whom he asks; and the one who is given is distinct from him by whom he is given.

Q. 7. How else does it appear that the three Persons are distinct among Themselves?

A. Because each of the three has certain personal properties which the others have not; and we can say with truth of the one what cannot be said of the others.

Q. 8. What are the personal properties of the Father which cannot be said of the Son or of the Holy Ghost?

A. That the Father is from no other, neither made, nor created, nor begotten; but is the Origin or Principle from whom the other two Persons proceed, and therefore He is called it first Person, and the Father.

Q. 9. What are the personal properties of the Son?

A. That He is begotten of the Father from all eternity, and proceeds from the Father only, and therefore is called the second Person, the Word, and the Son of God; according to that text, "Thou art My Son, this day have T begotten Thee,"Ps. ii. 7. And again, "The Lord said to my Lord, . . . from the womb, before the day-star, I begot Thee," Ps. cix. 1 , 3. Also, "This is My beloved Son in whom I am well pleased," Mat. iii. 17 . And, "God so loved the world, that He gave His only begotten Son," John, iii. 16 .

Q. 10. What are the personal properties of the Holy Ghost?

A. That He proceeds both from the Father and the Son, and therefore is the third Person, and is called the Holy Ghost, and the Spirit of God, and the Spirit of Truth: thus God the Son says: '• When the Paraclete Cometh, whom I will send you from the Father, the Spirit of Truth, who proceedeth from the Father," John, xv. 26 ; where it is plain that the Holy Ghost is sent by the Son from the Father, and therefore must proceed from both. Again He says: "The Holy Ghost, whom the Father will send in My name, He will teach you all things," John, xiv. 26 . Here the Holy Ghost is said to be sent by the Father in the name of the Son; in the former texts. He is said to be sent by the Son from the Father, which shows He is equally sent by both, and therefore proceedeth or comes from both. Lastly, God the Son says, - He (the Spirit of Truth) shall receive of Mine, and shall show it you," John, xvi. 14 .

Q. 11. Does the distinction of the Persons appear in any thing else than in Their personal properties?

A. Yes; it appears also from this, that God the Father "spared not even His own Son, but delivered Him up for us all," Rom. viii. 32 . And God the Son being thus delivered up by His Father, was made man, and died upon the Cross for the sins of the world; but it cannot be said that the Father or the Holy Ghost was delivered up, or made man, and died for us; which evidently shows the Son to be a distinct Person from the Father and the Holy Ghost. In like manner the Holy Ghost appeared in the form of a dove upon our Saviour after His baptism, Mat. iii. i6; and in the form of fiery tongues upon the Apostles on Pentecost , Acts, ii. 3 ; but it cannot be said that either the Father or Son appeared in this manner; which shows the Holy Ghost to be a distinct Person from them.

Q. 12. Is the second Person really and truly God, equal to the Father from all eternity, and of the same substance or nature with Him?

A. Yes, He is; our holy faith assures us of this in the strongest terms. Thus, "In the beginning was the Word, and the Word was with God, and the Word was God. . . . And the Word was made flesh," John, i. 1 , 14. In which text the Word, or the second Person, the same that was made flesh, is expressly declared to be God, and the Word was God. So God the Son declares, "I and the Father are one," John, x. 30 - that is, one in substance, one in nature, one God. Of the Redeemer, the ruler in Israel, it is said, "His going forth is from the beginning, from the days of eternity," Mich. v. 2 . Of Christ, St Paul says, "Who being in the form of God, thought it no robbery to be equal with God," Philip, ii. 6 ; and again, "Christ is over all things, God blessed for ever. Amen," - Rom. ix. 5 .

Q. 13. Is the Holy Ghost also true God?

A. Our holy faith assures us of this also. Thus St Peter first said to Ananias, "Why hath Satan tempted thy heart, that thou shouldst lie to the Holy Ghost?" and then adds, "Thou hast not lied to men, but to God," Acts, V. 3 , 4. The Divine perfections, also, are attributed to the Holy Ghost in Scripture - to wit, immensity: "The Spirit of the Lord hath filled the whole world," Wis. i. 7 ; and omniscience, "The Spirit (of God) searcheth all things, yea the deep things of God," i Cor. ii. 10 ; and He is associated with the Father and the Son in baptism, as being the same God with Them.

Q. 14. If all the three Persons be God, and at the same time be distinct among Themselves, why are They not three distinct Gods?

A. Because They all three, though distinct Persons, have but one and the self-same Divine nature, the same Divine substance, the same Godhead. Now the Divine nature being infinite and immense, cannot possibly be multiplied or more than one, but is the self-same in all the three Persons; who, therefore, are but one and the self-same God, have all the same Divine perfections, and are equal in all things.

Q. 15. But how can we conceive or comprehend this?

A. It is impossible for us to comprehend it. In the simplicity of our heart
we believe it is so, because God Himself has revealed it. He alone perfectly
knows and comprehends Himself: it is impossible for us, poor finite creatures, to know more of Him than what He is pleased to discover of Himself
to us. Seeing, then, that He has revealed that there is but one only God,
and that in God there are three distinct Persons, this we are to believe as a
certain and Divine truth, without presuming to search further, or to know
more about Him than He is pleased we should know; for the Scripture says,
"He that searcheth into Majesty, shall be overwhelmed by glory," Prov. xxv.
1 .

CHAPTER III.

Of The Creation And Providence

Q. What do you mean when you say that God is the Creator and Sovereign Lord of all things?

A. I mean that this one only living and true God, one in substance, and three in Persons, created the heavens and the earth, and all that they contain, all things visible and invisible; and that He still continues to preserve, govern, and dispose of all things according to His own good will and pleasure.

Q. 2. What do you mean by created all things?

A. I mean that God made all things out of nothing, by His word alone; for, as the Scripture expresseth it, "He calleth those things that are not, as those that are," Rom. iv. 17 . "He spoke, and they were made; He commanded, and they were created," Ps. cxlviii. 5 . "And God said. Be light made; and light was made. . . , And God said. Let the waters that are under the heaven be gathered into one place, and let the dry land appear; and it was done so," Gen. i. 9 . "And God said, Let the earth bring forth the green herb; . . . and it was done so,"; Gen. i. 11. And of the Son it is said, "All things were made by Him, and without Him was made nothing that was made," John, i. 3 . Also, "In Him were all things created, in heaven and in earth, visible and invisible. . . . All things were created by Him and in Him," Col. i. 16 . Lastly, of the Holy Ghost the Scripture says: "In the beginning God created the heaven and the earth; . . . and the Spirit of God moved over the waters," Gen. i. 2 . "His Spirit hath adorned the heavens, and His artful hand hath brought forth the winding serpent," Job, xxvi. 13 . "By the word of the Lord the heavens were established, and all the power
of them by the Spirit of His mouth," Ps. xxxii. 6 . "There is one most high Creator, almighty and a powerful King, and greatly to be feared, who sitteth upon His throne, and is the God of dominion, He created her (to wit, wisdom) in the Holy Ghost," Ecclus. i. 8 , 9.

Q. 3. Had, then, this world a beginning?

A. Yes, it had; and the Scripture says, "In the beginning God created the heaven and the earth," Gen. i. 1 .

Q. 4. What was there before this world began?

A. Nothing but God alone, who had no beginning, but was from all eternity, perfectly happy in Himself, and in His own Divine perfections.

Q. 5. Why did God create this world?

A. Not out of any necessity, or through force, but out of His own free will
and good pleasure, and for His own glory: "for the Lord hath made all
things for Himself," Prov. xvi. 4 . And "Every one that calleth upon My
name, saith He, I have created him for My glory, I have formed him and
made him," Isa. xliii. 7 . Hence the saints in heaven continually cry out to
Him, "Thou art worthy, O Lord, to receive glory, and honour, and power;
for Thou hast created all things, and for Thy pleasure they are and were created," Rev. iv. 11 .

Q. What do you mean by these words, for His own glory?

A. I mean that God, by creating intelligent beings, capable of knowing
and loving Him, and inferior creatures for their use and benefit, displays
to those beings His own Divine perfections, His infinite power, wisdom,
and goodness, that they may give glory to Him, and render Him the just
homage of love, gratitude, obedience, and praise. Thus the Holy Scripture,
speaking of the creation of man, says, "God set His eyes upon their hearts,
to show them the greatness of His works, that they might praise the name
which He hath sanctified, and glory in His wondrous acts," Ecclus. xvii. 7 ,
8.

Q. 7. Does God still continue to preserve all things in the being which He
gave them, or can they subsist without Him, once they are made?

A. As God alone has being essentially and of Himself, and is independent of any other, so no creature has any being at all of itself, but is wholly
dependent upon God, without whose continual preservation no creature
could subsist for one instant; so that, were God for an instant to withdraw
His almighty hand from any creature, it would immediately fall back to
its primitive nothingness; for "He upholdeth all things by the word of His
power," Heb. i. 3 . "He is before all, and by Him all things consist," Col. i.
17 . And therefore the wise man justly said to God, "How could anything
endure if Thou wouldst not? or be preserved, if not called by Thee?" Wis.
xi. 26 . On this account, God the Son declares that He and His Father are

always working - to wit, by the continual preservation of all creatures. "But Jesus answered them, My Father worketh until now, and I work,'" John, v. 17 .

Q. 8. Can God destroy the whole world if He will, and in what manner soever he pleases?

A. Most undoubtedly; for as all creatures depend entirely on Him, and have their very being and all their powers and faculties only from Him, and at His pleasure; so He is sole master, to do with all and every one of them what He wills, nor is there anything that can resist or oppose Him. Hence He says Himself, "My word which shall go forth from My mouth, shall not return to Me void; but it shall do whatever I please, and shall prosper in the things for which I sent it," Isa. lv. II. And the royal Prophet declares that "the Lord is great, and our God is above all gods; whatsoever the Lord pleased. He hath done in heaven, in earth, in the sea, and in all the depths," Ps. cxxxiv. 5 , 6. "All the inhabitants of the earth are reputed as nothing before Him; and He doth according to His will, as well with the powers of heaven as among the inhabitants of the earth; and there is none that can resist His hand, and say to Him, Why hast Thou done it?" Dan. iv. 32 . This was the comfort of the servants of God in their distress: "We trust, said they, in the Almighty Lord, who at a beck can utterly destroy both them that come against us, and the whole world," 2 Mac. viii. 18 . And the Holy Scriptures are full of the wonderful effects of His almighty power, and of His absolute dominion over all His creatures. There we are informed that at one time he stopped the course of the sun for several hours, that at another He made it even go back for ten degrees on the dial, and that He deprived it of its light at the death of Christ; that He divided the Red Sea into two, and gave His people a passage through the midst of it on dry ground; that He rained down food to them from heaven in the desert; that He gave them water out of the hard rock; that He changed the waters in Egypt into blood, and at the marriage of Cana into exquisite wine; that He hindered the fiery furnace from touching His faithful servants who were thrown into it; that He raised the dead to life, commanded the winds and sea, cured all diseases, cast out devils, with many other such wonders, in an instant, and by His word alone; - so that the Scripture justly declares, that "the Lord is terrible and exceeding great, and His power is admirable," Ecclus. xliii. 31 ; for "He only is mighty, the King of kings, and Lord of lords," I Tim. vi. 15 .

Q. 9. Can creatures produce any effect, or do anything of themselves, without the concurrence of Almighty God?

A. All the powers which creatures have to produce anything are given them by God, and depend entirely on His preservation; they therefore are only as instruments in His hand for accomplishing His will, of which, however, he has no need. They, indeed, can act with His concurrence, according to the powers He has given them; but He is the original cause on which they and all the effects they produce depend. Thus it is God "who covereth the heavens with clouds, and prepareth rain for the earth; who maketh grass to grow on the mountains, and herbs for the service of man," Ps. cxlvi. 8 . Also, "The Most High hath created medicines out of the earth, . . . but all healing is from God," Ecclus. xxxviii. 2 . 4. For "it was neither herb nor mollifying plaster that healed them; but Thy word, O Lord, which heals all things," Wis. xvi. 12 . So, also, Isaiah says: "Lord, Thou wilt give us peace, for Thou has wrought all our works for us," Isa. xxvi. 12 . And St Paul: "There are diversities of operations; but it is the same God which worketh all in all," i Cor. xii. 6 . "Neither he that planteth is anything, nor he that watereth; but God that giveth the increase," i Cor. iii. 7 . For "without Me, saith God Himself, you can do nothing," John, xv. 5 ; and "it is God that worketh in you, both to will and to accomplish, according to His good will," Philip, ii. 13 .

Q. 10. Does, then, Almighty God rule, govern, and dispose of all creatures according to His will?

A. He certainly does; all things belong to Him: "The earth is the Lord's, and the fulness thereof; the world, and all that dwell therein," Ps. xxiii. 1 . He disposes of all things according to His own pleasure; for "He doth according to His will, as well with the powers of heaven as among the inhabitants of the earth," Dan. iv. 2 . He is the King, Lord, and Master of all creatures, and rules and governs them, and everything that happens among them, according to His eternal purposes: "There is one most high Creator, Almighty, and a powerful King, and greatly to be feared, who sitteth upon His throne, and is the God of dominion," Ecclus. i. 8 . "He that liveth for ever created all things together; God only shall be justified, and He remaineth an invincible King for ever," Ecclus. xviii. 1 . "God is the King over all the earth: God shall reign over the nations," Ps. xlvi. 8 , 9. "The Lord shall reign to eternity, yea, for ever and ever," Ps. ix. 16 . "The Lord is a great God, and a great King above all gods; for in His hand are all the ends of the earth, and the heights of mountains are His; for the sea is His, and He made it, and His hands formed the dry land," Ps. xciv. 3 , 4, 5. "The Lord He hath reigned, He hath corrected the world, which shall not be moved; He will judge the people with justice," Ps. xcv. 10 . "He is the King of kings, and the Lord of lords," Rev. xix. 16 .

Q. II. Does the care and attention of this Sovereign Lord extend to all creatures without exception?

A. The eternal Providence of God watches over all His creatures, the least as well as the greatest, with equal care and attention; for "He made the great and the little, and He hath equally care of all," Wis. vi. 8 . "He hath ordered all things in number, weight, and measure," Wis. xi. 21 . "He telleth the number of the stars, and calleth them all by their names," Ps. cxlvi. 4 . "Are not two sparrows sold for a farthing? and not one of them shall fall on the ground without your Father," Mat. x. 29 . Also, "Are not five sparrows sold for two farthings? and not one of them is forgotten before God. Yea, the very hairs of your head are all numbered," Mat. x. 30 ; and without Him "a hair of your head shall not perish," Luke, xxi. 18 .

Q. 12. What do you mean by the Providence of God?

A. The Providence of God is His eternal will, by which He disposes of all things whatsoever that come to pass, according to his own pleasure, and conducts His creatures in the way that He sees most proper towards the ends and purposes for which He created them. It includes three things: First, His infinite wisdom, by which He knows all His creatures, and all the good of which they are capable, and the ends to which they can serve, as also the ways and means by which they can acquire that good, and arrive at those ends, with the impediments that can hinder them from either. Secondly, His infinite goodness, which inclines Him to will and choose for them those means of acquiring the ends for which He creates them, that are the most proper and conducive thereto, and the fittest and best proportioned, and most conformable to the nature and capacity of each creature; and to remove or diminish the hindrances they may meet with in doing so. And, thirdly, His infinite power, by which He most effectually puts in execution, in time, those means which, from all eternity, He knew and made choice of, for enabling His creatures to obtain the ends He thus proposed to Himself in creating them. Thus the Scripture says: "O Lord God, Thou hast done the things of old, and hast devised one thing after another, and what Thou hast designed hath been done; for all Thy ways are prepared, and in Thy providence Thou hast placed Thy judgments," Judith,

ix. 4 , 5. "For in His hands are both we and our works, and all wisdom, and the knowledge and skill of works," Wis. vii. 16 . "Wherefore give not thy mouth to cause thy flesh to sin, and say not before the angel there is no providence, lest God be angry at thy words and destroy all the works of thy hands," Ecclus. v. 5 .

Q. 13. Can the Divine Providence be ever mistaken, or use improper means for obtaining Its ends, or be disappointed in obtaining Its designs?

A. No, by no means. It is absolutely impossible God should either mistake the means or be disappointed in His designs; His infinite wisdom is incapable of mistake, and His infinite power quashes all opposition to His will: "No evil can overcome His wisdom, it reacheth from end to end mightily, and ordereth all things sweetly," Wis. vii. 30 , and viii. 1. "All things are in His power, and there is none that can resist His will in what He determines to be done,"Esther, xiii. 9. "I am God," says He, "who show from the beginning the things that shall be at last, and from ancient times the things that as yet are not done, saying. My council shall stand, and all My will shall be done," Isa. xlvi. 10 . "For He will do all that pleaseth Him, and His word is full of power," Ecclus. viii. 3 .

Q. 14. Can anything happen by chance in the creation?

A. A thing is said to happen by chance when it is supposed to happen without any cause, or without being foreseen or expected, or without design or intention. Now, with regard to men, numbers of things happen, as it were by chance, in some one or other of these ways; but with regard to God this is absolutely impossible; for the Scripture assures us that "nothing upon earth is done without a cause," Job. v. 6 ; that His infinite wisdom "sees from eternity to eternity;" that "nothing is hid from His eyes;" that "He knows the works of all flesh." (See above. Chap. I. Q. 8.) So that it is impossible for anything to happen but what He foresees from all eternity; and that "He has made all things in wisdom," Ps. ciii. 24 ; and that He orders "all things in number, weight, and measure," Wis. xi. 21 . Consequently everything that happens is foreknown by Him, enters into the plan of His operations, and is disposed by the Divine Providence, according to His eternal purposes. Hence "lots are cast into the lap, but they are disposed of by the Lord," Prov. xvi. 11 ,; and this the royal Prophet well knew when he said, "Thou art my God, my lots are in Thy hands," Ps. xxx. 16 ; "The heart of the king is in the hand of the Lord, whithersoever He will He shall turn it," Prov. xxi. 1 . Thus it was not by chance that the asses of Saul were lost, or that the Ishmaelite merchants passed by when Joseph's brethren were going to kill him, but by the particular disposition of God's Providence, for accomplishing the ends He had in view.

Q. 15. Does, then, the Providence of God dispose of and direct everything that happens in the creation?

A. Yes, it does; it extends to all creatures, and to all things, whether good or evil; all which it disposes of and directs in the way and manner which He knows to be most conducive to His own wise ends and purposes; so that, whatever be the immediate cause by which anything is done or produced, Almighty God is the first supreme disposer of the whole, and against whose will nothing that is, or happens, could possibly exist. In this, however. He acts in the most admirable manner, without encroaching in the smallest degree on the free-will of man, or hindering second causes from going on in their natural course; but making use of man's free-will and all second causes to accomplish most sweetly, but, at the same time, most assuredly, whatever He pleases.

Q. 16. How does the Providence of God manifest and exert itself for the good of His creatures?

A. The Scripture assures us that God is the author of all good to His creatures, and "that every best gift, and every perfect gift, is from above, coming down from the Father of lights," James, i. 17 . And this He manifests chiefly in three ways: First, In providing for and bestowing upon all and every one of His creatures whatever is necessary for, and conducive to, their good and happiness, conformable to their state and condition, and according to the ends He has in view for them. Secondly, In preserving them or delivering them from the evils that are contrary to these ends. Thirdly, In guiding and governing them towards these ends. All which the Scripture points out to us in the clearest and most affecting manner. And, first, that He provides all the good things that we enjoy: "The eyes of all hope in Thee, O Lord, and Thou givest them meat in due season; Thou openest Thy hand and fillest with Thy blessing every living creature," Ps. cxliv. 15 , 16. "Who provideth food for the raven when her young ones cry to God, wandering about, because they have no meat?" Job, xxxviii. 41 . "Who hath sent out the wild ass free," says God, "and who hath loosed his bounds? to whom I have given a house, in the wilderness, and his dwelling in the barren land," Job, xxxix. 5 , 6. "Behold the birds of the air, for they neither sow, nor do they reap, nor gather into barns, and your heavenly Father feedeth them. . . . Consider the lilies of the field, how they grow; they labour not, neither do they spin; but I say to you, that even Solomon in all his glory was not arrayed like one of these. And if the grass of the field, which to-day is, and to-morrow is cast into the oven, God doth so clothe, how much more you, O ye of little faith?" Mat. vi. 26 , etc. "All things work together for good to them that love God," Rom. viii. 28 ; and therefore "cast all your care on Him, for He hath care of you,"I Pet. V. 7. "Cast thy care upon the Lord, and He shall sustain thee. He will not suffer the just to waver for ever," Ps. liv. 23 ; "It was neither herb nor mollifying plaster that healed them, but Thy word, O Lord, which healeth all things," Wis. xvi. 12 . Secondly, that He preserves and delivers His creatures from evil: "God is our refuge and strength, a helper in troubles, which have found us exceedingly," Ps. xlv. 1 . "Blessed is he who hath the God of Jacob for his protector - Who executeth judgment for them that suffer wrong; Who giveth food to the hungry: the Lord looseth them that are fettered; the Lord giveth sight to the blind: the Lord keepeth ' the strangers; He will support the fatherless and the widow," Ps. cxlv. 9 . "The Lord healeth the broken of heart, and bindeth up their bruises," Ps. cxlvi. 3 . "He hath given His angels charge over thee, to keep thee in all thy ways: in their hands they shall bear thee up, lest thou dash thy foot against a stone," Ps. xc. 11 , 12. And indeed the whole Scripture is full of this truth, and of the most striking examples of His Divine Providence, in preserving His creatures from evil, and even of turning the trials of His servants to their greater good. Witness His conduct towards His people in the wilderness, the history of Joseph, Job, Daniel, the three children, Elijah, and many others. 3rdly, That He guides and governs His creatures towards their good, and the ends He has in view for them: the Divine wisdom "goeth about seeking such as are worthy of her, and she showeth herself cheerfully to them in the ways, and meeteth them with all providence," Wis. vi. 17 . "In all thy ways think on God, and He will direct thy steps," Prov. iii. 6 . "Thus saith the Lord, I am the Lord thy God, that teach thee profitable things, that govern thee in the way that thou walkest," Isa. xlviii. 17 . •' The Lord ruleth me, and I shall want nothing. He hath set me in a place of pasture. He hath brought me up on the waters of refreshment; He hath converted my soul. He hath led me on the paths of justice," Ps. xxii. 1 . 2, 3.

Q. 17. How does the Providence of God enter into the evils of creatures?

A. The evils of creatures are of two kinds - to wit, the evil of sin, and the evil of suffering. The evil of sin resides in the perverse will of man consenting to anything which is against the law of the Almighty: all evils of this kind God only permits. The evil of suffering includes all the afflictions, pains, and miseries, by which creatures suffer, whether in mind or body: all evil of this kind, from whatever immediate occasion it arises, is ordained, intended, and expressly willed by Almighty God.

Q. 18. How does God permit the evil of sin?

A. The Scripture assures us that God hates sin, that He abhors it as a most grievous injury done to Himself, that He cannot look upon iniquity, and that He expressly forbids His creatures ever to commit it, under pain of the severest and most dreadful punishments

Hence it is manifestly impossible that He should ever, will sin, or intend it in any creature, and much less that He should be the cause or author of it; for this would be acting against Himself, which is totally inconsistent with His infinite perfection. Seeing, however, that sin is actually committed by His creatures, and His laws numberless times are transgressed by them, all which God could hinder, if He pleased, but does not hinder, it necessarily follows that He only permits this to happen. That is to say, God has endowed some of His creatures with knowledge and free-will, and from them He requires a voluntary service; He sets good and evil, life and death, before them, and leaves them to the freedom of their own will to choose the one or the other; He proposes to them the most powerful motives to induce them to choose the good, and threatens them with the worst of miseries to deter them from choosing the evil: "Consider," says He, by the prophet Moses, "that I have set before thee this day life and good, and on the other hand death and evil; "and a little after, "I call heaven and earth to witness this day, that I have set before you life and death, blessing and cursing; choose, therefore, life, that both thou and thy seed may live," Deut. XXX. 15 , 19. And the wise man assures us "that God made man from the beginning, and left him in the hand of his own counsel. ... He hath set water and fire before thee; stretch forth thy hand to which thou wilt. Before man is life and death, good and evil; that which he chooseth shall be given him," Ecclus. xv. 14 . He is always ready, however, to assist them to choose and execute the good; for "God is faithful. Who will not suffer you to be tempted above what you are able, but with the temptation will also make issue (that is, a way to escape), that you may be able to bear it," i Cor. x. 13 ; but He will not force them to this, nor oblige them to good against their free-will. When, therefore, they choose the evil, He leaves them to their own choice, and permits the sin they commit; for "He hath commanded no man to do wickedly, and He hath given no man license to sin," Ecclus.

XV. 21 . But in thus permitting sin, we must not imagine He does so either out of sloth, impotence, or negligence. Man often permits things that are disagreeable to him out of mere indolence, or through carelessness and indifference, or because he cannot help it; it is not so with God. God is incapable of sloth or carelessness, and is far from being indifferent about what His creatures do; at the same time He is perfectly able to hinder and prevent them from sinning, if He pleases. But He permits sin, because it is His will to permit it, because He has the most just and wise reasons to permit it, because it enters into the plan of His providence, and contributes to the great end of His creating this universe; and therefore He has, from all eternity, resolved and decreed to permit it; and in permitting it He displays, in the most admirable manner. His Divine perfections, by making it an occasion of infinitely greater good, both for exalting His own glory, and advancing the perfection of His creatures.

Q. 19. What do you mean when you say that God wills the evil of suffering?

A. That all the pains, sufferings, and afflictions, of whatever kind, that any creatures endure, whether in mind or body, are ordained, decreed, and sent upon them by God; that He expressly wills all their sufferings, is the chief cause and author of them, and the first and sovereign source from which they flow, whatever be their immediate cause or occasion. This is a truth everywhere displayed to us in the sacred Scriptures. "Good things and evil, life and death, poverty and riches, are from God," Eccles. xi. 14 . "The Lord killeth and maketh alive. He bringeth down to the grave and bringeth back again. The Lord maketh poor and maketh rich. He humbleth and He ex- alteth," i Kings (Sam.), ii. 6. 7. "See ye that I alone am, and there is no other God besides Me; I will kill and I will make alive, I will strike and I will heal; and there is none that can deliver out of My hand," Deut. xxxii. 39 . "I am the Lord, and there is none else; I form the light and create darkness; I make peace and create evil, I the Lord that do all these things," Isa. xlv. 6 , 7. "Shall there be evil in a city which the Lord hath not done? "Amos, iii. 6 . And wherever we find Almighty God foretelling by His prophets the sufferings and calamities of His people, He always declares Himself to be the author of them: "I will visit you with poverty; . . . I will send in upon you the beasts of the field to destroy you; . . . I will bring in upon you the sword, I will send the pestilence in the midst of you; . . . I will destroy your land - I will scatter you among the Gentiles," Lev. xxvi. "I will raise up evil against them," and the like, are the expressions He uses on such occasions. And hence we find that all the holy servants of God, whenever they met with any disasters, immediately referred them all to God as the sovereign cause and author, and received them with resignation, as coming from His hand. Thus Job, in the midst of his severe afflictions, cried out, "The Lord gave and the Lord hath taken away; as it hath pleased the Lord so is it done; blessed be the name of the Lord," Job, i. 21 . And a little after he adds, "If we have received good things at the hand of God, why should we not receive evil?" Job, ii. 10 . So when God, by His prophet Samuel, foretold to the high priest, Heli, all the ruin and misery that He was to send upon his family, he immediately replied, "It is the Lord, let Him do what is good in His sight," i Kings (Sam.), iii. 18. David also, when cursed by Semei, acknowledged this great humiliation to be from God, and said, "The Lord hath command-ed him to curse David, and who shall dare say. Why hath He done so? "2 Kings (Sam.), xvi. 10. And Christ Himself acknowledged all His sufferings as coming from God His Father, when He said, "The cup that My Father hath given Me, shall I not drink it?" John, xviii. 11 . Hence Solomon, com-prehending all the goods and evils of this life under the expression of the good and the evil day, says, "For God hath made both the one and the oth-er, that man may not find against Him any just complaint," Eccles. vii. 15 .

Q. 20. But how is it consistent with the goodness of God to render His crea-tures miserable by sufferings and afflictions?

A. It is impossible that the infinite goodness of God should render His creatures miserable from any pleasure He takes in their sufferings as such; or that He should directly intend or will their sufferings as an object which is in itself agreeable to Him. He, therefore, never sends any affliction upon them but with a view to some greater good, relating either to His own glory, which is the supreme end of the creation, or the happiness of the creatures themselves; either for the exaltation of His own Divine justice in punishing sinners, for the correction of the wicked, or for the preservation and improvement of the good; either in punishing past sins in those whom He afflicts, or in preserving them from sin for the time to come. Hence all the sufferings of this life are the effects of sin; and the voluntary abuse we make of our free-will is the cause that obliges or moves Almighty God to send them. Thus the holy Sarah, in her prayer to God, says, "For Thou art not delighted in our being lost; because after a storm Thou makest a calm; and after tears and weeping Thou pourest in joyfulness," Tob. iii. 2 2. Where we see that God takes no delight in our sufferings, and only sends them with a view to good, bringing from them peace and joy, so also "God made not death, neither hath He pleasure in the destruction of the living, for He created all things that they might be, and He made the nations of the earth for health; and there is no poison or destruction in them, nor kingdom of hell upon earth (for justice is perpetual and immortal). But the wicked with works and deeds have called it to them," Wis. i. 13 . "As I live, saith the Lord, I desire not the death of the wicked, but that the wicked turn from his way and live,"Ezech. xxxiii. 11. And therefore He declares, by another prophet, "Destruction is thy own, O Israel; thy help is only in Me," Hosea, xiii. 9 .

Q. 21. That all those sufferings which arise from natural or innocent causes - such as diseases, famine, pestilence, death, and the like - are sent expressly from God, and that He is the principal cause and author of them, it is easy to conceive; because there is no sin in these things, and the occasions of them are incapable of sin; but as for those sufferings which arise from our own sins, or from the sins of others, from their malice, hatred, injustice, or cruelty, how can God be the author of these, since they arise not from natural or innocent causes, but from wickedness and crimes, of which God cannot possibly be the author?

A. This difficulty often proves a stumbling-block to souls, and leads to a pernicious delusion; for falsely imagining that God cannot be the author or cause of those sufferings which arise from the crimes of men, they attribute them solely to the mistake, hatred, or malice of their fellow-creatures, and seek from this to justify their own impatience, passion, and desire of revenge. But this is a very great mistake; for it is a certain truth, that though God only indeed permits the crimes, of which our sufferings are the effects, yet these sufferings He as positively wills, and has from all eternity as expressly decreed to send upon us, as any others which flow from the most innocent cause. To understand this, we must carefully distinguish between the sin committed, and the effects which flow from it. The sin resides precisely in the perverse will of him committing it. The effects which flow from the sin are the sufferings which it occasions in others. The sin in him who commits it, God only permits, because He is incapable of willing sin, or of being the cause or author of it; yet from all eternity He foresaw it, and from all eternity, for His own most wise and just reasons, decreed to permit it. Now, what were these reasons? He foresaw that this sin, if permitted, would be the occasion of sufferings to others. He takes no pleasure in the sufferings of His creatures, and would never allow them to be afflicted, unless for some good end, either in justice or in mercy. No sufferings can come upon them against His will; for "not a hair of our head falls to the ground without Him." It is equally impossible that He should be indifferent to the sufferings of His creatures; this His infinite goodness forbids. We must conclude, therefore, that as all the sufferings of this life, as

we have seen above. Question 20, are either punishments or benefits, and
as such expressly willed and decreed from eternity by God - the punishments by His justice, the benefits by His mercy - consequently, though God
only permits the sin in the one who commits it, yet He expressly wills the
sufferings of others, which are its effects; and the reason of the sin being so
permitted is, that it may serve as an instrument in the hand of God for executing upon those who suffer what He has decreed from eternity to inflict
upon them. Hence we find in Scripture that when God Almighty foretells,
by His prophet, sufferings and afflictions. He always declares Himself to
be the author of them, even though the means by which they are inflicted
are of the most criminal nature. Thus, when the prophet Nathan reproved
David for the sins of adultery and murder which he had committed, he
says, in the name of God, "Thus saith the Lord, Behold, I will raise up evil
against thee out of thy own house, and I will take thy wives before thy eyes,
and give them to thy neighbour, and he shall lie with thy wives in the sight
of the sun," 2 Kings (Sam.), xii. 11. Here is a most severe sentence passed
upon David by the Divine justice, which God foretells He Himself would
execute upon him; and, therefore, which He positively wills and decrees
that David should undergo. His infinite wisdom could have executed this
sentence by many different means; but He foresaw that David's own son
Absalom, pushed on by his ambition, would rebel against his father, and
abuse his wives. God could easily have hindered Absalom from committing
such crimes, or have prevented the execution of them; but He was pleased
to leave him to the freedom of his own will, and make use of his crimes as
the instrument for executing the punishment He had decreed to inflict on
David.

When Jeroboam, king of Israel, provoked God to anger by his idolatry,
the prophet Ahias declared to him, in the name of God, the punishment
which God had decreed to send upon him. "Thus saith the Lord, Behold I
will bring evils upon the house of Jeroboam, . . . and I will sweep away the
remnant of the house of Jeroboam, as dung is swept away, till all be clear,"
3 Kings, xiv. 10 . How was this sentence executed? By rebellion, conspiracy,
and the most shocking cruelty. "In the reign of Nadab son of Jeroboam,
Baasa conspired against him, and slew him, and reigned in his place; and
when he was king, he cut off all the house of Jeroboam. He left not so much
as one soul of his seed till he had utterly destroyed him, according to the
word of the Lord, which He had spoken in the hand of Ahias the Silonite,"
3 Kings, xv. 27 . The crimes of Baasa, in conspiring against his sovereign
and killing him, were the effects of his ambition; and his cruelty in murder-
ing all the family of Jeroboam was a stroke of worldly policy to secure his

own possession of the throne; but whilst thus gratifying his own passion, he was, though unknown to himself, only an instrument of the Divine justice in punishing the sins of Jeroboam, and executing the decrees of the Almighty on the family of that unhappy prince. No doubt God could have prevented the crimes of Baasa, and have executed His own sentence on Jeroboam by other means; but knowing Baasa's perverse heart. He permitted him to follow its suggestions, so that the crimes he committed were from himself, by God's permission; but the effects which they produced in the family of Jeroboam were expressly willed, decreed, and foretold by Almighty God. In like manner when Satan, by God's permission, after having brought so many miseries upon Job, and reduced him to the most distressing state, appeared a second time before God, "The Lord said to Satan, Hast thou considered My servant Job . . . still keeping his innocence? But thou hast moved Me against him, that I should afflict him without a cause," Job, ii. 3 . In which words God Himself declares that He was the author of his afflictions - Satan and the other means being only instruments for executing His will.

Many other examples of the same kind are found in holy writ; but the following one is particularly conclusive. When St Peter and St John, having been taken up and examined regarding the cure of the lame man, were set at liberty, and returned "to their own company, they related all that the chief priests and ancients had said to them. Who having heard it, with one accord they lifted up their voice to God, and said. Lord, thou art He that didst make heaven and earth, the sea, and all things that are in them, who by the Holy Ghost, by the mouth of our Father David, hast said, Why did the Gentiles rage, and the people meditate vain things? the kings of the earth stood up, and princes assembled together against the Lord, and against His Christ. For, of a truth, there assembled together, in this city, against Thy holy child Jesus, whom Thou hast anointed, Herod, and Pontius Pilate, with the Gentiles, and people of Israel, to do what Thy hand and counsel decreed to be done," Acts, iv. 23 , (S:c. And St Peter, in his first sermon to the Jews on Pentecost, affirms the same truth, in these words: "Jesus of Nazareth . . . being delivered up by the determinate counsel and fore-knowledge of God, you, by the hands of wicked men, have crucified and slain," Acts, ii. 23 . In both which places it is positively declared that all the sufferings and death of Christ were expressly decreed by God, who had previously foretold them by the mouth of His holy prophets; yet the sins of the Jews and Gentiles, in what they did to Christ, were of the deepest dye; these sins were not from God, but from the malice of their own hearts, and the abuse of their free-will; this God only permitted, but He expressly willed the consequences of their crime in the sufferings and death of Jesus, The same is to be said in all similar cases: whatever troubles and afflictions come upon us by the malice, hatred, mistakes, or sins of others, or even of ourselves, we are to consider them all as positively willed and sent upon us by Almighty God; the sins committed He only permits, but our sufferings which flow from them He expressly wills, and has, from all eternity, decreed; and whereas, if He thought proper. He could inflict these sufferings by many other means, yet knowing the voluntary abuse which we or our fellow-creatures will make of our free will. He permits it, and thus uses our sins as the instruments of executing His will.

This is precisely the light in which all the holy servants of God consider their afflictions; for, from whatever immediate source they come, they receive them all as from the hand of God - they look upon the malice and crimes of those who injure them merely as the instruments which He uses for their punishment, or correction and advancement in virtue, and as such they love them and do them good. To the examples of this truth mentioned above, Q. 19, add these others: When Joseph made himself known to his brethren, considering all the cruel treatment he had received from them as the orders of the Divine Providence, he comforted them, and said, "Be not afraid, and let it not seem to you a hard case that you sold me into these countries, for God sent me before you into Egypt for your preservation." A little after he repeats the same, and adds, "not by your counsel was I sent hither, but by the will of God," Gen. xlv. 5 , 8. And after his father's death, when they feared he would then revenge the injuries they had done him, and sent a message, asking his forgiveness, he wept for concern on their account, and said, "Fear not; can we resist the will of God? you thought evil against me; but God turned it into good, that He might exalt me as at present you see, and might save many people: Fear not, I will feed you and your children; and he comforted them, and spoke gently and mildly," Gen. 1. 21. And our Saviour received the cup of His passion in no other light but as sent by His Father, and considered His enemies only as the instruments made use of by Him. He also earnestly prayed for them with His last breath upon the Cross, instead of bearing any resentment against them. Oh, happy those who seriously consider these truths, and imitate these holy examples! They already enjoy a foretaste of heaven itself, even in the midst of this valley of tears; no evil can come near them; for what the mistaken world calls evil is to them a real good, a source of joy and consolation. In everything they see the finger of God, in everything they adore His Divine Providence, in everything they rejoice for the accomplishment of His will: and hence they learn, by the most endearing experience, that "all things work together for good to them that love God," Rom. viii. 28 .

CHAPTER IV.

On The Creation And Fall Of The Angels

Q. I. What are the principal creatures that God made in the world?

A. Angels and men.

Q. 2. Why are they the principal or chief of all others?

A. Because they are endowed with understanding and free-will, by which they are capable of knowing and loving God, of which none of the other creatures are capable.

Q. 3. For what end, then, were the other creatures made?

A. For the use and benefit of man, to excite him to love, praise, and adore his Creator, for the numberless services he receives from these creatures.

Q. 4. Who are the angels?

A. Pure spirits without any body: "He made his angels spirits," Ps. ciii. 4 .

Q. 5. In what state did God create the angels?

A. In a most excellent and happy state; for (1.) He made them of a spiritual and incorruptible nature. (2.) He gave them a most sublime understanding, capable of, and endowed with, exceeding great knowledge. (3.) He made them Almighty his strength" Ps. cii. 20 . And (4.) Besides these natural excellences, He adorned them with the supernatural gift of His Divine grace and heavenly beauty.

Q. 6. For what end did He create them?

A. That they might be always in His own presence, "Their angels always see the face of My Father who is in heaven," Mat. xviii. 10; assisting at His throne, for "Thousands of thousands ministered to Him, and ten thousand times a hundred thousand stood before Him," Dan. vii. 10; and executing His orders throughout the rest of the creation, for they "Executed His word, hearkening to the voice of His orders," Ps. cii. 20

Q. 7. Did they continue in this happy state?

A. The greater part of them did, and are now confirmed in glory: but many of them fell by sin, and are now devils in hell.

Q. 8. What was the sin by which they fell?

A. It was pride, arising from the great beauty and sublime graces which God had bestowed upon them. For, seeing themselves such glorious beings, they fell in love with themselves, and, forgetting the God that made them, wished to be on an equality with their Creator.

Q. 9. What were the consequences of their crime?

A. They were immediately deprived of all their supernatural graces and heavenly beauty: they were changed from glorious angels into hideous devils; they were banished out of heaven, and condemned to the torments of hell, which was prepared to receive them.

Q. 10. Who was the chief of these fallen angels?

A. He was called Lucifer before his fall, which signifies one that carries light along with him, from the exceeding great splendour with which God had adorned him above his fellows; and since his fall, he is called Satan, or the Adversary, because he is the enemy both of God and man; he is also called the Devil.

Q. 11. What account doth the Scripture give of all this?

A. It is as follows: In the prophet Ezekiel, under the figure of the king of Tyre, the beauty and fall of the angels is thus described: "Thus saith the Lord God, Thou wast the seal of resemblance, full of wisdom, and perfect in beauty: Thou wast in the pleasure of the paradise of God. . . . Thou wast a cherub stretching out thy wings. . . . Thou wast perfect in thy ways from the day of thy creation until iniquity was found in thee. Thou wast filled with iniquity; thou hast sinned, and I cast thee out from the mountain of God and destroyed thee, O covering cherub. And thy heart was filled up with thy beauty. I have cast thee to the ground," Ezech. xxviii. And the prophet Isaiah thus speaks to Lucifer, the chief of the fallen angels, under the figure of the king of Babylon: "How art thou fallen from heaven, O Lucifer! . . . Thou saidst in thy heart, I will ascend into heaven, I will exalt

my throne above the stars of God, I will sit in the mountain of the covenant, in the sides of the north. I will ascend above the height of the clouds.
I will be like the Most High. But yet thou shalt be brought down to hell,
into the depth of the pit," Isa. xiv. 12 . And at the last day the Judge will say
to the wicked, "Depart from Me, ye cursed, into everlasting fire, prepared
for the devil and his angels," Mat. xxv. 41 . Their fall is also thus described
by St John: "And there was a great battle in heaven, Michael and his angels
fought with the dragon, and the dragon fought and his angels. And they
prevailed not, neither was their place found any more in heaven; and the
great dragon was cast out, that old serpent, who is called the Devil and
Satan, who seduceth the whole world," Rev. xii. 7 , 8, 9; for "God spared not
the angels that sinned, but delivered them, drawn down by infernal ropes,
to the lower hell into torments," 2 Peter, ii. 4 . "And the angels who kept
not their principality, but forsook their own habitation, He hath reserved
under darkness, in everlasting chains, unto the judgment of the great day,"
Jude, verse 6. "And the devil, who seduced them, was cast into the pool
of fire and brimstone, where both the beast and the false prophet shall be
tormented day and night, for ever and ever," Rev. xx. 9.]

CHAPTER V.

Of The Creation And Fall Of Man

Q. 1. What kind of a being is man?

A. Man is a being composed of soul and body.

Q. 2. What is his body made of?

A. The dust of the earth.

Q. 3. What is his soul made of?

A. It is created by God out of nothing.

Q. 4. For what end did God create man?

A. To know, love, and serve Him during the short course of his pilgrimage in this world, and then to be taken up to heaven, and be happy in the possession and enjoyment of God Himself for all eternity.

Q. 5. Is this possession of God in heaven due to the nature of man?

A. By no means; it was wholly an effect of the infinite goodness of God, to create man for such a glorious and supernatural end; to communicate to him the riches of His mercy, and make him supremely blest in the clear vision and enjoyment of Himself for ever.

Q. 6. Who were the first of mankind that God created?

A. Adam and Eve, who are our first parents, and from whom all mankind are descended.

Q. 7. In what manner did God create them?

A. He formed the body of Adam "out of the dust Of the earth, and then breathed into him the breath of life," Gen. ii. 7 - that is, created his soul out of nothing to animate that body, "and Adam became a living soul," Ibid. 'Then causing a deep sleep to fall upon Adam, He took out one of his ribs, filling up its place with flesh; and the Lord God built the rib which He took from Adam into a woman, and brought her to Adam," Gen. ii. 21 .

Q. 8. To whose image and likeness did He create man?

A. "God created man to His own image; to the image of God He created him; male and female He created them," Gen. i. 27 .

Q. 9. In what does this likeness consist?

A. In several things: for (1.) as there is but one only God, and three Persons in one God; so in man there is but one soul, and in this one soul there are three powers, the will, memory, and understanding, by which man, in some sense, resembles the ever-blessed Trinity. (2.) As God is a Spirit, and immortal, so the soul of man is a spirit, and will never die. (3.) As God is the sovereign Lord of all things, and. does in all creatures whatever He pleases, so He endowed man with free-will, and made him the visible sovereign over all the other creatures of this earth. "Let Us make man," says God, "to Our image and likeness; and let him have dominion over the fishes of the sea, and the fowls of the air, and the whole earth, and every creeping creature that moveth upon the earth," Gen. i. 26 .

Q. 10. In what state did God create our first parents?

A. In the state of innocence, grace, and happiness.

Q. 11. What do you mean by the state of innocence?

A. That at their creation they were free from the smallest pollution of sin, and pure and unspotted before God. "This I know, that God made man upright," Eccles. vii. 30 .

Q. 12. What do you mean by the state of grace?

A. That they were adorned with the grace of God, called also original Justice, or righteousness, which God communicated to their souls, making them beautiful and truly holy before Him. Thus St Paul, exhorting us to be renewed in the spirit to that original justice in which our first parents were created, says, "Put on the new man, who, according to God, is created in justice and holiness of truth," Eph. iv. 24 .

Q. 13. Was this original righteousness due to their nature?

A. By no means; it was a free gift of the goodness of God.

Q. 14. Why did He bestow it upon them?

A. Because, as He was pleased out of His great goodness to create them for a supernatural end - to wit, the enjoyment of Himself in heaven; so out of the same goodness He bestowed original justice upon them, as the necessary help to enable them to attain that end.

Q. 15. What benefit did they receive from this original justice?

A. (1.) It sanctified them, or made them truly holy before God, objects of His delight and complacency. (2.) It subjected all their senses, appetites, and passions to reason. (3.) It rendered their reason and their whole soul subject to the will of God; and (4.) It was the source and support of the happiness they enjoyed.

Q. 16. What do you mean by the state of happiness?

A. That being free from all stain of sin, and adorned with original justice, they were on that account free from sufferings, and enjoyed a perfect happiness both in soul and body, suitable to their nature and the state they were in.

Q. 17. In what did this happiness consist?

A. Chiefly in the following particulars: (1.) They were endowed with great knowledge of everything relating to their state and the rest of the creatures. Thus "God created man, and created of him a helpmate like to himself; He gave them counsel, and a tongue, and eyes, and ears, and a heart to devise, and He filled them with the knowledge of understanding; He created in them the science of the spirit; He filled their heart with wisdom, and showed them both good and evil," Ecclus. xvii. 5 ,6. (2.) They were free from all those passions, irregular desires, and appetites which so violently torment our souls; for "God made man upright," Eccles. vii. 30 , and of course they enjoyed a perpetual peace and serenity of mind. (3.) Their hearts were inclined to all good, and their wills united to God by holy love. (4.) Their bodies were free from all sickness and pain, and enjoyed a perpetual health. (5.) They were not subject to death; but, after serving God for a time upon earth, were to have been translated, both soul and body, without passing through the gates of death, to enjoy Him for ever in heaven; for "God created man incorruptible," Wis. ii. 23 .

Q. 18. Where did God place our first parents when He had created them?

A. "The Lord God had planted a paradise of pleasure from the beginning, wherein He placed man whom He had formed. And the Lord God brought forth from the ground all manner of trees, fair to behold and pleasant to eat of. . . . And the Lord God took man, and put him into the paradise of pleasure, to dress it and to keep it," Gen. ii. 8 , 9, 15. This was a garden planted by the hand of God, and filled with everything that could make them happy.

Q. 19. Were they allowed to eat of all the fruit of this garden?

A. They were allowed to eat of everything this garden produced except the fruit of one tree, which God forbade them, under pain of death, to touch. And God "commanded him, saying: Of every tree of paradise thou shalt eat; but of the tree of knowledge of good and evil thou shalt not eat; for in what day soever thou shalt eat of it, thou shalt die the death," Gen. ii. 16 .

Q. 20. "What means, thou shalt die the death?

A. It means, in the day thou eatest of that fruit thou shalt immediately die the death of the soul, by committing a mortal sin; thou shalt be subjected to the death of the body, and return to the dust from whence thou art made: and after that to the death, both of soul and body, in hell-fire for all eternity.

Q. 21. Why did God lay this command upon them?

A. To exercise their obedience, and be a continual testimony of their subjection to God, and of their dependence upon Him.

Q. 22. Did our first parents continue in this happy state?

A. No; they fell from it, by transgressing this easy command of God their maker, and eating this forbidden fruit.

Q. 23. Who tempted them to commit this crime?

A. Satan, the chief of the fallen angels, who, appearing to Eve in the serpent, seduced her to eat of the fruit, and she having eaten it herself, carried it to her husband, and persuaded him to do the same.

Q. 24. What account does the Scripture give of this?

A. "And the serpent said to the woman. Why hath God commanded you that you should not eat of every tree of paradise? And the woman answered him, saying, Of the fruit of the trees that are in paradise we do eat; but of the fruit of the tree which is in the midst of paradise, God hath commanded us that we should not eat, and that we should not touch it, lest perhaps we die. And the serpent said to the woman, No, you shall not die the death; for God doth know, that in what day soever you do eat thereof, your eyes shall be opened, and you shall be as gods, knowing good and evil. And the woman saw that the tree was good to eat, and fair to the eyes, and delightful to behold, and she took of the fruit thereof, and did eat, and gave to her husband, who did eat," Gen. iii.

Q. 25. What moved the devil to tempt them to this sin?

A. Envy at their happiness; for "God created man incorruptible - but by the envy of the devil death came into the world," Wis. ii. 24 ; and it was by tempting them to this sin that death was introduced, for "By one man sin entered into the world, and by sin death," Rom. v. 12 .

Q. 26. What were the consequences of their disobedience? Did they become as gods?

A. Quite the reverse. Instead of that, they immediately lost "their innocence," bringing upon themselves the dreadful guilt of mortal sin; they were deprived of the sublime treasure of "original justice; "for by this sin the grace of God was banished from their souls, and they lost "their happiness," and became miserable both in soul and body. In consequence of this, they became objects of the wrath and indignation of God, whom they had offended, slaves of the devil, whose service they had voluntary preferred to the service of God, and they lost all right and title to eternal happiness.

Q. 27. In what respect did they become miserable as to their soul?

A. Their understanding was darkened, and subjected to ignorance and error; their will was turned away from God, and violently bent upon evil, and their passions rebelled against reason, and tormented their minds.

Q. 28. How did they become miserable as to their bodies?

A. Their bodies were subjected to all manner of sickness and disease, to innumerable pains and torments, to death itself in this world, and to be reduced to the dust from which they were made, and at last both soul and body to hell-fire.

Q. 29. What does the Scripture say of this?

A. "And to the woman God said, I will multiply thy sorrows and thy conceptions; in sorrow shalt thou bring forth children, and thou shalt be under thy husband's power, and he shall have dominion over thee. And to Adam He said - Cursed is the earth in thy work; with labour and toil shalt thou eat thereof all the days of thy life. Thorns and thistles shall it bring forth to thee. . . . In the sweat of thy brow shalt thou eat bread, till thou return to the earth out of which thou wast taken: for dust thou art, and into dust thou shalt return," Gen. iii.

Q. 30. Are all mankind born under the guilt of this sin of our first parents?

A. Yes, they are; for "By one man sin entered into the world, and by sin death, and so death passed upon all men, in whom all have sinned," Rom. v. 12 .

Q. 31. What is this sin called in us?

A. Original sin.

Q. 32. Why so?

A. Both because we inherit it from our first parents, who were the origin or beginning of all mankind, and also because we contract it from the first origin of our being - that is, the very moment we are conceived in our mother's womb, according to that of the prophet, "Behold, I was conceived in iniquity, and in sin did my mother conceive me," Ps. 1. 7.

Q. 22. Are we also subjected to all these miseries, both of soul and body, which this sin brought upon our first parents?

A. Yes, we are; "For we are by nature children of wrath," Eph. ii. 3 , being all born under the guilt of this their sin, and deprived of that original justice in which they were created, and on that account subjected to the dominion of Satan, and without any right or title to heaven, where we can never enter so long as this original guilt remains upon our souls - our minds are darkened with error and ignorance, as experience itself shows; "The thoughts of our hearts are bent upon evil at all times," Gen. v. vi., by which we are daily hurried on to the numberless sins we commit ourselves; and as for the torments and pains to which we are liable, both in mind and body, who can enumerate them? "Man born of a woman," saith Job, "living for a short time, is filled with many miseries," Job, xiv. i. "For what profit hath man of all his labour and vexation of spirit, with which he has been tormented under the sun? All his days are full of sorrows and miseries; even in the night he doth not rest in mind: and is not this vanity?" Eccles. ii. 22 ,

CHAPTER VI.

Of The Promise Of A Redeemer,
And The State Of Mankind Till His Coming

Q. 1. As man, in his fallen state, able to make his peace with God, and remedy his own miseries?

A. No. Fallen man was utterly incapable of taking any effectual step towards that end, much less of attaining it.

Q. 2. Why so?

A. Because, to make his peace with God, it was necessary the Divine justice should first be satisfied for the grievous injury done to God by his disobedience in preferring the suggestions of Satan to the command of God. And to remedy his miseries, it was necessary he should regain the grace of God which he had lost by sin; neither of which was it possible for man, in his fallen state, to do.

Q. 3. Why could he not satisfy the justice of God for the offence he had committed against Him?

A. Because, considering on the one hand the vileness of man, who of himself is a mere nothing; and, on the other, the infinite Majesty of God, whom this nothing had so grievously injured, the malice of the offence was in a manner infinite; and therefore the Divine justice required a satisfaction of infinite value to equal the offence, and make the offender's peace. Now man, a poor sinful creature, was incapable of this in the smallest degree.

Q. 4. Why could not he of himself regain the grace of God?

A. Because the grace of original justice, which he lost by sin, was a free gift of the goodness of God, to which man could have no right nor title, even when innocent, and was a gift of infinite value; but by his fall he was become positively unworthy of that or any other grace, and utterly incapable of doing anything that could move God to bestow it upon him.

Q. 5. Was it possible for the good angels to make man's peace with God, and bring a remedy to his evils?

A. No. It was impossible for any mere creature, though ever so pure and holy, to satisfy for the offence committed by man in the manner the Divine justice required, or to obtain for him the grace he had lost by sin. None but God Himself could apply an effectual remedy to so great an evil.

Q. 6. What, then, must have become of our first parents if no remedy had been found?

A. They, and all of us their posterity, must have been lost for ever.

Q. 7. Were they left, then, by the Divine justice to the punishment they deserved, without all remedy?

A. God Almighty, out of His incomprehensible justice, was pleased to pursue the fallen angels with immediate punishment without remedy; but of His infinite goodness He had pity and compassion on fallen man, and provided a Redeemer for him.

Q. 8. Who is this Redeemer?

A. No less a person than God the Son, whom the Father promised to send into this world in the fulness of time, to remedy all the evils of their fall.

Q. 9. When was this promise first made?

A. When passing sentence on our first parents after their fall; He even then showed the greatness of His mercy by promising to send them a Redeemer, who should overcome their enemy that had seduced them, saying to the serpent, "I will put enmity between thee and the woman, and thy seed and her seed; she shall crush thy head; and thou shalt lie in wait for her heel,'" Gen. iii. 15 . And St John tells us that, "For this purpose the Son of God appeared, that He might destroy the works of the devil," i John, iii. 8 .

Q. 10. Was it long after the fall before this promise was fulfilled, by the coming of the Redeemer?

A. It was about four thousand years after the creation and fall before He appeared in the world, though the promise of sending Him was frequently renewed, during that time, to the holy servants of God, and all the circumstances of His appearance and office were revealed to several among them, and by them communicated to others.

Q. II. In what condition was mankind during that long space of time?

A. Soon after the world began to be peopled, men began to forsake God, and follow the bent of their corrupted nature; and though God always had a succession of good people who adhered to Him, yet vice at last became so universal that, "God seeing that the wickedness of men was great on the earth, and that all the thought of their heart was bent upon evil, at all times, it repented Him that He had made man upon the earth: and being touched inwardly with sorrow of heart, He said, I will destroy man, whom I have created, from the face of the earth. But Noah found grace before the Lord, for Noah was a just and perfect man in his generation, and he walked with God. . . And God said to Noah, The end of all flesh is come before me; the earth is filled with iniquity through them, and I will destroy them with the earth. Make thee an ark of timber planks - behold I will bring the waters of a great flood upon the earth to destroy all flesh, wherein is the breath of life under heaven. . . . And I will establish My covenant with thee, and thou shalt enter into the ark, thou and thy sons, and thy wife, and the wives of thy sons with thee; and of every living creature of all flesh, thou shalt bring two of a sort into the ark, that they may live with thee. . . . For yet a while, and after seven days, I will rain upon the earth forty days and forty nights, and I will destroy every substance that I have made from the face of the earth. And Noah did all things which the Lord commanded him. . . . And after seven days the waters overflowed the earth. . . . All the fountains of the great deep were broken up, and the flood-gates of heaven were opened; and the rain fell upon the earth forty days and forty nights. . . . And the waters overflowed exceedingly, and filled all the face of the earth - and they prevailed beyond measure upon the earth, and all the high mountains under the whole heaven were covered. The water was fifteen cubits higher than the mountains which it covered. And all flesh was destroyed that moved upon the earth. . . . And all men, and all things wherein there was the breath of life on the earth, died. . . . And Noah only remained, and they that were with him in the ark," Gen. vi. vii.

Q. 12. What became of them after this?

A. When the waters of the deluge were abated, and the earth was again dried, "God spoke to Noah, saying, Go out of the ark, thou and thy wife, thy sons and the wives of thy sons, and all living things that are with thee of all flesh . . . bring out with thee, and go ye upon the earth; increase and multiply upon it," Gen. viii. 15 . And they did so, "and God blessed Noah and his sons, and said to them. Increase and multiply, and fill the earth," Gen. ix. 1 .

Q. 13. After so dreadful an example of the Divine justice, did the posterity of Noah continue faithful to God?

A. For some time they did; but at last the effects of corrupt nature, and the delusions of Satan, began again to prevail, and by degrees spread over the whole world, insomuch that, after some time, the very knowledge of the true God was almost extinguished from the face of the earth, and mankind was drowned in idolatry and all manner of crimes, worshipping idols instead of God, and sacrificing their own children to devils; of which the Scriptures give us the following description: "They did works hateful to God by their sorceries and wicked sacrifices; they were merciless murderers of their own children, and eaters of men's bowels, and devourers of blood; the parents sacrificing with their own hands helpless souls," Wis. xii. 4 . St Paul also describes the state of their idolatry before the coming of Christ, in these words: "They changed the glory of the incorruptible God into the likeness of the image of a corruptible man, and of birds, and of four-footed beasts, and of creeping things; they changed the truth of God into a lie, and worshipped and served the creature rather than the Creator," Rom. i. 23 , 25. And as the Holy Ghost declares, "That the beginning of fornication is the devising of idols, and the invention of them is the corruption of life," Wis. xiv. 12 ; so the apostle goes on to declare the shocking abominations which were the consequences of their idolatry: "as they liked not to have God in their knowledge, God delivered them up to a reprobate sense, to do those things which are not convenient, being filled with all iniquity, malice, fornication, covetousness, wickedness; full of envy, murder, contention, deceit, malignity, whispers, hateful to God, contumelious, proud, haughty, inventors of evil things," &:c., Rom. i. Such is the description which the Word of God gives us of the deplorable situation that mankind was in before the Redeemer was sent among them.

Q. 14. "Why did Almighty God leave mankind in this sad condition, and so long delay the coming of the Redeemer?

A. To teach us, by sad experience, our own extreme perverseness, and the dreadful corruption of our nature by sin; to cure the deep wound of pride which sin had made in our souls, by letting us see what we are capable of when left to ourselves; to convince us of the great need we have of a Redeemer, and to make us receive Him with the greater readiness when He should come amongst us.

Q. 15. Did God totally abandon mankind to their wicked ways during all that time?

A. Far from it; for (1.) He raised up holy men from time to time to warn the wicked of their evil ways, and exhort them to repentence. (2.) He often punished them in a visible and dreadful manner for their crimes, as when He drowned the whole world by the deluge, and rained down fire and brimstone from heaven to consume the wicked cities of Sodom and Gomorrah. And (3.) When wickedness was still more and more spreading over the face of the earth. He chose a whole people, whom He separated from the rest of mankind, and by a special providence preserved from the general corruption.

Q. 16. Who was this so highly favoured people?

A. The posterity of His faithful servant Abraham, whose fidelity and obedience God tried many different ways, and finding him always constant and uniform in his duty, He made choice of him to be the father of His chosen people, renewed to him the promise of the Redeemer, and assured him that He should come of His posterity: "And the Lord appeared to Abraham, and said unto him, I am the Almighty God: walk before Me and be perfect; and I will make My covenant between Me and thee, and I will multiply thee exceedingly. . . . And thou shalt be father of many nations. . . . And kinds shall come out of thee. . . . And I will establish My covenant between Me and thee, and between thy seed after thee, in their generations, by a perpetual covenant, to be a God to thee and to thy seed after thee," Gen. xvii. And again, "By Myself have I sworn, saith the Lord," to Abraham, "I bless thee, and I will multiply thy seed as the stars of heaven, and as the sand that is on the sea-shore; thy seed shall possess the gates of their enemies; and in thy seed shall all the nations of the earth be blessed, because thou hast obeyed My voice," Gen. xxii. i6, 17, 18.

Q. 17. What did God do for this people, the posterity of Abraham?

A. He multiplied them into a great nation. He watched over them by a special providence, and wrought numberless and most amazing miracles in their favour and for their defence. He settled them in a most excellent land, "flowing with milk and honey," as the Scripture expresses it. He gave them by His servant Moses a holy law to direct them, written with His own hand on tables of stone. He taught them the way in which He would be worshipped by them, revealing to them His holy religion for that end. He gave them His Holy Scriptures for their instruction and consolation. He sent among them from time to time His holy prophets to declare His will to them, and keep them steady in His service. He often renewed His promise of a Redeemer to several of His holy servants among them, and foretold by His prophets all the circumstances of His coming, and what He was to do for mankind. For all which, see their whole history in Scripture.

Q. 18. How was this people called?

A. They were sometimes called Israelites, or the children of Israel, from the name of one of their patriarchs; sometimes Jews, from one of their principal tribes, out of which the Redeemer was to come; and sometimes the people of God, from the care and protection which God had of them, choosing them for His inheritance from among all the nations of the earth, and preserving them from that deplorable corruption into which all the other nations fell.

Q. 19. Did this people always continue faithful to God, and grateful to Him for such special protection shown by Him to them?

A. Far from it; they often rebelled against Him, forsook His service, and fell into idolatry and other abominations, for which He most severely punished them, till by their repentance they regained His favour, and returned again to the faithful observance of His law.

Q. 20. What kind of religion did God institute among them?

A. The full and perfect manifestation of the will of God to man was reserved to be the work of the Redeemer; but to this people God gave an imperfect revelation of the truths of eternity, such as the grossness of their minds and the hardness of their hearts were able to receive: their religion, therefore, principally consisted in the several kinds of sacrifices of beasts and other creatures which God instituted to be offered for His honour, and in their obedience to the law He had given them.

Q. 21. Had these sacrifices of beasts and other creatures any worth or value in themselves before God?

A. All these sacrifices, and, indeed, all the religion which God instituted among this people, were but types and figures of the Redeemer then to come, and of the perfect religion which was afterwards to be instituted by Him, and as such they were agreeable to God; and when offered by the people with a view to the Redeemer, and with faith in Him, were most beneficial to them; for from the beginning "there is no other name under heaven given to man -whereby we must be saved but the name of Jesus only," Acts, iv. 12 , So that from the beginning, before the Redeemer appeared among men, none could be saved but by faith in Him, who was then to come; as none can be saved since His coming but by faith in Him, as already come.

Q. 22. In what condition were the Jews when the Redeemer came among them?

A. They still retained the knowledge and worship of the true God, according to the law of Moses; but had corrupted the true sense of the law in many things by human opinions, and were divided into several different sects among themselves.

Q. 23. In what condition was the rest of mankind when the Redeemer came into the world?

A. All the other nations of the earth, who in Scripture language are called the Gentiles at the time our Saviour appeared, and for many ages before, were sunk in those miserable vices which are mentioned above ((2- 13), and wholly ignorant of the God that made them, and of everything else concerning their eternal salvation.

Q. 24. What are those truths of eternity of which they were so ignorant, and the knowledge of which is so necessary for salvation?

A. They may all be reduced to these heads: the knowledge of the one true living God that created us; the way of worshipping this great God according to His will; the cause of all our miseries, which is sin or disobedience to His law; the only remedy of sin, and of all our miseries, which is the grace of a Redeemer; the great end for which we were created, which is the possession and enjoyment of God in heaven; and the means on our part to obtain this end of our being, which are faith and obedience. Of these great and important truths all the nations of the earth were wholly ignorant, the Jews only excepted; and they had, by their depraved opinions in many things, corrupted even that imperfect knowledge of them which God had given them.

Q. 25. Could not man, by the strength of reason and study, have attained the knowledge of these things?

A. No; that was absolutely impossible; for these truths are all supernatural; they belong to another world; they do not fall under our senses or reason, so as to be examined or investigated by them; and some of them flow entirely from the free-will and appointment of Almighty God: so that it was impossible man should ever come to the knowledge of them, except God Himself had discovered them to him. And this is proved to a demonstration by experience itself, not only from the ancient heathens before the Redeemer came, among whom there were many great men remarkable for their strength of genius and learning, who yet could never acquire any rational knowledge of the above great truths, though they often applied themselves with great assiduity to study them; but also from many different nations in the remoter regions of the globe, to whom the revelation of these truths has not yet reached, and who, though endowed with sense and reason not inferior to our own, have never been able, to this day, to arrive at any degree of knowledge of them.

Q. 26. Did, then. Almighty God ever reveal those truths to mankind?

A. He did; and it was one of the principal offices of the Redeemer to bring from heaven to men the knowledge of these Divine truths, and to deliver them from the miserable darkness in which they had been involved. The deplorable situation they were in before He came, with the admirable light He brought among them, is thus beautifully described in the Holy Scriptures: Isaiah, foretelling this happy effect of His coming, says, - "The people that walked in darkness have seen a great light; to them that dwelt in the region of the shadow of death, to them light is risen," Isa. ix. 2 . And God thus speaks to the Redeemer by the same prophet: "I have given Thee for a covenant of the people, for a light of the Gentiles; that Thou mightest open the eyes of the blind, and bring forth the prisoner out of prison, and them that sit in darkness out of the prison-house," Isa. xlii. 7 . Zacharias also, in his prophecy at the birth of St John the Baptist, says of the Redeemer: "Through the bowels of mercy of our God, the Orient from on high hath visited us, to enlighten them that sit in darkness and in the shadow of death, and to direct our feet in the way of peace," Luke, i. 78 . The holy Simeon, holding the Redeemer, then a child, in his arms, said He was the salvation of God, "which Thou, O Lord," said he, "hast prepared before the face of all people, a light to the revelation of the Gentiles, and the glory of Thy people Israel," Luke, ii. 31 , And the Redeemer Himself, when He appeared to St Paul, and authorised him to carry the light of His revelation to the Gentiles, said He sent him to the nations "to open their eyes, that they may be converted from darkness to light, and from the power of Satan to God, that they may receive forgiveness of sins, and a lot among the saints by the faith that is in me," Acts, XXV. 18 . Hence the same holy apostle, describing the misery and blindness of the Gentiles, says: "They walk in the vanity of their mind, having their understandings darkened, being alienated from the life of God, through the ignorance that is in them, because of the blindness of our hearts," Eph. iv. 18 ; but that God, by the Redeemer, "has made us worthy to be partakers of the lot of the saints in light, and delivered us from the power of darkness, and hath translated us into the kingdom of His beloved Son, in whom we have redemption through His blood, the remission of sins," Col. i. 12 . St Peter declares to Christians - that is, to the followers of the Redeemer - "You are a chosen generation, a kingly priesthood, a holy nation, a purchased people, that you may declare His virtues who hath called you out of darkness into His admirable light; who in time past were not a people, but are now the people of God,"I Pet. ii. 9.

Q. 27. What are the principal offices of the Redeemer?

A. They are chiefly these two: (1.) To redeem us from our sins, and from the captivity of Satan, to which mankind has been reduced by sin. (2.) To enlighten our minds by revealing to us the great truths of eternity, which we could never have known without such a teacher, and upon the knowledge of which our eternal happiness depends.

Q. 28. What is the Redeemer's name?

A. Jesus Christ. The name Jesus signifies a Saviour, and was given Him by God Himself, as foretold by the prophet Isaiah many ages before His coming, when he said, "Thou shalt be called by a new name, which the mouth of the Lord shall name," Isa. lxii. 2 . And it was brought immediately from heaven before He was born; for when the angel discovered the mystery of His incarnation to St Joseph, he said, "Thou shalt call His name Jesus, for He shall save His people from their sins," Mat. i. 21 and not only from their sins, but also from the fatal effects of sin, the slavery of Satan, and the torments of hell. The name Christ signifies anointed, and implies that the Redeemer is anointed with all kind of grace, and with the Divinity Itself; for "in him it hath well pleased the Father that all fulness should dwell," Col. ii. 9 ; and "in Him dwelleth all the fulness of the Godhead bodily," ii. 9. By this Divine unction He is consecrated to be "a priest for ever according to the order of Melchisedech," Ps. cix. 4; as also "to be king over Sion His holy mountain," Ps. ii. 6 ; and "to reign in the house of Jacob for ever; for of His kingdom there shall be no end," Luke, i. 32 . It also implies that He is anointed with all the graces of the Holy Ghost, according to Isaiah: "And the Spirit of the Lord shall rest upon Him, the spirit of wisdom and of understanding, the spirit of counsel and of fortitude, the spirit of knowledge and of godliness, and He shall be filled with the spirit of the fear of the Lord," Isa. xi. 2 Hence St Peter says that "God anointed Him with the Holy Ghost and with power," Acts, x. 38 .

CHAPTER VII.

Of Jesus Christ Our Redeemer

Q. 1. IS it necessary to know Jesus Christ the Redeemer?

A. It is most necessary to know both what Jesus Christ is and what He has done for us; for "there is no other name under heaven given to men whereby we must be saved," Acts, iv. 12. And Christ Himself, speaking to His eternal Father, says, "This is eternal life, that they may know Thee, the only true God, and Jesus Christ whom Thou hast sent," John, xvii. 3.

Q. 2. Who is Jesus Christ?

A. Jesus Christ is God the Son, the second Person of the ever-blessed Trinity, who, taking our nature upon Him, became man in order to redeem lost man.

Q. 3. Where doth it appear that Jesus Christ is God the Son, the second Person of the blessed Trinity?

A. From many plain texts of Scripture. Thus the angel declared to the blessed Virgin Mary, before He was conceived in her womb, "The holy One that shall be born of thee shall be called the Son of God," Luke, i. 35. St Peter, inspired by God Himself, said to Christ, "Thou art Christ, the Son of the living God," Mat. xvi. 16. St John declares "that- the Word was God," and that this "Word," or Son of God, "was made flesh, and dwelt among us, and we saw His glory, the glory as of the only begotten of the Father," John, i. 14. St John the Baptist, by particular revelation from the Holy Ghost, says of Jesus Christ, "I saw, and I gave testimony that this is the Son of God," John, i. 34. God the Father, at the transfiguration, by a voice from heaven, declared, "This is my beloved Son, in whom I am well pleased," Mat. xvii. 5. All the miracles He performed are recorded in the Gospel in proof of this truth. "Many other signs Jesus did; but these are written that you may believe that Jesus is the Christ, the Son of God," John, XX. 30. And St Paul declares that "Christ is over all things, God blessed for ever," Rom. ix. 5.

Q. 4. Is Jesus Christ true man?

A. Jesus Christ is also true man; for whereas He was always God, equal to His Father from all eternity, when the fulness of time was come He became man by taking our nature upon Him, and uniting it to His Divine nature in His own person; so that He is also true man, having the nature of man - that is, having a soul and a body like unto us. Thus "the Word," or Son of God, "which in the beginning was with God, and was true God, was made flesh, and dwelt among us," John, i. "Jesus Christ being in the form of God, thought it no robbery to be equal with God, but debased Himself, taking the form of a servant, being made in the likeness of men, and in fashion found as a man," Philip, ii. 6. God sent His own Son in the likeness of "sinful flesh," Rom. viii. 3. "For nowhere doth He take hold (that is, take upon Him the nature) of the angels, but of the seed of Abraham He taketh hold," Heb. ii. 16. "And hence we are sanctified by the oblation of the body of Jesus Christ once - for this Man offering one sacrifice for sins, for ever sitteth on the right hand of God," Heb. x. 10 , 12. "Forasmuch then as the children were partakers of flesh and blood, He (Jesus Christ) also Himself, in like manner, partook of the same, that through death He might destroy - the devil," Heb. ii. 14. And that He has a human soul as well as a body. He assures us Himself when He says, "My soul is sorrowful even unto death," Mat. xxvi. 38. Lastly, Jesus Christ Himself declares He is a true man, capable of being put to death, when he says, "You seek to kill me, a man who have spoken the truth to you," John, viii. 40.

Q,. 5. Was Jesus Christ, in His human nature, subject to all the infirmities of man?

A. Yes; Jesus Christ, as man, was pleased to subject Himself to all our infirmities and miseries, sin only excepted, of which He was incapable, that He might thereby manifest to us the more abundantly the infinite riches of His goodness and mercy towards us. Thus He subjected Himself to suffer hunger, and thirst, and weariness; to be afflicted with grief and sorrow of mind; to be tempted and tried; to suffer pain and torment in His body, and to undergo death itself, and that in the most cruel and ignominious manner. "It behoved Him in all things to be made like to His brethren, that He might become a merciful and faithful high priest, with God, to make a reconciliation for the sins of the people. For in that wherein He himself hath suffered and been tempted, He is able to succour them also that are tempted," Heb. ii. 17. "For we have not a high priest, who cannot have compassion on our infirmities, but one tempted in all things like as we are, yet without sin," Heb. iv. 15. For "He did no sin, neither was guile found in His mouth," i Pet. ii. 22. On the contrary, "He was holy, innocent, undefiled, separated from sinners," Heb. vii. 26.

Q. 6. Why did Jesus Christ subject Himself to all the infirmities of human nature?

A. That He might be able to suffer for our sins; for whereas the Divine justice demanded a satisfaction for sin equal to the injury done to God by sin, which none but God could give; and, on the other hand, God Himself was incapable of suffering in His own nature, in order to give that satisfaction; therefore He took our nature upon Him, with all its infirmities, that in His flesh He might suffer and die for us: Christ "His own self bore our sins in His body upon the tree, that we being dead to sin, should live to justice; - by Whose stripes you are healed," i Pet. ii. 24 : "Christ also died once for our sins, the Just for the unjust, that He might offer us to God, being put to death, indeed, in the flesh,"I Pet. iii. 18. "Christ therefore suffered in the flesh,"I Pet. iv. 1; and Isaiah long before His coming hath foretold, that "He was wounded for our iniquities. He was bruised for our sins,... and by His bruises we are healed," Isa. liii. 5.

Q. 7. What was it that moved Almighty God to provide such a Redeemer for lost men?

A. It was the effect of His pure love and mercy towards us. He was not obliged to do it; He might have pursued us with all the rigour of His justice, if He had been pleased to do so, as He did the fallen angels; but He had compassion upon our miseries, and, of His own free will, out of pure love to us, provided the Redeemer for us. Thus Isaiah, foretelling the sufferings of the Redeemer, says, "He was offered because it was His own will," Isa. liii. 7. And Jesus Christ says on this subject, "No man taketh away My life from Me, but I lay it down of Myself; and I have power to lay it down, and I have power to take it up again," John, x. 18.

And therefore, though His enemies on different occasions sought to apprehend Him, "yet no man laid hands on Him, because His hour was not yet come," John, vii. 30. Now that it was pure love for us, and compassion for our miseries, which moved God to send us such a Redeemer, is often declared in holy writ: "God so loved the world as to give His only begotten Son, that whosoever believed in Him may not perish, but may have life everlasting. For God sent not His Son into the world to judge the world, but that the world may be saved by Him," John, iii. 16. "By this hath the charity of God appeared towards us; because God hath sent His only begotten Son into the world that we may live by Him. In this is charity: not as though we had loved God; but because He first loved us, and sent His Son to be a propitiation for our sins," i John, iv. 9. "God, who is rich in mercy, for His exceeding great charity wherewith He loved us, even when we were dead by sins, hath quickened us together in Christ (by whose grace you are saved),... that He might show, in the ages to come, the abundant riches of His grace in His bounty towards us in Christ Jesus," Eph. ii. 4. "In this we have known the charity of God; because He hath laid down His life for us," i John, iii. 16. "God commendeth His charity towards us; because, when as yet we were sinners, according to the time, Christ died for us," Rom. V. 8. "Christ also loved us, and hath delivered Himself for us an oblation and a sacrifice to God," Eph. V. 2. And in this we see the greatness of His love for us; for, as He Himself declares, "Greater love than this no man hath, that a man lay down his life for his friends," John, xv. 13.

Q. 8. In what manner did God the Son take the nature of man upon Him?

A. He made choice of the blessed Virgin Mary to be His Mother, and, when the fulness of time was come, in her sacred womb, and of her most pure blood, a human body was formed, by the operation of the Holy Ghost, and a most perfect soul was created to animate this body; and in the same instant of time the Divine nature was united to this soul and body, in the person of God the Son, by the power of. the Most High, which overshadowed this blessed Virgin for that purpose. Jesus Christ, God and man, being thus conceived in her sacred womb, remained there for the space of nine months, and then was born of her in the stable of Bethlehem, she still remaining a pure virgin.

Q. 9. What account does the Scripture give of this?

A. St Paul says, that "when the fulness of time was come, God sent His Son, made of a woman," Gal. iv. 4 , to show that He took flesh of her, or that His body was formed of the substance of her body; so also the Scripture says that He was born of Mary, - "Jacob begat Joseph, the husband of Mary, of whom was born Jesus, who is called Christ," Mat. i. 16. And that she was a Virgin, both when she conceived and when she brought Him forth, was foretold long before by the prophet Isaiah, saying, "Behold a Virgin shall conceive and bear a son, and His name shall be called Emmanuel," Isa. vii. 14 ; "which, being interpreted, is God with us," Mat. i. 23. And in what manner this was done is thus told by St Luke: "And the angel Gabriel was sent from God, unto a city of Galilee, called Nazareth, to a Virgin espoused to a man whose name was Joseph, of the house of David; and the Virgin's name was Mary. And the angel being come in, saith to her, Hail, full of grace, our Lord is with thee; blessed art thou among women. And when she had heard, she was troubled at his saying, and thought with herself what manner of salutation this should be. And the angel said to her, Fear not, Mary, for thou hast found grace with God: behold, thou shalt conceive in thy womb, and shalt bring forth a son, and thou shalt call His name Jesus: He shall be great, and shall be called the Son of the Most High.... And Mary said to the angel, How shall this be done, because I know not man? And the angel answering, said to her. The Holy Ghost shall come upon thee, and the power of the Most High shall overshadow thee, and therefore, also, the Holy One which shall be born of thee shall be called the Son of God.... And Mary said. Behold the handmaid of the Lord; be it done unto me according to thy word." Luke, i. 38.

Q. 10. Has Jesus Christ two natures?

A. Yes; Jesus Christ has two natures, the nature of God and the nature of man, united together in one person, which is the Person of God the Son; for, as the Athanasian creed expresses it, "as the rational soul and flesh is one man, so God and man is one Christ."

Q. II. How does it appear from Scripture that there is but one person in Christ?

A. Because the same person who is there declared to be Christ, according to the flesh, is also declared to be God; thus St Paul, speaking of the Israelites, says, "Of whom is Christ according to the flesh, who is over all things, God blessed for ever," Rom. ix. 4. He also says that the same person, "who being in the form of God thought it no robbery to be equal to God, was made in the likeness of man, and in fashion found as a man," Philip, ii. 6 ; and Jesus Christ Himself, who says on one occasion "I and the Father are one," John, x. 30 , says at another time, "I go to the Father, for the Father is greater than I," John, xiv. 28 ; where the same person of Christ, the same, declares that He is one and the same with the Father, speaking of Himself as God, and as to His Divine nature; and that He is also inferior to His Father, speaking of Himself as man, and as to His human nature: so that in these expressions is declared both that there is but one person in Christ, and that in this one person the two natures are united.

Q. 12. Does it appear from any other texts of Scripture that there are two natures in Christ, the Divine and human natures?

A. Most evidently; for, as Ave have seen above that Christ is both true God and true man, all the texts which show those two truths show that He has both the nature of God and the nature of man; for, being true God, He must of necessity have the nature of God, and being true man. He must of necessity have the nature of man, since the being anything and the having the nature of that thing is one and the self-same.

Q. 13. Will this union of the Divine and human natures in the person of Christ be ever dissolved?

A. It will never be dissolved; for the Holy Scripture assures us that Jesus Christ, true God and true man, is "a priest for ever," and that He is a "king for ever "; that He will reign over His faithful, and over all His enemies, "for ever "; that all things are subjected to Him, and that "of His kingdom there shall be no end." Thus, "the Lord hath sworn, and He will not repent, Thou art a priest for ever," Ps. cix. 4 ; which St Paul declares was said by God the Father to Christ in these words: "So also Christ did not glorify Himself to be made a high priest, but He that said to Him, Thou art My Son, this day have I begotten Thee," as he says also in another place, "Thou art a priest for ever," Heb. v. 5 ; and a little after adds that Christ is made priest, "not according to the law of a carnal commandment, but according to the power of an indissoluble life; for He testifieth, Thou art a priest for ever," Heb. vii. 17. And with regard to His kingdom, Isaiah says: "A child is born to us, and a son is given to us, and the government is upon His shoulders.... His empire shall be multiplied, and there shall be no end of peace; He shall sit upon the throne of David, and upon His kingdom, to establish it, and strengthen it with judgment and with justice, from henceforth and for ever," Isa. ix, 6 , 7. And Ezekiel, speaking of Christ's kingdom, says: "Thus saith the Lord God - and My servant David shall be king over them, and they shall have one shepherd - and David My servant shall be their prince for ever," Ezek. xxxvii. 24 , 25. Hence the angel Gabriel says to the blessed Virgin: "Thou shalt conceive in thy womb, and bring forth a son, and thou shalt call His name Jesus; and the Lord God shall give Him the throne of His father David, and He shall reign in the house of Jacob for ever, and of His kingdom there shall be no end," Luke, i. 31. The Jews themselves were very sensible of this truth, and therefore said, "We have heard out the law that Christ abideth for ever," John, xii. 34. From all which St Paul declares, that "Jesus Christ, yesterday and to-day, He is the same for ever," Heb. xiii. 8.

Q. 14. Is the blessed Virgin truly and properly the Mother of God?

A. Yes, she is truly and properly the Mother of God; because she conceived in her womb, and brought forth, in due time, that Divine Person who is both true God and true man, as the angel declared to her, when he said, "Thou shalt conceive in thy womb, and shalt bring forth a son; and the Holy One which shall be born of thee shall be called the Son of God," Luke, i. Now, to conceive and bring forth a son is surely to be his mother. It is true the divinity of Jesus Christ was from all eternity, and as God He was begotten of the Father before all ages, without any mother; so that it cannot be said that the blessed Virgin begot the Divine nature of Jesus Christ. But this is nowise necessary to make her the Mother of God; for our own mothers do not beget our souls, yet they are truly our mothers, both as to soul and body, because our souls, though created immediately by Almighty God, are united to our bodies in our mothers' womb, where we are conceived, and in due time brought forth by them. In like manner as the Divine nature was united to the human nature in the person of Jesus Christ within the womb of the blessed Virgin, and He who is true God was conceived and born of her, this makes her truly and properly the Mother of God. Hence St Elizabeth, inspired by the Holy Ghost, gave her this sacred title, when she said, "Whence is this to me, that the Mother of my Lord should come to me?" Luke, i. 43.

CHAPTER VIII.

The Office And Dignities Of The Redeemer

Q. I. What do you mean by the office of the Redeemer?

A. I mean all that Jesus Christ did, said, and suffered for the redemption of mankind, in quality of our Redeemer; which includes all the mysteries of His birth, life, passion, death, resurrection, and ascension.

Q. 2. Where was our Saviour born?

A. In the stable of Bethlehem, of which the Scripture gives this account: "In those days there went out a decree from Caesar Augustus, that the whole world should be enrolled. And all went to be enrolled, every one into his own city. And Joseph also went up from Galilee, out of the city of Nazareth, into Judea, to the city of David, which is called Bethlehem, because he was of the house and family of David, to be enrolled, with Mary his espoused wife, who was with child. . . . And it came to pass, that, when they were there, the days were accomplished that she should be delivered; and she brought forth her first-born son, and wrapt Him in swaddling-clothes, and laid Him in a manger, because there was no room for them in the inn," Luke, ii. 1 .

Q. 3. When was our Saviour born?

A. On the twenty-fifth day of December, the most inclement season of the year.

Q. 4. What are we principally to observe in this account of the birth of Jesus?

A. First, The wonderful and overruling providence of God, which makes use of the very vices and passions of men to accomplish His own designs. Augustus Caesar, the Roman Emperor, was moved by his pride and avarice to cause all his subjects to be numbered throughout his vast empire. In obedience to this decree, Joseph and Mary, who were living in Galilee, at a great distance from Bethlehem, the city of their family, came to that city to be numbered with their own family, just about the time of her being delivered; all which was so disposed by the Divine Providence, in order to accomplish what had been foretold by the prophets, that Christ should be born in that city: "And thou, Bethlehem Ephrata, art a little one among the thousands of Judah; out of thee shall He come forth unto Me that is to be the ruler in Israel," Mich. v. 2 .

Secondly, The infinite love of Jesus Christ to us, in beginning at so early a period, even at His very first entrance into the world, to suffer for us, and to give us, in His most tender infancy, the most perfect example of poverty, humility, and mortification; those darling virtues of His, which He knew were so necessary for us to practise, in order to cure all the spiritual maladies of our souls.

Q. 5. How did He practise these virtues at His birth?

A. He practised humility, in being rejected by all the rich and great ones in Bethlehem, none of whom would admit His Virgin Mother to their houses, notwithstanding her condition of being great with child, which obliged her to take up her abode in a stable, where He chose to be born. He practised poverty, in so ordering matters by His Divine Providence, that He. should be born at a distance from the place where His Mother dwelt, and on that account be deprived of all those conveniences which the poorest people have on such occasions; so He chose to be born in a stable instead of a palace, and laid in a manger instead of a soft bed. He practised mortification, in being exposed to much pain from the inclemency of the weather at that cold season, from the open stable in which He was born, and the hard manger in which He was laid.

Q. 6. What became of Him after He was born?

A. In His infancy He was circumcised, in obedience to the law, Luke, ii. 21 . He discovered Himself to the shepherds by an embassy of angels from heaven, to show that He came to be the Saviour of the Jews , Luke, ii. 9 . He afterwards manifested Himself to the Gentiles by a star in the heavens, to show He was also come to be the Saviour of the Gentiles, Mat. ii. And He was persecuted by King Herod, who, hearing of His birth from the wise men, sought to destroy Him, Mat. ii. After this He lived in private with His Virgin Mother and St Joseph, her spouse and guardian, and "subjected Himself to them," Luke, ii. 51 ; and continued to live in a poor, private, and retired manner, till He was thirty years of age, faithfully observing all the law of Moses, to give us an example of humility, submission, and obedience; and because He came, as He Himself tells us, "not to destroy the law, but to fulfil it," Mat. v. 17 .

Q. 7. At the thirtieth year of His life what did He do?

A. He then began His public life, preaching the Gospel, doing good to all, healing their diseases, casting out devils, and working the most stupendous miracles, to prove His Divine mission, and that He was the Messiah, or Saviour of the world, promised to mankind from the beginning: "God anointed Jesus of Nazareth with the Holy Ghost, and with power, who went about doing good, and healing all that were oppressed with the devil," Acts, x. 38 . "He was a prophet mighty in work and word before God and all the people," Luke, xxiv. 19 . "The Spirit of the Lord, saith He Himself, is upon Me, wherefore He hath anointed Me; to preach the Gospel to the poor He hath sent Me, to heal the contrite of heart, to preach deliverance to the captives, and sight to the blind, to set at liberty them that are bruised, to preach the acceptable year of the Lord, and the day of reward," Luke, iv. 18 . And when St John the Baptist sent two of His disciples to Him to ask if He was the Christ, He appealed to the miracles which He then wrought in their presence: "And answering. He said to them. Go and relate to John what you have heard and seen. The blind see, the lame walk, the lepers are made clean, the deaf hear, the dead rise again, to the poor the Gospel is preached," Luke, vii. 22 . Hence the testimony given of His public employment in the Gospel is this: "And Jesus went about all Galilee, teaching in their synagogues, and preaching the Gospel of the kingdom, and healing all manner of sickness, and all manner of diseases among the people. . . . And they brought to Him all sick people that were taken with divers diseases and torments, and such as were possessed by devils, and lunatics, and those that had the palsy, and He healed them," Mat. iv. 23 . "And there came to Him great multitudes, having with them the dumb, the blind, the lame, the maimed, and many others; and they cast them down at His feet, and He healed them," Mat. xv. 30 . "And whithersoever He entered into towns, or into villages, or cities, they laid the sick in the streets, and be sought Him that they might touch but the hem of His garment; and as many as touched Him were made whole," Mark, vi. 56 .

Q. 8. Were the miracles wrought by Jesus Christ a full and sufficient proof of His Divine mission, and of His being the Redeemer?

A. They certainly were a full and convincing proof of it, for several reasons, (1.) Because the very miracles He wrought had been foretold many ages before by the prophets, as the signs of the Redeemer. Thus Isaiah says, "Behold your God will bring the revenge of recompense. God Himself will come and save you; then shall the eyes of the blind be opened, and the ears of the deaf shall be unstopped; then shall the lame man leap as a hart, and the tongue of the dumb shall be free," Isa. XXXV. 5 . All which are the very things which Jesus did as proofs of His being the Redeemer. (2.) Because the works which Jesus did were done in the name of God the Father, on purpose to prove that He was the Messiah. Thus when "the Jews came round about Him, and said to Him, How long dost Thou hold our souls in suspense? if Thou be Christ, tell us plainly: Jesus answered them, I speak to you, and you believe not; the works that I do in the name of My Father give testimony of Me," John, x. 24 . Now it is impossible that Almighty God should allow any miracles to be wrought in His name in favour of falsehood. (3.) Because the works He did were such as none but God could perform; and therefore He appeals to them as the highest proofs that He is the Son of God. "Do you say," says He, "of Him whom the Father hath sanctified and sent into the world. Thou blasphemest, because I said I am the Son of God? If I do not the works of My Father, believe Me not; but if I do, though you will not believe Me, believe the works, that ye may know and believe that the Father is in Me, and I in the Father," John, X. 36 . "The works," says He again, "which the Father hath given Me to perform, the works themselves which I do, give testimony of Me that the Father hath sent Me; and the Father Himself who hath sent Me hath given testimony of Me," John, v. 36 . Also, "The words that I speak to you I speak not of Myself. 'But the Father who abideth in Me, He doth the works. Believe you not that I am in the Father, and the Father in Me? otherwise believe for the very works' sake," John, xiv. 10 . Lastly, Because Christ declares that the Jews were inexcusable for not believing Him on so convincing a proof as His miracles were. "If I had not come and spoken to them, they would not have sin; but now they have no excuse for their sin. He that ' hateth Me, ha-teth My Father also. If I had not done among them the works that no other man hath done, they would not have sin; but now they have both seen, and hated both Me and My Father," John, xv. 22 .

Q. 9. How long did Jesus Christ continue in His public ministry?

A. For about three years; and then He delivered Himself up to the will of His enemies, to be put to death for the sins of the world.

Q. 10. How did this happen?

A. From the beginning of His public life the chief priests and princes of the Jews had conceived an implacable hatred against Him; the sanctity of His life, the purity of His doctrine, and the splendour of His miracles, which gained Him the hearts of all the people, imbittered theirs with the most malignant envy, and they continually sought an opportunity to destroy Him.

Q. II. How could they destroy or hurt Him who was God as well as man, and had all creatures at His command?

A. So long as He pleased they could not touch a hair of His head; for though "they sought to apprehend Him, yet no man laid hands upon Him, because His hour was not yet come," John, vii. 30 . But when His own time was come. He said to His disciples in the garden, "It is enough, the hour is come; behold the Son of Man shall be betrayed into the hands of sinners," Mark, xiv. 41 . And when He was taken in the garden, He said to His enemies, "This is your hour, and the power of darkness," Luke, xxii. 53 - that is, the hour in which He was pleased to deliver Himself up to their will; for, as St Paul assures us, "Christ loved us, and delivered Himself up for us an oblation and a sacrifice to God, for an odour of sweetness," Eph. v. 2 . St Peter also declares that "He delivered Himself to him that judged Him unjustly," i Pet. ii. 23 . And Christ Himself declared to Pilate, "Tho»u shouldst not have any power against Me unless it were given thee from above," John, xix. II.

Q. 12. When, therefore, His hour was come, what did He suffer for us?

A. To show the greatness of His love for us, and the plenteous redemption which He brought us, He was pleased to suffer during His passion every kind of torment with which human nature could be afflicted. He suffered in His soul, in His body, in His goods, in His honour, in His reputation. He suffered in all His senses, and in all His members; He suffered from all kinds of persons - from the highest to the lowest, all were combined against Him; He suffered also from His own friends, being betrayed by one of His bosom friends, denied by another, and forsaken by the rest. Having gone through all these different torments with the most amazing patience, meekness, and charity, at last, to crown the whole, He was nailed to a disgraceful cross, and died a cruel and ignominious death, between two thieves, as is related at large in the four Gospels.

Q. 13. What became of Him after His death?

A. Death is the separation of the soul from the body; and to assure us that Christ died a true and real death, all the four Gospels declare, that after hanging in torments on the Cross for three long hours, "He bowed down his head, and gave up the ghost," John, xix. 30 - that is, gave up his soul and died. Now, after his death, "Joseph of Arimathea, who also himself was a disciple of Jesus, went to Pilate and begged the body of Jesus. And Pilate commanded that the body should be delivered; and Joseph, taking the body, wrapt it in a clean linen cloth, and laid it in his own new monument, which he had hewn out in a rock; and he rolled a great stone to the door of the monument, and went his way," Mat. xxvii. 57 . In what manner this was done is thus related by St John: And Nicodemus "also came, he who at first came to Jesus by night, bringing a mixture of myrrh and aloes, about a hundred pound weight. They took, therefore, the body of Jesus, and wound it in linen cloths with the spices, as the manner of the Jews is to bury. Now there was a garden in the place where He was crucified, and in the garden a new sepulchre, wherein no man had yet been laid: there therefore they laid Jesus, because the sepulchre was nigh at hand," John, xix. 39 .

Q. 14. And what became of His soul when it left His body?

A. It descended into hell - which word, in the original Hebrew language, is sheol, and signifies a place below, or in the bowels of the earth. It is thus interpreted by St Paul, when he said that "Christ descended to the lower parts of the earth," Eph. iv. 9 . And therefore hell is applicable to all the different places that are there.

Q. 15. How many places does the Scripture point to us, as in the bowels of the earth, which go by the general name of hell.

A. Chiefly these three: (1.) The place of the damned, which is also called in Scripture Gehenna, and the abyss, or bottomless pit, and hell-fire; this is hell properly so called, as being the deepest of all, and at the greatest distance from heaven. St John, describing a vision he had of this place, says, that when "a star that fell from heaven opened the bottomless pit, the smoke of the pit arose, as the smoke of a great furnace," Rev. ix. 2 . And again, "The beast . . . shall come out of the bottomless pit, and go into destruction; and the inhabitants of the earth shall wonder," Rev. xvii. 8 . (2.) The prison of Purgatory, where the souls of those "who have not made agreement with their adversary, whilst in the way with him, and therefore are cast into this prison," are detained till they are cleansed from all smaller stains and imperfections, and have fully satisfied for what they owe to their adversary, the Divine justice, by "paying the utmost farthing," Mat. v. 25 . (3.) The prison of Limbo, where the souls of those saints were detained who died before Christ came into the world. To this last place it was that the soul of Christ descended at His death, to preach redemption to these blessed souls, to free them from their long captivity and carry them up with Him to heaven.

Q. 16. Had none of the ancient saints gone to heaven at their death?

A. They had not; and this is expressly declared by Jesus Christ Himself, who, in His conversation with Nicodemus, says, "No man hath ascended into heaven but He that descended from heaven, the Son of Man, who is in heaven," John, iii. 13 . In which words He positively says, that at the time when He was speaking, no man had ever gone to heaven but He Himself alone, whom He calls "the Son of Man," and whose blessed soul, from its union with the Divine nature, was always in heaven - that is, was always enjoying the clear Vision of God. This is also declared by St Peter, in his first sermon to the Jews, after receiving the Holy Ghost; where, proving the ascension of Jesus Christ to the right hand of God, from this prophecy of David, "The Lord said to my Lord, Sit Thou on My right hand," he shows that this prophecy could not be understood of David himself; "for," says he, "David did not ascend to heaven," Acts, ii. 34 . Now, if David did not ascend to heaven, neither did any other who died before our Saviour. And St Paul, speaking of all the saints before Christ, expressly affirms, that "all these being approved by the testimony of faith, received not the promise, God providing some better thing for us, that they should not be perfected without us," Heb. xi. 39 , 40.

Q- 17. Are we not told in Scripture that Elijah was taken up to heaven when he left this world?

A. As all the places beneath us in the bowels of the earth go by the general name of Hell, so, in Scripture language, all the places above us go by the general name oi Heaven. Hence St Paul tells us that he was "taken up to the third heaven," 2 Cor. xii. 2 - which shows that there are different places above that go by that name. Now the most noble of all these is that glorious heaven where God shows Himself in all His majesty and beauty to the blessed; for the Scripture tells us that Christ, at His ascension, "is set on the right hand of the throne of Majesty in the heavens," Heb. viii. 1 ; "at the right hand of God," Rom. viii. 34 . Of which throne He Himself says, "To him that shall overcome I will give to sit with Me in My throne, as I also have overcome, and am set down with My Father in His throne," Rev. iii. 21 . Before which throne St John "saw a great multitude, which no man could number, standing in the sight of the Lamb; "and adds, that "they are before the throne of God, and serve Him night and day in His temple, and that they shall no more hunger nor thirst, neither shall the sun fall on them, nor any heat; for the Lamb, which is in the midst of the throne, shall rule them, and lead them to the living fountains of water, and God shall wipe away all tears from their eyes," Rev. vii. 15 . Now that this heaven of heavens is above all other places that go by the name of heaven, St Paul assures us when he says that the place to which Christ ascended was "above all the heavens," Eph. iv. 10 . When, therefore, our Saviour declares that "no man hath ascended into heaven "before Him, He means the highest heaven, where God is seen and enjoyed by the blessed; where He Himself, as man, always was, in this sense, that He always enjoyed the Beatific Vision, by reason of His union with the Divine nature; but Elijah, and also Enos, were only taken up to some of the lower heavens, where they shall remain till the last days, when they shall come again and be put to death by antichrist, but where they do not enjoy the Vision of God.

Q. 18. Why had no man gone to that heaven where God is seen and enjoyed, before Christ?

A. Because the gates of heaven were shut to man by Adam's sin, and could not be opened to us till the price of our redemption should be paid, which was the Blood of Jesus shed upon the Cross.

Q. 19. Were these blessed gates opened again to man when that price was paid?

A. Yes, they were; and hence, in the hymn called Te Deum, acknowledged and used by the Church of England, it is said to Christ, "when Thou hadst overcome the sharpness of death, Thou didst open the kingdom of heaven to all believers."

Q. 20. How is that place called in which the souls of the saints were detained who had died before our Saviour had paid the price of our redemption?

A. In the Creed and in the Scripture it is called by the general name of Hell. Thus, when Jacob believed that his son Joseph was dead, and that a wild beast had devoured him, he said in his grief, "I will go down to my son into hell mourning," Gen. xxxvii. 35 ; where it is evident that, by the word hell, he could not mean the grave, since he believed that his son was devoured by a wild beast, and therefore that even his body was not in the grave, much less his soul; and he says he "would go down to him," to be with him, to be where he was, to enjoy his company. The same language was used by Joseph's brethren when he sought to detain Benjamin, that, if they should return without him to their father, "thy servants," said they, "shall bring down his grey hairs with sorrow into hell," Gen. xliv. 31 . It is also in Scripture called "the lower part of the earth"; so St Paul, speaking of Christ's going down to this place, says, "He descended to the lower parts of the earth," Eph. iv. 9 . Hence, when the soul of Samuel appeared to the witch of Endor, and she was astonished, and cried out, Saul asked her, "What hast thou seen? The woman answered, I saw a god ascending out of the earth. And he said, What form is he of? and she said, An old man cometh up, and he is covered with a mantle. And Samuel said to Saul, Why hast thou disturbed my rest, that I should be brought up?" i Kings (or Sam.), xxiii.12, xxviii. 15. Which expressions show that the place of rest where the soul of Samuel had been was in the bowels of the earth. The wise man also, giving the praises of Samuel, concludes thus: "And after this he slept, and he made known to the king, and showed him the end of his life, and he lifted up his voice from the earth in prophecy," Ecclus. xlvi. 23 . It is likewise called in Scripture Abraham's bosom, because it was a place of rest and peace; for the blessed souls there had no sufferings, but rather were comforted after all their sufferings in their mortal life. Thus the rich glutton in hell, "lifting up his eyes when he was in torments, he saw Abraham afar off, and Lazarus in his bosom. . . . And Abraham said to him, Son, remember that thou didst receive good things in thy lifetime, and likewise Lazarus evil things; but now he is comforted, and thou art tormented," Luke, xvi. 22 . Finally, in the language of the Church, this place is called Limbus, to distinguish it from the hell of the damned and from Purgatory.

Q. 21. How does it appear that Christ went down to this place?

A. The Creed affirms that at His death "He descended into hell." Christ Himself expressly foretold it when He said, "As Jonas was in the whale's belly three days and three nights, so shall the Son of Man be in the heart of the earth three days and three nights," Mat. xii. 40 . St Paul also declares it thus, "Now that He ascended, what is it but because He also descended first into the lower parts of the earth?" Eph. iv. 9 . And St Peter assures us that, "in His spirit. He went and preached to those spirits who were in prison," i Pet. iii. 19 .

Q. 22. For what purpose did Christ descend to this place?

A. First, That He might preach the Gospel to these holy souls, and bring them the happy tidings that the price of their redemption was paid, and the time of their deliverance was come, which they had for so long a time desired with so much ardour. Thus St Peter having told us that "He went and preached to those spirits that were in prison "(i Pet. iii. 19), a little after adds-" The Gospel was preached also to the dead, that they might be judged, indeed, according to men in the flesh, but may live according to God in the spirit," i Pet. iv. 6 . And this the Divine wisdom, God the Son, foretold long before, by the mouth of the wise man, saying, "I wisdom . . . will penetrate to all the lower parts of the earth, and wall behold all that sleep, and will enlighten all that hope in the Lord," Ecclus. xxiv. 45 . Secondly, That He might deliver those blessed souls from their long imprisonment in which they had been detained, as was foretold by the prophet, saying, "Thou also, by the blood of Thy testament hast sent forth Thy prisoners out of the pit wherein is no water,"Zach. ix. 11. Thirdly, To carry them up with Him to heaven at His ascension, as the first-fruits of His redemption, and the triumphs of His victory over sin and death, as was foretold by David, saying, "Thou hast ascended on high. Thou hast led captivity captive," Ps. lxvii. 19 , which prophecy is also cited by St Paul , Eph. iv. 8 , who also says that, after His death, "having spoiled principalities and powers, He made a show of them confidently, triumphing openly over them in Himself,'" Col. ii. 15 .

Q. 23. Did his presence occasion great joy to those holy souls?

A. Most undoubtedly. These holy souls had nothing more at heart than to be delivered out of their long confinement, and admitted to the clear sight and enjoyment of God. This was the great object of all their desires; and the delay of this was the only thing that could give them any pain, according to that saying of the wise man, "Hope that is deferred afflicteth the soul," Prov. xiii. 12 . But as it is there immediately added, "Desire when it cometh is a tree of life," so the sight of the Redeemer coming in among them - the beholding the beauty of His Divine presence, and receiving from Him the happy tidings that their redemption was paid, and the day of their release was come - was indeed "a tree of life to them," filled them with the most exquisite joy and gladness, and turned their dreary prison into a paradise of delight, according to what our Saviour said to the good thief upon the cross, "This day thou shalt be with Me in paradise; "' because he was, at his death, to follow Jesus Christ to this place, and there enjoy His Divine presence, and all the fruits of His redemption.

Q. 24. How long did Christ continue dead?

A. Part of three days - to wit, from Friday about mid-afternoon till Sunday morning.

Q. 25. On the third day after His death, what did He do?

A. He rose again from the dead - that is. His blessed soul, by His own Divine power, returned into His body, was reunited to it, and raised it to life again. "T lay down My life," said He, "that I may take it up again. No man taketh it away from Me, but I lay it down of Myself; and I have power to lay it down, and I have power to take it up again," John, x. 17 . And when the Jews asked a sign from Him of His authority for cleansing the temple of those who profaned it, "Jesus answered and said to them. Destroy this temple, and in three days I will raise it up. . . . But He spoke of the temple of His body; when, therefore, He was risen again from the dead, His disciples remembered that He said this," John, ii. 19 . The history of what happened at this great event is thus given by St Matthew: "And, behold, there was a great earthquake; for an angel of the Lord descended from heaven, and coming, rolled back the stone, and sat upon it: and his countenance was as lightning, and his raiment as snow; and for fear of him the guards were struck with terror and became as dead men. . . . And the angel answering said to the women, Fear not you, for I know that you seek Jesus who was crucified: He is not here, for He is risen, as He said. Come and see the place where the Lord was laid," Mat. xxviii. 2 .

Q. 26. Is the resurrection of Jesus an important article of the Christian faith?

A. It is one of the most important and fundamental articles of the Christian religion, and the groundwork and proof of all the rest. Hear how St Paul speaks of it on occasion of some that denied the resurrection of the dead, in order to confirm and show the importance of this article of our faith: "I delivered to you first of all what I also received, how that Christ died for our sins, according to the Scriptures; and that He was buried and rose again according to the Scriptures; and that He was seen by Cephas, and after that by the eleven; then was He seen by more than five hundred brethren at once, of whom many remain until this present, and some are fallen asleep. . . . Last of all, He was seen also by me. . . . Now, if Christ be preached that He rose again from the dead, how do some among you say that there is no resurrection of the dead? For if there be no resurrection of the dead, then Christ is not risen again; and if Christ be not risen again, then is our preaching vain, and your faith is also vain. Yea, and we are found false witnesses of God, because we have given testimony against God, that He hath raised up Christ, whom He hath not raised up, if the dead rise not again. For if the dead rise not again, neither is Christ risen again; and if Christ be not risen again, your faith is vain, for you are yet in your sins. . . . But now Christ is risen from the dead, the first-fruits of them that sleep," i Cor. xv. 3 .

Q. 27. How comes the resurrection of Christ to be of so great importance to the Christian Faith?

A. Because it is the most convincing proof that Jesus Christ is the Son of God, and that His doctrine is Divine and true. For (1.) During His public ministry. He often foretold that He would be put to death, but that He would rise again the third day: "I lay down My life," said He, "that I may take it up again," John, X. 17 . "From that time forth Jesus began to show to His disciples that He must go to Jerusalem, and suffer many things from the ancients, and the scribes, and chief priests, and be put to death, and the third day rise again," Mat. xvi. 21 . "And Jesus said to them. The Son of Man shall be betrayed into the hands of men, and they shall kill Him, and the third day He shall rise again," Mat. xvii. 21 . Now this prediction was spread among the people before His death, insomuch that after He was laid in the grave, "the chief priests and the Pharisees came together to Pilate, saying, Sir, we have remembered that that seducer said, while He was yet alive. After three days I will rise again. Command, therefore, the sepulchre to be guarded till the third day, lest His disciples come and steal Him away, and say to the people He is risen from the dead; so the last error shall be worse than the first. Pilate said to them, Go guard it as you know: so they departing made the sepulchre sure, sealing the Stone, and setting guards," Mat. xxvii. 62 . Seeing, then, that He did rise again, as He had foretold, this evidently shows that He is the very person whom He called Himself, - the Messiah, the Son of God, made man for the redemption of the world; for who but God could raise Himself to life? who but God could foretell beforehand that He was to do so? (2.) When the Pharisees pressed Him to give them a sign of His being the Messiah, and of the authority by which He acted. He referred them to His resurrection as the most convincing sign of any: "An evil and adulterous generation," said He, "seeketh for a sign, and a sign shall not be given it but the sign of Jonas the prophet; for as Jonas was in the whale's belly three days and three nights, so shall the Son of Man be in the heart of the earth three days and three nights," Mat.

xii. 39. "Destroy this temple of My body, and in three days I will raise it up again," John, ii. 19. (3.) Because the apostles were most assiduous and earnest in establishing this point as the most essential article of Christianity, and alone sufficient to convince the world of the truth of it. This was the great scope of their preaching, and the miracles they wrought were chiefly intended to confirm and establish this article. Thus, when St Peter cured the lame man, he said to the people, "But the Author of life you killed, whom God hath raised from the dead, of which we are witnesses, and His name, through the faith of His name, hath made this man strong," Acts iii. 15. Again, "With great power did the apostles give testimony of the resurrection of Jesus Christ our Lord," Acts, iv. 1 . And in the first sermon which St Peter preached to the Jews on Pentecost, after the coming of the Holy Ghost, at which no less than three thousand were converted, he insists in a particular manner on this article, and proves it from the prophecy of David, which he cites at large, and especially from these words, - "Thou wilt not leave My soul in hell, nor suffer Thy Holy One to see corruption; "on which he speaks thus, - "Him God hath raised up, having loosed the sorrows of hell, as it was impossible that He should be holden by it." Then, reciting the prophecy, he goes on: "Whereas, therefore, he (David) was a prophet - foreseeing he spoke of the resurrection of Christ, for neither was He left in hell, neither did His flesh see corruption. This Jesus hath God raised up again, whereof all we are witnesses," Acts, ii. 32 .
Q. 28. How long did Christ continue upon earth after His resurrection?

A. For the space of forty days, and then He ascended up in a glorious manner into heaven, in the sight of His apostles and other disciples, of which the Scripture gives this account: "He showed Himself alive (to them) after His passion, by many proofs, for forty days, appearing to them, and speaking of the kingdom of God, and eating with them," Acts, i. 3 . And on the fortieth day, after having instructed them in all the mysteries of His kingdom, "opening their understandings that they might understand the Scriptures," Luke, xxiv. 45 , he gave them commission "to preach the Gospel to all nations, baptising them in the name of the Father, and of the Son, and of the Holy Ghost," Mat. xxviii. 19 ; and power to work all miracles in confirmation of their doctrine , Mark, xvi. 17 . He then "led them out as far as Bethania, and, lifting up His hands, He blessed them; and it came to pass, whilst He blessed them, that He departed from them, and was carried up into heaven," Luke, xxiv. 50 ; and a cloud received Him out of their sight. "And while they were beholding Him going up to heaven, behold two men stood by them in white garments, who also said, Ye men of Galilee, why stand you looking up to heaven? this Jesus, who is taken up from you into heaven, shall so come as ye have seen Him going up to heaven," Acts, i. 9 .

Q. 29. Why did Christ ascend to heaven?

A. First, To take possession, even as man, of that eternal glory which His Father had prepared for Him in heaven, as the reward of all He had done and suffered for His Father's glory, and in obedience to His will, according to what He said Himself to the two disciples going to Emaus, "Ought not Christ to have suffered these things, and so to enter into His glory?" Luke, xxiv. 26 . How great this glory was He also shows by the prayer He made to His Father, when He said, "I have glorified Thee on earth, I have finished the work which Thou gavest Me to do, and now glorify Me, O Father, with Thyself, with the glory which I had, before the world was, with Thee," John, xvii. 4 . To receive this Divine, this infinite glory, Jesus Christ "ascended above all the heavens," Eph. iv. 10 ; His Father "setting Him at His own right hand in the heavenly places, above all principality and power, and virtue and dominion, and every name that is named not only in this world, but also in that which is to come, and He hath put all things under His feet," Eph. i. 20 , and has bestowed the highest dignities upon Him, suitable to that immense glory which He enjoys, and conformable to all He did and suffered in obedience to His Father's will. Second, To prepare a place in His kingdom for all His faithful followers, and draw up our hearts to heaven after Him. Thus comforting His apostles, who were in great affliction at the news of His going to leave them, He said, "Let not your hearts be troubled - in My Father's house there are many mansions; if not, I would have told you, that I go to prepare a place for you. And if I shall go and prepare a place for you, I will come again and take you to Myself, that where I am you also may be," John, xiv. I. And in His prayer for His followers, He says to His Father, "Father, I will that where I am, they also whom Thou hast given Me may be with Me, that they may see My glory which Thou hast given Me," John, xvii. 24 .

Q. 30. What are these dignities which Jesus Christ, as man, is honoured with in heaven by His Father?

A. Chiefly these following: (1.) His very name itself; for as "He humbled Himself, becoming obedient unto death, even the death of the cross, therefore God hath exalted Him, and hath given to Him a name which is above every name, that in the name of Jesus every knee should bow, of those that are in heaven, on earth, and under the earth, and that every tongue should confess that the Lord Jesus Christ is in the glory of God the Father," Philip,

ii. 8 . (2.) The royal dignity of being King over all creatures, with the most absolute power and dominion over them. This He foretold by the royal prophet, saying, "I am appointed King by Him over Zion His holy mountain. . . . The Lord said to Me - ask of Me and I will give Thee the Gentiles for Thy inheritance, and the utmost parts of the world for Thy possession, and Thou shalt rule them with a rod of iron," Ps. ii. 6 . "He shall have dominion from sea to sea, and from the river unto the ends of the earth," Ps. lxxi. 8 . And in the Gospel He says to His apostles, "All things are delivered to Me by My Father," Mat. xi. 27 ; "All power is given unto Me in heaven and in earth," Mat. xxviii. 18 . And to His Father He says, "Father - glorify Thy Son, that Thy Son may glorify Thee, as Thou hast given Him power over all flesh," John, xvii. 1 . Hence St Peter concludes his first sermon to the Jews thus: "Therefore let all the house of Israel know most assuredly, that God hath made this same Jesus, whom you have crucified, both Lord and Christ," Acts, ii. 36 ; and in his epistles he says, that "He is on the right hand of God swallowing down death, that we might be made heirs of life everlasting; being gone into heaven, the angels, and powers, and virtues, being made subject to Him," i Pet. iii. 22 . St Paul also assures us, that "to this end Christ died and rose again, that He might be Lord both of the dead and of the living," Rom. xiv. 9 . And how great and tremendous His majesty is, appears from this description given of Him by St John: "And I saw heaven opened, and beheld a white horse, and He that sat upon Him was called Faithful and True, and with justice does He judge and fight: and His eyes were as a flame of fire, and on His head were many crowns, and He hath a name written which no man knoweth but Himself; and He was clothed with a garment sprinkled with blood, and His name is called The Word of God; and out of His mouth proceeded a sharp two-edged sword, that with it He may strike the Gentiles; and He shall rule them with a rod of iron; and He treadeth the wine-press of the fierceness of God the Almighty; and He hath on His garment and thigh written, King of kings, and Lord of lords" Rev. xix.

Q. 31. What are the other dignities of Jesus Christ?

A. They are, (3.) That He is the Head of the Church, which is His body, and of which we all are members: "He hath put all things under His feet," and "hath made Him Head over all the Church, which is His body," Eph. i. 22 , "that . . . we may in all things grow up in Him, who is the Head, even Christ, from whom the whole body, compacted and fitly joined together, by what every joint supplieth, according to the operation in the measure of every part, maketh increase of the body," Eph. iv. 15 . "We being many,

are one body in Christ, and members one of another," Rom. xii. 5 . "Now
you are the body of Christ, and members of member," i Cor. xii. 27 . "Christ
is the Head of the Church; He is the Saviour of the body; . . . Christ cher-
isheth the Church, for we are members of His body, of His flesh, and of His
bones," Eph. V. 23 , 30; "for He is the head of the body, the Church, Who
is the beginning, the first-born from the dead, that in all things He may
hold the primacy," Col. i. 18 . (4.) He is the sovereign Judge of all mankind;
"neither doth the Father judge any man, but hath committed all judgment
to the Son, that all men may honour the Son as they honour the Father; ...
and He hath given Him authority to execute judgment, because He is the
Son of Man," John, v. 22 , 27. Hence St Peter declares, that he and the other
apostles received an express command from God, "to preach to the people,
and to testify that He (Christ) it is who is appointed by God to be the judge
of the living and of the dead," Acts, X. 42 .

Q. 32. In what manner does Christ perform the office of Head of His
Church?

A. In several ways, but particularly the following: (1.) By the continual protection of His Divine Providence; of which the royal prophet says,
"Behold, He shall neither slumber nor sleep that keepeth Israel. The Lord
is thy keeper; the Lord is thy protection upon thy right hand. The sun shall
not burn thee by day, nor the moon by night; the Lord keepeth thee from
all evil," Ps. cxx. 4 . And Zacharias, speaking of the glories of the Church,
and the providence of God over her, says: "I will raise up thy sons, O Sion,
above thy sons, O Greece, and I will make thee as the sword of the mighty;
and the Lord God shall be seen over them, . . . and the Lord of hosts will
protect them; . . . the Lord their God shall save them in that day," Zach. ix.
"In that day shall the Lord protect the inhabitants of Jerusalem, and he that
hath offended among them shall be as David (to wit, shall return to God by
sincere repentance as David did), and the house of David as that of God,
as an angel of the Lord in their sight. And it shall come to pass in that day,
that I will seek to destroy all the nations that come against Jerusalem. And I
will pour out upon the house of David, and upon the inhabitants of Jerusalem, the spirit of grace and of prayers,"Zach. xii. 8. Now this continual protection is exercised by ordering and disposing all things for the good of His
Church, and the sanctification of her members, establishing her in justice
and judgment, defending her from all her enemies, preserving her in peace,
and increasing her dominion to the utmost bounds of the earth; all which
was foretold by the prophets many ages before Christ came into the world.
Thus, "of the increase of His government and peace there shall be no end;

He shall sit upon the throne of David, and upon His kingdom, to establish it with justice and with judgment, from henceforth, even for .ever. The zeal of the Lord of hosts will perform this," Isa. ix. 6 . "Fear not, for thou shalt not be ashamed; neither be thou confounded, for thou shalt not be put to shame. . . . For thy Maker is thine husband, the Lord of hosts is His name: and thy Redeemer, the Holy One of Israel, the Lord of the whole earth shall He be called. . . . And thou shalt be founded in justice: depart far from oppression, for thou shalt not fear; and from terror, for it shall not come near thee. . . . No weapon that is formed against thee shall prosper, and every tongue that resisteth thee thou shalt condemn," Isa. liv. "I will make thee to be an everlasting excellence, a joy unto generation and generation; and thou shalt suck the milk of the Gentiles, and thou shalt be nursed with the breasts of kings; and thou shalt know that I am the Lord thy Saviour and thy Redeemer, the Mighty One of Jacob," Isa. lx. 15 . "This shall be the covenant that I will make with the house of Israel, after those days, saith the Lord: I will give My law in their bowels, and I will write it in their heart; and I will be their God, and they shall be My people," Jer. xxxi. 22 . These and many other such glorious promises made to the Church, Jesus Christ fulfils as Head of the Church, by His Divine Providence, watching over her at all times, "loving her and cherishing her," as St Paul expresses it, Eph. v. 25 , 29. (2.) By the continual communication of His Divine grace to all her members, according to their wants and necessities; for, "to every one of us is given grace according to the measure of the giving of Christ," Eph. iv. 7 ; and "of His fulness we have all received, and grace for grace," John, i. 16 . He being always ready on His part to communicate His grace to their souls, to beautify, nourish, and enliven them, and to enable them to bring forth good fruit in abundance; just as the trunk of the tree always sends forth nourishing juice to all its branches, in order to beautify them with leaves and flowers, and enable them to produce good fruit in its season: and this is the similitude which Christ Himself makes use of to explain this matter to us, when He says, "Abide in Me and I in you: as the branch cannot bear fruit of itself, unless it abide in the vine, neither can you unless you abide in Me. I am the vine, you the branches; he that abideth in Me and I in him, the same beareth much fruit," John, xv. 4 . (3.) By the special protection which He has over her pastors, who are her principal members, and to whom the care of all the others is committed. Over these He watches with a most particular providence, to assist them in the important office of preserving and propagating the great truths of His holy Faith, and conveying them pure and undefiled to the latest posterity; for this purpose He has passed His sacred promise, that He Himself "will be with them all days, even to the consummation of the world," Mat. xxviii. 20 . And, soon after

His ascension into heaven, He sent down His Holy Spirit upon them, "the Spirit of truth," on purpose "that He might abide with them for ever, and teach them all truth," John, xiv. 16 , 17, and xvi. 13.

Q. 33. In what manner did the Holy Ghost first come down upon the apostles and Christians?

A. Ten days after our Saviour went to heaven, during which time the apostles and other disciples "continued with one accord in prayer, with Mary the mother of Jesus and His brethren "(Acts, i. 14), "when the days of Pentecost were accomplished, . . . suddenly there came a sound from heaven, as of a mighty wind coming, and it filled the whole house where they were sitting. And there appeared to them parted tongues, as it were of fire, and sat upon every one of them. And they were all filled with the Holy Ghost, and they began to speak with divers tongues, according as the Holy Ghost gave them to speak," Acts, ii. 1 .

Q. 34. What were the principal ends for which our Saviour sent the Holy Ghost to His Church?

A. The Scripture points out these following: (r.) To comfort her members in all their distresses and afflictions. "I will ask the Father," says He, "and He will give you another Comforter, the Spirit of truth, whom the world cannot receive, because it seeth Him not, nor knoweth Him; but you shall know Him, because He shall abide with you, and be in you," John, xiv. i6. (2.) To purify and cleanse them from their sins, and strengthen their souls against- all temptations: "but you are washed, but you are sanctified, but you are justified in the name of the Lord Jesus Christ, and in the Spirit of our God," I Cor. vi. 11 ; "for the law of the spirit of life in Christ Jesus hath freed me from the law of sin and of death, . . . that the justification of the law might be fulfilled in us who walk not according to the flesh, but according to the Spirit; . . . likewise the Spirit helpeth our infirmity," Rom. viii. 2 , 4, 26. (3.) To teach and enable them to pray, by which they may obtain all good things from God: "for we know not what we should pray for as we ought, but the Spirit Himself asketh for us with unspeakable groanings; and He that searcheth the hearts knoweth what the Spirit desireth, because He asketh for the saints according to God," Rom. viii. 26 . (4.) To adorn their souls with Divine charity, or the love of God, and with all manner of virtues, "because the charity of God is poured abroad in our hearts by the Holy Ghost, who is given to us," Rom. v. 5 ; and "the fruit of the Spirit is charity, joy, peace, patience, benignity, goodness, longanimity, mildness, faith, modesty, continence, chastity," Gal. V. 22 . (5.) To enlighten their understandings with the knowledge of heavenly things; for "the things that are of God no man knoweth, but the Spirit of God; now we have received not the spirit of this world, but the Spirit that is of God, that we may know the things that are given us from God," i Cor. ii. 11 . And "the Comforter," says our Saviour, "the Holy Ghost, whom the Father will send in my name. He will teach you all things, and bring all things to your mind, whatsoever I shall have said to you," John, xiv. 26 . Hence He is called by Isaias, "the Spirit of wisdom and of understanding, the Spirit of counsel and of fortitude, the Spirit of knowledge and of godliness, and the Spirit of the fear of the Lord," Isa. xi. 2 ; which are the Sevenfold precious graces that Divine Spirit bestows upon those in whom He dwells, in such measure and proportion as He sees fitting, and as the disposition of their souls is capable of receiving. (6.) To raise them up to the glorious dignity of being the adopted children of God, "for whosoever are led by the Spirit of God, they are the sons of God; for you have not received the spirit of bondage again in fear; but you have received the spirit of adoption of sons, whereby we cry, Abba (Father); for the Spirit Himself giveth testimony to our spirit that we are the sons of God," Rom. viii. 14 . So that "if any man have not the Spirit of Christ, He is none of His," Ibid. 9. (7.) To make them the temples of God and of His Holy Spirit: "Know ye not that you are the temple of God, and that the Spirit of God dwelleth in you? But if any man violate the temple of God, him God will destroy; for the temple of God is holy, which you are," i Cor. iii. 16 . "Know you not that your members are the temple of the Holy Ghost, who is in you, whom you have from God, and that you are not your own?" i Cor. vi. 19 . (8.) To bear witness to, and give testimony of, Jesus Christ; for, says our Saviour, "when the Comforter Cometh, whom I will send you from the Father, the Spirit of truth, who proceedeth from the Father, He shall give testimony of Me, and you shall give testimony, because you are with Me from the beginning," John, xv. 26 . Now the apostles gave testimony of Jesus Christ, because they declared to the world as eyewitnesses what they knew concerning Him, and the truths they had heard from Him. And the Holy Ghost gave testimony of Jesus Christ, by confirming what the apostles preached, with numberless miracles which He wrought through them for "by the hands of the apostles were many signs and wonders wrought among the people, . . . insomuch that they brought the sick into the streets, and laid them on beds and couches, that when Peter came, his shadow, at least, might overshadow them, and they might be delivered from their infirmities," Acts, v. 12 , 15. Hence St Paul declares that "he was the minister of Christ Jesus among the Gentiles, ... by the virtue of signs and wonders in the power of the Holy Ghost," Rom. xv. 16 , 19; that "his speech and his preaching was not in the persuasive words of human wisdom, but in the showing of the Spirit and in power, that our faith might not stand on the wisdom of men, but on the power of God," i Cor. ii. 4 ; that though he himself was nothing, yet, "the signs of his apostleship were wrought in all patience, in signs and wonders and mighty deeds," 2 Cor. xii. 12 ; "and that his gospel was not in word only, but in power also, and in the Holy Ghost, and in much fulness," 1 Thess. i. 5 ; for this is the way that the Holy Ghost gave testimony to, or confirmed the doctrine of, Christ, preached by the pastors of His Church according to that text, "The Lord gave testimony to the word of His grace, granting signs and wonders to be done by their hands," Acts, xiv. 3] and "they going forth preached every-where, the Lord working withal, and confirming the word with signs that followed," Mark, xvi. 20 ; for "the testimony of Jesus is the Spirit of proph-ecy," Rev. xix. 10 ; which is one of the greatest of miracles. Now the Holy Ghost bestows these miraculous powers on whom and in what manner He pleases; to some He gives one kind, to others another, as St Paul observes at large, i Cor. xii.: but "the manifestation of the Spirit is given to every one unto profit," verse 7; and "all these things the same Spirit worketh, dividing to every one according as He will," verse 11. Lastly, One of the principal ends for which Christ sent down His Holy Spirit upon His Church was to confirm her and establish her for ever, "building her upon the rock "of His Divine protection, so that "the gates of hell shall not prevail against her," Mat. xvi. 18 ; "to abide with her for ever, and teach her all truth," I Tim. iii. 15 ; and to enable her to preserve the purity of the doctrine of Jesus Christ unstained, unaltered, uncorrupted, to the end of ages; so that the words once put into her mouth should never depart from her to the end of time, according to that glorious promise made by the Almighty God many ages before, and recorded by the prophet Isaias, of the continual assistance of His Holy Spirit, and preservation of the doctrine of the Redeemer for ever: "And there shall a Redeemer come to Sion, and to them that return from iniquity in Jacob, saith the Lord: This is My covenant with them, saith the Lord. My Spirit that is in thee, and My words which I have put in thy mouth, shall not depart out of thy mouth, nor out of the mouth of thy seed, nor out of the mouth of thy seed's seed, saith the Lord, from henceforth and for ever," Isa. lix. 20 .

Q. 35. Did the Holy Ghost produce all these glorious effects in the apostles and first Christians, when He came upon them?

A. He did, in a most eminent degree; for, (1.) immediately upon His de-scent, the apostles became altogether new men: from poor ignorant fishermen that they were before, they were enlightened by that Divine Spirit with the most sublime knowledge of all Divine truths, and became the masters and teachers of the whole world. Their hearts were inflamed with an ardent love of God, and zeal for the salvation of souls; and all manner of Christian virtues, humility, meekness, patience, brotherly love, and the like, shone forth in them in the highest perfection; whereas before, they were afraid to stand by their Master in His sufferings, and "all forsook Him and fled," when He was taken in the garden; and, during His passion, shut "themselves up, for fear of the Jews." Now they thought it their greatest glory to lay down their very lives for His sake, and went away rejoicing to be "counted worthy to suffer ignominy for the name of Jesus." Such were the fortitude and grace with which the Holy Ghost endowed them! (2.) The Jews themselves, the hardened Jews, who had for three years resisted all the charms of the sanctity, eloquence, and miracles of the Son of God, immediately upon the coming of the Holy Ghost, were converted from their evil ways in great numbers, renounced their errors, adored as their God that Jesus whom a little before they had crucified upon a tree, embraced His heavenly doctrine with all their souls, and became His most zealous followers. No less than three thousand were converted at once on hearing the first sermon St Peter preached to them, and five thousand at hearing another. Such power and force did the Holy Ghost give to the word, such light and understanding to those who heard it! (3.) The sanctity of their lives, after their conversion, was no less conspicuous than their conversion itself. The account the Scripture gives of them is most affecting; "And they were persevering in the doctrine of the apostles, and in the communication of the breaking of bread, and in prayers. . . . And all they that believed were together, and had all things in common. They sold their possessions and goods, and divided them all according as every one had need; and were continuing daily, with one accord, in the temple, . . . praising God, and having favour with all the people," Acts, ii. 42 . "And the multitude of the believers had but one heart and one soul; neither did any one say that aught of the things which he possessed was his own, but all things were common to them; . . . for neither was there any one among them that wanted. For as many as were owners of lands and houses sold them, and brought the price of the things they sold, and laid it down before the feet of the apostles; and distribution was made to every one according as he had need," Acts, iv. 32 ; "and every day they ceased not in the temple, and from house to house, to teach and preach Christ Jesus," Acts, V. 42 .

Q. 36. By what means may we invite and draw down the Holy Ghost to our souls, so as to receive the blessed effects of His presence?

A. The Scripture points out to us these following: (1.) We must live innocent lives, flying from all sin, especially sins of malice, and all breaches of
charity to our neighbour, and all duplicity and deceit; for the Holy Spirit, who is the Spirit of "wisdom, will not enter into a malicious soul, nor
dwell in a body subject to sins; for the Holy Spirit of discipline will fly from
the deceitful, and will withdraw Himself from thoughts that are without
understanding, and He shall not abide when iniquity cometh in," Wis. i.
4 . (2.) By self-denial, and mortification of our passions, we must divest
ourselves of the wisdom of the flesh; for, "the wisdom of the flesh is death;
"but the wisdom of "the Spirit is life and peace; because the wisdom of the
flesh is an enemy to God; for it is not subject to the law of God, neither
can it be, and they who are in the flesh cannot please God," Rom. viii. 6 .
Consequently, so long as we willingly adhere to the wisdom of the flesh, we
cannot expect the Spirit of God will come to dwell in us. Now, the wisdom
of the flesh is that which esteems and seeks after all the pleasures of the
flesh, and in eating and drinking, and all carnal delight and sensual enjoy-
ments, and seeks satisfaction and happiness in them. This, therefore, we
must mortify and destroy; for, as the Scripture declares, "the sensual man
perceiveth not the things that are of the Spirit of God; for it is foolishness
to him, and he cannot understand," I Cor. ii. 14 ; and therefore, "If you live
according to the flesh, you shall die; but if by the Spirit you mortify the
deeds of the flesh, you shall live," Rom. viii. 13 - (3-) One must also divest
ourselves of the spirit of the world, which bears an essential opposition to
the Spirit of God. St Paul shows this opposition when he says, "we have
received not the spirit of this world, but the Spirit which is of God," i Cor.
ii. 12 . Nay, our blessed Lord declares, that "the world cannot receive the
Comforter, the Spirit of truth," John, xiv. 17 . Again, the Scripture assures
us that "the wisdom "of this spirit "of the world, is foolishness with God," i
Cor. iii. 19 ; that "the friendship of this world is the enemy of God; whosoever, therefore, will be a friend of this world, becomes an enemy of God,"
James, iv. 4 . And the beloved disciple exhorts us in this earnest manner:
"Love not the world, nor the things that are in the world. If any man love
the world, the love of the Father is not in him. For all that is in this world
is the concupiscence of the flesh, and the concupiscence of the eyes, and
the pride of life, which is not of the Father, but is of the world; and the
world passeth away and the concupiscence thereof," i John, ii. 15 . We must
therefore mortify all inordinate love of the world, all pride, vanity, and
ambition, and all attachment to riches and honours, to all which the spirit
of the world strongly inclines and ties us, if we wish that the Spirit of God
should come and dwell in our souls. (4.) Another powerful means to draw
down this Divine Spirit to our hearts is, to have a sincere love for Jesus

Christ, and to give proof of it by keeping His commandments, this being the very condition He requires of us for this purpose. "If you love Me," says He, "keep My commandments; and I will ask the Father, and He will give you another Comforter, that He may abide with you for ever, the Spirit of truth," John, xiv. 16 . (5.) Lastly, by fervent and earnest prayer, we must endeavour to move the Father to send His Holy Spirit upon us, prayer being a most powerful means for obtaining this Holy Spirit from the Father; for, "if you being evil," says our Saviour, "know how to give good gifts to your children, how much more will your Father from heaven give the Good Spirit to them that ask Him?" Luke, xi. 13 .

Q. 37. In what manner does Jesus Christ exercise the office of Judge of the living and the dead?

A. Chiefly in three ways, (1.) While men are in this life, Jesus Christ, as supreme Judge, rewards those who serve Him faithfully, and improve the talents and graces He gives them, both by the temporal rewards He often bestows upon them, and also by giving them still more abundant graces; according to what is recorded by St Luke, when He ordered the pound (a piece of money) to be taken from the slothful and unprofitable servant, and given to the faithful servant, who had doubled what his Lord had given him, by his diligence and industry: "To every one," says He, "that hath, shall be given, and he shall abound," Luke, xix. 26 . That is, to every one that hath, and makes a good use of what he hath, as that profitable servant did, more shall be given, that he may still more and more abound. In like manner He punishes those who abuse His graces, both by temporal miseries which He often sends upon them, and especially by withdrawing these graces from them, and leaving them to the hardness of their own hearts, to follow their own inventions, according to what He adds on the same occasion: "and from him that hath not "(that is, who is unprofitable in what he hath, as that slothful servant was), "even that which he hath shall be taken from him," Ibid. Now, to bestow rewards and punishments is an act of judicial power, and presupposes a judgment made of the merits of the persons. (2.) At the particular judgment of each one immediately after death, when the soul shall be presented before the tribunal of Jesus Christ, and receive that sentence from Him which His justice sees fit. (3.) At the day of general judgment, when He shall come "with great power and majesty," to judge all mankind, and confirm their eternal doom.

Q. 38. Shall every man be judged immediately on his death?

A. Yes; for the Scripture says, "It is easy before God, in the day of death, to reward every one according to his ways; the affliction of an hour maketh one forget great delights, and in the end of a man is the disclosing of his works," Ecclus. xi. 28 . And still more expressly, "It is appointed for men once to die, and after this the judgment," Heb. ix. 27 . The same truth is also strongly pointed out to us by the parable of the unjust steward, whom his master called to account, and put out of his stewardship at the same instant of time. Now, when we die, our stewardship is at an end; therefore, then is the time when we must give an account. Besides, it is certain that the rich glutton was condemned to hell immediately at his death; and likewise Lazarus, at his death, was carried by angels to Abraham's bosom, a place of rest and peace: but, to punish or reward according to justice, necessarily requires a previous act judgment, which therefore must have happened at the hour of their death to the rich glutton and to Lazarus.

Q. 39. If each one be judged at his death, what need is there of the general judgment at the last day?

A. Several causes are assigned for this: (1.) To vindicate the Divine Providence before all creatures. In this life, "the works of the Most High are glorious, and secret and hidden," Ecclus. xi. 4 . Proud haughty man, not being able to comprehend them, impiously presumes to call the conduct of the Almighty to the bar of his human reason, and often proceeds so far in his censures upon it, as sometimes "to say in his heart. There is no God," Ps. xiii. 1 ; sometimes to deny His Divine Providence and concern about His creatures, and "to say in his heart, God hath forgotten; He hath turned away His face, not to see the end," Ps. x. 11 ; or to doubt of His providence, by saying, "How doth God know? - He judgeth as it were through a mist; the clouds are His cover, and He doth not consider our things," Job, xxii. 13 .; and sometimes even to deny His justice, and greatly "provoke God, by saying in his heart He will not require it," Ps. x. 13 . Nay, the secrets of the Divine Providence are so amazing, especially in the adversity of the good and the prosperity of the wicked, that even holy people are confounded, when they consider it, as David was, when he said, "Behold, these are sinners, and yet abounding in the world, they have obtained riches; and I said, Then have I in vain justified my heart, and washed my hands among the innocent. ... I studied that I might know this thing; it is a labour in my sight, until I go into the sanctuary of God, and understand concerning their last ends." Now it is at the last end that all this mystery will be discovered; at the general judgment, when God will appear in all His majesty in the presence of all mankind, and when all the wondrous ways of His

Divine Providence shall be revealed, and His justice manifested in all His doings; for "He hath prepared His throne in judgment; He shall judge the world in equity, He shall judge the people in justice. . . . The Lord shall be known when He executeth judgment," Ps. ix. 8 , 17.

(2). To do justice to Jesus Christ Himself in His human nature, and to fulfil the promises made to Him by His Father for this end: for, whereas "He became a worm and no man, the reproach of men and the outcast of the people, so that all that saw Him laughed Him to scorn," Ps. xxi. 7 ; "and was despised, and the most abject of men, a man of sorrows, and acquainted with infirmity," Isa. liii. 3 ; "so as at last to humble Himself to death, even the death of the cross," Philip, ii.; and suffered all this for the glory of His heavenly Father; - justice requires that He who was so much humbled before men, should also be glorified before them, according to that promise related by the prophet, "Behold, My servant shall understand. He shall be exalted, and extolled, and exceeding high," Isa. lii. 13 . This will be done before the whole universe at the general judgment, as foretold by the same prophet, "Behold My servant, I will uphold Him; My elect, My soul delighteth in Him; I have given My Spirit upon Him; He shall bring forth judgment to the Gentiles; . . . He shall bring forth judgment unto truth; . . . He shall set judgment on the earth," Isa. xlii. 1 . At that great day will fully be accomplished these sacred promises made to Him by His Father: "The Lord said to my Lord, Sit Thou on My right hand, till I make Thy enemies Thy footstool. The Lord will send forth the sceptre of Thy power out of Sion, rule Thou in the midst of Thy enemies; with Thee is the principality in the day of Thy strength, in the brightness of Thy saints," Ps. cix. 1 ; for "this Man offering one sacrifice for sins, for ever sitteth on the right hand of God, from henceforth expecting until His enemies be made His footstool," Heb. x. 12 . Again, "One in a certain place hath testified, saying, . . . Thou hast put all things in subjection under His feet: for, in that He subjected all things to Him, He left nothing not subject to Him. But now we see not as yet all things subject to Him," Heb. ii. 6 , 8; but this shall be completely done at the end, at the day of judgment, "when He shall have brought to nought all principality, and power, and virtue; for He must reign until He hath put all enemies under His feet; and the enemy death shall be last destroyed," i Cor. xv. 24 . At that great day, then, all things shall be perfectly subjected to Him, and at the sacred "name of Jesus every knee shall bow "before Him, "of those that are in heaven, and on earth, and under the earth; and every tongue shall confess that the Lord Jesus Christ is in the glory of God the Father," Philip, ii. 10 .

(3.) To do justice to all His holy saints, that they who in this life have for His sake suffered numberless afflictions and calamities before men, might be glorified and rewarded by Him before the whole universe, in a manner worthy of Himself, and so as to justify, in the eyes of all mankind, the whole of His conduct towards them. At present, by a particular disposition of the Divine Providence, the elect of God, who are the righteous, are often confounded with the wicked, and not to be distinguished from hypocrites: His saints, who are the meek and humble of heart, far from being honoured and respected, are often despised and insulted; His servants, who are the poor in spirit, instead of being relieved and comforted, are abandoned and neglected: but will it be always so? By no means: "The poor man shall not be forgotten to the end; the patience of the poor shall not perish for ever," Ps. ix. 19 ; "Thou wilt be a helper to the orphan. . . . The Lord hath heard the desire of the poor; Thy ear hath heard the preparation of their heart, to judge for the fatherless and for the humble," Ps. x. 14 , 17. At that great day the just shall be separated from the wicked, and placed on the right hand of the Judge in great glory. All their glorious virtues and acts of piety shall be manifested to men and angels, and they shall be enriched with eternal treasures; and so admirable will their exaltation be, that their enemies, the wicked, who oppressed and afflicted them in their mortal life, seeing their great glory, "shall be troubled with terrible fear, and shall be amazed at the suddenness of their unexpected salvation; saying within themselves, repenting and groaning for anguish of spirit: These are they whom we sometimes had in derision, and for a parable of reproach; we fools esteemed their life madness, and their end without honour; behold how they are numbered among the children of God, and their lot is among the saints! "Wis. v. 1 .

(4.) To execute judgment upon the whole man; for, at the particular judgment after death, the soul alone is judged; but, as both soul and body are companions, in all man does in his mortal life, it is fitting that, at the resurrection, when both shall be rejoined, both should be judged, and both together receive their eternal doom.

Q. 40. What account does the Scripture give of the general judgment?

A. As this is one of the most important truths revealed by God to man. He has been pleased to give us a most minute and awful description of everything concerning it: "The great day of the Lord is near," says the prophet Sophonias; "it is near and exceeding swift; the voice of the day of the Lord is bitter; the mighty man shall there meet with tribulation. That day is a day of wrath, a day of tribulation and distress, a day of calamity and misery, a day of darkness and obscurity, a day of clouds and of whirlwinds, a day of the trumpet and alarm against the fenced cities, and against the high bulwarks; and I will distress men, and they shall walk like blind men, because they have sinned against the Lord; their blood shall be poured out as earth, and their bodies as dung,"Soph. i. 14. In like manner the prophet Isaias describes it in these awful terms: "Behold, the day of the Lord shall come, a cruel day, and full of indignation, and of wrath, and fury, to lay the land desolate, and to destroy the sinners thereof out of it. For the stars of heaven and their brightness shall not display their light; the sun shall be darkened in his rising, and the moon shall not shine with her light; and I will visit the evils of the world, and against the wicked for their iniquity, and I will make the pride of infidels to cease, and will bring down the arrogance of the mighty. . . . For this I will trouble the heaven, and the earth shall be moved out of her place, for the indignation of the Lord of hosts, and for the day of His fierce wrath," Isa. xiii. 9 . And how justly it deserves this awful description will appear from the history given of it; whether we consider the signs that will go before the judgment itself, or the sentence of the Judge which shall conclude the whole.

Q. 41. What are the signs that shall go before the day of judgment?

A. The Scripture lays them down as follows: "When you shall hear of wars and seditions, be not terrified; these things must come to pass, but the end is not yet presently. Nation shall rise against nation, and kingdom against kingdom; and there shall be great earthquakes in divers places, and pestilences and famines, and terrors from heaven, and there shall be great signs," Luke, xxi. 9 . "Now, all these are the beginnings of sorrows," Mat. xxiv. 8 ; "and because iniquity hath abounded, the charity of many shall grow cold, . . . and this gospel of the kingdom shall be preached in the whole world, for a testimony to all nations, and then shall the consummation come," Ibid., vers. 12, 14; "and there shall be signs in the sun, and in the moon, and in the stars; and upon the earth distress of nations, by reason of the confusion of the roaring of the sea and of the waves. Men withering away for fear and expectation of what shall come upon the whole world," Luke, xxi. 25 ; for "I will show wonders in heaven and in earth, blood, and fire, and vapour of smoke; the sun shall be turned into darkness, and the moon into blood, before the great and dreadful day of the Lord doth come," Joel, ii. 30 : "And immediately after the tribulation of those days, the sun shall be darkened, and the moon shall not give her light, and the stars shall fall from heaven, and the powers of the heavens shall be moved," Mat. xxiv. 29 . "And the heavens departed as a book folded up, and every mountain and the islands were moved out of their place; and the kings of the earth, and the princes, and the tribunes, and the rich men and the strong men, and every bond man, and every free man, hid themselves in the dens and in the rocks of the mountain; and they say to the mountains and to the rocks. Fall upon us, and hide us from the face of Him that sitteth upon the throne, and from the wrath of the Lamb; for the great day of their wrath is come, and who shall be able to stand?" Rev. vi. 14 . After all those dreadful forerunners of this great day, a raging fire like a torrent shall spread over the whole world, and execute the final sentence of destruction upon all creatures that shall then be on the face of the earth, and reduce the whole to smoke and ashes. "Our God shall come manifestly, our God shall come and shall not keep silence: a fire shall bum before Him, and a mighty tempest round about Him," Ps. xlix. 3 . "Clouds and darkness are round about Him, justice and judgment are the establishment of His throne; a fire shall go before Him, and shall burn His enemies round about. His lightnings have shone forth to the world; the earth saw and trembled, the mountains melted like wax at the presence of the Lord of all the earth," Ps. xcvi. 2 . "The day of the Lord shall come as a thief, in which the heavens shall pass away with great violence, and the elements shall be melted with heat, and the earth and the works that are in it shall be burnt up," 2 Pet. iii. 10 . "The day of the Lord cometh, because it is nigh at hand; a day of darkness and of gloominess, a day of clouds and whirlwinds. . . . Before the face thereof a devouring fire, and behind it a burning flame; the land is like a garden of pleasure before it, and behind it a desolate wilderness; neither is there any one that can escape it," Joel, ii. 1 . These are the forerunners of this great day, which shall precede the judgment, and bring along with them the final destruction of this world.

Q. 42. What account does the Scripture give of the judgment itself?

A. The account given of the judgment contains the resurrection, the appearance of the Judge, and the judgment. For, first the angel of God shall come down from heaven to summon all the posterity of Adam to rise from the dead and come to judgment: "And He shall send His angels with a trumpet and a great voice, and they shall gather together His elect from the four winds, from the farthest parts of the heavens to the utmost bounds of them," Mat. xxiv. 31 . "For the Lord Himself shall come down from heaven with commandment, and with the voice of an archangel, and with the trumpet of God," I Thess. iv. 15 . "And in a moment, in the twinkling of an eye, at the last trumpet, for the trumpet shall sound, and the dead shall rise again incorruptible; and this corruption must put on incorruption, and this mortal must put on immortality," i Cor. xv. 52 . "And the sea gave up the dead that were in it, and death and hell gave up the dead that were in them," Apoc. xx. 13 . "The hour Cometh wherein all that are in the graves shall hear the voice of the Son of God, and they that have done good shall come forth unto the resurrection of life, but they that have done evil unto the resurrection of condemnation," John, V. 28 . "I know that my Redeemer liveth, and in the last day I shall rise out of the earth, and I shall be clothed again with my skin, and in my flesh I shall see my God, whom I myself shall see, and my eyes shall behold, and not another," Job, xix. 25 .

Then all mankind shall be assembled together in the valley of Josaphat, within sight of Mount Calvary, that where He underwent the greatest excess of His sufferings and humiliations, there He may appear in the full splendour of His majesty and glory, according to the prophet: "And I will gather together all nations, and will bring them down to the valley of Josaphat; ... for there will I sit to judge all nations round about," Joel, iii. 2 , 12. "And then shall appear the sign of the Son of Man in heaven; and then shall all the tribes of the earth mourn, and they shall see the Son of Man coming in the clouds of heaven with great power and majesty," Mat. xxiv. 30 .

For "Jesus Christ shall be received from heaven with the angels of His power in a flame of fire, yielding vengeance to them who know not God, and who obey not the gospel of our Lord Jesus Christ," 2 Thess. i. 7 . "Behold, He cometh with the clouds, and every eye shall see Him, and they also who pierced Him; and all the tribes of the earth shall bewail themselves because of Him," Apoc. i. 7 . "Behold, the Lord cometh with thousands of His saints, to execute judgment upon all, and to reprove all the ungodly for all the works of their ungodliness, whereby they have done ungodly, and for all the hard things which ungodly sinners have spoken against God," Jude, ver. 14. "He put on justice as a breastplate, and a helmet of salvation upon His head; He put on the garments of vengeance, and was clad with zeal as with a cloak. ... As unto revenge as it were to repay wrath to His adversaries, and a reward to His enemies," Isa. lix. 17 . And so great will be the splendour of His majesty, that "the moon shall blush and the sun shall be ashamed, when the Lord of hosts shall reign in Mount Zion and in Jerusalem, and be glorified in the sight of His ancients," Isa. xxiv. 23 .

The Judge being now seated in His glory, the grand separation shall be made of the good from the bad. At present, the kingdom of Christ in this world is likened, in Scripture, to a barn floor, in which the good com and chaff are mixed together in one heap; to z. field of corn, in which the good grain and tares grow up together till the harvest; to a net cast into the sea, and enclosing all kinds of fishes, both good and bad; and to a flock, composed both of sheep and goats; because in this life the just and the unjust, the saints and the sinners, the children of God and the children of Satan, are mixed together in one body, and seldom to be distinguished the one from the other; but at that great day, the Judge, "whose fan is in His hand, will thoroughly cleanse His floor, and gather His wheat into His barn, but the chaff He will burn with unquenchable fire," Mat. iii. 12 . And when the harvest comes, "the Son of Man shall send His angels, and they shall gather out of His kingdom all scandals and them that work iniquity," Mat. xiii. 41 ; "for at the end of the world the angels shall go and separate the wicked from among the just," Ibid. ver. 49; which is thus particularly described in St Matthew: "And when the Son of Man shall come in His majesty, and all the angels with Him, then shall He sit upon the seat of His majesty, and all nations shall be gathered together before Him, and He shall separate them one from another, as the shepherd separates the sheep from the goats, and He shall set the sheep on His right hand, but the goats on the left; "Mat. xxv. 31 . This separation will be made without any respect of persons, and purely according to what each one deserves; so that parents and children, husbands and wives, friends and companions, shall then be separated from one another for ever, and the one placed on the right hand, the other on the left; for "in that night there shall be two men in one bed (intimate friends) the one shall be taken and the other left; two women shall be grinding together (fellow-servants), the one shall be taken and the other shall be left; two men shall be in the field (dear companions), the one shall be taken and the other shall be left," Luke, xvii. 34 . What joy and delight will then fill the hearts of the righteous! but what anguish shall pierce the souls of the wicked! "The wicked shall see, and shall be angry; he shall gnash with his teeth and pine away," Ps. cxi. 10 . "There shall be weeping and gnashing of teeth, when you shall see Abraham, and Isaac, and Jacob, and all the prophets, in the kingdom of God, and you yourselves thrust out," Luke, xiii. 28 . (See above, Q. 39).

The separation being made, the judgment will follow, which is thus described in Scripture: "I beheld till thrones were placed, and the Ancient of Days sat down: His garment was white as snow, and the hair of His head like clean wool; His throne like flames of fire, and the wheels of it like a burning fire; a swift stream of fire issued forth from before Him; thousands of thousands ministered to Him, and ten thousand times a hundred thousand stood before Him; the judgment sat, and the books were opened," Dan. vii. 9 . "And I saw a great white throne, and One sitting upon it, from Whose face the earth and the heavens fled away, and there was no place found for them. And I saw the dead, great and small, standing in the presence of the throne, and the books were opened: and another book was opened, which is the book of life; and the dead were judged by those things which were written in the books, according to their works," Rev. xx. 11 . These books are the books of conscience, from which the whole conduct of every one during His mortal life, all the sins he has ever been guilty of, however secret and hidden from the eyes of the world, shall then be manifested in their most glaring colours, before the whole universe, before God and His holy angels; for "every idle word that man shall speak, they shall render an account of it in the day of judgment," Mat. xii. 36 . "There is not anything secret that shall not be made manifest, nor hidden that shall not be known, and come abroad," Luke, viii. 17 ; for "we shall all stand before the judgment-seat of Christ, and then every one of us shall render an account to God for himself," Rom. xiv. 10 , 12. The Lord will come, "who will both bring to light the hidden things of darkness, and will make manifest the counsel of hearts," i Cor. iv. 5 ; and then shall be fulfilled what was spoken by the prophets against sinners - "Thy nakedness shall be discovered, and thy shame shall be seen; I will take vengeance, and no man shall resist Me," Isa. xlvii. 3 , "Behold, I come against thee, saith the Lord of hosts, and I will discover thy shame to thy face, and will show thy nakedness to the nations, and thy shame to kingdoms, and I will cast abominations upon thee, and will disgrace thee, and will make an example of thee," Nahum, iii. 5 , Oh, how miserable a condition will the Christian sinner be in at that day when he shall find himself thus covered with all his sins, and condemned in this great judgment as a traitor to his God, a rebel against the King of heaven, and a murderer of Jesus Christ! when the men of Nineveh shall rise up against him and condemn him; and the people of Sodom and Gomorrah shall be more mercifully dealt with than he!

Q. 43. What effect will all these things have upon the just?

A. Our Saviour, after describing to the apostles the signs that shall go before this great day, says to them, "But when these things begin to come to pass, look up and lift up your heads, because your redemption is at hand," Luke, xxi. 28 . And the Scripture says that at that day "the just shall stand with great constancy against those that have afflicted them, and taken away their labours; . . . they shall live for evermore, and their reward is with the Lord, and a care of them is with the Most High,"Wis. v. i. 16. Every circumstance of this awful day will contribute to their honour and happiness, and they shall be exalted in great glory; "for behold the day shall come kindled as a furnace, and all the proud, and all that do wickedly, shall be stubble; and the day that cometh shall set them on fire, saith the Lord of hosts; it shall not leave them root nor branch. But unto you that fear My name the Sun of Justice shall arise, and health in His wings, and you shall go forth, and shall leap like calves of the herd, and you shall tread down the wicked, when they shall be ashes under the sole of your feet, in the day that I do this, saith the Lord of hosts," Mai. iv. 1 . And this their happiness shall be completed beyond expression, when the sentence of eternal bliss shall be pronounced by the great Judge upon them.

Q. 44. What account does the Scripture give of the last sentence?

A. Christ Himself declares it to us in these words: "Then shall the King say to them that shall be on His right hand. Come, ye blessed of My Father, possess the kingdom prepared for you from the foundation of the world. . . . Then shall He say to them also that shall be on His left hand, Depart from Me, ye cursed, into everlasting fire, which was prepared for the devil and his angels." And immediately shall these two sentences be executed; for "these last shall go into everlasting punishment, but the just into life ever-lasting," Mat. xxv. 34 . "At the end of the world the Son of Man shall send His angels, and they shall gather out of His kingdom all scandals, and them that work iniquity, and shall cast them into the furnace of fire; there shall be weeping and gnashing of teeth: then shall the just shine as the sun in the kingdom of their Father," Mat. xiii. 41 . Thus the whole posterity of Adam shall receive their eternal doom either in heaven or hell, in eternal happiness or eternal misery.

CHAPTER IX.

Of The Benefits Of Our Redemption

Q. 1. What are the benefits which we receive from the Redeemer?

A. They are all comprehended in these three general heads; to wit, satisfaction or propitiation, redemption, and impetration - that is to say, that, by the infinite merits of what He did and suffered for us. He fully satisfied the Divine justice for our sins; He rendered God propitious to us, and inclined to mercy; He redeemed us from sin, from the tyranny of the devil, and from the torments of hell; and He obtained for us all spiritual benedictions and graces in this life, and the kingdom of heaven in the life to come.

Q. 2. Were the merits of Christ of infinite value?

A. By the word mercy is understood the right or title that one person acquires by his services, to receive any favour or reward from another. This right may either be a right of congruity or a right injustice. A right or title of congruity is when the person to whom the service is done is no-wise obliged to reward it, by any promise or agreement, but is at liberty to reward it or not as he pleases, and in what manner or proportion he sees proper. A right injustice is when the person to whom the service is done is bound by promise or agreement to reward it; for by this the other, who does the service, acquires a full right and just title to the reward. Now, what Jesus Christ did and suffered for the glory and service of His Father was of infinite value in itself, and deserved an infinite reward; and His eternal Father Himself laid these sufferings upon Him, and engaged, on His undergoing them, to give the reward which He demanded, both in regard to Himself and us. Hence the merits of Christ were of infinite value; and He has acquired a full title in justice to everything He demands from His Father in reward of them.

Q. 3. How comes the merit of what Christ did and suffered to be of infinite value in itself?

A. This arises chiefly from three causes: (1.) The infinite dignity of His person; for the more exalted any person is, the more meritorious and valuable is any act of obsequiousness which he does to please another. (2.) The infinite value of what He gave and dedicated to the service of His Father, which was no less than the actions, sufferings, life and death of God made man. (3.) The fervour of His charity and love with which He served His Father; for, from the moment He was conceived in His Mother's womb, till the moment He expired on the cross, everything He did, said, and suffered, was all done out of the most perfect obedience to His Father's will. Thus, "when He cometh into the world, He saith. Sacrifice and oblation Thou wouldst not; but a body Thou hast fitted to go; holocausts for sin did not please Thee. Then said I, Behold, I come, in the head of the book it is written of Me, that I should do Thy will, O God," Heb. x. 5 . And this His fervent charity to do the will of His Father, was so agreeable to Him, that St Paul immediately adds, "By the which will we are sanctified by the oblation of the body of Jesus Christ once," ver. lo. This perfect obedience He carried on through the whole of His life, in everything He did; so that it was "His meat to do the will of Him that sent Him, and to perfect His work," John, iv. 34 . "I do nothing of Myself," says He, "but as the Father has taught Me, I speak these things; .... for I do always the things that please Him," John, viii. 28 . And He laid down His life at last, in the midst of torments, from the same Divine motive of obedience to His heavenly Father; "He humbled Himself, becoming obedient unto death, even the death of the cross," Philip, ii. 8 . Now, a person of such dignity offering to His Father a gift of infinite value, and employing Himself with such infinite love, and through such dreadful sufferings for His Father's glory, most certainly deserves an infinite reward for such services; and therefore His merits are in themselves of infinite value.

Q. 4. How does it appear that God the Father laid all the sufferings of Christ upon Him, and promised Him a reward for them?

A. This is expressly declared by the prophet Isaias, who also assures us that this was done in punishment for our sins, to make our peace with God, and heal our bruises. "Surely He hath borne our infirmities and carried our sorrows, and we have thought Him as it were a leper, and as one struck by God and afflicted: but He was wounded for our iniquities. He was bruised for our sins, the chastisement of our peace was upon Him, and by His bruises we are healed. . . . And the Lord hath laid upon Him the iniquity of us all; . . . for the wickedness of My people have I struck Him; . . . and the Lord was pleased to bruise Him in infirmity." Then follows the promise of the reward: "If He shall lay down His life for sin. He shall see a long-lived seed, and the will of the Lord shall be prosperous in His hand. Because His soul hath laboured, He shall see and be filled; by His knowledge shall this My just servant justify many, and He shall bear their iniquities; therefore will I distribute to Him very many, and He shall divide the spoils of the strong," Isa. liii. Hence Jesus Christ claimed from His Father an infinite reward as His due for what He had done for Him - to wit, the eternal glorification of His human nature in heaven, promised in the words of the prophet, "He shall see and be filled. I have glorified Thee on earth," says He, "I have finished the work which Thou gavest Me to do; and now glorify Thou Me, O Father, with Thyself, with the glory which I had, before the world was, with Thee," John, xvii. 4 . And He made the same demand for all His faithful followers, who should believe in Him. "Father, I will that where I am they also whom Thou hast given Me may be with Me, that they may see My glory which Thou hast given Me," verse 24.

Q. 5. What is properly meant by the satisfaction and propitiation of Christ?

A. To give satisfaction for an offence committed, is to offer to the person off"ended some gift or service equal or more pleasing than the offence was displeasing. The rigour of justice demands that the satisfaction be equally agreeable to the displeasure given by the offence; and, if it be more so, the satisfaction is superabundant. In either case the person offended is appeased and satisfied, and willing to be reconciled to the offender and to forgive the offence. Now, what Jesus Christ did and suffered, was of infinite value in the eyes of His Father, and therefore infinitely agreeable to Him; and as it was the condition required by the Divine justice to satisfy for the sins of men, therefore His satisfaction was not only equal to the offence but infinitely superabundant, and on that account fully appeased the wrath of God against man, made Him willing to be reconciled with man, and to forgive the offence received by his sins. Inasmuch as this satisfied the demands of justice, it is properly called satisfaction; and inasmuch as it rendered God propitious, or inclined to mercy, it is called propitiation. Now, the Scripture everywhere proposes the sufferings and death of Christ as a satisfaction to the justice of God, and on that account taking away the effects of His justice against man, and as a propitiation for our sins, appeasing the wrath of God and reconciling us with Him. Thus St Paul declares, that "God hath set forth Jesus Christ to be a propitiation through faith in His blood, to the showing of His justice through the remission of former sins, through the forbearance of God, for the showing of His justice in this time," Rom. iii. 25 . But that justice being now satisfied by the sufferings of Christ, He hath "blotted out the handwriting of the decree that was against us, and He hath taken the same out of the way, fastening it to the Cross," Col. ii. 14 . St John also says, "Jesus Christ the just, He is the propitiation for our sins," i John, ii. 2 . "And God loved us first, and sent His Son to be a propitiation for our sins," i John, iv. 10 . "When enemies, we were reconciled to God by the death of His Son," Rom. v, 10 . "All things are of God, who hath reconciled us to Himself by Christ," 2 Cor. v. 18 . "Christ is our peace," says St Paul, "and died both for Jews and Gentiles, that he might reconcile both to God in one body by the Cross," Eph. ii. 14 , 16. "It hath well pleased the Father, through Him, to reconcile all things to Himself, making peace through the blood of His Cross," Col. i. 20 . "The God of our Fathers," said St Peter to the Jews, "hath raised up Jesus, whom you put to death, hanging Him upon a tree. Him hath God exalted with His right hand to be a Prince and Saviour, to give repentance to Israel, and remission of sins," Acts, v. 30 . In Christ "we have redemption through His blood, the remission of sins," Eph. i. 7 .

Q. 6. What is understood by the redemption of Christ?

A. To redeem is, properly speaking, to buy anything again, which was formerly one's own, but had gone into the possession of another; and, when applied to men, it signifies to buy one out of slavery, who had been formerly free. Now, God at the beginning created man in a state of freedom, serving God indeed, but with voluntary obedience, and out of love as a son, not by force and out of fear as a slave; for to serve God is the only true liberty. But man, by sin, withdrawing himself from the easy service of God, became the servant of sin, according to the words of our Saviour, "Amen, amen, I say unto you, that whosoever committeth sin is the servant of sin," John, viii. 34 ; and was so tyrannised over by that cruel master, that "all the thought of his heart was bent upon evil at all times," Gen. vi. 5 . "Without his being sufficient of himself, as of himself, to think any good," 2 Cor. iii. 5 . Besides, as in committing sin he had been overcome by the devil, and obeyed him in preference to God; therefore he was also enslaved to the devil; for "by whom a man is overcome, of the same also is he the slave," 2 Pet. ii. 19 ; and, "to whom you yield yourselves servants to obey, his servants you are whom you obey," Rom. vi. 16 ; and being by this means entangled in the snares of that cruel master, "was by him held captive at his will," I Tim. ii. 26 . Not that God had lost His supreme dominion and power over man, but that He justly delivered him up to be tyrannised over by sin and Satan, as the executioners of the Divine justice, in punishment of having voluntarily left the easy and delightful service of his heavenly Father. Nor did the miserable slavery of man end with this life; for, as by sin he had become an object of the Divine vengeance, he was condemned by the justice of God to suffer the eternal punishment of hell in the life to come, under the never-ending tyranny of Satan. Now, from this miserable and never-ending slavery, Jesus Christ came to redeem us, by paying a price for us of infinite value to the Divine justice; for "you were not redeemed with corruptible things, such as gold or silver, . . . but with the precious Blood of Christ, as of a lamb unspotted and undefiled,"I Pet. i. 18. "But Christ being come, . . . neither by the blood of goats, nor of calves, but by His own Blood, entered once into the holies, having obtained eternal redemption. For if the blood of goats and of oxen, and the ashes of an heifer being sprinkled, sanctify such as are defiled to the cleansing of the flesh, how much more shall the Blood of Christ, who, through the Holy Ghost, offered Himself without spot to God, cleanse our conscience from dead works to serve the living God?" Heb. ix. 11 ; for He also partook of flesh and blood, that through death He might destroy him who had the empire of death, the devil; and might deliver them who, through the fear of death, were all their lifetime subject to bondage," Heb. ii. 14 .

Q. 7. What is the principal effect of our redemption by Christ?

A. As the first cause and source of our slavery is sin - because by sin we are enslaved to the devil, and condemned to hell - so the principal effect of our redemption by Christ is the delivering us from sin, by which we are, of course, delivered both from Satan and hell. Hence the Scripture always speaks of this as the greatest of benefits, and Christ is styled our Redeemer and Saviour chiefly on this account. Thus the angel Gabriel declared to St Joseph, before He was born, "Thou shalt call His name Jesus "(or Saviour), "for He shall save His people from their sins," Mat. i. 21 . "A faithful saying, and worthy of all acceptation, that Christ Jesus came into this world to save sinners," i Tim. i. 15 . For this He was raised up and exalted by His Father; for "Him hath God exalted with His right hand to be Prince and Saviour, to give repentance to Israel and remission of sins. Acts, v. 31 . "To Him all the prophets gave testimony, that through His name all receive remission of sins who believe in Him," Acts, x. 43 . "Be it known therefore to you, men and brethren, that through Him remission of sins is preached to you, and from all the things from which you could not be justified by the law of Moses," Acts, xiii. 38 . Him "God hath sent forth to be a propitiation through faith in His Blood, for the remission of former sins," Rom. iii. 25 . "In whom we have redemption through His Blood, the remission of sins," Eph. i. 7 . "The Blood of Jesus Christ His Son cleanseth us from all sin," i John, i. 7 . "But you are washed, but you are sanctified, but you are justified in the name of our Lord Jesus Christ," i Cor, vi. 11 . "The Blood of Christ cleanseth our consciences from dead works," Heb. ix. 14 . Jesus Christ hath "loved us and washed us from our sins in His own Blood," Apoc. i. 5 . Now, whereas "our wrestling is not against flesh and blood, but against principalities and powers, against the rulers of the world of this darkness, against the spirit of wickedness in high places," Eph. vi. 12 ; against "the devil, who goeth about as a roaring lion, seeking whom he may devour," i Pet. v. 8 ; and whereas, "for this purpose the Son of God appeared, that He might destroy the works of the devil," i John, iii. 8 , by delivering us from our sins; consequently by so doing, He also has delivered us from the tyranny of that cruel master, and taken our nature upon Him, "that through death He might destroy him who hath the empire of death, that is the devil; and might deliver them who, through fear of death, were all their lifetime subject to bondage," Heb. ii. 14 . And therefore He Himself declares, "Now is the judgment of this world, now shall the prince of this world be cast out," John, xiii. 31 . In consequence of this we are also delivered by Him from that eternal punishment to which we must otherwise have been condemned for our sins; for "Christ died for us; much more, therefore, being now justified by His Blood, shall we be saved from wrath through Him," Rom. v. 9 , "who hath delivered us from the power of darkness," Col. i. 13 , and "who hath delivered us from the wrath to come," i Thes. i. 10 .

Q. 8. Was it necessary that Christ should do and suffer as much as He did in order to purchase this redemption for man?

A. Far from it; for, considering the infinite dignity of His Person, and the ardent charity with which He always acted according to His Father's will, the smallest action or suffering of His was of infinite value in itself, and sufficient to redeem ten thousand worlds. But it was the will of the Almighty that He should do and suffer so much, and at last die on the Cross, and shed the last drop of His precious Blood for us, that He might the more efficaciously demonstrate the greatness of His love for us; for "greater love than this no man hath, that a man lay down his life for his friend," John, xv. 13 : and "God commendeth His charity to us; because, when as yet we were sinners, Christ died for us," Rom. V. 8 ; also that He might the more abundantly glorify His eternal Father, by the supereminent greatness of His merits, and the more perfectly accomplish the work His Father gave Him to do in redeeming mankind; and that He might the more effectually encourage and excite us to love Him, and repose a perfect confidence in His infinite goodness. Hence we find it expressly declared in Scripture: (1.) That what Christ did for our redemption was not only sufficient, but superabundant. Thus Jesus Christ "is the propitiation for our sins; and not for ours only, but also for those of the whole world," I John, ii. 2 . "With the Lord there is mercy, and with Him plentiful redemption," Ps. cxxix. 7 . "By one oblation He hath perfected for ever them that are sanctified,"

Heb. X. 14 . "In whom we have redemption through His Blood according to the riches of His grace, which hath superabounded in us," Eph. i. 7 . "But not as the offence so also is the gift; for if by the offence of one many have died, much more the grace of God, and the gift in the grace of one man Jesus Christ, hath abounded unto many; . . . where sin abounded, grace hath abounded more," Rom. v. 15 , 20. "God, who is rich in mercy, for His exceeding great charity wherewith He loved us, even when we were dead by sins, hath quickened us together in Christ, . . . that He might show in the ages to come the abundant riches of His grace in His bounty towards us in Christ Jesus," Eph. ii. 4 . (2.) That it was the express decree of the Almighty that He should lay down His life in order to procure the redemption of mankind. "If He shall lay down His life for sin. He shall see a long-lived seed." Is. liii. "This same Jesus being delivered up by the determinate counsel and foreknowledge of God, you, by the hands of wicked men, have crucified and slain," Acts, ii. 23 , said St Peter to the Jews in his first sermon. "For of a truth," said the whole Church to God, "there assembled together in this city, against Thy Holy Child Jesus, whom Thou hast anointed, Herod and Pontius Pilate, and the Gentiles, with the people of Israel, to do what Thy hand and Thy counsel decreed to be done," Acts, iv. 27 . Hence Christ Himself, speaking of His Passion to His apostles, always speaks of His sufferings and death as what He must undergo. "From that time Jesus began to show to His disciples that He must go to Jerusalem, and suffer many things, . . . and be put to death," Mat. xvi. 21 ; and to the disciples, after His resurrection. He said, "Thus it behoved Christ to suffer, and to rise again the third day," Luke, xxiv. 46 . That it was on this condition He was to bring forth much fruit by the redemption of mankind, and enter Himself into glory. He shows in these texts: "The hour is come that the Son of Man should be glorified. Amen, amen, I say unto you, unless the grain of wheat fall into the ground and die, it remaineth alone; but if it die, it bringeth forth much fruit," John, xii. 23 ; and "ought not Christ to have suffered these things, and so to enter into His glory?" Luke, xxiv. 26 .

Q. 9. What is meant by the benefit of Christ's impetration?

A. It means that Christ, by the infinite merits of His passion and death, obtained for us all spiritual benedictions and graces in this life, all the means necessary for attaining eternal happiness, and eternal happiness itself in the life to come. Insomuch that it is only in and through Him that any favour, grace, or blessing is bestowed upon us by God, or that anything we do can be agreeable or acceptable to God, or conducive to our eternal salvation. Hence we find it declared in Scripture that all the graces we receive from

God, and our salvation itself, flow only from this source. Thus (1.) with regard to all graces in general, St Paul says, "He that spared not even His own Son, but delivered Him up for us all, how hath He not also with Him given us all things?" Rom. viii. 32 , And therefore, "Blessed be the God and Father of our Lord Jesus Christ, who hath blessed us with all spiritual blessings in heavenly things in Christ," Eph. i. 3 . For "of His fulness we have all received, and grace for grace," John, i. 16 ; "and in Him dwelleth all the fulness of the Godhead bodily, and you are filled in Him, Who is the head of all principality and power," Col. ii. 9 . "As all things of His Divine power, which appertain to life and godliness, are given us through the knowledge of Him Who hath called us by His own proper glory and virtue, by whom He hath given us most great and precious promises, that by these you may be made partakers of the Divine nature," 2 Pet. i. 3 . (2.) The grace of our election; for "He hath chosen us in Him" (Christ) "before the foundation of the world, that we should be holy and unspotted in His sight in charity, Who hath predestinated us unto the adoption of children, through Jesus Christ," Eph. i. 4 . (3.) The grace of our vocation; for "He hath delivered us and called us by His holy calling, not according to our works, but according to His own purpose and grace, which was given to us in Christ Jesus before the times of the world," 2 Tim. i. 9 . ..." Wherefore, holy brethren, partakers of the heavenly calling, consider the Apostle and High Priest of our profession, Jesus," Heb. iii. 1 . "For God is faithful, by Whom you are called unto the fellowship of His Son Jesus Christ our Lord," i Cor. i. 9 . "In Whom we are called by lot, being predestinated according to the purpose of Him, Who worketh all things according to the counsel of His will," Eph. i. 11 . (4.) The grace of justification - to wit, that sanctifying grace which, applying to our souls the fruits and efficacy of the Blood of Jesus, washes and cleanses them from all the defilements and pollutions of sin, adorns us with the heavenly beauty of holiness, and makes us just before God; for "the Blood of Jesus Christ cleanseth us from all sins," I John, i. 7 ; but "we are justified freely by His grace, through the redemption that is in Christ Jesus," Rom. iii. 24 , Who "by one oblation, perfected for ever them that are sanctified," Heb. x. 14 . Indeed, "such some of you were" (to wit, guilty of many crimes), "but you are washed, but you are sanctified, but you are justified, in the name of our Lord Jesus Christ," i Cor. vi. 11 . "Who is made to us from God, wisdom and justice, and sanctification and redemption,"" i Cor. i. 30 . (5.) Habitual grace, by which we remain in Christ and He in us, which dignifies all our good works, and makes them acceptable and agreeable to God, and consequently meritorious of eternal life, and by which they become the works of Christ Himself, as the fruit produced by the branches is chiefly the fruit of the vine from which the branches receive their nourishment. "Abide in Me," says Christ, "and I in you. As the branch cannot bear fruit of itself, unless it abide in the vine; so neither can you, unless you abide in me. I am the vine, you the branches; he that abideth in Me, and I in him, the same beareth much fruit; for without Me you can do nothing," John, XV. 4 . What that fruit is St Paul tells us, saying, "But now being made free from sin, and become servants to God, you have your fruit unto sanctification, and the end everlasting life," Rom. vi. 22 . "For the fruit of the light is in all goodness, and justice, and truth," Eph. v. 9 - to wit, all manner of good works; and therefore St Peter exhorts us to labour the more, that by good works "we may make our calling and election sure," 2 Peter, i. 10 . (6.) Eternal glory in the salvation of our souls, which is represented to us as the end of all these other graces, and the ultimate effect in us of our redemption through Jesus. "Christ died for us when sinners, much more, therefore, being now justified through His Blood, shall we be saved from wrath through Him," Rom. v. 9 . For "Whom He predestinated, them He also called; and whom He called, them He also justified; and whom He justified, them He glorified," Rom. viii. 30 . "According to His mercy He saved us by the laver of regeneration, and the renovation of the Holy Ghost, Whom He hath poured forth upon us abundantly, through Jesus Christ our Saviour; that being justified by His grace, we may be heirs, according to hope, of everlasting life," Tit. iii. 5 . "The grace of God is life everlasting in Christ Jesus," Rom. vi. 23 ; "for God hath not appointed us to Avrath, but to the purchasing salvation by our Lord Jesus Christ, Who died for us, that we may live together with Him," I Thess. v. 9 . "And being consummated He became the cause of salvation to all that obey Him," Heb. v. 9 , and therefore we have a confidence in "the entering into the Holies by the Blood of Christ, a new and living way, which He hath dedicated for us through the veil, that is to say. His flesh,'" Heb. x. 19 , 20. Lastly, that Jesus Christ alone is the source of our salvation is expressly declared by St Peter: "Neither is there salvation in any other," says he, "for there is no other name under heaven given to men whereby we must be saved, but the Name of Jesus only," Acts, iv. 12 . And as "there is ' but "one God," so there is but "one Mediator of God and man, the Man Christ Jesus, Who gave Himself a redemption for all," i Tim. ii. 5 .

Q. 10. Why is Jesus Christ called a Mediator?

A. Because He is truly "the Mediator of God and man "in the most perfect sense of the word. A mediator is one who acts between two, either to obtain pardon, or to procure some benefit from the one for the other. Now a mediator may obtain this pardon or benefit either as a right in justice by paying an equivalent price, or as a favour through prayer and intercession. Man by sin had grievously offended God, and was an object of His wrath and indignation; Jesus Christ appears as a Mediator to obtain pardon from God to man; to purchase this He paid a price of infinite value, the merits of all His sufferings, and death upon the Cross, by which He acquired a right and title, in justice, to demand the pardon from His Father, and all other graces for us; but that nothing might be wanting to the perfection of His mediatorship, to His sufferings and death He also joined most fervent prayers for the same end. Hence the Scripture says, "Therefore He is the Mediator of the New Testament, that by means of His death for the redemption of those transgressions which were under the former Testament, they that are called may receive the promise of eternal inheritance," Heb. ix. 15 ; and, "in the days of His flesh, offering up prayers and supplications with a strong cry, and tears, to Him that was able to save Him from death, was heard for His reverence," Heb. V. 7 . By the former He is a Mediator of Redemption, and the only Mediator between God and man; by the latter He is also a Mediator of intercession, but so that He has a right in His own person to claim what He asks for us as His own due. When one man intercedes with God for another, he is also a mediator of intercession, but such a one has no right nor title in himself to demand what he prays for, but must expect to be heard only through mercy and favour; yea, this very mercy and favour he can look for only in and through the merits of Jesus Christ; so that all good to man must come from that source alone, whatever be the immediate instruments or means of applying to it.

Q. II. As Jesus Christ has done so much for the salvation of mankind, will all mankind be saved?

A. Far from it; on the contrary, the light which the Holy Scripture gives us on this point expressly declares that "many are called, but few are chosen; "which alarming truth Jesus Christ repeats on two different occasions, and further assures us, in the plainest terms, that "wide is the gate, and broad is the way, that leadeth to destruction, and many there are who walk therein; but oh, how narrow is the gate," says He, "and straight the way, that leadeth to life, and few there are who find it! "Mat. vii. 13 . By which it is plain that the number of those who are lost is much greater than of those who are saved.

Q,. 12. How comes this? Does not God will all men to be saved?

A. He certainly does. St Paul declares it in the plainest terms: "God will have all men to be saved, and come to the knowledge of the truth," i Tim. ii. 4 .

Q. 13. Did not Christ die for all mankind?

A. Most assuredly; "Jesus Christ gave Himself a redemption for all," I Tim. ii. 6 ; "and He is the propitiation for our sins, and not for ours only, but also for those of the whole world," i John, ii. 2 .

Q. 14. How comes it, then, that such numbers will be lost?

A. From their own fault alone. To understand this, we must observe that, as God created man a free agent, He therefore required from him a free and voluntary service, as we have seen above at large, Chap. III. 18. But man, abusing his free-will, rebelled against his God, and forfeited all the favours which God had bestowed upon him in this life, with all title to that eternal reward which He had prepared for him in the life to come; and also became utterly incapable of taking the smallest step towards making his peace with his Creator. Now, though Jesus Christ fully satisfied the Divine justice for the offence committed against God, and rendered Him propitious, and willing to be reconciled with us, obtaining grace to enable us to do on our part what should be required of us to complete our reconciliation; yet, it is manifest, that, if we still continue in our rebellion against God, refusing to return to His service, and to perform the conditions which He requires, the merits of Christ cannot be applied to our souls, so as to reinstate us in the favour of God, or secure our salvation. We lost His favour by the voluntary abuse of our free-will, and it is impossible to recover it without our voluntary performance of what He requires from us for that end. Though Christ died for all, and obtained so many benefits for all, yet He forces no one to accept these benefits; nor will all He did avail us unless His merits be applied to our souls, through the use of the means and the performance of the conditions which He has appointed. Hence the Scripture expressly declares, that "Christ is become the cause of eternal salvation to all that obey Him," Heb. v. 9 . Now as God wills all to be saved, and as Jesus Christ died for all, therefore God, through the merits of Christ, gives to all men, in the way He sees proper and suitable to their state, the necessary helps of His grace, to enable them to perform the conditions He requires from them, and by that means to secure their salvation. But, alas! the greatest number still continuing to abuse their free will, refuse to co-operate with that grace; and hence, as they do not perform the conditions required, they are therefore lost for ever!

Q- 15. What are the conditions which God requires of us to be saved?

A. They may all be reduced to two general heads: (1.) To believe what Christ teaches j and (2.) To obey what He commands; or, in other words, Faith and Love; for by Faith we believe, and by Love we obey. Hence St Paul lays down these two conditions as the only means by which we can reap any benefit from the redemption of Christ: "In Christ Jesus," says he, "neither Circumcision availeth anything, nor uncircumcision, but Faith that worketh by Charity," Gal. v. 6 .

CHAPTER X.

Of Faith In Jesus Christ

Q. I. What is Faith?

A. Faith, taken in the general sense of the word, is our belief of any truth founded on the testimony of others. To understand this, we must observe that there are different ways by which we can come to the knowledge of any truth. For some things can be known only by experience - that is, by the testimony of our two principal senses of touching and seeing; and this is generally the first source of our knowledge, and a very extensive one: by this we know the existence of all things about us, with all their sensible qualities and properties, and the like. Other things there are which can only be known by reason - that is, when from known principles we argue and draw conclusions which lead us to the knowledge of numberless truths, which the senses alone could never have acquired. Lastly, there are other things which can never be known, either by reason or experience, but only by hearing the testimony of those who know them; and the belief we have of such things is called Faith. By this means alone we can acquire the knowledge of all past matters of fact, of things that happen at a distance from us, and of all such things as do not fall under the examination of our senses, and are above the comprehension of human reason.

Q. 2. How many kinds of faith are there?

A. Two kinds - human faith and Divine faith. Human faith is belief in anything we learn from the testimony of man, and Divine faith is belief in anything we receive on the testimony of God.

Q. 3. Is faith a certain means of acquiring knowledge?

A. The certainty of what we learn from the testimony of others depends upon the authority of those who give the testimony - that is, upon their knowledge and veracity. Two things are necessary to make us certain of what we hear from another - that he be not mistaken himself in what he relates, and that he speak exactly according to his knowledge. Where we are persuaded of these two things, we can have no reasonable doubt of the truth of what we hear; but if either of these be wanting, we can have no certain faith in such testimony. Now, though in the ordinary course of life the testimony of other men is a very general and extensive source of knowledge, and in many cases must be entirely depended upon; yet, as all men are liable to be mistaken themselves, or to deceive us, therefore human faith, properly speaking, cannot be said to carry an absolute certainty along with it. But with Divine faith the case is otherwise; for as it is simply impossible that God should be deceived Himself, and no less impossible that He should mean to deceive His creatures, therefore everything we know from the testimony of God, we know with the most absolute certainty of its being true.

Q. 4. What description do the Scriptures give of Divine faith?

A. St Paul says that "faith is the substance of things to be hoped for, the evidence of things that are not seen," Heb. xi. He calls it "the substance of things to be hoped for," because the happiness we hope for in the next life is above all human comprehension; so that neither experience nor reason can give us any idea of it, and it is only by Divine faith we know it; but this Divine faith, founded on the infallible testimony of God Himself, gives us such a feeling conviction and persuasion of the greatness of it, that it renders it in a manner present with us, as St Chrysostom observes, so as to support and encourage us under all our afflictions, as if we already possessed it. He calls it also "the evidence of things not seen; "because though it be possible for us to see with our eyes, or comprehend by our reason the great truths of eternity which Jesus Christ has revealed to us, yet His Divine revelation gives us a more convincing evidence of their truth than if we saw them with our very eyes themselves. And it is in preferring His Divine word and authority in revealing them to anything our senses or reason can oppose to the contrary, that the merit of our faith precisely consists; because by this we do the greatest homage to the infinite wisdom and veracity of God, while we humble the proud idol of our own judgment to His Holy word, "and captivate our understandings in obedience to Him;" hence Jesus Christ says to St Thomas, "Because thou hast seen Me, Thomas, thou hast believed; blessed are they that have not seen and have believed," John, xx. 29 .

Q. 5. What is faith in Jesus Christ?

A. It is the firm belief of all those heavenly truths which He has revealed to man concerning God and eternity, and the salvation of our souls.

Q. 6, Could not man have acquired the knowledge of these heavenly truths by his own strength?

A. No. It was impossible for man, by his own abilities, ever to have attained the knowledge of them, as we have seen above, Chap. VI. 9, 25. These truths are above nature, they belong to another world, and many of them depend solely upon the will and good pleasure of God, and, therefore, could never have been known to man unless God had revealed them to him. Hence the Holy Scripture says, "Hardly do we guess aright at things that are upon earth, and with labour do we find the things that are before us; but the things that are in heaven who shall search?" Wis. ix. 16 . And Christ Himself, Who assures us that life eternal consists in "knowing the only living and true God, and Jesus Christ Whom He hath sent," John, xvii. 3 , declares also that "no man knoweth who the Son is but the Father, and who the Father is but the Son, and he to whom the Son will reveal Him," Luke, x. 22 . So that Jesus Christ Himself, the Son of God, made man, is the heavenly teacher, by Whom the knowledge of the Father, and of all the truths of salvation, is communicated to us.

Q. 7. Can we depend upon the truth of what He teaches?

A. Most undoubtedly; for as He is God, a Being of infinite wisdom. Who essentially knows all things, it is manifestly impossible He should ever be deceived Himself, or make the smallest mistake in anything He says; and as He is a God of infinite truth - nay, truth itself - and, at the same time, infinitely holy, incapable of the smallest imperfection, it is no less impossible for Him ever to deceive His creatures, so that whatever He says must be absolutely and infallibly true.

Q. 8. Are we then obliged to believe whatever He teaches?

A. Most certainly; for as everything taught or revealed by Him is absolutely true, whenever we know anything to be His doctrine, we must either believe it to be a real truth, or, by refusing to believe it, suppose Him guilty of telling a lie, which would be a manifest impiety, and the highest injury done to His infinite wisdom and veracity. Hence the Scripture says, "He that believeth not maketh God a liar, because he believeth not the testimony which God hath given of His Son," i John, v. 10 . Now how can we expect any part with Christ if we make God a liar?

Q. 9. Does He require of all men to believe in Him as a condition of salvation?

A. Yes, He does. As He is the only Saviour of mankind, who by shedding His precious blood redeems all men from their sins, and from the slavery of Satan, so all who wish to partake of His salvation must acknowledge Him as their Redeemer, and believe in Him; nay, this belief or faith in Him is the very first step towards our salvation, the foundation and groundwork of all the duties we owe Him.

Q. 10. How so?

A. Because it is self-evident that we can neither love Him, nor hope in Him, nor honour Him, nor obey Him, except we first believe in Him, and receive in faith what He teaches. Yet He has expressly declared that unless we love Him and obey Him, there is no salvation for us; and St Peter assures us that "there is no other name given to men, under heaven, by which we can be saved but the name of Jesus only," Acts, iv, 12 .

Q. 11. How were those saved who lived in the world before the time of Christ?

A. From the beginning there never was any other name given to men by which they could be saved but the name of Jesus only; so that all that ever were saved from the beginning were saved only by believing in Jesus I Christ the Redeemer, who was then to come, and obeying the law which God then gave them, as now we can be saved only by believing in the same Redeemer, who is already come, and obeying the law of His Gospel.

Q. 12. Is it enough to believe in the Person of Jesus Christ, "That He is the Son of God made man," in order to be saved?

A. We must not only believe in His Person, but we must also believe all that he has revealed - His whole doctrine; for how can we believe that Jesus Christ is God if we refuse to believe any one thing that He says, and by that means suppose Him either ignorant or a liar?

Q. 13. But is it not enough to have the faith of Peter: now his faith was, "Thou art Christ, the Son of the living God," for which Christ pronounced him blessed, and yet this was only faith in His Person?

A. The faith of Peter is certainly sufficient; and at that time Peter only made profession of his faith in the Person of Christ, because that was the only point proposed by our Saviour when He said, "Whom say ye that I am? "and it is the chief article of our faith in Christ, upon which all the rest depend. But the faith of Peter was by no means confined to this only, for afterwards, when some of the disciples left Him because they would not believe the sublime doctrine He was teaching them concerning the blessed Eucharist, and Christ asked His apostles, "Will you also leave Me? "Peter immediately answered, "Lord, to whom shall we go? Thou hast the words of eternal life," John, vi. 69 , which shows how firmly he believed His words also, even in things he did not understand as well as the Divinity of His Person.

Q. 14. Is the necessity of faith or belief in Jesus Christ and His doctrine declared in the Scripture?

A. As the virtue of faith in Jesus Christ and His doctrine is the foundation of all other Christian virtues, and of all Christian duties, Almighty God has been pleased that it should be laid down in the Holy Scriptures in the clearest and plainest terms.

Thus, with regard to his Person, "This is His command, that we believe in the name of His Son Jesus Christ," i John, iii. 23 . "He that believeth not is already condemned, because he believeth not in the name of the only begotten Son of God," John, iii. 18 . "He that believeth not the Son shall not see life; but the wrath of God remaineth in him," John, iii. t,6. "Many seducers are gone out into the world, who confess not that Jesus Christ is come in the flesh: this is a seducer and an antichrist," 2 John, ver. 7. "He that believeth not, makes God a liar, because he believeth not the testimony which God has given of His Son," i John, v. 10 .

With regard to His word or His doctrine, when He gave His apostles the commission to go and teach all nations those things which He had commanded them, He immediately adds, "He that believes and is baptised, shall be saved, and he that believes not, shall be condemned," Mat. , Mark. And on another occasion He says to them, "Whosoever shall not hear you or receive your words, when you depart out of that city, shake off the dust from your feet; verily I say unto you, it shall be more tolerable for the land of Sodom and Gomorrah in the day of judgment than for that city," Mat. x. "Whosoever shall be ashamed of Me and My words," says Christ, "in this sinful and adulterous generation, of him also the Son of Man shall be ashamed when He shall come in the glory of His Father, with His holy angels," Mark, viii. 38 ; Luke, ix. 26. "He that revolteth and continueth not in the doctrine of Christ, hath not God," 2 John, ix. . . . . "Jesus Christ shall be revealed from heaven with His mighty angels, in flaming fire, taking vengeance on them that know not God, and obey not the Gospel of our Lord Jesus Christ; who shall be punished with everlasting destruction, from the presence of the Lord, and from the glory of His power," 2 Thess. i. In all which plain testimonies we see that the receiving His words, the embracing His doctrine, and the obeying His Gospel, are laid down as necessary conditions of salvation, without which "everlasting destruction from the presence of the Lord "will undoubtedly be our portion.

Lastly. With regard to faith in general, both in His person and doctrine, and to the great crime and punishment of unbelievers, the Scriptures speak thus: "without faith it is impossible to please God," Heb. xi. 6 ; "As for unbelievers, and murderers, and fornicators, and adulterers, their portion shall be in a lake burning with fire and brimstone, which is the second death," Rev. xxi. 8 . Hence the holy apostle St Jude says, in the beginning of his epistle, "It is necessary to write, to beseech you to contend, earnestly for the faith once delivered to the saints;" and then goes on, in the rest of his short epistle, to expose, in the strongest colours, the wickedness and punishment of those who corrupt this true faith by false doctrine; and St Paul, writing to the Galatians, pronounces a curse, and repeats it a second time, upon any one who shall dare to change the Gospel of Jesus Christ, or in any one article teach another Gospel than what he had already taught them, Gal. i.

Q. 15. As true faith in Jesus Christ, or the belief of all those Divine truths which He has revealed, is so strictly required by Almighty God from all as a condition of salvation, how can we possibly know what those truths are which He has revealed, and which we are obliged to believe?

A. This can be known only by means of the rule which Jesus Christ established for that purpose.

CHAPTER XI.

Of The Rule Of Faith

Q. 1. Has Jesus Christ left us a rule by which we may know the truths He has revealed?

A. He has; and it is only by following this rule that we are preserved in that one true faith, of which the Scripture says, there is "one Lord, one faith, one baptism," Eph. iv. 5 , and "without which faith it is impossible to please God," Heb. xi. 6 . Hence St Paul, exhorting all to be of the same mind - that is, to believe the same truths and to have the same faith - commands us to continue in this rule, as the means to be so; "Nevertheless," says he, "whereunto we are already arrived, that we be of the same mind, let us also continue in the same rule," Philip, iii. 16.

Q. 2. Have we any description of this rule in the Scriptures?

A. Yes, we have. The prophet Isaiah, foretelling the glory of Christ's kingdom, describes this rule by which we are to walk under the Gospel, as a highway, plain, open, and easy to walk in; as a; way of holiness, containing everything necessary for making those holy who walk in it; as a certain and secure way, in which even fools shall walk without danger of error; and, finally, as a way that leads to daily happiness. The prophet's words are these: "And a path and a way shall be there, and it shall be called the holy way, . . . and this shall be to you a straight way, so that fools shall not err therein; . . . they shall walk there that shall be delivered; and the redeemed of the Lord shall return, and shall come into Sion with praise, and everlasting joy shall be upon their heads; they shall obtain joy and gladness, and sorrow and mourning shall flee away," Isa. xxxv. 8 .

Q. 3. What may be drawn from these words of the prophet?

A. That the rule which Jesus Christ has left for instructing us in what we are to believe and do, in order to be saved, has these three properties, (1.) It is easy and plain, fitted for all capacities. (2.) It is universal, and contains all revealed truth. (3.) It is certain, and may be securely depended upon.

Q. 4. Was it becoming the wisdom and goodness of God to leave us such a rule for our guide in these things?

A. It was not only becoming in Him to do so, but it was absolutely necessary for the end He proposed. For how could He require of man to believe His truths and obey His law, under pain of damnation, if He had not left us some plain and certain means by which we might know what all these truths are, and what His law requires from us?

Q. 5. What is the rule of our faith left us by Jesus Christ?

A. The Christian world, as it stands at present, is divided into two great bodies in regard to this point. All, indeed, agree in this, that the Holy Scriptures, being dictated by the Holy Ghost, are truly the Word of God, and therefore are infallibly true in what they teach, both as to what we are to believe, and as to what we are to do in order to be saved. But as the Divine truths contained in them cannot be known without understanding the true sense of these sacred writings, hence the great question arises, How is the true sense of the Scripture to he known? One of the two great bodies of Christians - to wit, Protestants - affirm that the true sense of the Scriptures maybe sufficiently known in all things necessary to salvation by every man of sound judgment who reads them with humility and attention; and therefore they hold that the rule left by Jesus Christ to man for knowing what we are to believe, and what we are to do, in order to be saved, is the written Word alone, interpreted by every man of sound judgment. The other great body of Christians - namely. Catholics - affirm that the true sense of the Scriptures cannot be sufficiently known by any private interpretation, but only by the public authority of the Church; and therefore they hold that the rule left us by Jesus Christ is the written Word, as interpreted by the Church.

Q. 6. How shall this great question be decided?

A. This is indeed a very great and important question, on the solution of which the whole difference between Protestants and Catholics depends. But the decision of it is far from being difficult; it is shown in a very plain and simple manner by comparing these two rules with the qualities which, as we have seen above, both Scripture and reason prove the rule left by Jesus Christ must have, and seeing to which of them those qualities belong. Now the qualities or the properties of the rule left by Jesus Christ are, that it is plain and easy, comprehensive, containing all truths, and certain, so that we can depend upon it.

Q. 7. Is the written Word alone a plain and easy rule, fitted for all capacities?

A. A little attention will show that it is far from it; for (1.) It is impossible it should be such to those who cannot read; and yet what vast multitudes of these are there in the world! To them it can be no rule at all, for they cannot use it. Before printing was invented, which was not for above thirteen hundred years after Christ, there were none but written books in the world, and, of course, very few learned to read - not one, perhaps,in some thousands. What must the great bulk of mankind have done during all that time if the written Word alone be the only rule? Did Jesus Christ leave a rule for knowing His truths which could be used only by the learned, while yet He obliges all, under pain of damnation, to believe these truths? (2.) With regard to those who can read, and who pretend to follow the written Word alone, as they interpret it for themselves, we see from experience that they never agree among themselves about the sense of it, but run into the most opposite and contradictory interpretations - the most convincing proof that it is far from being plain and easy; nay, on the contrary, that it is in many things obscure and difficult. (3.) The Scripture itself affirms, in express terms, that in the Epistles of St Paul there "are some things hard to be understood, which the unlearned and unstable wrest, as they do also the other Scriptures, to their own destruction," 2 Pet. iii. 16 . In which text it is declared that the Scriptures are "hard to be understood," and that not only the unlearned, but also the unstable, who presume to interpret them according to their own judgment, instead of finding their true sense, pervert and wrest them to false meanings, and by so doing bring destruction on themselves. Consequently, this rule of the written "Word alone is by no means a plain and easy rule, fitted for all capacities; on the contrary, it is a most dangerous thing for any one to pretend to follow it, for the number of the unlearned is immense, and even among those who are learned, who can answer for his own stability? Would Jesus Christ ever have left such a hard and dangerous rule to poor mortals?

Q. 8. Is the written Word alone a comprehensive rule?

A. It is very far from it: there are several things believed and practised by all Christians, for which no authority is found in Scripture; nay, which are contrary to the express words of Scripture; we shall only mention these three: - (1.) The law of God laid down in Scripture commands the seventh day of the week, which is Saturday, to be kept holy, and no manner of work to be done on it. There is not, in the whole Bible, one single text annulling that law, or dispensing with it; and yet all Christians think it lawful to break that law, by working upon the seventh day, and think it a duty to keep holy the first day of the week, or Sunday, in its place. (2.) The Scripture expressly forbids to eat blood, or things strangled, as a command of the Holy Ghost , Acts, XV. 28 . And yet this law is broken every day by Christians, without any scruple, though they have not the smallest authority from Scripture to do so. (3.) All Christians believe the Scriptures to be the Word of God, written by the inspiration of the Holy Ghost; and this belief is the very groundwork of religion to those who follow Scripture alone as their rule; yet there is not the smallest proof from the Scriptures themselves of their being so. Nay, it is simply impossible to prove from the Scriptures that the books therein contained were written by the persons whose names they bear; that these writers were inspired by God; that the books, as we have them, are such as were written by them, without addition, diminution, or corruption; or that the translations made of them are faithful, and agree with the originals. The Scriptures, then, are far from being a comprehensive rule, and far from containing all revealed truths, since the above particulars, and many others, are not to be found in them.

Q. 9. Is the written Word alone a certain rule?

A. It fails here no less than in the two former properties. The true sense of Scripture is, indeed, a most certain and infallible rule; but it is evident that those who interpret it by their own private judgment can have no certainty that the sense they put upon it is the true one; for (1.) The Scripture itself declares, "that the unlearned and the unstable wrest it to their own destruction," 2 Pet. iii. 16 . Now, how can any man be certain that he is not of this number? He may say he thinks he is right, but he can have no certainty. Nay, he cannot reasonably even think he is right; for (2.) Those who follow their own interpretation as their rule, are perpetually disagreeing among themselves, and giving the most contrary and often contradictory interpretation to the same text. How, then, can any man among them reasonably think that the sense he puts upon it is right, when he sees it contradicted by numbers of others every way as well qualified to understand it as himself? (3.) Very often the same persons alter their opinion about the sense they put on Scripture; and what they believe to be the true sense to-day, they reject as false to-morrow, being continually carried about with every wind of doctrine. Now, what certainty can they have for their opinion at one time more than another? Their very change is an evident acknowledgment that they were long before, though they were persuaded then that they were right, what certainty can they have of being right now? (4.) All those who follow this rule have the whole weight of the Catholic Church against them which condemns all their peculiar interpretations of Scripture as false and erroneous. What security, then, can they have of being right, when such a numerous and respectable body of Christians condemns them?

Q. 10. What is the consequence of these reasonings?

A. That seeing the written Word alone, as interpreted by every man's private judgment, has not one of those qualities which the rule of our faith ought to have; therefore this cannot be the rule left us by Jesus Christ for teaching us the truths revealed by Him.

Q. 11. What is the rule of faith held by Catholics?

A. Catholics hold that Jesus Christ, well knowing that the dead letter of the Scriptures could never serve the purpose of a rule by which men could come to the knowledge of the truth revealed by Him, if left to every private person to interpret according to his own fancy, and that, on the contrary, such private interpretation must prove an unavoidable source of contentions and divisions among them, was therefore pleased to authorise the pastors of His Church to be the interpreters of His Word, and the depositaries of all the sacred truths He had revealed to the world: that He gave them power and commission to teach the people the truths of salvation, and requires all to receive their faith from them; and, in consequence of this, they hold that the rule of faith ordained by Jesus Christ is the Word of God as interpreted by the Church - that is, by the great body of the pastors of His Church spread throughout the world.

Q. 12. Is this rule plain and easy, and fitted for all capacities?

A. Nothing can be more plain, or more adapted to the infirmity of human nature. For let a person be ever so illiterate, and of ever so mean a capacity, if he have but the smallest degree of common sense, he can always be instructed in what is necessary for him to know by the living voice of his pastors, who can vary the manner of their instructions in every different shape, to adapt them to his capacity, and make him comprehend them. It was by this means alone that thousands and thousands, in all ages, have been instructed in the true faith, and in the practice of all Christian duties, though they had never learned to read a single letter. It is by this means alone that thousands are daily instructed in the truths of religion, who, though they have learned to read, have neither judgment nor capacity to understand what they do read; and it is by this means alone that all, even the most learned, have been instructed in the first rudiments of religion in their infancy. So that this is evidently a plain easy rule, fitted for all capacities, and for persons of every age, condition, and sex.

Q. 13. Is this rule comprehensive, so that all revealed truths can be learned by it?

A. It is; for as Jesus Christ taught all revealed truths to His apostles by word of mouth, so it was perfectly easy for them to teach their disciples everything they had learned from Him in the same manner. Thus, from generation to generation, the pastors of the Church, being thoroughly instructed in all revealed truths themselves by those before them, can communicate the whole, without exception, to their people. And, in fact, it is by this means alone we know for certain that the Scriptures are the Word of God; that the books we have for Scripture are genuine; that it is lawful to keep the first day of the week holy instead of the seventh, though there be no authority for doing so in the Scripture; and that it is lawful to eat blood and things strangled, though contrary to the express command of the Scripture; and, in general, it is by this means alone we come to know the true sense of Scripture, and every other point of religion which the written Word either does not or could not contain.

Q. 14. Is this rule certain so that we may safely depend upon it?

A. It is in this that the beauty and excellency of this rule chiefly shine forth, and show it to be the rule left us by Jesus Christ, and truly worthy of His Divine wisdom and goodness. The certainty of this rule appears chiefly from three considerations: (1.) From the nature of the rule itself; for this does not consist in the private opinion of a few particular persons, but in the unanimous doctrine of the great body of the pastors of the Church spread throughout the whole world. Now these pastors are exceedingly numerous; they are spread throughout all nations, and they differ from one another in their country, language, manners, government, and worldly interests, and even in their opinions about other matters of knowledge and learning. When, therefore, they all agree in giving us the same interpretation of Scripture, or in declaring to us any truth of religion, is it not infinitely safer to follow their decision than to trust to our own private judgment in opposition to them? Would not a man be a fool to prefer his own interpretation of the civil law of the land in opposition to the unanimous decision of the whole body of judges and lawyers? Besides, in so delicate a matter as religion, in which experience shows how jealous men commonly are of their own opinions, does not such unanimity evidently show the finger of God to be there? What but an overruling Providence could keep such multitudes of men united in religion who so widely differ in everything else? Among those who do not follow this rule, we can scarcely find two of the same opinion in every article, though of the same nation and language - yea, though of the same family; which evidently shows the uncertainty of their rule. How is it possible, then, that such vast multitudes, differing so much in all things else, should agree in every article of revealed truth, if the rule they follow were not perfectly secure? This will appear still further if we consider (2.) The method they observe in declaring these truths; for when the pastors of the Church declare any article of religion, they never give it as their own private opinion, or as what they believe on their own private judgment, but they all declare and protest that what they teach their people is precisely the same, without addition or diminution, which they received by tradition from their forefathers. Their predecessors, from whom they learned these truths, declared the same, and pledged their salvation for the truth of their declaration; every preceding generation did the same, till we arrive at the apostles themselves; assuring us, in all ages, that they hold it as a damnable sin to add or diminish one single iota of the faith once delivered to the saints. Now, it is manifest, that a body of people faithfully observing this rule of tradition can never vary, alter, or change any article of their religion; and, therefore, that the faith they hold at present is the self-same that was held in all preceding ages, and first taught by Christ and His apostles. But what places the certainty of this rule beyond all dispute is - (3.) The sacred character of infallibility promised by Christ to His Church, and laid down in the plainest terms in the Holy Scriptures themselves.

Q. 15. How does this infallibility of the Church appear from Scripture?

A. Among the numberless passages that show this, we shall here consider only these following: (1.) Almighty God, by the prophet Isaiah, lays down the covenant He makes with Jesus Christ and His church in these beautiful terms: "There shall come a Redeemer to Sion, and to them that return from iniquity in Jacob, saith the Lord. This is My covenant with them, saith the Lord. My Spirit that is in Thee, and My words that I have put in Thy mouth, shall not depart out of Thy mouth, nor out of the mouth of Thy seed, nor out of the mouth of Thy seed's seed, saith the Lord, from henceforth and for ever," Isa. lix. 22 . Here two things are promised, as a covenant made by

God with the Redeemer, in the most absolute and unconditional manner: first, that the Spirit of the Lord should never depart from the Redeemer, nor from His posterity; and, secondly, that the words put into His mouth, and by Him revealed to His seed, should never depart from His mouth, nor from the mouth of His seed, from henceforth and for ever. The seed or posterity of the Redeemer are His followers, or His Church; consequently. Almighty God here engages His most sacred promise that the Holy Ghost shall ever remain with the Church of Christ, and that the true doctrine of revealed truths shall never cease to be held and taught by her; for they shall never "depart out of her mouth." (2.) This divine promise is renewed and confirmed in both its parts by Jesus Christ Himself in the Gospel, for, speaking to the pastors of His Church in the persons of the apostles, He says, "I will ask the Father, and He shall give you another Comforter, that He may abide with you for ever, the Spirit of truth," John, xiv. 16 , And a little after He adds, "But when He, the Spirit of truth, is come. He shall teach you all truth," John, xvi. 13 . Here we see a positive promise that the "Spirit of Truth "should be sent upon His Church, and "abide with her for ever," and that the office of this Spirit should be "to teach her all truth." Now, the first part of this promise was visibly accomplished on Pentecost, when the Holy Ghost came down upon the apostles and first Christians; it was frequently after repeated in the same visible manner upon the first converted Gentiles, Acts, x., and other converts. There can be no doubt, then, of the perfect accomplishment of the other parts of it also, that He will continue with the Church "for ever," and "teach her all truth." (3.) Jesus Christ declares "that He builds His Church upon a rock," and positively assures us that "the gates of hell shall not prevail against her," Mat. xvi. 18 . Now, what He means by saying He builds His Church upon a rock He Himself explains when He says, "Whosoever heareth these My words, and doeth them, shall be likened to a wise man that built his house upon a rock; and the rain fell, and the floods came, and the winds blew, and they beat upon that house, and it fell not, for it was founded upon a rock," Mat. vii. 24 . Christ, then, is the wise builder, and by building His Church upon a rock gives her an absolute security against all storms, tempests, or assaults whatever, that may be made to destroy her; therefore He assures us that she shall never fail, never cease to be His Church, and, consequently, never be corrupted, never fall into error. In the other part of this text, He confirms this conclusion, positively declaring that "the gates of hell shall not prevail against her."

Q. 16. What is the consequence of these reasonings?

A. That, seeing that the Church of Christ, teaching her children by the mouth of her pastors, is z plain easy way of instructing them in all the truths of religion, and THAT with the most perfect certainty, so that even fools can walk without danger of error under her direction, therefore she is the rule left us by Jesus Christ, by which we are to know what we are to believe and what we are to do in order to secure our salvation; by which also we know the Scriptures themselves, and the true sense of them.

Q. 17. Are there any other direct proofs to show that the Church is this rule?

A. Yes; we have also these following, among many others: - (1.) Because Jesus Christ did not give His apostles any commission to write the Gospel, but only to teach and preach it; which plainly shows that His intention was, that preaching and teaching by the living voice of His pastors should be our rule, and not the dead letter of the Scripture. (2.) It is a certain truth that it was by preaching and teaching, and not by writing, that the world was converted unto Christianity; that several of the apostles wrote nothing; and that those among them who did write never converted any person or nation by their writings, but first converted them, and established the faith among them by their preachings, and then wrote to those whom they had before converted, for their instruction, on some particular occasion, and for their consolation. (3.) Because the Scripture nowhere sends us to the Scripture itself, as to our rule, but, on the contrary, it expressly declares that "no prophecy of Scriptures comes by private interpretation," 2 Pet. i. 20 . (4.) Because the Scripture, as we shall see by-and-by, sends us only to the Church and to her pastors for our instructions; and obliges all, under the severest penalties, to submit to her doctrine in all things relating to religion. (5.) Because the same Scripture expressly assures us that the pastors of the Church were instituted and ordained by Jesus Christ, to bring us all to "the unity of the Faith," and prevent us from "being carried about by strange doctrines," Eph. iv. All this will appear more fully when we have explained the nature of tradition.

Q. 18. What is meant by tradition?

A. The handing down from one generation to another, whether by word of mouth or by writings, those truths revealed by Jesus Christ to His apostles, which either are not contained in the Holy Scriptures or at least are not clearly contained in them; of which we have seen above several instances.

Q. 19. What is the principle upon which tradition proceeds?

A. It is the laying down, as an invariable rule, to be observed in every generation, that it should firmly adhere to the doctrine received from the preceding, and carefully commit the same to the succeeding one, without addition or diminution.

Q. 20. Was this principle of tradition established by the apostles?

A. It was most firmly established by them, and they used the most efficacious means to preserve it.

Q. 21. What were these means?

A. We find the following laid down in their sacred writings: - (1.) They warmly exhorted the faithful, and strictly commanded them to stick close to the doctrine which they had delivered to them, and to teach the same inviolate to those after them. Thus, "O Timothy," says St Paul, "keep that which is committed to thy trust, avoiding the profane novelties of words, and oppositions of knowledge, falsely so called, which some promising, have erred concerning the Faith," i Tim. vi. 20 . "Hold the form of sound words, which thou hast heard of me, in faith, and in the love which is in Christ Jesus. Keep the good things committed to thy trust by the Holy Ghost, Who dwelleth in us," 2 Tim. i. 13 ; "And the things which thou hast heard of me before many witnesses, the same commend to faithful men, who shall be fit to teach others also," 2 Tim. ii 2. "Continue thou in those things which thou hast learned, and which have been committed to thee, knowing of whom thou hast learned them," 2 Tim. iii. 14 . Such are the injunctions which he laid upon the pastors of the Church in the person of his disciple Timothy. And to show that the bishops, or chief pastors, are particularly charged with the obligation of adhering to the doctrine delivered to them from the apostles, when relating to Titus the qualities of these chief pastors, among others, he says that a bishop ought to "embrace that faithful Word which is according to doctrine, that he may be able to exhort in sound doctrine, and convince the gainsayers, - who must be reproved, who subvert whole houses, teaching things which they ought not for filthy lucre's sake," Tit. i. 9 ; where we see the strict charge laid upon the pastors, both to adhere to the true doctrine themselves, and to defend it against seducers. The same injunction of adhering to the doctrine they had received, by tradition, from the apostles, he lays upon all the faithful in these words: "Therefore, brethren, stand fast, and hold the traditions which you have learned, whether by word or by our epistle," 2 Thess. ii. 14 . St Jude also writes his epistle expressly to enforce this duty, and says, "I was under a necessity to write to you, to beseech you to contend earnestly for the Faith once delivered to the saints," Jude, ver. 3. Such strong and repeated injunctions laid upon all, and especially upon the pastors of the Church, who are appointed by Jesus Christ to be the guardians and teachers of the Faith, could not fail to make the deepest impression upon their minds, and have in all ages been considered as the great rule of their conduct in preserving the true doctrine inviolate.

(2.) Not content with laying such strict commands upon the faithful to adhere firmly to the old doctrine handed down from the beginning, they also warn them against all broachers of new doctrine, describe their manners, foretell their reprobation and damnation, and command the faithful to avoid them. St Paul writes to Timothy: "Now the Spirit manifestly saith, that in the last times some shall depart from the Faith, giving heed to spirits of error, and doctrines of devils, speaking lies in hypocrisy, and having their consciences seared," i Tim. iv. 1 . What an impression must this description make upon the minds of all serious Christians! what a horror must it raise in them against all innovations! "Know this also," says the same apostle, "that in the last days shall come on dangerous times; for men shall be lovers of themselves, covetous, haughty, proud, blasphemers, - lovers of pleasure more than of God; having an appearance indeed of godliness, but denying the power thereof: now these avoid, for of this sort are they - who resist the truth, men corrupted in mind, reprobate concerning the Faith," 2 Tim. iii. 1 . St Peter also is very strong upon this head, when he says, "There shall be among you lying teachers, who shall bring in sects of perdition" (damnable heresies, as the Protestant translation has it) - "bringing upon themselves swift destruction - whose judgment now of a long time lingereth not, and their destruction slumbereth not," 2 Pet. ii. 1 . St Paul also to the Romans saith, "Now I beseech you, brethren, to mark them who cause dissensions and offences, contrary to the doctrine which you have learned, and to avoid them; for they that are such serve not Christ our Lord, but their own belly," Rom. xvi. 17 ; and in his epistle to Titus he says, "A man that is a heretic, after the first and second admonition, avoid; knowing that he that is such an one is subverted, and sinneth, being condemned by his own judgment," Tit. iii. lo. Again, to Timothy he saith, "If any man teach otherwise, and consent not to the sound words of our Lord Jesus Christ, and to that doctrine which is according to goodness, he is proud, knowing nothing, but sick about questions and strifes of words, . . . corrupted in mind, and destitute of the truth," i Tim. vi. 3 . St John also speaks to the same purpose, saying "Whosoever revolteth, and continueth not in the doctrine of Christ, hath not God. ... If any man come to you, and bring not this doctrine, receive him not into thy house, and say not to him, God speed you; for he that saith to him, God speed you, communicateth with his wicked works," 2 John, 9. Could anything more efficacious have been uttered than these oracles of the Holy Ghost, to excite in the hearts of the faithful the strongest aversion to the very smallest deviation from the doctrine they had received? Could anything more firmly establish the sacred principle of tradition?

(3.) But to fix this principle upon the most solid footing, besides what is above, these sacred writers pronounce a dreadful curse upon, and deliver over to Satan, all those who shall dare to alter or corrupt the Faith once delivered to the saints, though but in one single article. Thus when some false brethren, in St Paul's absence, had persuaded the Galatians that it was necessary to unite circumcision with the Gospel, he wrote his epistle to them, on purpose to correct this delusion; and though it was but an error in one point, and that in everything else they adhered to his doctrine, yet he calls it a "removing from the grace of Christ, . . . and a perverting the Gospel of Christ," Gal. i. 6 , 7. And then he adds, "But though we, or an angel from heaven, preach a Gospel to you, besides that which we have preached to you, let him be accursed; as we said before, so I say now again, If any one preach to you a Gospel besides that which you have received, let him be accursed," Gal. i. 8 . So also he mentions two heretics of his own time, who erred only in one point, and says, "Their speech spreadeth like a canker, of whom are Hymeneus and Philetus, who have erred from the truth, saying that the resurrection is past already, and have subverted the faith of some," 2 Tim. ii. 17 . But he had told his disciples before in what manner he had dealt with Hymeneus and Alexander, who "had made shipwreck of their faith; whom," says he, "I have delivered to Satan, that they may learn not to blaspheme," I Tim. i. 20 . Nothing surely could more effectually imprint in the minds of the faithful the firmest attachment to the truths of the Gospel than this judgment of the apostle, or more excite their attention and solicitude to preserve these sacred truths whole and undefiled, and to deliver them entire and uncorrupted to their posterity.

Q. 22. All this is exceedingly strong indeed; but how can it be applied to show the preservation of the truths revealed by Jesus Christ throughout all ages?

A. It is manifest, from these Scripture oracles, that the great principle or rule of tradition was laid down and established by God Himself at the beginning, and that it was delivered by the apostles to their disciples, along with the other truths of the Gospel, as the fence and safeguard ordained by God for the preservation of the Faith throughout all generations; and it is no less evident that as long as this rule is faithfully observed, any change in the faith is absolutely impossible. For if the Christians of the second age believed nothing as revealed truth but what they had received from their predecessors of the first age, then it is manifest that the faith of the first and second age was exactly the same. And if those of the second age delivered the sacred deposit entire and unchanged to their successors, then their faith can have differed in nothing from that of the two preceding ages. The same may be said of every succeeding age to the present time, and even to the end of the world.

Q. 23. Is it certain that the Church always adhered to this rule of tradition, and never deviated from it?

A. Nothing can be more certain, for several reasons, (1.) Because the Church, in the apostolic age, most certainly adhered to it, as all the above testimonies of Scripture show. In every succeeding age she professed her constant adherence to it, as the acts of her councils and the writings of the holy Fathers in every age declare; and at the present time she openly avows the same, protesting that she received this rule, along with the other truths of Christianity, from those before her, as handed down to them from the preceding generations; therefore she has never, in any age, deviated from it. (2.) Because this rule, as we have seen, is so strongly, so frequently, and under such dreadful penalties, inculcated in the Holy Scriptures, that it is morally impossible the whole Christian world should, in any age, renounce it, unless we suppose the whole world at once renouncing all concern for their salvation. (3.) Because no deviation from this rule could be introduced by degrees; for the first that should begin to teach such a deviation would immediately be condemned by all those adhering to it. (4.) Because by this rule alone the Church ever condemned all who broached new doctrines, as is manifest from her councils and the writings of Christians in every age, some of whom, as St Vincent of Lerins and Tertullian, wrote entire books on this very subject, as the shortest and easiest means of confuting all novelties in doctrine. (5.) Because it is manifest from the writings of Christians in every age since the apostles, that the doctrine of Faith has ever been uniformly the same in the Catholic Church; and that those revealed truths which the apostles delivered by word of mouth only, as well as the true sense of their sacred writings themselves, have been handed down throughout every age, not only by the constant teaching of the pastors, but also by the writings of many of her members who were eminent for their sanctity, and distinguished by their learning. Which evidently shows that she has never departed from this rule; and that by adhering to it, the sacred "words of God, once put into her mouth, have never departed from her," as God, in His covenant with her, had expressly promised by the prophet Isaiah, chap. lix. 21.

Q. 24. Can it be evidently proved that the Church never altered or corrupted any of the truths revealed to her at the beginning?

A. We observed in the last question. No. 5, that this is manifest from the writings of Christians, in all preceding ages, and in all the different nations of the world; in which writings we uniformly find the same sacred truths taught, explained, and inculcated, which the Church teaches at this day. It also follows as a necessary consequence from the principle of changing nothing, neither adding to nor taking from the sacred body of Divine truths, but delivering the same inviolate to every generation, for it is evident that a Church which constantly adheres to this rule can never change her faith. Besides, as her attachment to this principle and practice is itself one of the very points delivered by tradition, it is evident that a Church professing to believe and follow this principle must have strictly observed it, and must always have maintained the same faith. Add to this the number of persons interested in the preservation of this rule, spread from the beginning through all nations, and differing from each other in everything but religion. Add also how tenacious men commonly are of their religion, especially those who hold it as an article of their faith itself that not one iota of it may be changed. Join to all this how vigilant and careful the Church has ever been to oppose the slightest attempt to alter or corrupt her doctrine, and it will easily appear how impossible it is that she should ever change one point of revealed truth. And if we also consider the promised assistance of the Holy Ghost, to teach her all truth and abide with her for ever, the matter is put beyond the possibility of doubt.

Q. 25. In what does this promised assistance of the Holy Ghost properly consist? To what does it extend?

A. To understand this, we must observe that Jesus Christ revealed to His apostles, by word of mouth, all those Divine truths, both regarding faith and morals, which God was pleased to communicate to man. This He Himself declares when He said, "But I have called you friends; because all things whatsoever I have heard of My Father I have made known to you," John, xv. 15 . Now these truths the apostles taught to the world, partly in their writings and partly byword of mouth; but as both are equally the Word of God, and revealed by Him, therefore both are equally to be received and believed. "Therefore, brethren," says St Paul, "stand fast, and hold the traditions which you have learned, whether by word or by epistle," 2 Thess. ii. 14 . In these sacred traditions, both written and unwritten, some things are not so clearly and explicitly expressed as others. There are many, as the Scripture itself says, "hard to be understood;" and there are also others, essentially connected with what is there expressed, which are not mentioned there at all; but which, nevertheless, are implicitly revealed by God, in those with which they are necessarily connected. When, therefore, a difficulty arises on any point of doctrine, the Church immediately has recourse to revelation, contained in the written and unwritten Word, in Scripture and tradition, and examines the point in question by this sacred rule; in doing which, she is so effectually assisted by the Spirit of God, as infallibly to discover whether or not the point in question be contained in, connected with, or conformable to, revelation. If it be, she adopts it as a sound doctrine; and if not, she condemns it as false and erroneous. So that the Church never proposes to her children any new article of faith, but only brings to light and unfolds the truths originally revealed by Jesus Christ; but which, till her declaration, had been obscurely or ambiguously contained in Scripture and tradition; and this is the principal thing in which the Holy Ghost gives her His infallible assistance. All this is manifest from our Saviour's own declaration, "He had made known to His apostles all things whatsoever He had heard of His Father;" but many of those things were little understood by them, and many were so delivered that they could not understand them - at least, as to the full extent of what His words meant. To remedy this. He promises to send them the Holy Ghost, and shows what His office would be, in these words: "But the Paraclete, the Holy Ghost, whom the Father will send in my Name, He will teach you all things, and bring all things to your mind, whatsoever I shall have said to you," John, xiv. 26 . And again, "I have yet many things to say to you: but you cannot bear them now; - but when He, the Spirit of truth, is come.

He will teach you all truth," John, xvi. 12 . This then is the office of the Holy Ghost; and as Christ declared that He "would abide with His Church for ever," this office He continually performs, teaching the pastors of the Church all truth, and bringing to their mind, as occasion may require, all those things contained in the revelation which Christ made at the beginning to His apostles.

Q. 26. What conclusion follows from all this?

A. From this we see still more fully the perfect security we have in relying upon the authority of the Church, as the guide which Jesus Christ has ordained to conduct us in the way of salvation, and by which alone we can come to the certain knowledge of all those Divine truths which He has revealed, whether with regard to faith or morals.

Q. 27. Is it therefore necessary for the Christian people to be well instructed in what our holy Faith teaches concerning the Church?

A. The knowledge of the Church is certainly one of the most necessary points of the Christian religion, because the Church is the very foundation of all the rest, being the sacred rule appointed by Jesus Christ by which we come to the knowledge of all the truths of revelation, even of the Scriptures themselves, and of the true sense and interpretation of them; the Church is the organ of God, by which He speaks to His people, and discovers to them the great truths of eternity; and the true doctrine concerning the Church being once properly established, an end is put to all uncertainty, doubt, and controversy on religion. Hence we find that, in the Apostles' Creed, after professing our belief in the ever-blessed Trinity, the Incarnation, and other mysteries of our redemption, the article which follows is that of the Holy Catholic Church as next in importance and as firmly to be believed as the sacred truths of the Trinity and Incarnation; it stands upon the same ground with them, the Divine revelation; and is the sacred channel by which the revelation of those Divine truths is conveyed to us.

Q. 28. Is this article of the Creed, The Holy Catholic Church, a proof of the continual existence of the Church upon earth?

A. It is certainly a most convincing proof both of the continuance of the Church of Christ and of all those sacred prerogatives with which her Divine Spouse has adorned her. For the Apostles' Creed is universally admitted, by Christians of all denominations, to contain the fundamental articles of the Christian religion, as revealed by Jesus Christ to His apostles, consequently all the articles of the Creed are Divine truths, and, as the Church of England teaches in her thirty-nine articles, ought thoroughly to be received and believed, for they may be proved by most certain warrants of Holy Scripture, Art. VIII.; therefore they must be true at all times and in all places. Consequently, as it was a Divine revealed truth, when the Creed was made by the apostles, that Christ had then a Holy Catholic Church upon earth, so it is no less a Divine truth that He has a Holy Catholic Church upon earth at present, that He has had such a Church ever since the Creed was made, and will have to the end of the world. And as this Church never could cease to be the true Church of Christ, so never could she cease to be what Christ at first made her, nor fail in any of those sacred prerogatives with which Christ at first adorned her; consequently she is always Holy, always Catholic, always a visible body, consisting of pastors teaching and people taught by them - always one, always apostolical, always infallible in what she teaches, for these, as we have seen in part, and shall see more fully by-and-by, are the sacred prerogatives which He bestowed upon her. For if ever she lost any of these, she could no longer be the Church of Christ, and then that article of the Creed would be false, which it were blasphemy to suppose.

CHAPTER XII

Of The Church

Q. 1. What is the Church of Christ?

A. It is the congregation or society of all the true followers of Jesus Christ throughout the whole world united together in one body, under one head for "we, being many," says St Paul, "are one body in Christ, and every one members one of another," Rom. xii. 5 . "And there shall be one fold and one Shepherd," John, x. 16 .

Q. 2. In what are all the members of the Church united together, so as to compose one body in Christ?

A. Chiefly in these three things: (1.) In one and the same Faith, believing and teaching all those Divine truths which Jesus Christ revealed and His apostles taught, and no other; for there is but "one Lord, one Faith, one Baptism," Eph. iv. 5 ; and of the Church, in the time of the apostles, it is said that "they were persevering in the doctrine of the apostles," Acts, ii. 42 . (2.) In the participation of those Sacraments which Jesus Christ ordained for the sanctification of our souls; thus St Paul, speaking of the Sacrament of Baptism, says, "In one Spirit were we all baptised into one body," i Cor. xii. 13 ; and of the Holy Eucharist he says, "Because the bread is one, all we, being many, are one body, who partake of that one bread," i Cor. x. 17 . (3.) In being all governed by one head, and by pastors under him, ordained and authorised by Jesus Christ; for He Himself declares, that all who belong to Him "shall be one fold, and one Shepherd," John, x. 16 , And St Paul assures us that all the different orders of pastors, apostles, evangelists, and teachers, were ordained by Jesus Christ Himself, "for edifying the body of Christ," Eph. iv. 12 - that is, for building up and preserving the Church in one body.

Q. 3. Of whom is the Church composed?

A. Of pastors teaching, and of the people who are taught.

Q. 4. "Who are the pastors of the Church?

A. The successors of the apostles, ordained and authorised by Jesus Christ to teach the people the truths of salvation, and to rule the Church.

Q. 5. How do you prove that Jesus Christ authorised the pastors to teach the people?

A. From His own commission to them, laid down in several places of the Holy Scripture, as follows: (1.) He declares that He Himself was sent by God His Father to preach the Gospel , Luke, iv. 18 ; and He says to His apostles, "As My Father hath sent Me, I also send you," John, xx. 21 . (2.) He revealed to His apostles all Divine truths: "All things," says He to them, "whatsoever I have heard of My Father, I have made known unto you," John, xv. 15 . And before He left the world He gave them commission to teach the same to all nations; "Go ye," says He, "unto the whole world, and preach the Gospel to every creature," Mark, xvi. 15 ; and again, "Go ye therefore and teach all nations, . . . teaching them to observe all things whatsoever I have commanded you," Mat. xxviii. 19 .

Q. 6. Was this commission of teaching to continue with the successors of the apostles?

A. Most certainly it was; for (1.) When Christ gave the apostles the commission "to teach all nations," He immediately added, "And behold ' I am with you all days, even to the consummation of the world," Mat. xxviii. 20 . Now, as the apostles neither did nor could teach all nations in their own persons, nor were to continue upon earth till the end of the world, it is manifest that this commission was not confined to their persons, but given to their office - that is, to them and their successors in office, who should continue to the end of the world, and complete the work of teaching all nations, which the apostles began. (2.) St Paul was not one of those to whom the above commission was given personally, and yet he declares of himself, "I am appointed a preacher and an apostle (I say the truth, I lie not), a doctor of the Gentiles, in faith and truth," Tim. ii. 7 ; and "that Christ sent him to preach the Gospel," i Cor. i. 17 - (3-) St Timothy was ordained by St Paul to be a pastor of the Church, and a successor of the apostles, and St Paul conjures him faithfully to discharge this duty of teaching: "I charge thee before God and Jesus Christ, Who shall judge the living and the dead, by His coming and His kingdom, preach the word; be instant in season, out of season; reprove, entreat, rebuke, with all patience and doctrine," 2 Tim. iv. r. (4.) He also orders the same Timothy to appoint others to succeed him in the same office of teaching: "The things," says he, "which thou hast heard of me, before many witnesses, the same commend to faithful men, who shall be fit to teach others also," 2 Tim. ii. 2 .

Q. 7. In what light do the Scriptures represent to us the pastors of the Church?

A. (1.) As the ambassadors of Christ, sent by Him to declare to us His will, and reconcile us with God. "For Christ, therefore," says St Paul, "we are ambassadors, God as it were exhorting by us. For Christ we beseech you, be reconciled to God,'" 2 Cor. v. 20 . (2.) As the organs of Christ by whom He speaks to us, "He that hears you," says Christ, "hears Me, and he that despises you despises Me," Luke, x. 16 . (3.) As the angels of God, from whom we are to know His law; for, "the lips of the priest shall keep knowledge, and they shall seek the law at his mouth, because he is the angel of the Lord of hosts," Mai. ii. 7 . "I preached the Gospel to you heretofore," says St Paul, "and you received me as the Angel of God, even as Christ Jesus," Gal. iv. 13 . Great, indeed, is this dignity; but woe to those priests who disgrace it by their conduct!

Q. 8. Are we obliged to hear the pastors of the Church, and to receive the doctrine of our Faith from them?

A. Nothing is more strongly commanded, or more clearly expressed in Scripture, than this obligation; for - (1.) The pastors are expressly authorised by Christ to teach us; consequently, we are obliged to be taught by them. (2.) They are instituted by Jesus Christ, to preserve us all in the unity of the Faith; consequently we are obliged to receive our Faith from them. (3.) When Christ gave the commission of teaching to the pastors of His Church, He immediately adds, "He that believeth and is baptised shall be saved, but he that believeth not shall be condemned," Mark, xvi. 16 ; consequently, Ave are obliged by Jesus Christ Himself to believe what the pastors of His Church teach, under pain of damnation. (4.) He further declares to the pastors of His Church, "He that hears you hears Me, and he that despises you despises Me, and he that despises Me despises Him that sent Me," Luke, x. i6. (5.) He condemns those that "will not hear His Church as heathens and publicans," Mat. xviii. 17 - that is, as "worshippers of the devil," for such were the heathens; and "as people abandoned by God," and given up "to a reprobate sense," for such the publicans were reputed among the Jews. (6.) The Holy Ghost gives the same command to all by the mouth of St Paul: "Remember your prelates, who have spoken the Word of God to you, whose faith follow . . . and be not led away by various and strange doctrines," Heb. xiii. 7 , 9. (7.) St John, speaking of himself and the other pastors in his time, gives our submission to them as the sign to distinguish the Spirit of truth from the Spirit of error, and of our belonging to God:

"We are of God," says he; "he that knoweth God heareth us, he that is not of God heareth us not; in this we know the Spirit of truth and the Spirit of error," i John, iv. 6 .

Q. 9. What are we to think of any doctrine which is contrary to what the Church teaches?

A. As, by what we have seen above, we are undoubtedly assured that Jesus Christ will never permit His Church to fall into error or teach false doctrine, but will continue to preserve the sacred truths which He revealed to her, and put into her mouth, at the beginning, unchanged and uncorrupted to the end of the world; so it is evident that the doctrine which the Church teaches is infallibly true; consequently, any doctrine which is contrary to this must necessarily be a false doctrine; and, if false, it cannot be from God, for God is truth, and cannot deny Himself, by speaking contrary to the truth.

Q. 10. From whom, then, does all false doctrine come?

A. Our blessed Saviour says to the Jews who opposed His doctrine, "You are of your father the devil. . . . He abode not in the truth, because truth is not in him; ... for he is a liar, and the father thereof," John, viii. 44 . St Paul also assures us that "in the last times some shall depart from the Faith, giving heed to spirits of error, and doctrines of devils, speaking lies in hypocrisy," I Tim. iv. 1 ; and St James says, "Be not liars against the truth; for this is not wisdom descending from above, but earthly, sensual, devilish," James, iii. 14 , 15.

Q. 11. What other powers belong to the pastors of the Church besides that of teaching?

A. They are also commissioned and authorised by Jesus Christ to rule and govern the Church, and have received from Him all the spiritual powers of the priesthood for this purpose.

Q. 12. How is it proved that the pastors are authorised by Jesus Christ to rule the Church?

A. From the words of St Paul, who, speaking to the chief pastors of the Church at Ephesus, says, "Take heed to yourselves and to the whole flock, wherein the Holy Ghost hath placed you bishops to rule the Church of

God, which He hath purchased with His own Blood," Acts, XX. 28 .

Q. 13. What does this power of ruling the Church comprehend?

A. It includes the whole of their authority, and is described by St Paul, Eph. iv. 12 , under three heads. For He declares that the different order of pastors were instituted by Jesus Christ: (1.) "For the perfecting the saints" - that is, for conducting souls in the road of Christian perfection, by prescribing such rules to them and giving them such advice as is necessary or conducive to that end. (2.) "For the work of the ministry" - that is, for the preaching of the Word and the administration of the Sacraments. (3.) "For the edifying of the body of Christ "- that is, for regulating the externals of religion, by prescribing such rules and ordinances as they judge necessary for the decorous performance of all the outward service of the Church, for preventing or punishing all scandals, and for keeping the Christian people in virtuous discipline; so that everything may contribute to give edification to the whole body, and to promote the honour of God in His Church.

Q. 14. For what end did Christ give such powers to the pastors of the Church?

A. St Paul goes on, in the same place, to tell us that all this was done by Christ: (1.) To bring "all to the unity of the faith;" (2.) To enable us all "to become perfect men;" and, (3.) "To prevent us being tossed to and fro like children, and carried about with every wind of doctrine by the wickedness of men, by cunning craftiness, by which they lie in wait to deceive," Eph. iv. 13 ,

Q. 15. Are the people obliged in conscience to obey the commands of the pastors of the Church in things concerning religion, and subjected to their authority?

A. Most certainly they are; for St Paul says expressly, "Let every soul be subject to higher powers; for there is no power but from God, and those that are, are ordained of God. Therefore he that resisteth the power resisteth the ordinance of God. And they that resist purchase to themselves damnation," Rom. xiii. 1 . Now if this be the case with all lawful powers, though they be immediately of human institution, and may be changed and altered by man, both as to their form and the extent of their authority, how much more must it be with regard to the pastors of Christ's Church, whose power is immediately from Christ Himself, instituted expressly by

Him, and which can be altered by no other whatsoever? Hence, (2.) Jesus Christ Himself says to the pastors of His Church, in the persons of His apostles, "He that hears you hears Me, and he that despises you despises Me," Luke, x. 16 . (3.) He declares the greatness of the sin of disobeying His Church in these strong terms: "He that will not hear the Church, let him be to thee as a heathen and a publican," Mat. xviii. 17 . (4.) St Paul "went through Syria and Cilicia, confirming the churches; "and the means he used to confirm them was by "commanding them to keep the precepts of the apostles and the ancients," Acts, xv. 41 . Hence, (5.) He expressly requires this obedience and subjection to our pastors, when he says, "Obey your prelates, and be subject to them, for they watch as being to render an account of your souls," Heb. xiii. 17 .

Q. 16. Who is the Chief Pastor, or Head of the Church?

A. Jesus Christ is the invisible supreme Head of the Church; for God "hath put all things under His feet, and hath made Him Head over all the Church, which is His body," Eph. i. 22 ; and therefore He assures us that He is "with her all days, even to the consummation of the world; "and that He animates her by His Holy Spirit, "the Spirit of truth, Who abides with her for ever;" and by this means He communicates to her and to all her members the heavenly influence of grace and charity, to preserve them in life, and enable them to bring forth fruit, as the vine communicates nourishment to the branches, John, xv.; for "the charity of God is poured abroad in our hearts by the Holy Ghost, Who is given to us," Rom. V. 5 . But though Christ be thus the invisible Head of the Church Himself, yet He has also been pleased to appoint another under Him to be His vicegerent upon earth, the Chief Pastor among men, and the visible Head of His Church.

Q. 17. Whom did Christ appoint for this high office?

A. St Peter the apostle, and his successors after him.

Q. 18. How does it appear from Scripture that Christ made St Peter visible head of the Church?

A. From the following testimonies, among many others: (1.) Christ gave him the name of Peter, which signifies a Rock; and declared, that upon him, as "a rock, he would build His Church;" Mat. xvi. 18 . (2.) Christ gave to him in particular, and to none of the other apostles, "the key of the kingdom of heaven," Mat. xvi. 19 . Now, the power of the keys is the emblem of supreme power and authority, according to the prophet, "I will lay the key of the house of David upon His shoulders, and He shall open, and none shall shut; and He shall shut, and none shall open," Isa. xxii. 22 . This was prophesied of Christ Himself, Who also says on this subject, "Thus saith the Holy One, and the True One, He that hath the key of David; He that openeth, and no man shutteth; shutteth, and no man openeth," Rev. iii. 7 ; consequently, by saying to St Peter, "To thee I will give the keys of the kingdom of heaven," He manifestly communicates to him this supreme power, as to His vicegerent upon earth. (3.) After His resurrection He gave him the formal commission to feed His whole flock in these express words, "Feed My lambs; feed My sheep," John, xxi.; by which He constituted him the Chief Pastor of His fold, of which He had said before, "There shall be one fold and one Shepherd," John, x. 16 . (4.) When Satan sought to have the apostles in his power, "that he might sift them as wheat," Christ prayed only for St Peter, "that his faith should not fail," and left him as head of the whole, "to confirm his brethren," Luke, xxii. 31 . (5.) In the lists of the apostles given in the Gospel, St Peter is always named first in order, and the others are named sometimes in one order, sometimes in another; yet it is certain St Peter was not first called to Christ, for his brother Andrew was called before him, and introduced him to Christ. (6.) St Matthew, St Mark, and St Luke, in their lists of the apostles, take particular notice of the name of Peter, which Christ gave him, for his own name was Simon, which indicates the particular privilege annexed to that name; and therefore St Matthew expressly calls him the frist. (7.) St Peter acted in this supreme capacity as Head of the Church, both when he called the brethren to deliberate about choosing one in the place of Judas, Acts i., and also when he gave the definitive sentence in the council of Jerusalem, after "there had been much disputing," Acts, xv. 7 ; but when he had spoken, all "the multitude held their peace," verse 12, and submitted to his decision, as did also St James, who assented to and confirmed what he had said. (8.) The Christian writers and holy fathers in every age have always attested it as a truth revealed by God, that Jesus Christ did constitute St Peter prince of the apostles, and visible Head of His Church. (9.) It is an undoubted fact that his successors have always claimed this supreme authority, and have exercised it throughout the whole Church, as occasion required, in every age, from the very beginning. Now, considering the nature of man, it is evidently impossible that any one bishop of the Church should have acquired such authority ever all the others even in the most different nations and the most distant kingdoms, or that he could have exercised it everywhere among them, if it had not been given him from the beginning, and ordained by Jesus Christ.

Q. 19. Why did Christ institute one visible Head of His Church upon earth?

A. Because, as the Church is a visible body, or society of men, it was most becoming they should have a visible supreme Head among them, like to the members of whom the body is composed. Besides, as the Church was ordained to be spread over all nations, differing from one another in language, customs, government, and everything but religion, it would have been morally impossible to have kept them all united in one body, if there had not been one common visible Head or supreme authority among them, to which all must submit. So that this Head of the Church is the centre of unity, by which the Church of Christ, throughout the whole world, is united in one body.

Q. 20. Who are the successors of St Peter as head of the Church?

A. The Bishops of the city of Rome, of which St Peter was the first Bishop, and suffered martyrdom in that city for the Faith of Christ, leaving his successors there the heirs of all his power and authority.

Q. 21. Wherein consists the power of the Bishop of Rome, as Head of the Church?

A. As he is appointed by Jesus Christ to be the supreme Head and Pastor of the Church under Him, to be the spiritual Father and Teacher of all Christians, with full power to feed and govern the whole flock, therefore he is the supreme judge and lawgiver, in all things relating to religion, whether as to faith, morals, or discipline. The primacy, both of honour and jurisdiction, over all the other bishops, belongs to him; and all the members of the Church are obliged to pay the greatest respect, veneration, and obedience to his decrees and orders in all things belonging to religion.

Q. 22. How is the Head of the Church commonly called?

A. He is called the Pope, which word signifies Father, and is given to the Head of the Church; because, being the Vicar of Jesus Christ, he is the common spiritual Father of all Christians.

Q. 23. As the power of teaching resides in the pastors of the Church, does the infallibility of the Church, preserving the true doctrine, reside only in them?

A. The promises of infallibility, in preserving the true doctrine of Jesus Christ, are of two sorts. Some are made to the Church in general, such as these, "I will build My Church upon a rock, and the gates of hell shall not prevail against her. My words which I have put in His (the Redeemer's) mouth shall not depart out of His mouth, nor out of the mouth of His seed, from henceforth and for ever." "The Church is the pillar and ground of truth." By these promises infallibility is secured to the whole Church, pastors and people; so that they shall never cease to believe and profess the true Faith of Jesus Christ. But whereas the people are commanded to receive the Faith from their pastors, and to believe what they teach, so that the Faith of the people depends upon the teaching of the pastors, therefore the second class of promises are made to the pastors in particular; for to the pastors, in the persons of the apostles, our Saviour said, "Behold, I am with you all days, even to the consummation of the world; ""The Father will send you the Spirit of truth, to abide with you for ever, and teach you all truth." By which both pastors and people are assured that Jesus Christ and His Holy Spirit will always remain with the pastors of His Church, and so assist them, by the continual protection of His overruling providence, in the great work of teaching the people, that they shall never alter nor corrupt the true doctrine of Christ, but teach it whole and undefiled, to the end of time.

Q. 24. In whom then does the infallibility properly reside?

A. In the body of the pastors, joined with their head.

Q. 25. How so?

A. In either of these two ways: (1.) When the pastors of the Church are called together by the Chief Pastor, in a general council, to decide anything about religion, whether regarding faith or morals, they are then infallible in their decisions, and their decrees are considered as dictated by the Holy Ghost, according to the example of the apostles, in their council at Jerusalem, who begin their decrees with these words, "It hath seemed good to the Holy Ghost and to us," Acts, xv. (2.) When the Head of the Church, without calling together the other pastors, publishes any decree concerning faith or morals, and this decree is accepted and received by the body of the pastors, either expressly or tacitly, it then becomes a decree of the whole Church, and of the same infallible authority as if it had been made in a general council.

Q. 26. When the Head of the Church publishes any decree concerning faith or morals, to which he requires submission from all the faithful, is he himself infallible in what he there teaches?

A. This is not proposed as an article of Divine faith, nor has the Church ever made any decision concerning it.[See Appendix B] Great numbers of the most learned divines are of opinion, that in such a case the Head of the Church is infallible in what he teaches; but there are others of a contrary opinion, who think that his decree is not to be considered as infallibly certain, till the body of the bishops receive it, either by their express approbation, or their tacit submission when it becomes a decree of the whole Church, whose infallibility is undoubted.

Q. 27. On what grounds do those divines found their opinion, who believe that the Pope himself, when he speaks to all the faithful as Head of the Church, is infallible in what he teaches?

A. On several very strong reasons, both from Scripture, tradition, and reason.

Q. 28. What proofs do they bring from Scripture?

A. These following: (1.) Because this privilege of the particular direction and assistance of God in teaching true doctrine was given to the High Priest in the old law; and the synagogue being only a figure of the law of grace, and of the Church of Christ, the same privilege must certainly be given to the High Priest of the Church also; otherwise the type would have been more perfect than the reality, the shadow more privileged than the substance. Now that the High Priests were so privileged in the old law appears from this, that in all their disputes or doubts about religion the people were referred to them as the supreme judges, with the assurance that they would declare to the people the truth of the judgment, and with the corresponding obligation "to do whatsoever they shall say that preside in the place which the Lord shall choose, and what they shall teach, according to His law, and to follow their sentence; and not to decline to the right hand or to the left; "adding, "But he that will be proud, and refuse to obey the commandment of the priest who ministereth at that time to the Lord thy God, and the decree of the judge, that man shall die, and thou shalt take away the evil from Israel. And all the people hearing it shall fear, that no one swell with pride," Deut. xvii. 8 .

(2.) Because Jesus Christ said to St Peter, whom He constituted the Head of His Church, "Thou art Peter "(that is, a rock), "and upon this rock will I build My Church, and the gates of hell shall not prevail against her," Mat. xvi. 18 . From this text, as we have seen above, the infallibility of the Church, in always teaching the true Faith, is most solidly proved; and the grounds of this proof are given by Christ Himself, when He says that the firmness and stability of the wise man's house against all storms and tempests, winds and rain, was precisely owing to this; "for it was founded on a rock," Mat. vii. 25 - that is, on a solid and immovable foundation. Seeing then that St Peter, as Head of the Church, is the rock, under Christ, on which she is built, and seeing that she is therefore infallible, because built on a rock, it necessarily follows that the foundation itself must be infallible also.

(3.) Because our Lord said also to St Peter, "Simon, Simon, behold, Satan hath desired to have you, that he may sift you as wheat; but I have prayed for thee, that thy faith fail not, and thou being converted, confirm thy brethren," Luke, xxii. 32 . Here our Saviour shows the rage of Satan against all His followers; but, to disappoint him, Christ prayed for St Peter, in particular, that his faith should not fail, and then commissions him, as the Head, to confirm all the rest. Now, when our Saviour prayed to His Father to raise Lazams from the dead, He said, "Father, I give Thee thanks that Thou hast heard Me, and I knew that Thou hearest Me always," John, xi. 41 . If, therefore, the prayer of Christ was always heard by His Father, the above prayer, that the faith of Peter should not fail, was without doubt heard also. Whence it follows that St Peter, as Head of the Church, and consequently his successors in office, shall never fail in faith, nor teach false doctrine. Besides, our Saviour, in the very text itself, shows that this very prayer for Peter was heard by His Father: "I have prayed for thee," says He; "you have nothing to fear." In consequence of My prayer, you shall be confirmed in the faith; and when you are so, "strengthen your brethren, and confirm them also." Now this very commission of confirming others necessarily presupposes that the prayer of Christ was heard, by which Peter was confirmed in the Faith himself. Neither does the subsequent fall of Peter, in denying His Master that very night, in the smallest degree weaken this argument: it rather corroborates it, because it shows that this promise of our Saviour, that Peter's faith should not fail, was made to him, not as a private person, but as the Head of the Church, and therefore to stand firm in all his successors; because, like all the other promises made to the Church itself, it was not to be fulfilled till the coming of the Holy Ghost, Who was sent on purpose to establish the Church, and fulfil all the promises Christ made to her, and for that end to "abide with her for ever."

Q. 29. What proofs of the infallibility of the Head of the Church do they bring from tradition?

A. From the testimony of the holy Fathers from the very earliest ages, which shows that this was the belief of the Church in their days. Thus Origen, a celebrated writer in the third age, explaining the text, "Thou art Peter," etc. says, "It is true, though not said expressly, that neither against Peter, nor against the Church, shall the gates of hell ever be able to prevail; for if they could prevail against Peter, in whom the Church is founded, they would also prevail against the Church. St Irenseus, Bishop of Lyons, in the second age, confutes all heresies, and all false doctrine, from the authority of the Holy See alone: "By declaring," says he, "the tradition and faith of that Church which she received from the apostles, and has handed down to our days," Adv. Her. 1. 3. cap. 5. And then adds, "To this Church all must have recourse; for in her the apostolical tradition is always preserved." So St Cyril, Patriarch of Alexandria, from the text, "Thou art Peter," concludes thus: "According to this promise, the apostolical Church of Peter remains immaculate, free from all seduction and heretical circumvention." Great numbers of others are omitted for brevity's sake. Only we must add St Augustine, who, when the Pelagian heresy was condemned by the Pope, says, "The answer of Rome is come; the ca:use is ended," Serm. 3. de Verb. Apost. "Jam enim de hac causa duo concilia missa sunt ad Sedem Apostolicam, inde etiam rescripta venerunt. Causa finita est."

Q. 30. What proofs are brought from reason?

A. The proofs from reason are founded on facts, and on principles received by all members of the Church as Divine truths; for (1.) There never was an instance of any Pope who proposed any doctrine to be believed by the Church, that was contrary to the sacred truths of faith revealed by Christ; for though a few, and only a few Popes have been disedifying in their lives, yet the most inveterate adversaries of the Catholic Faith have never yet been able to show that any Pope ever taught false or pernicious doctrine. (2.) Never yet did any Pope issue any decree concerning the truths of faith or sound morality, but it was immediately received by the great body of the bishops as containing the most solid and wholesome doctrine. (3.) Many different heresies that have arisen in different ages in the Church have been proscribed and condemned by the authority of the Head of the Church alone, both before the first general council was held, and since.

(4.) In all controversies of moment that have arisen in the Church about points of faith, the bishops have always had recourse to the Head of the Church, as the supreme tribunal for settling them; and if the obstinacy of the party condemned by him made it advisable to have recourse to general councils, these councils never were found to do anything else, after the most mature examination, but confirm the sentence already passed by the Head. Besides, (5.) It is a truth received by all Catholics, as Toumely, a French divine, who writes against the infallibility of the Holy See, expresses it, "That as the Roman and apostolical See is the bond of Catholic unity and of Catholic communion, no man can be held to be a Catholic, unless he be joined with that See in the unity of Faith and doctrine." And then, showing that this union is of two kinds, both in the external profession and the internal assent of the mind, he concludes, - "To be united in both ways with the See of Rome was always necessary, and looked upon in all ages as the most certain sign and proof of true Faith and pure doctrine," tom. i. De Eccl. a. 6. This same truth is handed down from the very beginning in the writings of the holy Fathers, in every age, in the strongest terms. Thus St Jerome, writing to the Bishop of Rome, says: "I am joined in communion with your Holiness - that is, with the chair of Peter: upon that rock I know the Church is built. Whoever eats the lamb out of this house is profane; whoever is not in his ark shall perish in the deluge; . . . whosoever gathers not with thee scatters - that is, he who is not of Christ belongs to Antichrist," Epist. 56 ad Damas. And St Augustine, in his psalm against the Donatist schismatics, says to them: "Come, brethren, if you have a mind to be ingrafted in the vine.

'Tis a pity to see you lie in this manner lopped off from the stock. Reckon up the prelates in the very See of Peter; and in that order of Fathers see which has succeeded which. This is the rock over which the proud gates of hell prevail not." (6.) The same celebrated Tournely acknowledges, that if a division among the bishops should happen about any point of Faith, "without doubt," says he, "we must adhere to that part which is united with the Head, which is always to be esteemed the better and the sounder part." From all which, the infallibility of the Head of the Church naturally flows; for, if Christ obliges all to be united with Him in Faith and doctrine, He surely is obliged to preserve him from teaching false doctrine. From the command of Christ to hear His Church under pain of being considered as heathens and publicans, it is justly inferred that the Church can never err. This argument has an equal weight, when applied to the obligation of being united with the Church's Head in Faith and doctrine.

Q. 31. These are very strong arguments indeed: but what proofs do the others bring for their opinion, that the Head of the Church is not infallible?

A. They bring not a single text of Scripture nor almost one argument from tradition to prove it. Indeed they seem to aim rather at invalidating the proofs from Scripture and tradition in favour of infallibility, than at directly establishing the contrary. However, as this is a question in which faith is not concerned, the Church having given no decision regarding it, any person may believe it or not according as he thinks the reasons on either side preponderate.[See Appendix B.]

Q. 32. What consequences flow from these Scripture truths concerning the Church of Christ?

A. The consequences that necessarily flow from all that has been said in this and the preceding chapter, are chiefly these three: (1.) That the Church of Christ is the sacred Rule of Faith, and the supreme judge of controversy, instituted and ordained by Him to preserve inviolate to the end of time all those Divine truths which He revealed to man, and on the knowledge and belief of which the salvation of our souls depends; and that she is fully qualified by her Divine Spouse to discharge this office, so as to pronounce sentence upon every point of revelation, clearly and distinctly, and with infallible certainty. (2.) That this Church of Christ is one body, having one and the same Faith, and governed by one and the same supreme Church authority; so that whatever sect is divided from this body, by professing a faith different from hers, is no part of the Church of Christ, but, at best, a human invention; and the faith they profess is falsehood and error, arising from the father of lies. (3.) That the Church of Christ is the only road to salvation; both because it is only in her communion that the true Faith of Christ can be found, "without which it is impossible to please God," Heb. xi. 6 ; and because Christ has declared, that all who refuse to hear her are condemned by Him as heathens and publicans, and that those who despise her pastors despise Christ Himself, and His Father who sent Him.

Q. 33. Is there any other direct proofs from Scripture to show that out of the Church of Christ there is no salvation?

A. Yes, there are several; of which we shall only mention these two here: (1.) Christ, speaking of those who were not yet joined in the communion of His Church, but whom He foreknew would make a good use of the graces He would give them for that purpose, says, "Other sheep I have who are not of this fold, them also I MUST BRING, and they shall hear My voice, and there shall be one fold and one shepherd," John, x. 16 ; where He plainly declares, that all those of His sheep who are not yet of His fold must be brought into it, as a necessary condition of their salvation. (2.) In consequence of this fixed disposition of the Divine providence, no sooner did the apostles begin to preach the Gospel, than immediately "the Lord added daily to the Church such as should be saved," Acts, ii. 47 ; which evidently shows that all who are not added to the Church are out of the way of salvation.

Q. 34. Is it lawful to have any communication in things of religion with those who are separated from the Church of Christ?

A. By no means; all communication or fellowship in religious duties with those who are out of the Church of Christ is repeatedly and strictly forbidden in the Word of God, both by Christ Himself and by His holy apostles.

Q. 35. Among the many different sects of Christians who pretend to be the Church of Christ, how can one distinguish which is really the true Church?

A. By the marks laid down in the Holy Scriptures, by which the true Church of Christ can easily be distinguished from all separate congregations.

CHAPTER XIII.

Of The Marks Of The Church

Q. What are the marks of the Church of Christ laid down in the Scriptures?

A. They are chiefly these four, as declared in the Nicene creed - that she is one, holy, catholic, and apostolic.

Q. 2. How does it appear that the Church of Christ is one?

A. This we have seen in the preceding chapter, where the Church is shown to be one body, of which Christ is the Head, and that all her members are united to Him in His body, by having all one and the same Faith, being all in one communion, and subject to one supreme Church authority. It also appears manifest, from the manner in which the Church is constantly represented to us in Scripture; for there she is called the kingdom of God "that shall never be destroyed, that shall not be delivered up to another people, . . . but shall stand for ever," Dan. ii. 44 . She is also called "the city of the living God, . . . the Church of the first-born," Heb. xii. 22 ; of which God says, by His prophet David, "The Lord hath chosen Sion, He hath chosen it for His dwelling. This is My rest for ever and ever; here will I dwell, for I have chosen it," Ps. cxxxi. 13 . St Paul also calls her "the house of God, the Church of the living God, the pillar and ground of truth," i Tim. iii. 15 . Seeing, therefore, that this kingdom, this city, this house of God, shall never be destroyed, but shall stand for ever, it necessarily follows that she can never be divided against herself, cannot possibly consist of jarring sects or separate communions, contradicting and condemning one another, but must always be one body, and all her members must be perfectly united in one faith and one communion; for Christ Himself expressly declares "that every kingdom divided against itself shall be made desolate; and every city or house divided against itself shall not stand," Mat. xii. 25 . St Paul also shows this unity of the Church, when he affirms that "we, being many, are ONE body in Christ," Rom. xii. 5 ; and that there is but "one body, one Spirit, one Lord, one Faith, one baptism," Eph. iv. 4 ; and Christ Himself, in plain terms, says, that "there shall be one fold and one shepherd," John, X. 16 ; which clearly shows that all the members of the Church of Christ make but one body, having all one faith, and are governed by one shepherd.

Q. 3. How is it proved that the Church of Christ is holy?

A. By holiness is meant that the Church of Christ teaches nothing but what is holy and tends to holiness; that she proposes to her children the most powerful motives to induce them to become holy, that she affords them the most efficacious means to enable them to be so, and that great numbers of her children, by following her instructions and using these means, do actually become holy. Now, that all this is essential to the true Church of Christ is manifest from many texts of Scripture: (1.) The prophet Isaiah, foretelling the glories of the Church, as the way or rule to conduct us to eternal happiness, says: "And a way shall be there, and it shall be called the Holy way," Isa. xxxv. 8 ; or, as the Protestant translation has it, "the way of holiness; "and that "the unclean shall not pass over it," to show that it is both holy in itself and conducts to holiness all those that walk therein, and brings them at last to eternal happiness; for it is added: "They shall walk there that shall be delivered; and the redeemed of the Lord shall return, and shall come to Sion with praise; and everlasting joy shall be upon their heads; they shall obtain joy and gladness, and sorrow and mourning shall flee away," ver. 9, 10. (2.) David also foretells the holiness of the Church, when he says, "Holiness becomes Thy house, O Lord, unto length of days," Ps. xcii. 5 . (3.) St Paul assures us that Christ died for this very purpose, to purify His Church and make her holy: "Christ loved the Church," says he, "and delivered Himself up for it, that He might sanctify it, cleansing it by the laver of water in the word of life; that He might present it to Himself a glorious Church, not having spot or wrinkle, nor any such thing; but that it should be Holy and without blemish," Eph. v. 25 . (4.) The same holy apostle also teaches that Christ died for the sanctification of her members, and that He "gave Himself for us, that He might redeem us from all iniquity, and might cleanse to Himself a people acceptable, a pursuer of good works," Tit. ii. 14 ; and hence St Peter says, "You are a chosen generation, a Holy nation, a purchased people," i Pet. ii. 9 .

Q. 4. How does it appear that the Church of Christ is Catholic?

A. The word Catholic signifies universal, and means that the Church of Christ is not confined to one corner of the world, or to one nation, as the Jewish church was, but is made for all nations and for all countries, so as to embrace the whole world; which is explained in the following manner from the Scripture: (1.) That the Church -was instituted by Jesus Christ to be diffused through all nations, and propagated to the utmost bounds of the earth. Thus He gave the pastors of the Church express commission to carry the light of His Gospel everywhere: "Go ye," says He, "and teach all nations," Mat. xxviii. 19 . "Going into the world, preach the Gospel to every creature," Mark, xvi. 15 . "And you shall be witnesses to Me in Jerusalem, and in all Judea, and Samaria, and even to the uttermost parts of the earth," Acts, i. 8 . Yea, Christ Himself assures us that He suffered for this very end: "Thus it behoved Christ to suffer," said He to the eleven, "and to rise again from the dead the third day; and that penance and remission of sins should be preached in His name among all nations, beginning at Jerusalem," Luke, xxiv. 46 . (2.) That the Church being intended for this purpose, and being of this diffusive nature, must possess in herself the means and qualifications necessary for propagating the faith of Christ among all nations, and for converting all mankind to Christianity. These in the beginning were apostolic men, men burning with zeal for the glory of God and the salvation of souls, who, leaving all to follow Christ, cheerfully sacrificed their own ease, their life itself, and undenvent all dangers and difficulties, in order to convert souls to Christ: men eminent for their holiness of life, and on whom God bestowed the gift of miracles, as proofs of their commission, and to confirm the truth of what they taught. Apostolic men of this kind, then, must never be wanting in the true Church of Christ, as the means appointed by Him for converting the world to His Church. Thus the prophet Isaiah foretells the perpetuity of apostolic pastors in the Church, and their continual zeal for the propagation of the Gospel, in these words: Upon thy walls, O Jerusalem, I have appointed watchmen all the day and all the night; they shall never hold their peace. You that are mindful of the Lord, hold not your peace," Isa. lxii. 6 . And the success of their labours is thus described: "Thy gates shall be open continually: they shall not be shut day nor night, that the strength of the Gentiles may be brought unto thee, and their kings may be brought," Isa. lx. 11 .

That the gift of miracles shall not be wanting to many of these apostolic labourers Christ Himself assures us; for when He gave the apostles and their successors the commission of teaching all nations, He immediately adds, "And these signs shall follow them that believe. In My Name they shall cast out devils, they shall speak with new tongues, they shall take up serpents, and if they drink any deadly thing it shall not hurt them; they shall lay their hands upon the sick and they shall recover," Mark, xvi. 17 . And that this gift of miracles was chiefly promised to those who preached the Word, in confirmation of what they taught, is plain, from the first performance of the promise; for it is immediately added that "they going forth preached everwhere, the Lord working withal, and confirming the Word with signs that followed," ver. 20. On another occasion He says: "Amen, amen, I say unto you, he that believeth in Me, the works that I do he shall do also, and greater than these shall he do, because I go to the Father," John, xiv. 12 . (3.)

In consequence of this, the Church must, from the beginning, be propagating the faith of Christ, and from time to time be converting nations, till at last she be spread over the whole universe; thus, "From the rising of the sun to the going down thereof. My name is great among the Gentiles," Mai. i. 2 . "All the ends of the earth shall remember, and shall be converted to the Lord, and all the kindred of the Gentiles shall adore in His sight; for the kingdom is the Lord's, and He shall have dominion over the nations," Ps. xxi. 28 . "Ask of Me, and I will give Thee the Gentiles for Thy inheritance, and the uttermost parts of the earth for Thy possession," Ps. ii. 8 . And of the kingdom of Christ, according to the Protestant translation, Isaiah says: "Of the increase of His government and peace there shall be no end, upon the throne of David, and upon His kingdom, to order it, and establish it with judgment and with justice, from henceforth even for ever," Isa. ix. 7 . And, in the New Testament, St Paul says to the Colossians, "The truth of the Gospel is come to you, as also it is in the whole world, and bringeth forth fruit and groweth," Col. i. 6 . From which it is evident, that to be Catholic or universal is an essential quality of the Church of Christ; that she is not and cannot be confined to one corner or nation, but is more or less spread over all the known world, and is the Church of all nations.

Q. 5. How does it appear that the Church of Christ is Apostolical?

A. By the word Apostolical is meant, that the Church of Christ was founded by the apostles, and received the doctrine of her Faith, the powers of the priesthood, and the mission of her pastors from them at the beginning; and that she must continue to the end of the world in the profession of the same Faith and doctrine, and in a continual uninterrupted succession of the priesthood, and mission of her pastors, so that the apostolical doctrine, priesthood, and mission, remain with her for ever.

That the Church shall always preserve the apostolical doctrine we have seen above, when explaining the rule of faith; and that she shall never want a succession of true pastors, inheriting the same priestly powers and mission which she received at first from the apostles, is manifest from these considerations: (1.) Because true pastors, properly empowered and lawfully sent, are a necessary part of the Church, and instituted by Jesus Christ, "for the perfecting the saints, for the work of the ministry, for the edification of the body of Christ," Eph. iv. 12 ; consequently such pastors will never be wanting in her, according to the Prophet: "Upon thy walls, O Jerusalem, I have appointed watchmen; all the day and all the night they shall never hold their peace," Isa. lxii. 6 . (2.) Because the Scripture assures us that "no man taketh the honour of the priesthood upon himself but he that is called by God, as Aaron was," Heb. V. 4 ; much less can any man possess the powers of the priesthood, unless they be given to him by those who have power to confer them. Thus St Paul writes to Titus, "For this cause I left thee at Crete, that thou shouldst set in order the things that are wanting, and shouldst ordain priests in every city, as I also appointed thee," Tit. i. 5 , (3.) That none who have these priestly powers can lawfully exercise them unless they be authorised and commissioned to do so by being lawfully sent. Thus the apostles received their mission from Christ, who said to them, "As my Father sent me I also send you," John, xx. 21 . In like manner they sent others to succeed themselves, with power also to send others after them, as St Paul and Barnabas were sent by the pastors of the church at Antioch, and their doing so was declared to be the work of the Holy Ghost: "Then they, fasting and praying, and imposing their hands upon them, sent them away. So they, being sent by the Holy Ghost, went to Seleucia," Acts, xii. 3

Paul himself sent Titus as above - that is, authorised and commissioned him to govern the church in Crete, and ordain pastors in it under him; and he says, in another place, "How can they preach unless they be sent?" Rom. x. 15 . This, then, is the door by which the true pastors of Christ's flock enter - to wit, when lawfully ordained and sent, or commissioned by the chief pastors of the Church: for all who take that office upon themselves, without entering by the door, are declared by Christ Himself to be "thieves and robbers," John, x. I. From which it is manifest, that as true pastors are an essential part of the Church of Christ, and will never be wanting in her, therefore there will be in the Church a continued uninterrupted succession, or transmission of the priestly powers and mission given at the beginning by Jesus Christ Himself to His apostles, to the end of time.

Q. 6. Are there any other proofs to show that these four marks belong to the true Church of Christ?

A. There are several other texts of Scripture which show it; and it is also proved from the creeds: for the Apostles' creed contains, as an article of Divine faith, that the Church is holy and Catholic. "I believe in the Holy Ghost, the Holy Catholic Church." And the Nicene creed contains all the four; I believe "One, Holy, Catholic, and Apostolic Church." Now the Church of England affirms, in the eighth of her 39 Articles, that these "creeds ought thoroughly to be received and believed, for they may be proved by most certain warrants of Holy Scripture."

Q. 7. Are there any other marks of the Church of Christ besides these four contained in the creed?

A. There are also two others which deserve a particular notice, because they serve, in a most convincing manner, to distinguish the true Church of Christ from all separate congregations; and these are, that she is perpetiial in her duration, and infallible in her doctrine. We have seen above, in the chapter on the rule of faith, that the Church of Christ is infaUible in what she teaches; that "the words once put in her mouth at the beginning shall never depart from her from henceforth and for ever;" that Jesus Christ is "with her pastors to the end of the world; '" and that the "Holy Ghost," the "Spirit of truth, abides with her for ever," to "teach her all truth." All which not only show her infallibility, but also her perpetual duration to the end of time. But, besides these, we have also many other testimonies of Scripture, which directly prove that the Church of Christ can never fail, but will continue upon earth, as long as the world endureth. Thus, Christ "shall reign over the house of Jacob for ever, and of His kingdom there shall be no end," Luke, i. 32 . And this was foretold by the royal prophet in these words, spoken by God Himself: "Thy seed will I settle for ever, and I will build up Thy throne unto generation and generation. . . . I will make Him My first-born high above the kings of the earth, and I will keep My mercy for Him for ever, and My covenant faithful to Him. And I will make His seed to endure for evermore; and His throne as the days of heaven. And if His children forsake My law, and walk not in My judgment; if they profane My justice, and keep not My commandments, I will visit their iniquities with a rod, and their sins with stripes; but My mercy I will not take away from Him, nor will I suffer My truth to fail; neither will I profane My covenant, and the words that proceed from My mouth I will not make void. Once have I sworn by My holiness: I will not lie unto David; His seed shall endure for ever; and His throne as the sun before Me; and as the moon perfect for ever, and a faithful witness in heaven," Ps. lxxxviii. 5 , 28.

What this covenant is which God makes with Christ, the true David, we are told by the prophet Isaiah as follows: "And there shall come a Redeemer to Sion, and to them that return from iniquity in Jacob, saith the Lord. This is My covenant with them, saith the Lord. My spirit that is in Thee, and My words that I have put in Thy mouth, shall not depart out of Thy mouth, nor out of the mouth of Thy seed, nor out of the mouth of Thy seed's seed, saith the Lord, from henceforth and for ever," Isa. lix. 20 . In which texts we see a most solemn promise of Almighty God, both that the seed of Christ, His Holy Church, shall continue for ever, and that she shall never fail to teach the true doctrine once put in her mouth. The prophet Daniel also declares the perpetuity of Christ's kingdom upon earth in these strong terms: "In the days of those kingdoms the God of heaven will set up a kingdom that shall never be destroyed, and His kingdom shall not be delivered up to another people; and it shall break to pieces and consume all these kingdoms, and itself shall stand for ever," Dan. ii. 44 .

Q. 8. In which of all the Christian societies which at present divide the Christian world, are all these marks of the Church of Christ found?

A. The smallest attention will immediately show that they are to be found in the Catholic Church, and in no other society of Christians whatsoever, and therefore, that she alone is the true Church of Christ:

(1.) The Catholic Church is one body, whose members are all united together in one and the same faith, in the same communion, and governed by one and the same supreme authority. And this is the more to be remarked, when we consider that, though those of her communion be exceedingly numerous, and spread throughout the whole known world, and differ from one another in almost everything else - in their country, in their language, in their customs, in their government, and in their worldly interests, yet they are all most perfectly united in religion: they everywhere believe the same Divine truths, profess the same faith, teach the same doctrine, preach the same Gospel; so that, wherever any one of that Church goes, throughout the whole world, he always finds himself at home with those of that communion, as to religion. But, on the other hand, no sooner does any sect break off from that Church, as several have done in all preceding ages, than immediately the curse of division seems to be entailed upon them. We need only consider those of our own day, the followers of Luther and Calvin, who are divided and subdivided without end, and every day are splitting more and more, insomuch that, even in those who are of the same country, under the same government, using the same language, having the same customs and the same common interest, yea, very often in the same family, you will scarcely find half-a-dozen holding the same belief on all points of religion. The different sects among them mutually condemn each other, and refuse to join in communion, and those who live under the same denomination seldom or ever have in all points one common faith. No wonder: the very principle upon which all separate sects proceed, leaving every one at liberty to judge according to his own fancy, without any fixed ground to stand upon, must necessarily lead them to endless divisions; whereas the Catholic Church has in its own bosom the principle of union among all its members - a fixed, invariable, and infallible rule, instituted by the Son of God to bind it together.

Neither do they differ in matters of small importance only, but in tenets which they themselves hold to be of the greatest consequence to Christianity: such as church government, the blessed Eucharist, free-will, and the like; so that, according to some, it is a Divine truth that Jesus Christ instituted bishops, priests, and deacons, with due subordination to govern His Church; but, according to others, that is a falsehood and an error; for they hold it as a Divine truth that Jesus Christ put all the pastors of the Church upon a perfect equality. According to some, none have power to preach the Word, and administer the Sacraments, but such as are lawfully ordained by a bishop who has received his authority by a continual uninterrupted succession from Christ and His apostles. According to others, any man may take upon himself the ministry, preach the Word, and administer the Sacraments as lawfully and as validly as any bishop in England. The Lutherans teach as a Divine truth, that the true Body and Blood of Christ are really and substantially present in the blessed Eucharist, along with the bread and wine. The Calvinists reject this as a false doctrine, and hold that there is nothing in the Holy Eucharist but mere bread and wine, as a figure of the Body and Blood of Christ; and so of other articles.

These sects have often carried their differences to such a height as to excommunicate and anathematise each other, scarcely looking upon one another as Christians. Thus Luther, the great apostle of the Reformation, anathematised Zuhiglius for denying the real presence, and declared him to be totally possessed by Satan on that account. Several attempts were made by these conflicting sects to bring about a reunion among themselves, and conferences were frequently held for that end, but all to no purpose; how much soever they pretended to agree in words, every one followed his own way. Their worldly interest was the mainspring of their seeking an agreement, as they were afraid, when disunited, of being overpowered by those Catholic states against which they had rebelled; and therefore their agreement was in appearance only. For whenever that fear was past, they divided as much as before, and have still continued to divide and subdivide to this day. Ashamed, however, of the contemptible figure they make on this account, when compared with the unity of the Catholic Church, the modern device they have fallen upon is the vain pretence that all their different parties, though holding such opposite and contradictory faiths, make up but one church of Christ; as if Christ had revealed one thing to one party, and the very reverse to another, and all their opposite tenets were equally the truths of God! There is, indeed, one point, and only one, on which they all agree, and that is, their inveterate aversion and opposition to the Catholic Church; for as Herod and Pilate, though enemies, combined together against the Lord and against His Christ, so all the various sects that ever separated from the spouse of Christ, however much they disagree among themselves, have never failed to join together in opposition to her, and to combine, as much as in them lay, for her destruction.

(2.) With regard to holiness: This shines forth in the Catholic Church in the most eminent degree. All her doctrines are consistent. Like the component parts of a perfect arch, they so fit and adhere together, mutually supporting and supported by each other, that no flaw can be detected, not a shadow of inconsistency or contradiction can be discovered in them - an evident mark of truth! Every article of her faith is holy in itself, and so conducive to true holiness that she challenges her greatest adversaries to show the slightest blemish or imperfection in anything she really teaches; and the strongest proof of their inability to do so is, that, not daring to attack her true doctrines, by calumny and misrepresentation they accuse her of things which she condemns and detests, and then combat phantoms of their own raising. As for holy persons, she justly glories in having great numbers of such in her communion, whose eminent virtues have been the admiration of all who know them, and have been frequently attested by God by innumerable miracles wrought through their means, and at their intercession. On the other hand, no sooner did any sects break off from her communion, and set up a separate faith, than evident contradictions and falsehoods appeared in their tenets. Many of them tended to the subversion of morals, or were insulting to the Divinity; and as for holiness of life among their members, attested by miracles, they never so much as pretend to it: nay, the general cry among them is to disclaim and deny all miracles whatsoever since the primitive ages, conscious of their own inability to procure them.

(3.) The Catholic Church alone possesses, as her undivided property, the glorious character of Catholic. In her communion alone, numbers of holy apostolic men have abounded in all ages, who, leaving all they possessed or could expect in this world, and burning with zeal for the conversion of souls to God, have dedicated themselves entirely to carry the light of the Gospel to those who "sat in darkness and in the shadow of death," and to bring heathen nations to the knowledge of Jesus Christ. In consequence of this, from the very beginning she has always been extending the sacred standard of the Gospel; and by her alone were all the heathen nations converted that have ever as yet been brought to the Christian faith: and though in different ages several who had enjoyed the happiness of being in her communion have, through the unsearchable judgments of God, been cut off from it, yet scarcely ever did this happen than other nations, in much greater numbers, were called in their place to her bosom. Witness the great defection in these latter ages, which had scarcely begun when the discovery of the East and West Indies opened a door to carry the Gospel to those parts, where multitudes were.__ converted to her faith, insomuch that at present she is spread over the whole known world. In many flourishing countries no other religion is known; and. in others, where a different religion is established, great numbers of her communion are generally to be found: by all which the very name of Catholic is so appropriated to her that no sect pretends to assume it. The various sects are seldom to be found entire throughout one whole nation. They are generally confined to one province or corner; they take their names from their founders, their tenets, or some particular circumstances; and in several parts of Christendom their very names are unheard of and unknown.

(4.) The Catholic Church alone is truly apostolic, not only in the continual preservation of the sacred doctrine delivered to her by the apostles, which, by the very rule of her faith, can never be altered, but also in the constant uninterrupted succession of lawful pastors, with all the sacred powers of the priesthood and mission derived from the same source. This is so palpable a truth, that the Church of England (which alone among the modem religions claims the power of ordination) acknowledges that whatever she has of the priestly powers she received from the Catholic Church, in which alone they have been transmitted to the present time, without interruption, from the apostles. It is true, indeed, that the Church of England claims the power of holy orders in her ministers, but this is at best a very doubtful point, and absolutely denied by the Catholic Church. As for all the other sects, they do not so much as pretend to it; and their founders, conscious of their own total want of the priestly powers, endeavoured to turn orders and missions into ridicule, rejecting the very name of Priest from their communion, and usurping an authority to which they could show no title, much less could they derive their assumed authority from the apostles. They paid no regard to the words of St Paul: "How shall they preach unless they be sent?" Rom. X. 15 . But, taking this office upon themselves, they must be classed with those false prophets of whom Almighty God complains: "I have not sent these prophets, yet they ran; I have not spoken to them, yet they prophesied," Jer. xxiii. 21 . They did not enter by the door appointed by Jesus Christ, and used by the apostles. What, then, can they say to show they are not the thieves and robbers mentioned in St John, X. 1 , instead of true pastors?

(5.) The Catholic Church alone has had a perpetual being from the times of the apostles to this present day, without the smallest alteration or innovation of her faith in any one article of revealed truth. Her most inveterate adversaries are forced to acknowledge her existence for many ages before the Reformation, but they could never show any period when she first began to be what she now is. Some carry her up to the fifth, fourth, third, or second ages; and some admit that she began to put on her present form even in the time of the apostles. But she justly despises all their conflicting statements; and as she certainly was the true Church of Christ when St Paul wrote his epistle to the faithful of the city of Rome, and declared that "their faith was spoken of through the whole world," Rom. i. 8 , so she holds that she has never ceased to be so since that time. The very rule of faith she follows, the promises of Jesus Christ, the history of all ages, the writings of the great lights of Christianity, the Holy Fathers, which remain to this day, the numbers of heresies which have always broken off from her, and the fruitless attempts of her adversaries to show the contrary, convincingly prove that she is still the same, and that her faith has never varied. On the other hand, all the separate communions that ever have been, or are at present in the Christian world, can never trace back their existence beyond a period long after the apostles. They all went out from the great body of Christians that was before them, and had been from the beginning. Those who appear in the earlier ages of the Church have long since sunk into oblivion, and now exist no longer. Those of more modern date were many ages after Christ before they were so much as heard of in the world, and their authors, separation, and particular tenets, the opposition they met with, their subsequent divisions and subdivisions, are all recorded in the histories of their times, and show how far they are from having even the shadow of a claim to a perpetual existence from the times of Christ and his apostles.

(6.) As to infallibility in preserving the faith once delivered to the saints, the Catholic Church is the only society of Christians which not only claims it, but has always exercised it, and acted on all occasions as alone possessing that high prerogative. Others are obliged not only to renounce all claim to it themselves, but even to deny that Christ left such a privilege to His Church; and they make their separation on the ground that the Church had actually fallen into error. The very groundwork of their defection is the assumption that the gates of hell have prevailed against the Church of Christ; that the "words once put in her mouth" have gone out of her mouth; that "Jesus Christ has not continued with her pastors in teaching all nations; "that the "Spirit of truth has failed to teach her all truth; "that she is no longer "the pillar and ground of truth: "in a word, that God Almighty has abandoned His Church, broken His covenant with her, and failed to fulfil all the sacred promises. While they thus deny infallibility to the Church of Christ, they renounce, indeed, all claim to it themselves; but tell us that we must receive their fallible word, and, in opposition to all God's sacred promises, must believe, because they assert it, that the Church of Christ has fallen even into damnable errors, and that they are sent to reform her!

Thus it appears that all the marks and characters of the true Church of Christ are to be found in the Catholic Church, and in her alone: therefore we justly conclude that she alone is the true Church of Christ, the house of the living God, the pillar and ground of truth, out of whose communion there is no ordinary possibility of salvation; and consequently, that from her we are to receive the true Faith of Christ - that is, the knowledge of those great truths of eternity which He revealed to the world, and the belief of which He requires of all as an essential condition of salvation.

Q. 9. Is this true Faith, or the belief of those sacred truths which Christ revealed, alone sufficient to save us?

A. By no means; it is, indeed, one condition, and a most necessary one, being the foundation of all other duties; but it is not the only condition. In order to obtain salvation, Christ absolutely requires not only that we believe what He has taught, but also that we obey what He has commanded in His holy law. Thus He expressly says, "If thou wilt enter into life, keep the commandments," Mat. xix. 17 ; and St Paul assures us that "Christ is become the cause of eternal salvation to all that obey Him," Heb. v. 9 .

Q. 10. On what must our obedience be grounded?

A. On charity, or the love of God, which must be the motive of our obedience, according to the words of our Saviour, "If you love Me, keep My commandments," John, xiv. 15 ; and hence St Paul declares, that in Christ Jesus nothing will avail us without these two essential conditions of faith and love that shows itself by works: "In Christ Jesus," says he, "neither circumcision availeth anything, nor uncircumcision, but faith that works by charity," or love, Gal. v, 6 . Again, he says, "Though I should have all faith, so that I could remove mountains, and have not charity, I am nothing," i

Cor. xiii. 2 . St James also declares that "faith without works is dead, being alone," and that "by works a man is justified, and not by faith only," James, ii. 17 , 24. This clearly shows that these two conditions, faith and obedience through love, are both expressly required by Almighty God as conditions of salvation; and these two include the whole sum of our duties.

CHAPTER XIV.

Of The Law Of God In General

Q. 1. What is the law of God?

A. It is the manifestation of the Divine will to man, declaring what he is required to do and to avoid, in order to please God and save his own soul.

Q. 2. In what light ought we to consider the law of God?

A. We ought to consider it, (1.) As our rule and guide given to direct us in our pilgrimage through the wilderness of this world, and to conduct us to true happiness both here and hereafter. (2.) As our Judge, because it is by this law that we shall be judged at the last day, and be either rewarded with eternal happiness, or condemned to eternal misery, according as we have obeyed this law, or transgressed it in our present life.

Q. 3. When did God give His law to man?

A. At three different times: First, at the creation, by what is called the light of nature, or of reason; by which he imprinted in the heart of man the sense of right and wrong, the knowledge of good and evil, and gave him that inward monitor his conscience, moving him to do the one and avoid the other. By the sin of Adam, and the subsequent corruption of our nature, this light was greatly diminished; and, as the world advanced in years, the wickedness of man becoming greater and greater, it was still more and more obscured, so as in the generality of mankind to be almost extinguished; for which reason, when the posterity of Abraham were grown into a great nation, and God took them under His particular protection, to preserve them from the general corruption, He made a second publication of His law to them, comprising the whole in Ten Commandments, which He wrote on two tables of stone, and gave them for their rule and direction. They continued to be so for many years; but their carnal hearts in process of time overcoming their sense of duty, they very much corrupted the meaning of the law by the interpretations they put upon it; for, as the law itself was given in the words, and contained many duties which were not clearly expressed in it, they explained it, with regard to these duties, in the way most agreeable to their own inclinations; and therefore, when Jesus Christ came into the world. He published it a third time in His Gospel, with the full explanation of its true sense and meaning; and established it on such a solid foundation in His Church, that it shall continue now uncorrupted among His followers to the end of the world, as the sum of all their duties, and the guide to conduct them to eternal happiness.

Q. 4. Are we strictly obliged to obey the law of God and His Gospel?

A. Undoubtedly we are; because, (1.) God, Who is the Lawgiver, is our sovereign Lord and Master, "Who created us out of nothing, and gave us all we are and all we have. Who has the most absolute dominion over us, and can do with us whatever He pleases; consequently we are wholly at His disposal, and therefore are strictly obliged to do whatever He requires of us. (2.) We have seen above that He has made our obedience to His law an essential condition of our salvation; and consequently, if we refuse this obedience, we shall be punished with eternal misery. (3.) Because the Scripture assures us that "the Lord Jesus shall be revealed from heaven, with the angels of His power, in a flame of fire, yielding vengeance to them who know not God, and who obey not the Gospel of our Lord Jesus Christ; who shall suffer eternal punishment in destruction," 2 Thess. i. 7 .

Q. 5. Are we obliged to obey the whole law in order to be saved?

A. We are; for the Holy Scripture says, "Whosoever shall keep the whole law, but offend in one point, is become guilty of all," James, ii. 10 - that is, he becomes a transgressor of the law in such a manner, that the observing of all the other points will not avail him to salvation.

Q. 6. Are we able, by the strength of nature alone, to keep the commands of God?

A. By our own natural strength alone, without the help of God's grace, we are not able to keep His commands, nor, indeed, so much as to think a good thought towards our salvation. Thus the Scriptures declare "that we are not sufficient to think anything of ourselves, as of ourselves, but our sufficiency is from God," 2 Cor. iii. 5 . "And no man can say the Lord Jesus, but by the Holy Ghost," I Cor. xii. 3 - that is, no man can say it, so as to be conducive to his salvation. And our Saviour Himself, to show our total inability of doing any good of ourselves, and without His Divine assistance, says, "Without Me you can do nothing," John, xv. 5 ; and He confirms the same truth by the similitude of a vine and its branches, saying, "As the branch cannot bear fruit of itself unless it abide in the vine, so neither can you, unless you abide in Me," ver. 4.

Q. 7. Are we able to keep the commandments by the help of God's grace?

A. Yes, we are; and God, who requires us to keep His commands, is never wanting on His part to give us sufficient grace for that purpose. The tmth of this is shown from several reasons: (1.) The Scriptures are full of the warmest exhortations to all to keep the commandments, which certainly would be unbecoming the Divine wisdom if it were impossible to keep them with the help of God's grace, or if that grace were ever refused us. (2.) God everywhere obliges man to keep His commandments, under pain of eternal punishment. Now it is totally inconsistent with his justice, and makes God a cruel tyrant, to say He would punish us for breaking His commands, if it were impossible to keep them. (3.) We read of several in the Scripture who actually did keep them perfectly, and are highly praised on that account, such as Abraham and Job, and particularly the parents of St John Baptist, of whom the Scripture says, that "they were both just before God, walking in all THE COMMANDMENTS and justifications of the Lord without blame," Luke, i. 6 . (4.) God Himself declares, in the very first commandment, that He "shows mercy to thousands of those that love Him and keep His commandments," Exod. XX. 6 . (5.) And St Paul assures us that God is never wanting on His part to give us all necessary assistance to keep them, saying, "God is faithful. Who will not suffer you to be tempted above what you are able to bear, but will make also, with the temptation, issue," (that is, a way to escape), "that you may be able to bear it," i Cor. x. 13 .

Q. 8. How are the Ten Commandments divided?

A. Into two tables: of which the first consists of three commandments, and contains all the duties we owe to God; and the second includes the other seven, in which are laid down all the duties we owe to our neighbours and to ourselves.

Q. 9. Why do you say the first table contains only three commandments?

A. Because, though some people divide the first commandment into two, and by this means place four in the first table; yet in reality it is only one and the same: for when God says, "Thou shalt have no other gods but Me," He plainly forbids us to worship any other being whatsoever as God, but Himself alone; and when afterwards He says, "Thou shalt not make to thyself any graven thing, etc. Thou shalt not adore them, nor serve them: for I am the Lord thy God," - He only explains in particular what He had before declared in general terms, and forbids the worship of idols as gods.

Q. 10. But what need was there for this particular explanation?

A. Because, as the worship of idols was then prevalent in the world, and the people of Israel were exceedingly prone to this vice, as appears from their whole history, it pleased Almighty God to caution them in particular against so detestable a breach of it.

Q. II. How then do you make out all the Ten Commandments, if this be joined in one?

A. Those who divide this first commandment into two are obliged to join the two last together; for, "Thou shalt not covet thy neighbour's wife," and "Thou shalt not covet thy neighbour's goods," are manifestly two distinct commands.

Q. 12. How can this be shown?

A. Because they forbid the internal acts of two totally different and distinct sins - the one a sin of lust, the other a sin of injustice; and as the external acts of these sins are forbidden by two distinct commandments, "Thou shalt not commit adultery," and "Thou shalt not steal," because they are two distinct sins, so the inward acts, or desires of these vices, being equally distinct sins, require likewise to be forbidden by two distinct commands.

CHAPTER XV.

Of the Commands of the Church

Q. I. What do you mean by the commands of the Church?

A. The commands of the Church, in general, signify all those laws, rules, and regulations, which the pastors of the Church have made for the perfecting of the saints, for the work of the ministry, and for the edification of the body of Christ; but what is meant in particular by the commands or precepts of the Church are six general laws, which are of more eminent note in the Church, both on account of their antiquity, having been observed, as to their substance, from the very first ages, and on account also of their universality, as obliging every member of the Church, without exception, whom they concern.

Q. 2. Are the people obliged, in conscience, to obey the laws of the Church?

A. We have seen this obligation proved at large in the chapter on the Church (which see), and hence it is the constant doctrine of the Church, that all her children are obliged in conscience to obey her commands; that it is always a sin wilfully to trangress them, and a mortal sin if it be done in a matter of moment, or out of contempt. And the council of Trent, one of the greatest and most respected general councils that have been in the Church, condemns, and pronounces anathema upon all those who shall teach the contrary. This obligation will appear still more fully if we consider the light in which the sacred Scripture represents these commands.

Q. 3. In what light does the Scripture represent the commands of the pastors of the Church?

A. As the commands of God Himself, more than as the commands of men. For, (1.) Christ declares to the pastors of the Church, "he that hears you hears Me;" consequently they are the ministers of Christ, by whom He discovers His will to His people. (2.) When the apostles and other pastors, in the council of Jerusalem, gave orders to abstain from "blood, and things strangled," they began their decree in this manner: "It has seemed good to the Holy Ghost, and to us, to lay no further burden upon you than these necessary things," Acts, xv. 28 ; where they plainly affirm that this command of abstinence was a command of the Holy Ghost, published by this decree of the pastors of the Church. (3.) St Paul also, writing to the Thessalonians concerning the commands he had laid upon them, says, "You know what precepts I have given you by the Lord Jesus;" and a little after he adds, "Therefore, he that despises these things despiseth not man but God, Who also hath given His Holy Spirit in us," i Thess. iv. 2 , 8; alluding to what our Saviour said, "he that despises you, despises Me." (4.) Our Saviour also declares to the pastors of the Church, in the persons of His apostles, "Whatsoever you shall bind on earth shall be bound in heaven," Mat. xviii. 18 ; consequently, when the pastors of the Church make laws for the Christian people, and bind them, by their commands, to do what they judge necessary for "the edification of the body of Christ," the people are bound in heaven to obey these commands, as being ratified and confirmed by God Himself. (5.) When we consider the six principal commands of the Church in particular, we shall see that the duties prescribed by them are duties which God Himself expressly demands from us, and that all the part the Church has in them is only to determine the particular time, place, or manner, in which we ought to practise them, lest, if left to ourselves, we should neglect them entirely.

Section I: Of The First Command Of The Church

Q. 4. What is the first command of the Church?

A. To hear Mass on Sundays and Holidays, and to rest from servile work.

Q. 5. What is the end and design of this command?

A. To direct us in the manner in which we ought to employ the time set apart for the service of God.

Q. 6. Does God Himself require that we should set apart some of our time to be wholly dedicated to His service?

A. He does; and has expressly commanded one day in seven to be allotted for that purpose. Besides which, under the old law. He also ordained six great solemnities to be kept holy throughout the year, in memory of the great temporal favours He had bestowed upon His people, as is related at large in the twenty-third chapter of Leviticus, and in the twenty-eighth and twenty-ninth chapters of the book of Numbers; all which He commanded to be kept with the same strictness as the Sabbath itself, and two of them lasted for eight days together.

Q. 7. Are these holidays of God's appointment under the old law binding upon Christians under the Gospel?

A. By no means: they were instituted in memory of the particular temporal benefits bestowed on the people of Israel, and were binding on them alone; and, like the rest of the exterior of their religion, which was all a figure of the good things to come under the Gospel, they were types of the Christian holidays which were to be ordained by the Church of Christ, in memory of the spiritual benefits bestowed by Him on Christians, and therefore were fulfilled and abrogated when the Christian religion was established.

Q. 8. By whom are the Christian holidays appointed?

A. By the Church of Christ; which also, by the authority and power given her by her Divine Spouse, ordained the Sunday, or first day of the week, to be kept holy, instead of Saturday, or the seventh day, which was ordered to be kept holy among the Jews by God Himself

Q. 9. For what end does the Church appoint holidays?

A. For the same ends for which the seventh day and the holidays of the old law were instituted by God Himself, Whose example in this she follows. These ends are, (1.) To dedicate a portion of our time to the service of God alone, to Whom the whole belongs. (2.) To have leisure from our worldly affairs that we may apply ourselves more earnestly to the concerns of our souls. God takes to Himself the glory of having these days dedicated to His service, as is most due; but He gives all the profit to us. (3.) To keep up the continual remembrance of the great spiritual benefits we have received from God in the different mysteries of our redemption, and to adore and thank God for them; as we should be very apt to forget them entirely, were it not for the return of these sacred solemnities. (4.) To honour God in His saints, and to be encouraged by their example, and helped by their prayers to live a life of piety and virtue. (5.). That those who have litde or no leisure on other days, on account of the duties of their state of life, to receive instruction in their religion, may have time, on these holidays, for so necessary an employment.

Q. 10. In what manner does the Church command these holidays to be kept?

A. In the same manner as the Sundays; by abstaining from all unnecessary servile work, and employing such a portion of the day in exercises of piety and devotion, that we may be truly said to keep the day holy, and particularly by assisting at the holy sacrifice of the Mass.

Q. II. Why are the holidays commanded to be kept in the same way as Sundays?

A. Because (1.) the intention of instituting both Sundays and holidays is the same. (2.) God commanded the holidays of the old law to be kept in the same way as the Sabbath; and as these were only types of the Sundays and holidays of the new law, if this was done in the figure, where only temporal benefits were commemorated, much more ought it to be done in the substance, which regards the great spiritual benefits of our redemption.

Q. 12. Why is hearing Mass only, and no other particular exercise of piety, commanded on Sundays and holidays?

A. We are commanded, both by the law of God and the law of His Church, to keep these days holy 3 but as all the various exercises of piety are not always fit for every one, therefore it is left to each one's own devotion to spend these days in such exercises as may be most proper for himself. Yet, as assisting at the holy sacrifice of the Mass is the duty of all, especially upon these days, therefore the Church obliges all her children, by an express command, to do so. Not as if this alone were enough to keep the day holy, but that this must be done by all as an essential duty of the day, other pious exercises being left to each one's devotion.

Q. 13. Would it be a mortal sin to work upon holidays?

A. It would, except necessity, or the small quantity of the work done, excused from the guilt of a grievous sin: because it would be a transgression of the laws of the Church of Christ, whom He commands us to obey, under pain of being condemned as heathens and publicans. It would also be a profanation of those sacred days, set apart for the service of the Almighty, by doing what is expressly forbidden to be done upon them.

Q. 14. Would it be a mortal sin to omit hearing Mass on a Sunday or a holiday?

A. Most certainly, unless we were hindered by a just necessity; for it would be a transgression of the law, a disobedience to the highest spiritual authority upon earth, and a depriving God of that homage which we are commanded to give Him on these sacred days.

Q. 15. What is the proper idea of this first precept of the Church?

A. It is this, that Almighty God absolutely requires in general certain portions of our time to be set apart for His service and the concerns of our souls: that He has Himself appointed one day in seven to be allotted for that purpose, and has left power to His Church to determine others as circumstances may require; and that the Church, in virtue of this power, having appointed several holidays, we ought to consider them as decisions of the general law of God concerning the portions of our time we should give to Him.

Q. 16. But is it not a great loss to the people to leave off their work on these days?

A. In answer to this, let us consider (1.) Is it not an infinitely greater loss for their souls, to lose the grace and favour of God, by robbing Him of that portion of their time which He demands from them, and by bringing upon themselves the guilt of mortal sin? (2.) How many days and hours do they throw away in idleness and sinful occupations without any regret? Is it not a shame for Christians to throw away their time, with pleasure, when serving the devil, and ruining their souls; and only to regret it when spent in the service of God, and the concerns of salvation? (3.) Has not God a thousand ways of making up that loss, by giving a blessing to their affairs, and causing things to proceed prosperously with them? And is it not a criminal distrust in His Providence, to imagine He would allow us to suffer loss in our affairs, by our attention to His service; especially when He has often promised, in His Holy Scriptures, to bless our temporal affairs, if we are careful to sanctify the days set apart for His service; and has expressly said, "Seek ye first the kingdom of God, and His justice, and all these things shall be added to you"? Matt. vi. 33 . (4.) Has He not often threatened, in His Holy Scriptures, to punish us in our temporal affairs, if we profane His holy days? Has He not numberless ways of putting these threats into execution, unknown to us? And will not this be an infinitely greater loss than that of a day's work? Where then is our faith, if we are deterred from our duty by such unchristian fears?

Q. 17. What is the second command of the Church?

A. To fast during the time of Lent, on Ember Days and Vigils, and to abstain from flesh on Fridays and Saturdays.

Q. 18. What is the end and design of this command?

A. It is to direct us in the times and manner in which we are to perform the duty of fasting, which God, by a general command, lays upon all.

Q. 19. What is meant by fasting?

A. The not taking our usual food, either as to quality or quantity. The not taking our usual food as to the quality, or the abstaining from certain kinds of food, is properly called abstinence; the diminishing the usual quantity of our food is properly called fasting; though fasting, in general, includes both.

Q 20. Is it agreeable to the spirit of religion, and to the word of God, that we sometimes abstain from certain kinds of food, for some good end?

A. Nothing can be more so; for (1.) The very first, and the only, command which God laid on man in the state of innocence, was that of abstinence, forbidding our first parents to eat the fruit of the tree of knowledge in the garden of Paradise. (2.) When Noah came out of the ark, God gave him leave to eat animal food, but expressly commanded him to abstain "from flesh with blood," Gen. ix. 4 . (3.) When God brought His people out of Egypt, He laid a most strict command upon them of abstaining from leavened bread during the seven days of the solemnity of the Passover, He even forbade them to have it in their houses, under pain of death. See Exod. xii. 15 . (4.) He commanded His priests, under pain of death, to abstain from wine and all strong drink, when they went to serve in the tabernacle , Lev. x. 9 . (5.) He laid a strict command on all His people, to observe a perpetual abstinence from several of the most delicate kinds of animal food; and ordered them to look upon all these forbidden creatures as unclean, and an abomination, declaring that the eating of them would defile their souls, and render them unclean: "Do not defile your souls," says He, after showing what they should abstain from, "nor touch ought thereof; for I am the Lord your God; be holy, because I am holy," Lev. xi. 43 . (6.) He commanded them, under pain of death, to abstain from eating the blood of any animal , Lev, vii. 26 . (7.) The Nazarites were commanded to abstain from wine, and everything that belongs to or comes from the grape, during all the time of their sanctification. Num. vi. 2 , 3. And the mother of Samson was ordered to abstain from wine, and all intoxicating liquors, during the time she was with child of him; because he was to be a Nazarite from his mother's womb. Judges, xiii. 7 . From which it is manifest, that abstinence from particular kinds of food, especially such as are more pleasing to flesh and blood, and more nourishing to the body, whether continually or for a time, is most agreeable to religion and to the word of God; and that when done in obedience to proper authority, and for a good end, it contributes to sanctify the soul, and unite us to God.

Q. 21. Did the people of God, in the old law, observe exactly this command of abstinence?

A. To the shame and confusion of Christians nowadays, who are so negligent in this duty, the servants of God, in the old law, observed it with such exactness, that they chose rather to die, upon occasion, than to break it. Thus Eleazar, a venerable old man, when a heathen king wished him to eat forbidden meat, and "he was pressed to open his mouth to eat swine's flesh, he, choosing rather a glorious death than a hateful life, went forward, of his own accord, to the torment . . . and when he was ready to die with the stripes, he groaned, and said, O Lord, Who hast the holy knowledge. Thou knowest manifestly that, whereas I might be delivered from death, I suffer grievous pains in body; but in soul I am well content to suffer these things, because I fear Thee," 2 Mac. vi. 18 , 30. After him seven brothers, with their mother, suffered most cruel torments, and cheerfully went to death for the same cause, the mother herself exhorting them to constancy, as is related in the following chapter. In like manner, Daniel and his companions, in their captivity, chose rather to live upon pottage and water than "be defiled with the king's table, and with the wine which he drank," Dan i. 8 , 12, contrary to the abstinence which their religion required from them. And the same holy prophet, when he sought to obtain understanding from God, had recourse to voluntary abstinence from things not forbidden by the law, but pleasing to flesh and blood, as a most powerful means to get his petition granted. "In those days," says he, "I, Daniel, mourned the days of three weeks; I ate no pleasant bread, and neither flesh nor wine entered my mouth; neither was I anointed with ointment till the days of three weeks were accomplished," Dan. X. 2 . And this voluntary abstinence was so agreeable to God, that at the end of three weeks an angel was sent from heaven to tell him all he desired to know, who said to him, "From the first day that thou didst set thy heart to understand, to afflict thyself in the sight of thy God, thy words have been heard, and I am come for thy words," ver. 12, Could anything more evidently show the great advantage of abstinence, and how agreeable it is in the sight of God?

Q. 22. Is there any authority for practising abstinence in the New Testament?

A. There is the strongest authority for it, from the apostles themselves; for they, being met in council at Jerusalem, gave out an express command to the newly-converted Gentiles, "to abstain from things sacrificed to idols, and from blood, and from things strangled," Acts, XV. 29 ; and declared at the same time that this command was dictated by the Holy Ghost.

Q. 23. But does not St Paul say, "that it is the doctrine of devils to forbid to marry, and to abstain from meats, which God hath created to be received with thanksgiving? "i Tim. iv. 3 .

A. Certainly St Paul cannot mean that the apostles taught the doctrine of devils, when they commanded "to abstain from blood and things strangled," Acts, xv. 29 . What he condemns is the doctrine of those heretics who taught that flesh and wine were evil in themselves, because not created by the true God, but by an evil principle; and, therefore, in confutation of these heretics, he adds, that "every creature of God is good, and nothing to be rejected that is received with thanksgiving; for it is sanctified by the word of God, and by prayer," I Tim. iv. 4 . These heretics were the Manicheans foretold here by the apostle, and who, when they afterwards appeared, were loudly condemned by the Church for this their impious doctrine; but it is evident this doctrine has nothing to do with abstaining from some of the creatures of God, which are more pleasing to our corrupt natures, from the motive of obedience, or of self-denial and mortification, at particular penitential times.

Q. 24. What then does St Paul mean when he says, "Whatsoever is sold in the shambles eat, asking no questions for conscience' sake"? i Cor. x. 25 .

A. He is there speaking of those who, from a scruple of conscience, were afraid of eating meats that had been offered to idols. Against this he argues strongly in the eighth chapter; and resuming it here, he concludes that whatever is publicly sold in the shambles they should buy and eat, without asking any questions, or troubling their minds whether it had been offered to idols or not. But it is manifest that this has nothing to do with abstaining from particular meats, at a time, for a good end.

Q. 25. Is there any command of God obliging us to fast?

A. There is a general command obliging all to the practice of fasting, but without prescribing the particular times or manner of doing it.

Q. 26. How does this command appear from Scripture?

A. In several ways; (1.) God expressly requires fasting, as a condition with which our repentance ought to be accompanied, in order to please Him. "Be converted to Me," says He, "with your whole heart, in fasting and in weeping and in mourning," Joel, ii. 12 . (2.) Our Saviour assures us, that after His ascension His followers should fast: "The days will come," says He, "when the Bridegroom shall be taken from them, and then they shall fast," Mat. ix. 15 . (3.) He also gives us rules about the intention with which we ought to fast, and promises a reward for doing it: "When thou fastest," says He, "anoint thy head and wash thy face, that thou appear not to men to fast, but to thy Father who is in secret, and thy Father who seeth in secret will repay thee," Mat. vi. 17 . (4.) St Paul requires fasting, among other virtues, as necessary to make us true servants of God; and exhorts us to it. "Let us in all things," says he, "exhibit ourselves as the ministers of God, in much patience ... in labours, in watchings, in fastings," 2 Cor. vi. 4

Q. 27. Do we find that the servants of God practised fasting?

A. Through the whole history of religion we find that all the servants of God have been most assiduous in the practice of this holy virtue. The forty days' fasts of Moses and Elias are well known to all. The royal prophet assures us that "his knees were weak with fasting, and that he mingled ashes with his bread, and tears with his drink." Daniel prayed to God "in fasting, sackcloth, and ashes," Dan. ix. 3 . Judith was remarkable for her constant fasting. Anna the prophetess is commended in the Gospel, because she "served God night and day in fasting and prayer," Luke, ii. 37 . St Paul tells us that his life was spent "in hunger and thirst, and often fasting," 2 Cor. xi. 27 . The apostles "ministered to the Lord, and fasted," Acts, xiii. 2 . And "when they had ordained priests in every church, they prayed with fasting,"

Acts, xiv. 22 . All which shows that they considered fasting as a necessary duty, which God required from His servants. To this practice we are also encouraged by the example of Christ our Lord, Who fasted forty days and forty nights in the desert, without tasting bread or drinking water.

Q. 28. Is fasting of any benefit to those who practise it?

A. Many and great are the advantages of fasting; for (1.) It obtains pardon of sins, as we see in the Israelites, I Kings, vii. 6. And in the Ninevites, Jonas, iii. And God requires it of sinners, in order to find mercy; "Be converted to me in your whole heart in fasting," Joel, ii. 12 . (2.) It causes our prayers to be heard, as we have seen above in Daniel, 9th and 10th chapters. Judith assured her people of this truth: "Know," says she, "that the Lord will hear your prayer, if you persevere in your fasting and prayer before the Lord," Judith, iv. 11 . And the angel Raphael declared to Tobias that "prayer is good when joined with fasting," Tobias, xii. 8. (3.) It obtains great strength against the temptations of the devil; some of which, as Christ Himself assures us, "cannot be cast out but by prayer and fasting;" and St Peter exhorts us "to be sober and watch," 2 Pet. v. 8, as the best preservative against his infernal assaults. (4.) It also obtains many temporal blessings: thus king "Jehosaphat, being exceedingly afraid" at the multitude of his enemies, "betook himself to pray to the Lord, and proclaimed a fast to all Juda," 2 Chron. xx. 3 , and on this account gained a most miraculous victory. Esdras, being much afraid on his journey, says, "Wherefore we fasted and prayed to the Lord, and it happened prosperously to us," i Esdr. viii. 23. Nehemias, having to intercede with the king for his people, says, "I wept and lamented many days, and fasted and prayed before the God of heaven," 2 Esdr. i. 4, 11; and he found mercy with the king, and got all he desired. Esther, by her fasting, obtained the preservation of her people, and so of many others.

Q. 29. Why did not Almighty God determine Himself the time and manner of fasting?

A. For a very obvious reason; because the circumstances of times, and places, and people's constitutions, are so various and changeable that no particular rules could be laid down to suit all; and therefore it was necessary that the determining the times and manner of fasting should be left to be accommodated to these circumstances, and to be altered as they might require.

Q. 30, To whom has God given power to determine this?

A. To the apostles and their successors, the pastors of the Church, to whom, as we have seen above, He has given the full power and authority of making laws and regulations for the Christian people, "for the work of the ministry, the perfecting the saints, and the edification of the body of Christ," Eph. iv. 12 .

Q. 31. Why was it not left to each one in particular to fast as he pleased?

A. Alas! the backwardness and aversion which too many have to the practice of this duty, and the too general neglect of it, even when we are obliged by the command of the Church to perform it, clearly prove that if it were left wholly to ourselves, we should soon give it up entirely; and therefore it was highly expedient that a living judge should be appointed, with power to enforce the exercise of so useful and necessary a duty, and prevent its being totally neglected.

Q. 32. What part does the Church act in her command of fasting?

A. She ordains the particular times and the manner in which we are to obey the general command which God lays upon all. So that, properly speaking, the obligation of fasting is laid upon us by God Himself, and the times and manner of doing it are prescribed by the Church according to circumstances.

Q. 33. Are the people then obliged to fast when and in what manner the Church commands?

A. Most undoubtedly; they are obliged to it under pain of mortal sin; because, as God has not specified the times and manner of fasting, but left this to be done by His Church, to whom He has given power and authority for this purpose, if we transgress her orders we resist the ordinances of God; of which the Scripture says, "He that resists, purchases to himself damnation," Rom. xiii. 2 . We despise the voice of Jesus Christ speaking to us by the pastors of His Church; "For he that despises you," says He, "despises Me, and He that despises Me despises Him that sent Me;" and, for refusing to hear His Church, we shall be classed by Him with heathens and publicans.

Q. 34. What is the rule prescribed by the Church for fasting?

A. The practice of the Church has been different, in this respect, in different ages, according to circumstances; and even in the same age it is not exactly the same in all places, especially with regard to the point of abstinence. In the primitive ages the general rule of abstinence, on fasting days, was to abstain from flesh, and all white-meats that come from flesh, and from wine; and the general rule for the quantity was to take only one meal in four-and-twenty hours, and that not till the evening. Thus St Basil, in his ' First Homily on Fasting,' says, "You eat no flesh, you abstain from wine, and you wait till the evening before you take your food." But in process of time, the fervour of Christians becoming cold, this ancient rule of fasting was much relaxed, insomuch that at present the general rule of abstinence is, (1.) On all fasting days out of Lent, and on all Fridays and Saturdays throughout the year, to abstain from fleshmeat, or other things made of flesh; and (2.) During Lent to abstain from flesh, and anything made of flesh, and also from all white-meats, as they come from flesh, such as eggs, milk, butter, cheese, etc. And the general rule for the quantity is, (1.) To take, indeed, but one full meal in the day; but (2.) To take it about mid-day, and not before; and (3.) a small collation is allowed at night, as a moderate support to the weakness of nature till next day at noon.

Q. 35. Does this general rule of fasting take place everywhere throughout the Church?

A. In general it does; though there are some exceptions in particular places, especially in those countries where people, having little or nothing else to eat with their bread but white-meats, these are more or less permitted in Lent itself, and in some places eggs also, by a particular ancient privilege.

Q. 36. Does this great indulgence of the Church make her children more fervent in observing this easy rule of fasting, which she lays upon them by her present discipline?

A. The rule of fasting which the Church prescribes at present is easy indeed, when compared with the ancient practice; and this ought in all reason to excite her members to comply, with the greatest exactness, with what is required of them. No doubt there are great numbers everywhere who observe it with the greatest attention; but it must be owned with regret that this is not the general custom; on the contrary, when one considers the lax opinions with regard to the obligation of fasting, and the consequent practices which everywhere prevail, one would be apt to fear that both the spirit and practice of fasting are every day disappearing more and more from amongst us. So many complaints we daily hear of the difficulty and hardship of it, and so many inconveniences found in observing it, such weakness of faith as to the spiritual benefits and advantages of it, such unchristian ideas of the greatness of the obligation of complying with it, and, in consequence of these dispositions, such liberties are everywhere taken in evading the law, both as to the quantity and quality, as must give the utmost grief and concern to every serious Christian, and call upon all. who have any zeal for the glory of God, and especially on those whose duty it is to conduct others in the road to salvation, to contribute their utmost, by their prayers and example, to stop the growing evil; lest, if that power- ful means of appeasing the wrath of God be banished from amongst us, His offended justice should fall upon us with redoubled vengeance. What would have been the fate of Ninive if fasting had not interposed to preserve it?

Q. 37. Why do not the pastors of the Church exert the authority Christ has given them to remedy this evil?

A. The late learned and pious Head of the Church, Pope Benedict XIV., was deeply sensible of this evil, and of the fatal consequences of it; and, in order to arrest its progress, he issued two different decrees, addressed to all the Bishops of the Church, containing several salutary- regulations, which, with all the weight of his supreme authority, as Head of the Church and Vicar of Jesus Christ, he enjoins to be observed by all her children through- out the whole world. And in his introduction he shows the high esteem we ought to have for this sacred duty, and laments the present unhappy dispo- sitions of Christians regarding it, in the following manner:

"We doubt not, Venerable Brethren, but that it is well known to all those who profess the Catholic Religion, that the fast of Lent has always been looked upon as one principal point of orthodox discipline throughout the Christian world. This fast was of old prefigured in the law and in the prophets, and consecrated by the example of our Lord Jesus Christ; it was delivered to us by the apostles, everywhere ordained by the sacred canons, and retained and observed by the whole Church from her very beginning. As we are daily offending God by sin, in this common penance we find a remedy; and, by partaking of the Cross of Christ, we perform, by this means, some part of what Christ did for us; and, at the same time, both souls and bodies being purified by this Holy fast, we are more worthily prepared for celebrating the most sacred mysteries of our redemption, the Passion and Resurrection of our Lord. This is, as it were, the banner of our spiritual warfare, by which we are distinguished from the enemies of the Cross of Christ, and by which we avert from ourselves the scourges of the Divine vengeance, and are daily strengthened with the assistance of Heaven against all the powers of darkness. Hence, if this sacred fast should come to be despised, it will certainly prove a detriment to the glory of God, and a disgrace to the Catholic Religion, and expose the souls of the faithful to great danger: nor can we doubt that this is one great cause of the calamities and miseries that oppress both states and individuals. But, alas! how different, how opposite is the prevailing practice of many at present, to the ancient respect and reverential observance of this Holy time, and of other fasting days, which were so deeply imprinted in the hearts of all Christians from the very beginning," etc. So far our Holy Father, out of his great zeal for the glory of God and the good of our souls. Is it possible to read with attention what he here says, without being penetrated with the like pious sentiments?

Q. 38. What are the regulations which this learned Pope prescribes?

A. He observes that one great cause of the present relaxation of this ancient discipline is the too importunate demand of many people to be dispensed with in the rule of fasting, or their imprudently taking dispensations at their own hand, and the too great easiness of their pastors in granting them; therefore, to put a stop to this, he declares: (1.) That it is unlawful, and a sin, for any person audaciously to usurp the power of dispensing himself in these laws of the Church. (2.) That none ought to importune their pastors to grant such dispensation, and endeavour, as it were, to extort it from them (3.) That no dispensation ought to be given without a real and just cause. (4.) That when a dispensation is granted to eat flesh on fasting days, it is absolutely forbidden to eat fish at the same time. (5.) That a dispensation to eat flesh on a fasting day docs not free the person from die strict obligation of eating but one meal: And (6.) He enjoins all pastors, and burdens their conscience with it, as they must account to their great Judge, to use all proper caution and discretion in granting these dispensations.

Q. 39. What rule is to be followed in taking the collation at night?

A. When the time of taking one meal on fasting days, was changed from the evening to about mid-day, the custom of taking a small collation was then introduced, chiefly for two reasons; first, because it was found too hard upon many constitutions to go without food from mid-day to mid-day; and, secondly, because many could not get their night's sleep if they went to rest fasting; and the collation was intended merely as a support to this weakness of human nature. Hence, as it is an infringement on the ancient rule of fasting, for a particular reason, it plainly follows, that it ought to be such, both as to the quantity and quality, as is merely necessary for answering the end proposed. At first, it consisted only of a little bread and drink; but as the heart of man is always prone to gratify and indulge the cravings of the sensual appetite, by degrees greater liberties were taken, and became customary. However, to put a stop to further relaxation, the late Pope, Benedict XIV., and his successor, Clement XIII., being severally applied to for this purpose, both declared that, even when a dispensation was granted for eating flesh or white meats at dinner, on any fasting days, this was no by means to be extended to the collation at night. Conformable, then, to this regulation, it follows that, in those countries where milk, and things that come from milk, are used on fasting days, by the common law of the place, and eggs only as a privilege, or by a dispensation, though the former may be used also at collation, yet eggs certainly cannot. As for the quantity allowed, this must depend upon circumstances, though the general voice of divines agrees that it ought not to exceed about eight ounces.

Q. 40. But what if any person, from his particular constitution, could not sleep after such a slight repast?

A. There is a very easy remedy for that; let him take his collation about mid-day, and his full meal at night.

Q. 41. Who are exempt from the obligation of fasting?

A. Both Almighty God and His Church, in laying upon us the obligation of fasting, intend by it to promote the real good of our souls, but by no means to destroy or even to impair the health of our body, or to hinder us from the lawful, much less from the virtuous, employments of our state of life. On this account, all are exempted from the law of fasting, as to the quantity, whose state of health, or weakness of age, or the necessary duties of their state of life, render fasting improper; such as young people under the age of twenty-one, because, till about that age, nature requires full sustenance for the growth of the body; also old people, who are able to take only a little at a time, but require it frequently; women with child, and those that give suck, because they have to support and nourish their child as well as themselves; people whose state of life subjects them to hard labour, and who require full nourishment to support them under it, such as husband-men and tradesmen; also those who are obliged to make journeys on foot, or assist the sick. But though these are exempted from the obligation of fasting, yet they are still obliged to observe the rules of abstinence, unless some other particular reason require the contrary, as is often the case with people in sickness, where not only the quantity but also the quality of the food must be dispensed with, as their disease, according to the opinion of physicians, may require it. On the other hand, where a person, on account of his health, is dispensed from the rule of abstinence, yet he is still obliged to observe the rule of fasting, as to the quantity, unless some other cause require a dispensation in this also. And when any such dispensation is given, it is sometimes enjoined, and always supposed, that they make up for this indulgence by other works of piety, such as more frequent prayer, and works of mercy towards their fellow-creatures in distress.

Q. 42. Is the pretence of health always a just excuse from fasting?

A. Sickness is certainly a just excuse; but where the fear of hurting the health is alleged as a motive for being dispensed from this duty, it is much to be suspected that it is often a mere pretext, without reality, and that such fears are much greater than the danger. For there is daily experience of people who were for some time afraid of hurting their health by abstinence, and on that account always seeking dispensations, who, upon a fair trial, have found their health much improved by it; and, in the strictest religious orders, it is found that the members are generally the most healthy, and the longest livers; so true it is, as the word of God declares, that "by surfeiting many have perished, but he that is temperate shall prolong life," Ecclus. xxxvii. 34 ; and, from this experience, many wise men of the world have even advised people to have one fasting day every week, merely on account of preserving their health. It is true indeed that, at the beginning of Lent, the change of diet, and the diminishing the usual quantity of food, may occasion a little uneasiness for a few days; but experience shows that this soon goes off, and no further hurt is felt from it. People therefore would do well to be very certain of the reality of this motive before they give way to it, lest what appears a just cause to them may prove a very insufficient one before God, and bring upon them the guilt of sin, besides depriving their souls of all the benefits of this holy exercise.

Q. 43. Is the fear of being ridiculed or laughed at by others a sufficient excuse for eating forbidden meat on days of fasting or abstinence?

A. The Scripture says, "There is a shame that bringeth sin, and there is a shame that bringeth glory and grace," Ecclus. iv. 25 . When a person is ashamed to do an evil action contrary to his duty, and therefore abstains from doing it, that is "a shame which brings glory and grace; "but when a man is ashamed of doing his duty, lest he may be laughed at or ridiculed by others, and therefore acts contrary to it, that is "a shame which bringeth sin," and this can never be an excuse. Of this last shame our Saviour says, "Whosoever shall be ashamed of Me, and of My words, in this sinful and adulterous generation, the Son of Man shall be ashamed of him when He -shall come in the glory of His Father, with the holy angels," Mark, viii. 38 . Now there is no part of the words of Christ - that is, of His doctrine - which He more inculcates, than obedience to His Church; and therefore, to be ashamed of obeying her, from fear of the ridicule of men, is a crime for which Christ will be ashamed of us at the last day. Besides, experience itself shows that, when a person transgresses this command of the Church in weak compliance with those of another religion, and in order to escape their ridicule, he only exposes himself to their contempt by acting contrary to his profession and principles: whereas, when on such occasions he stands firm to his duty, in their hearts they esteem and regard him the more.

Q. 44. But what answer should be given to those who say, in the words of our Saviour, "It is not that which goeth into the mouth that defiles a man," and that flesh is as good upon Fridays and Saturdays as on any other day, and is as much the creature of God?

A. Ask those who say this, if eating the forbidden fruit defiled our first parents? or if the Jews would have been defiled if they had eaten leavened bread on forbidden days? Ask them what Almighty God means, when, after forbidding His people to eat several kinds of creatures, He concludes, "Do not defile your soul, nor touch ought thereof?" Levit. xi. 43 . Ask them, if the first Christians would have been defiled if they had eaten blood, or things strangled, after the prohibition of the apostles? Ask, if all these forbidden meats were not as good in themselves as any others, and as much the creatures of God? But those who make this objection only show their own gross ignorance; for in eating flesh on forbidden days the sin does not consist in anything evil in the meat itself at those times more than at any other, but in disobedience to the command of God and His church, and in preferring our own unrestrained appetite, or the fear of the world, and what men will say, to the will of the most high God, and to the obedience which we owe to His commands.

Section III: Of The Third And Fourth Commands Of The Church

Q. 45. What is the third command of the Church?

A. To confess our sins, at least once a-year, to our own pastor.

Q. 46. What is the fourth command of the Church?

A. To receive the Holy Communion at least once a-year, and that about Easter.

Q. 47. What is the end and design of these two commands?

A. To direct us as to the time when we are obliged to obey the general command, given by our Lord Himself, of approaching the sacraments of penance and holy communion.

Q. 48. Has Jesus Christ given a general command for all to approach the sacrament of penance?

A. He has: For, as He has instituted the sacrament of penance as the ordinary means by which our sins are to be forgiven, and we restored to the favour of God, it follows of course that He obliges all to receive this sacrament, otherwise their sins will not be forgiven. And though it be true that, when a person has no opportunity of receiving it, perfect contrition, or repentance for sin, arising from a perfect love of God, and accompanied with an earnest desire of receiving the sacrament itself, is sufficient to cancel the guilt of sin, yet this perfect contrition is so difficult to be attained, so seldom to be met with, and one is so apt to deceive himself regarding his own disposition, that the command of approaching the sacrament obliges all, without exception; the receiving it, when possible, being an express condition, without which there is no forgiveness.

Q. 49. Has Jesus Christ given a general command for all to receive the holy communion?

A. He has: For He expressly says in the Gospel, "Except you eat the flesh of the Son of Man, and drink His blood, you shall not have life in you," John, vi. 54 ; consequently, all those who have come to the years of discretion, and are capable of discerning what they here receive, are commanded, under pain of eternal death, to partake of these Divine mysteries.

Q. 50. How often are we obliged to obey these Divine commands of receiving the sacraments of penance and Holy communion?

A. This our Lord Himself has not determined, because different circumstances render it necessary to follow different practices, and therefore no general rule could be laid down to suit all times. This He left to be done by His Church, which could vary her rules as circumstances might require. Accordingly we find that, in the primitive ages, the practice was to receive the Holy Communion every day; afterwards it came to be every Sunday; in process of time, as the fervour of charity began to wax colder, it became less frequent, and at last the Church, in the general council of Lateran, made a decree, by which she obliges all her children, who are capable, to receive these Holy Sacraments of Penance and the Eucharist at least once in the year, and that the Communion be about the Easter time, in memory of the great Paschal solemnity. So that these commands of the Church only point out the particular times at which we are to comply with the general precept given by Jesus Christ Himself.

Q. 51. Would it be a grievous sin to neglect our Easter duties?

A. Most certainly it would be a grievous mortal sin to omit them through negligence, and without a just cause; because it would be a breach of the general command given to all by Jesus Christ, and also of the command of His Church, which obliges us to put that general command of Jesus Christ in execution about the time of Easter.

Q. 52. What if a person be not properly prepared to perform these duties at the Easter time?

A. It is always in his power, with the help of God's grace and the assistance of his pastor, to prepare himself for them; and, therefore, the same command that obliges him to perform them, obliges him also to prepare himself: so that his neglecting to do so is itself a sin, and a continuance in the state of sin.

Q. 53. But what if a person endeavours to prepare himself, but cannot do so within the appointed time?

A. He must then follow the advice of his pastor, who has power to defer his communion till he be properly prepared; and, provided he be truly sincere in his endeavours, this delay will be no fault in him.

Q. 54. What is the fifth command of the Church?

A. To pay tithes to our pastors.

Q. 55. What is the end and design of this command?

A. It is to direct the Christian people in discharging their duty of supplying the temporal necessities of their pastors, who dedicate their time and labour to the spiritual good of the souls committed to their care.

Q. 56. From what does this obligation arise?

A. From the law of nature, and from the positive law of God, both in the Old and New Testament.

Q. 57. How does it arise from the law of nature?

A. This will easily appear from considering what a pastor of souls is; for a pastor of souls is one chosen by a special vocation of the Divine Providence, and ordained for men in the things that "appertain to God, that he may offer up gifts and sacrifices for sins," Heb. v. 1 ; that is, he is one whose business is to attend to the immediate service of God, and to the care of the souls of the people committed to his charge. The duties of his vocation are many and weighty. He is obliged to offer up daily prayers and frequent sacrifices for both these ends; to instruct the ignorant; to preach the Gospel; to assist the sick and dying; to comfort the afflicted; to administer the sacraments, and to be ready at all times, both by night and by day, to answer the calls of his flock, when their spiritual wants claim his assistance. That nothing may occupy his time or withdraw his mind from these important duties, he is prohibited from marriage, and binds himself by vow not to enter into the married state, lest the cares and solicitudes attending it should prove a hindrance to what he owes to God and his people. He is also strictly forbidden to follow any worldly business, trade, or employment; for "no man," says St Paul, "being a soldier of God, entangleth himself with secular business, that he may please Him to Whom he hath engaged himself," 2 Tim. ii. 4 ; because, were he to engage in these, he could neither attend to the service of God, as his office requires, nor to the necessary care of souls.

When, therefore, a person, following the vocation of God, engages in this sacred state, and from charity and zeal for the salvation of souls dedicates himself entirely to the spiritual service of his people, how is he to live? how is he to be maintained? He is not an angel: he is composed, like other men, of a frail body, which must be supported. His whole time and attention are occupied with his duties to God and his flock. It follows, therefore, from the very light of nature itself, that those who benefit spiritually by his labours are bound in justice to supply his temporal necessities. And, indeed, if magistrates and soldiers, though possessing private means, are justly entitled to be supported by the people whose temporal welfare they promote, how much more justly are the pastors of souls entitled to a like support, as they labour for the eternal happiness of others, and are deprived of every means of gaining a livelihood, that they may attend with greater diligence to the supreme end of their calling? Hence St Paul makes use of this very argument, and says, "Who serveth as a soldier at any time at his own charges? who planteth a vineyard, and eateth not the fruit thereof? who feedeth a flock, and eateth not of the milk of the flock?" i Cor. ix. 7.

Q. 58. How does this obligation appear from the command of God in the old law?

A. It is laid down there in the strongest terms; for no sooner did Almighty God institute a religion among His chosen people, than He spoke to Moses, saying "Take the Levites out of the midst of the children of Israel, and thou shalt purify them." Then, after describing the rite of their purification, he says, "And Aaron shall offer the Levites as a gift in the sight of the Lord, from the children of Israel, that they may serve in His ministry... and thou shalt separate them from the midst of the children of Israel, to be Mine... to serve Me for Israel in the tabernacle of the covenant, and to pray for them," Num. viii. 6 , 11, 14, 18. Here we see the whole tribe of Levi chosen, by a special vocation of God Himself, for His immediate service, to be the priests and pastors of the people. Being thus dedicated to Almighty God, He would not permit them to have any portion, possession, or inheritance in the land with the other tribes; for "the Lord said to Aaron, You shall possess nothing in their land, neither shall you have a portion among them. I am thy portion and inheritance in the midst of the children of Israel," Num. xviii. 20.

How then did He provide for their maintenance? He made a law that the tenth part of everything belonging to the people should be consecrated and devoted to God. He it was that gave them all that they possessed, and He required that they should give back a tenth part of the whole, as a tribute to Him. "All tithes of the land," says He, "whether of corn, or the fruits of trees, are the Lord's,... of all the tithes of oxen, or of sheep, or of goats, that pass under the shepherd's rod, every tenth that cometh shall be sanctified to the Lord," Levit. xxvii. 30 -32. The first-fruits also of all their substance He reserved for Himself: "Thou shalt give me," says He, "the first-born of thy oxen and sheep," Exo. xxii. 30 ; and "Thou shalt carry the first-fruits of the corn of thy ground into the house of the Lord thy God," Exo. xxiii. 19 ; and He was so strict in demanding this tribute from them, that He forbade them to taste these things until they had offered their first-fruits to God: "You shall not eat either bread, or parched corn, or frumenty of the harvest, until the day that you shall offer thereof unto your God. It is a precept for ever throughout your generations, and all your dwellings," Lev. xxiii. 14. This was the portion which God reserved for Himself; and all this He ordered to be given to His priests and Levites, who were His portion, from among the people, as a support and maintenance to them for their service. "And the Lord said to Aaron, Behold, I have given thee the charge of My first-fruits: All things that are sanctified by the children of Israel I have delivered to thee, and to thy sons, for the priestly office, by everlasting ordinances,... and I have given to the sons of Levi all the tithes of Israel in possession for the ministry' wherewith they serve Me in the tabernacles of the covenant," Num. xviii. 8 -21. And so jealous was He of this right, which He had reserved for Himself, that He declares any infringement of it to be an afflicting of God Himself, which He would punish, by sending the curse of poverty; and, on the contrary, assures His people that, if they be exact in giving Him what thus belonged to Him, He would bless them with plenty of all good things, even to abundance. "Shall a man afflict God?" says He, "for you afflict Me. And you have said, Wherein do we afflict Thee? In tithes and in first-fruits: and you are cursed with want. And you afflict Me, even the whole nation of you. Bring all the tithes into the storehouse, that there may be meat in My house; and try Me in this, saith the Lord, if I open not to you the flood-gates of Heaven, and pour you out a blessing, even to abundance," Mai. iii. 8.

Q. 59. How does this obligation appear from the Gospel?

A. We have seen above that St Paul makes use of the argument drawn from the law of nature to enforce this duty. But he does not stop there; he proceeds in the same chapter to show that it is an express command of God, and a law of Jesus Christ under the Gospel, that the pastors of His Church should be maintained by their flock. "Know ye not," says he, "that they who work in the Holy place eat the things that are of the Holy place, and they that serve the altar partake with the altar? So also hath the Lord ordained, that they who preach the Gospel should live by the Gospel," i Cor. ix. 13. Here we see the Holy Ghost, by the mouth of His apostle, declares that this duty is ordained by Jesus Christ; and, in fact, we find it expressly enjoined by Him, when He sent the apostles to preach the Gospel to the Jews: "Go," says He; "behold, I send you as lambs among wolves; carry neither purse, nor scrip, nor shoes,... into whatever house you enter,... in the same house remain, eating and drinking such things as they have; for the labourer is worthy of his hire," Luke, x. 3 , 5, 7. In which words He commands this duty, and lays down the natural reason of justice on which it is established. Hence St Paul repeats the same obligation on different occasions. Thus, "if the Gentiles have been made partakers of their spiritual things, they ought also, in carnal things, to minister unto them," Rom. xv. 27 ; and "Let him that is instructed in the Word communicate to him that instructeth him in all good things," Gal. vi. 6. Also, "Let the priests that rule well be esteemed worthy of double honour, especially they who labour in the Word and doctrine; for scripture saith. Thou shalt not muzzle the ox that treadeth out the corn, and the labourer is worthy of his hire," i Tim. v. 17. This scrip-ture he also cites for the same purpose to the Corinthians, and applies it thus, "Does God care for the oxen? or doth He say this for our sakes? For these things are written for our sakes." And a little after he concludes, "If we have sown unto you spiritual things, is it a great matter if we reap your carnal things?" i Cor. ix. ii. Thus we see how strongly the law of nature and the written law of God, both in the Old and New Testament, inculcate and enforce this duty.

Q. 60. How then does this law of the Church interpose in it?

A. This duty was so liberally and so cheerfully complied with, in the prim-itive ages, that no further authority was necessary to enforce it; and the necessities of the pastors of the Church were amply supplied by the vol-untary offerings of the people; but, in process of time, the charity of many waxing cold, and a worldly spirit springing up, they became remiss in the observance of this duty, and as our Saviour had only ordained, in gener-al, that "those who preach the Gospel should live by the Gospel," without specifying any particular amount to be ' given for this purpose; therefore the Church interposed her authority, and commanded a certain portion, called tithes, to be contributed by the people for the proper support of their pastors. This law was confirmed and promulgated by the civil powers of all Christian nations; some in one form, some in another, according to differ-ent circumstances; so that the duty of supporting pastors is established by all laws, Divine and human, civil and ecclesiastical.

Q. 61. Is this law strictly observed in the Church?

A. It is universally observed in all countries where the Catholic Religion is established; but where it is not, and especially where it is exposed to persecution, this duty is not enforced. In such places, the pastors study more the salvation of souls than their own worldly interest; and content themselves with what Providence provides, the voluntary benefactions and offerings which it pleases God to inspire their people to bestow. In this they imitate the example of that great model of apostolic men, St Paul, who after having established the right of pastors to be maintained by their flocks, declared, however, that he himself has never exacted this right, nor does he write for the purpose of doing so, but only to instruct the faithful, "So hath the Lord also ordained, that they who preach the Gospel should live by the Gospel; ""but I have used none of these things, neither have I written these, that they should be so done unto me; for it is good for me to die rather than to make my glory void," i Cor. ix. 15.

Section V Of The Sixth Command Of The Church

Q. 62. What is the sixth command of the Church?

A. Not to solemnise marriage at certain times, nor to marry within forbidden degrees of kindred.

Q. 63. What are the times in which it is forbidden to solemnise marriage?

A. From the first Sunday of Advent to the Epiphany; and from the first day of Lent, or Ash Wednesday, to Low Sunday, both included.

Q. 64. Why does the Church forbid her children to solemnise marriage at these times?

A. Because Advent and Lent are times set apart for humiliation, penance, and prayer; and therefore it is quite contrary to the spirit of those times to employ them in feasting, drinking, and dancing, which generally accompany the solemnising of marriage.

Q. 65. Would it be a sin to be present at marriage feasts in these forbidden times of Advent and Lent?

A. It would: because St Paul declares, that not only they are worthy of death who do things forbidden by the law, but also they who consent to those who do them. Now, to be present at such meetings, in these forbidden times, is not only to consent, but also to encourage them; besides the offence and scandal given to others.

Q. 66. Why does the Church forbid marriage between those who are within certain degrees of kindred?

A. Nature itself has an abhorrence to marriage-connections between persons nearly related in blood, which nothing but absolute necessity could excuse, as was the case at the first propagation of mankind; but afterwards, Almighty God made several laws forbidding such near connections among His chosen people: even the heathens themselves, from mere natural feeling, had an aversion to them. The Church, therefore, enforces this dictate of God and nature, by the particular law she has made for this purpose. For, as the light of nature only points out, in general, that people who are nearly connected in blood should not marry, the Church determines the particular degree to which this prohibition is extended, and forbids marriage as far as the fourth degree of kindred, counting in a direct line from the common stock, the father and mother, in which the parties are united.

Q. 67. How is this to be understood?

A. The father and mother are the common stock; their children - to wit, brothers and sisters - are in the first degree of kindred, because they are one degree removed from this common stock; the children of brothers and sisters, or cousins-german, are in the second degree of kindred, because they are two steps or degrees from the common stock; the children of cousins-german are in the third degree of kindred, because they are three degrees from the common stock; and the children of these last are in the fourth degree of kindred, being four steps from the common stock - that is, the same father and mother. Within these degrees the laws of the Church prohibit marriage; as also between those who are connected by affinity from lawful marriage within the same degrees.

Q. 68. What do you mean by affinity from lawful marriage?

A. The Scripture declares that husband and wife "are no longer two, but one flesh," Mat. xix. 5 ; consequently the blood relations of the one become equally connected with the other; and this connection which the husband contracts with the blood relations of his wife, and which the wife contracts with those of her husband, is called affinity.

Q. 69. Is the same connection contracted by cohabitation between people not married, and the relations of each other?

A. It is; for the Scripture says, "Know ye not that he who is joined to a harlot is made one body; for they shall be, says he, two in one flesh? "i Cor. vi. 16.

Q. 70. Does the prohibition of marriage extend to the fourth degree of affinity from cohabitation without marriage?

A. No; it only extends to the second degree.

Q. 71. Why is the prohibition of marriage extended to the fourth degree of kindred?

A. Chiefly for two reasons: (1.) That people being obliged to marry at a greater distance from their own blood relations, marriage connections may be more extended, and different families more united in the bonds of human society and Christian charity. (2.) Because persons nearly connected, being generally upon familiar terms, and frequently in each other's company, there is a danger lest the hope of marriage might prove a temptation and encouragement to unlawful familiarities and crimes; but all hopes of marriage being cut off, the most effectual bar is put to such conduct.

Q. 72. What is the effect of this prohibition of marriage between the above-named relations?

A. It renders marriage between them null and void in the sight of God; so that, were two persons within the prohibited degrees to marry, though they should live as husband and wife, and even be esteemed such in the eyes of men, yet before God they would be in a state of fornication and incest.

Q. 73. How can the prohibition of the Church hinder the validity of marriage, if the parties consent between themselves?

A. In the same way that this is done by the civil power; for in regard to the contract of marriage, both the Church and the State can impose conditions which, if not complied with, render the contract null and void in the eye of the law. Thus in certain countries children cannot legally contract marriage without the consent of parents, and in England the presence of the parish clergyman of the Established Church is required by law. In both cases where the condition is not complied with, the parties are deprived of all the legal and civil benefits of marriage. In like manner, by the laws of the Church of Christ, unless the parties be beyond the forbidden degrees, the marriage is null and void before God, by whose authority these laws are made.

Q. 74. Does the Church never dispense with this prohibition?

A. The laws of the Church are made for the edification, not for the injury of her children; therefore, when there are just and solid reasons, she dispenses with the prohibition in the third and fourth degrees, but very seldom in the second, and not without the strongest reasons.

Q. 75. To whom does it belong to grant such dispensations?

A. It properly belongs to the Head of the Church, and to others by commission and authority from him.

Q. 76. Have priests, who are the immediate pastors of the people, this authority?

A. In countries where the Catholic religion is exposed to persecution, and the number of the faithful but small, their immediate pastors have this commission communicated to them by their bishops, with regard to their own flock, in the third and fourth degrees; but to dispense in the second degree, or cousins-german, is reserved to the bishops only.

Q. 77. Why are the priests empowered to do this in the third and fourth degree?

A. Because in such countries the reasons for doing so more frequently occur, especially that of encouraging the faithful to marry with one another, which it were to be wished were always done, for many strong reasons.

Q. 78. Why are the dispensations in the second degree reserved to the bishops only?

A. Because the Church has a particular aversion to the marriage of persons so nearly related, and because experience shows that such marriages seldom or ever prove fortunate; and therefore the power of dispensing in them is reserved to the bishops, that the people may from this conceive the greater aversion to engage in them, and that the greater difficulty of obtaining the dispensation may deter them from attempting it; for it is expressly enjoined to the bishops not to grant dispensations in the second degree, except for the most urgent reasons.

Q. 79. Would it be a grievous sin for two cousins-german to marry without a dispensation?

A. It would be a very grievous mortal sin, and the marriage itself would be null and void.

Q. 80. If a bishop should give such dispensation without a just cause, would it be valid?

A. He would himself commit a grievous sin in granting it without a just cause, and the dispensation itself would be of no effect before God.

Q. 81. Is there anything more to be observed concerning the commands of God and His Church?

A. What we have seen is sufficient to give us a general idea of the most necessary things our faith teaches concerning the laws of God. But there are numberless things to be considered under the head of each particular duty, of which we ought to endeavour to acquire as perfect a knowledge as possible, by daily and serious meditation on this holy law; that by so doing we may be the more efficaciously excited, and the more powerfully enabled to keep it perfectly, and effectually to avoid the most dreadful of all evils, the transgression of the law of God by sin.

CHAPTER XVI.

Of Sin

Q. I. What is sin?

A. Sin is any thought, word, deed, or omission against the law of God.

Q. 2. How is sin in general divided?

A. Into original sin and actual sin.

Q. 3. What is original sin?

A. It is the sin of our first parents, under the guilt of which Ave are conceived and come into this world - as we have seen above, chap. v. Q. 30.

Q. 4. What is actual sin?

A. Actual sin is that which we commit ourselves.

Q. 5. Who are guilty of actual sin?

A. Those who willingly commit or consent to any thought, word, or deed which the law of God forbids, or who willingly omit any duty which the law of God enjoins.

Q. 6. How is actual sin divided?
A. Into mortal sin and venial sin.

Section I: Of Mortal Sin

Q. 7. What is mortal sin?

A. Mortal sin is a grievous transgression of the law, whether this grievousness arise from the nature of the thing done, or from the circumstances in which it is done, or from the will of the Lawgiver, Who strictly requires the observance of what is commanded, as was the case when our first parents ate the forbidden fruit.

Q. 8. What are the effects of mortal sin?

A. It banishes the grace of God from our souls, renders us hateful and abominable in the sight of God, and worthy of eternal punishment. For this reason it is called mortal because it kills the soul in this life by depriving it of the sanctifying grace of God, which is the spiritual life of the soul, and condemns it to eternal death in the life to come.

Q. 9. Is mortal sin a great evil?

A. It is the greatest of all evil, because infinitely opposed to the infinite goodness of God. It is a bottomless pit, which no created understanding can fathom; for as none but God Himself can fully comprehend His own infinite goodness, so none but God Himself can perfectly comprehend the infinite malice and enormity of this opposite evil. It is the parent both of the devil and of hell; for hell was only made for mortal sin, and Lucifer was an angel of light till he was transformed into a devil by mortal sin.

Q. 10. From what does the malice of mortal sin chiefly appear?

A. From several considerations: (1.) From the greatness of the injury done to God; (2.) From the hatred with which God abhors it; (3.) From the severity with which He punishes it, even in this world; (4.) From the ingratitude it involves against Jesus Christ; (5.) From the sad effects it produces in our souls in this life; and (6.) From the loss of heaven, of which it deprives us. and the torments of hell to which it condemns us in the life to come.

Q. 11. How does the malignity of sin appear from the injury done to God?

A. Because it strikes directly at God Himself; it is a rebellion and high treason against Him, and involves a most injurious contempt of all His divine perfections. The greatness of its malignity in this view will appear from the following considerations, (1.) God is a being of infinite perfection, goodness, dignity, and majesty, infinitely worthy in Himself of all possible honour, love, and obedience; in comparison of Him all created beings are a mere nothing. When, therefore, such wretched worms of the earth as we are presume to offend and insult this God of infinite dignity, by transgressing His commands, and preferring ourselves or any creature to Him, the malice of such conduct is in a manner infinite, for we find among ourselves that the grievousness of any injury always increases in proportion to the dignity of the person offended above the one who injures him. An injury which would be thought of very small consequence if done by a person to his equal, would be thought a great offence if done by him to a magistrate, still more if done to a prince or peer of the realm, and yet more so if done to the King's majesty. Seeing, therefore, that the dignity and majesty of God are infinitely above all creatures, an injury done to Him must increase in proportion to His dignity, and in this respect be of an infinite malice.

(2.) God is our Creator, Who gave us our very being; our souls and bodies, and all our powers and faculties, are the work of His hands, consequently He has an indisputable and unalienable tide to all our service. He is our First beginning and Last end. Who made us, and made us for Himself, and for His own glory. He is our Father, to Whom we owe infinitely more than to our natural parents. He is the sovereign Lord of us and of all creatures, the King of the whole universe. Who has the most absolute dominion over us, and can do with us whatsoever He pleases. We depend totally upon Him for our continual preservation, and for everything else that we possess and enjoy; when we had lost ourselves by sin He redeemed us and bought us with a great price, even His own most precious blood. Each of these titles gives God a supreme right to all our honour, love, and obedience, which it were the height of injustice to refuse, but sin at once breaks through them all, and most sacrilegiously alienates from God what is so strictly His. Parents, what do you feel in your own breasts when your children insult you, and despise your will? Masters, what is the indignation of your hearts when your servants disregard your orders, and reproach you? Kings, what feeling have you of the injury you receive when your subjects rebel against you? Judge, then, how great must be the injury done to God by sin, to Him in Whom all these titles are united, in a manner infinitely stronger than is possible between man and man! Hear how He complains of it Himself, "The son honoureth the father, and the servant his master; if, then, I be a Father, where is My honour? If I be a Master, where is My fear? saith the Lord of hosts," Mai. i. 6. Moses also says of his people, "They have sinned against Him, and are none of His children in their filth; they are a wicked and perverse generation. Is this the return thou makest to the Lord, O foolish and senseless people? Is not He thy Father, that hath possessed thee, and made thee, and created thee? "Deut. xxxii. 5.

(3.) God is our only true Friend, our best and kindest benefactor, Who has loved us with an eternal love, and is every hour bestowing the greatest favours on us; all we have, all we are, all we expect, is the pure effect of His goodness and love. To injure, then, so loving a friend, to insult and outrage Him by sin, involves the malice of basest ingratitude, of which God thus complains: "For even the man of My peace, in whom I trusted, who ate My bread, hath greatly supplanted Me," Ps. xl. 10.

(4.) To all the above ties of justice and gratitude, by which we are bound to love and serve God, is superadded that of the sacred vow of baptism, by which we were solemnly dedicated to Him, and engaged to His service, and became heirs of His kingdom, which vow is also broken by sin augmenting its malice by the basest perfidy.

(5.) Let us consider now the nature of sin itself, as opposed to all those sacred ties, and we shall clearly see how inconceivable a malice it must include. For by sin we withdraw ourselves from this Sovereign Good; we contemn and despise Him in the highest degree, by preferring our own will and passions to His Divine will; we insult His supreme dominion over us; we are guilty of the greatest injustice, ingratitude, and perfidy towards Him; we undervalue all His promises, laugh at His threats; we esteem the perishable riches, vain honours, and filthy pleasures of this world, more than Him, our Supreme Good; and we prefer the devil himself, and pleasing him, before the God of infinite goodness who made us!

Q. 12. How does the malice of sin appear from the hatred with which God abhors it?

A. From a very simple reason; for as God is a God of infinite goodness, He must necessarily love everything that is good, and cannot possibly hate anything but what justly deserves to be hated: now the hatred which God bears to sin is inconceivable, and expressed in the strongest terms in His Holy Scripture; consequently sin must be a monstrous evil when a God of infinite goodness so violently hates and detests it. "Thou art not a God," says David, "that wiliest iniquity; neither shall the wicked dwell near Thee, nor shall the unjust abide before Thy eyes: Thou hatest all the workers of iniquity," Ps. V. 6. "To God the wicked and his wickedness are hateful alike," Wis. xiv. 9. "The way of the wicked is an abomination to the Lord," Prov. xv. 9. "Thy eyes are too pure to behold evil; Thou canst not look upon iniquity," Hab. i. 13. "Evil thoughts are an abomination to the Lord," Prov. xv. 26. "Every proud man is an abomination to the Lord," Prov. xvi. 5. And the prophets, especially Jeremiah and Ezekiel, are full of the like expressions.

Q. 13. How does the malice of sin appear from the severity with which God punishes it in this world?

A. Because, as God is a God of infinite justice, it is impossible He should punish sin more than it deserves; nay, as in this life His infinite mercy is above His justice. He generally punishes it in the present time less than it deserves. Nothing, therefore, can show us more clearly the enormity of sin than the severity with which He pursues it, even in this world, of which there are several very remarkable instances in Holy Scripture, (1.) One sin in a moment stripped our first parents, and all their posterity, of that original justice, innocence, and happiness in which they were created, and of all the gifts of Divine grace with which they were adorned; it wounded them in all the powers of the soul, it gave them up to the tyranny of Satan, it cast them out of Paradise, condemned them both to a temporal and eternal death, and, in the mean time, let loose upon them that innumerable host of evils, both of soul and body, under which their posterity groan to this day. (2.) "God, seeing that the wickedness of men was great on the earth, and that all the thought of their heart has bent upon evil at all times, it repented Him that He had made man upon the earth. And being inwardly touched with sorrow of heart. He said, I shall destroy man whom I have created from the face of the earth,'" Gen. vi. 5 ; and accordingly He destroyed the whole world, in punishment of sin, by the waters of the Deluge. (3.) When the sin of Sodom and Gomorrah was multiplied, and became exceeding grievous, the Lord could not bear it longer, because it cried to heaven for vengeance: "And the Lord rained upon Sodom and Gomorrah fire and brimstone from the Lord out of heaven, and He destroyed these cities, and all the country about, all the inhabitants of the cities, and all things that spring from the earth," Gen. xix. 24. (4.) When Cora and his companions rebelled against the authority of Moses and Aaron, and claimed to themselves the priesthood, Almighty God was so displeased with them for this crime that He punished them in a most dreadful manner. For "the earth broke asunder under their feet, and opening her mouth, devoured them, with their tents and all their substance; and they went down alive into hell," Num. xvi. 31. Many other such examples are found in Scripture, both regarding the whole nation of the Israelites, and also many other particular persons, which show, to a demonstration, the great and inconceivable malignity of sin, from the severe punishments with which a just and merciful God pursues it, even in this world. But, above all, the sufferings and death of Jesus Christ clearly manifest this truth; for in them we see the Divine justice of God the Father inflicting the most dreadful torments upon His own innocent Son, for sins not His own, but ours, which He had taken upon Himself in order to satisfy our offended Creator. What, then, must be the enormous malignity of the monster sin, which a just and merciful God punishes in so unheard-of a manner in His own innocent Son?

Q. 14. How does the malice of sin appear from the ingratitude it involves
against Jesus Christ?

A. The obligations we lie under to Jesus Christ are immense, and beyond
conception. Without Him we must have been eternally miserable: He could
in all justice have left us to our unhappy fate; He had no need of us, He was
perfectly happy in Himself; He could have created thousands of worlds to
serve Him, though we had never existed; there was no force obliging Him
to do anything for us; He was perfectly free to do as He pleased. Out of
pure mercy, then, and compassion for our miseries. He undertook to save
us; and who can conceive what this undertaking cost Him? Count one by
one His dreadful torments, from His agony in the garden till He expires
upon the Cross; see the God of heaven, made man, agonising in the garden, buffeted, blindfolded, spit upon, and the most ignominious, insulting,
and blasphemous things done against Him; see Him scourged at a pillar,
tormented with a crown of thorns, and nailed to a disgraceful cross; consider the humility, the meekness, the patience, and, above all, the infinite
love for our souls with which He bears all these severe afflictions; behold
to what an excess His love for us goes, when He bows down His head and
expires upon the Cross for our salvation. Does not such immense love,
shown in so endearing a manner, and tending not only to free us from eternal damnation, but to procure for us everlasting joy and happiness, demand from us every possible return of gratitude and love that we can make
to such a benefactor? What shall we say, then, of the monstrous ingratitude
of sin, which not only refuses to make Him any return, but takes a fiendish
pleasure in wantonly renewing all His sufferings, and, as His Holy Word
expresses it, "crucifying again to themselves the Son of God, and making a
mockery of Him," Heb. vi. 6. Hear how He complains of this by His prophet David: "If My enemy had reviled Me, I verily would have borne with it:
and if he that hated Me had spoken great things against Me, I would perhaps have hid Myself from him; but thou, a man of one mind, My friend
and My familiar, who didst take sweetmeats together with Me, in the house
of God we walked with consent!" Ps. liv. 13. How aptly do all these expressions point to Christians, who are the familiar friends of Jesus Christ,
feast at His table, attend Him in the house of God, etc.! What a monster of
ingratitude, then, is sin in a Christian!

Q. 15. How does the malice of sin appear from its effects on our souls in
this life?

A. The effects which sin produces in our souls are many, and miserable indeed, showing to a demonstration the horrid malignancy of that fatal poison which causes them. To understand them properly, we must consider, (1.) That a soul in the state of grace is beautiful, like an angel, and a delightful object in the eyes of God and of His saints. Such a soul, in the language of the Scripture, is a Queen, the daughter of a King, the spouse of the Lamb, and her beauty is thus described: "The Queen stood on Thy right hand in gilded clothing, surrounded with variety. Hearken, O daughter, and see, and incline thy ear, - and the King shall greatly desire thy beauty; for He is the Lord thy God - all the glory of the King's daughter is within in golden borders, clothed round with varieties," Ps. xliv. lo. See also the beauty of the spouse of Christ described throughout the whole fourth chapter of the Song of Solomon: and, among the rest, he says, "How beautiful art thou, My love, how beautiful art thou! - thou art all fair, O my love, and there is not a spot in thee,"verse i, 7. And in the Revelations it is said of the spouse of the Lamb: "It is granted her that she should clothe herself with fine linen, glittering and white; for the fine linen are the justifications of the saints," Rev. xix. 8. What a noble idea does all this give us of the heavenly beauty of a soul in the state of grace! What an esteem and value ought we to put on that happy state! But no sooner does mortal sin enter into such a soul than immediately all this heavenly beauty is lost, the grace of God is banished from her, and she becomes an object of horror and detestation in the sight of God and of His saints, hideous and loathsome as the devils: "He that doth these things is abominable before God," Deut. xxii. 5. "How much more abominable and unprofitable is man that drinketh iniquity like water?" Job, xv. 16. "They are corrupted, and become abominable in iniquities," Ps. lii. 2. "A perverse heart is abominable to the Lord," Prov. xi. 20. "They are become abominable, as those things were which they loved," Hos. ix. 10. What a malignant monster, then, must sin be?

(2.) In consequence of this beauty, and of the love which God has for a soul in the state of grace. He raises her up to the exalted dignity of being a child of God, a spouse of Jesus Christ, a temple of the Holy Ghost; so that by grace she is intimately united with God, Who dwells in her, in a most especial manner. "Know ye not," says St Paul, "that you are the temple of God, and that the Spirit of God dwelleth in you? - the temple of God is holy, which ye are," i Cor. iii. 16. "If any one loves Me," says Jesus Christ, "he will keep My word; and My Father will love him, and We will come to him, and will make Our abode with him," John, xiv. 23. What an exalted dignity is this I what happiness to have God Himself dwelling in us as our Father, our Friend, our Spouse, our Protector! "If God be for us, who is against us?" Rom. viii. 31. But, alas! the moment such a soul consents to mortal sin she loses at once all this dignity and happiness; the grace of God is banished from her; God Himself forsakes her, and she becomes a slave of Satan, a vessel of filth and corruption, the habitation of unclean spirits. What a dismal change! what a sad misfortune to be deprived of her God! "Woe to them," says Almighty God, "when I shall depart from them," Hos. ix. 12. What a malignant monster is sin, to cause such a direful calamity.

(3.) The grace of God in the soul is "a living water, springing up to eternal life," John, iv. 14. It is an inexhaustible source of heavenly riches, which sanctifies all the good works of the just man, and makes them merit eternal life. It is that bond of union by which we abide in Jesus, and He in us. Now "he that abideth in Me, and I in him, the same beareth much fruit," says our Blessed Redeemer , John, xv. 5. When, therefore, a soul continues for a space of time in this happy state, what immense treasures may she not lay up for eternity! But if, after she has long exercised herself in holy works, and laid up stores of riches in heaven by their means, she should at last fall into one mortal sin, such is the venomous poison of that monster, that in an instant it consumes all the treasures of her past virtuous life, and reduces her to a deplorable state of the most abject poverty. This God Himself declares in these strong terms: "If the just man turns himself away from his justice, and do iniquity, according to all the abominations which the wicked man useth to work, shall he live? All his justices which he had done shall not be remembered. In the prevarication by which he hath prevaricated, and in his sin which he hath committed, in them he shall die,"Ezech. xviii. 24. To such as these our Saviour says, "Thou sayest I am rich, I am made wealthy, and I have need of nothing; and thou knowest not that thou art wretched, and miserable, and poor, and blind, and naked," Rev. iii. 17.

(4.) The grace of God is the spiritual life of the soul, and is preserved by innocence and a holy life; according to that text, "Keep the law and counsel, and there shall be life to thy soul, and grace to thy mouth," Prov. iii. 21 ; and the Wisdom of God says, "He that shall find Me shall find life, and shall have salvation from the Lord," Prov. viii. 35 ; and as the human person is beautiful and comely while in life, so a soul that is alive by the grace of God is beautiful and comely in His sight. But the moment sin enters the soul, the life of the soul is destroyed. It wounds, hurts, and kills the soul, and renders her more hideous and loathsome in the eyes of God than a dead carcase is in the eyes of man. "He that shall sin against Me," says the Wisdom of God, "shall hurt his own soul; all that hate Me love death," Prov. viii. 36. "When concupiscence hath conceived, it bringeth forth sin; but sin, when it is completed, begetteth death," James, i. 15 ; wherefore "flee from sin as from the face of a serpent; for if thou comest near them, they will take hold of thee; the teeth thereof are the teeth of a lion, killing the souls of men,'" Ecclus. xxi. 2. And of some more grievous sins in particular the Scripture says, "They lie in wait for their own blood; they practise deceits against their own souls; so the ways of every covetous man destroy the souls of the possessors," Prov. i. 18. "He that is an adulterer for the folly of his heart shall destroy his own soul," Prov. vi, 32. "Refrain your tongue from detraction, for an obscure speech shall not go for nought: and the mouth that belieth killeth the soul," Wis. i. 11. Behold the fatal venom of the monster sin!

Q. 16. How does the malice of sin appear from the I loss of heaven, and the condemnation of the sinner to hell?

A. From this plain reason, that as heaven is a place of infinite happiness and never-ending bliss, great must be the malignity of sin, which alone can deprive us of that kingdom, and banish us for ever from all good. And as hell is a place of infinite misery and never-ending woe, dreadful must be the malice of sin, which alone condemns a soul to that never-ending torment. Now sin is the only thing that can do either of these things. The malice of men and devils can never deprive us of heaven, nor bring us to hell, if we be free from the guilt of sin. But so dreadful is the malice of sin, that one mortal sin alone effects all this.

(1.) That sin for ever banishes us out of heaven is thus declared in Holy Writ: "Know ye not that the unjust shall not possess the kingdom of God? Be not deceived; neither fornicators, nor idolaters, nor adulterers, nor the effeminate, nor liers with mankind, nor thieves, nor covetous, nor drunkards, nor railers, nor extortioners, shall possess the kingdom of God," i Cor. vi. 9. "Now the works of the flesh are manifest, which are fornication, uncleanness, immodesty, luxury, idolatry, witchcraft, enmities, contentions, emulations, wrath, quarrels, dissensions, sects, envy, murders, drunkenness, revellings, and suchlike, of the which I foretell you, as I have foretold unto you, that they who do such things shall not obtain the kingdom of God," Gal. v. 9. "Know this and understand, that no fornicator, nor unclean, nor covetous person, which is a serving of idols, hath any inheritance in the kingdom of Christ and of God," Eph. V. 5. "Follow peace with all men, and holiness, without which no man shall see God," Heb. xii. 14.

(2.) That sin condemns those who are guilty of it to the eternal torments of hell is no less manifestly declared in these divine oracles. Thus the portion of sinners is described by the prophet: "Their land shall be soaked with blood, and their ground with the fat of fat ones,... the streams thereof shall be turned into pitch, and the ground thereof into brimstone, and the land thereof shall become burning pitch; night and day it shall not be quenched, and the smoke thereof shall go up for ever and ever," Is. xxxiv. 7. And Christ Himself thus assures us: "At the end of the world the Son of Man shall send His angels, and they shall gather out of His kingdom all scandals, and them that work iniquity, and shall cast them into the furnace of fire; there shall be weeping and gnashing of teeth," Mat. xiii. 40. For "they shall be cast into the hell of unquenchable fire, where their worm dieth not, and their fire is not extinguished,... for every one shall be salted with fire, and every victim shall be salted with salt," Mark, ix. 44 , 48. And at the last day the Judge will say to the wicked, "Depart from Me, ye cursed, into everlasting fire, prepared for the devil and his angels," Mat. xxv. 41. "But the fearful, and unbelieving, and the abominable, and murderers, and whore-mongers, and sorcerers, and idolators, and all liars, they shall have their portion in the pool burning with fire and brimstone, which is the second death," Rev. xxi. 8.

Q. 17. These truths are indeed dreadful, and show beyond reply what a monster sin must be; but is it not amazing that Christians who believe these truths should ever dare to sin?

A. Amazing it certainly is; but the reason is given us in the Holy Scripture - to wit, that they never seriously reflect. Bewitched by the pleasures and vanities and amusements of this world, they spend their lives in a continual round of unprofitable and hurtful dissipations, and never find a moment's time to consider the great truths which their Holy faith teaches them. On this account these truths make no impression upon them; they easily forget them, and therefore lead the lives of heathens, as if they believed them not. "With desolation is all the land made desolate, because there is none that considereth in the heart," Jer. xii. 11. "The harp, and the lyre, and the timbrel, and the pipe, and the wine are in your feasts; and the work of the Lord you regard not, nor do you consider the work of His hands,... therefore hath hell enlarged her soul, and opened her mouth without any bounds, and their strong ones, and their people, and their high and glorious ones, shall go down into it," Is. v. 14. That is, as Job expresses it, "They take the timbrel and the harp, and rejoice at the sound of the organ; they spend their days in wealth, and in a moment go down to hell," Job, xxi. 12. Oh that men would be wise, and think on these things!

Section II: Of Venial Sin

Q. 18. What is venial sin?

A. It is a smaller transgression of the law, a more pardonable offence, which, though it does not kill the soul, nor deserve eternal punishment, as mortal sin does, yet it obscures the beauty of the soul before God, displeases Him, and deserves a temporal chastisement.

Q. 19. How is this explained?

A. The grace of God, which beautifies the soul, may be in the soul in a greater or less degree; and of course the soul may be more or less beautiful in the eyes of God, more or less pure, more or less holy. Now the malignity of mortal sin is such that it banishes the grace of God entirely from the soul, and makes it positively hideous and loathsome in His sight; whereas venial sin does not entirely banish the grace of God from the soul, but it obscures its lustre, diminishes its splendour, and stains its brightness. It does not render the soul positively hateful to God, but it makes her less pure, less holy, less beautiful, and consequently less agreeable in His sight. It does not destroy friendship between God and the soul so as to make them enemies; but it cools the fervour of that charity and love which subsisted between them, and begets a degree of indifference on each side; and as even the smallest venial sin is contrary to the will of God, therefore it displeases Him, and deserves to be punished by Him.

Q. 20. How does it appear from Scripture that there are such venial sins, which do not break our peace with God?

A. That is plain from many parts of Scripture, (1.) It is said, "The just man shall fall seven times, and shall rise again," Prov. xxiv. 16 . Now by these falls cannot be meant mortal sins, otherwise he would be no longer the just man; but only smaller imperfections, such as even good people fall into, and which do not break their peace with God. To the same purpose St James says, "In many things we all offend," James, iii. 2 ; and St John, "If we say we have no sin, we deceive ourselves, and the truth is not in us," i John, i. 8 ; where both these apostles put themselves among the number of those who sin; yet nobody will say that they committed mortal sins, and were separated from Christ, or in a state of damnation; on the contrary, St Paul assures us of himself and brethren, that "nothing should ever be able to separate them from the love of God which is in Christ Jesus our Lord,"

Rom. viii. 39 ; nay, he declares that "there is now no condemnation"' (that is, clothing worthy of damnation) "to them that are in Christ Jesus, who walk not according to the flesh," Rom. viii. 1 . Now the apostles were the friends of Jesus Christ; and therefore any sins or imperfections in them were by no means mortal, or such as deserved damnation. The same truth we learn from our Lord's prayer; for in it He requires of His apostles, as well as of His followers, to pray, "forgive us our sins." Now we cannot suppose the apostles, and all the great saints of God, had mortal sins for which to ask forgiveness; yet they were not free from smaller imperfections, which, being sins, stood also in need of forgiveness. (2.) The Scripture makes the distinction between mortal and venial sins in very plain terms. Thus our Saviour says, "Whosoever is angry with his brother, shall be in danger of judgment; and whosoever shall say to his brother, Raca "(a word expressing contempt), "shall be in danger of the council; and whosoever shall say, Thou fool, shall be in danger of hell fire," Mat. v. 22 ; where He expressly distinguishes the different degrees of guilt in sin, and declares that the smaller degrees deserve not hell fire, but the greater do. Again He says, "Every idle word that men shall speak, they shall render an account for it at the day of judgment," Mat. xii, 36 ; but an idle word does not deserve hell fire; for even a word of anger does not deserve it, as He told us in the former text; yet an idle word is sinful, because we must give an account of it in judgment. Some sins are compared by Jesus Christ to beams in the eye, and others to small motes , Mat. vii. 3 , which shows the great difference between mortal and venial sins; for a beam in one's eye must destroy the sight entirely, whereas a mote only impairs it. To the same purpose He says: "You pay tithe of mint, and anise, and cummin, and have let alone the weightier things of the law; . . . blind guides, who strain out a gnat, and swallow a camel," Mat. xxiii. 23 ; yet at the same time He tells them that even these smaller things ought to be done, and therefore it was a sin to neglect them, though only like a gnat in comparison of a camel when compared to greater crimes.

Q. 21. Are there diff'erent kinds of venial sin?

A. Venial sins, in general, are divided into two kinds: (1.) Such as arise from human frailty, surprise, or inadvertency, and from objects to which the person has no inordinate attachment. (2.) Such as a person commits willingly and deliberately, or from an evil habit, which he fakes no pains to amend, or with affection to the sinful object.

Q. 22. Is venial sin a great evil?

A. Venial sins of the first kind, to which all men are more or less subject, and which arise from human frailty, without any inordinate attachment to them, show, indeed, the corruption of our heart, and our great weakness, and on that account ought to be the subject of our daily humiliation before God; but they are less evil in proportion as they are less deliberate and voluntary. But venial sins of the second kind, which a person commits deliberately and with affection, or out of an unresisted habit, though even these be but small sins compared to mortal sins, yet they are very great and pernicious evils.

Q. 23. How can the evil of deliberate venial sin be shown?

A. From the following considerations: (1.) It is an offence voluntarily committed against a God of infinite goodness and majesty, and on that account alone is a greater evil than all the miseries any creature can endure in time, insomuch that no man living can be permitted by any power in heaven or earth to commit one venial sin, though he might thereby save a kingdom, or even the whole world; because an evil done to the Creator is in itself a greater evil than the destruction or annihilation of the whole creation. (2.) Deliberate venial sins, especially if frequently repeated, show that the person who commits them has but a very weak and languid love for God when he makes so light of offending Him. True love has this constant property, that it makes the lover exceedingly attentive to please the beloved object, even on the most minute occasion, and studiously to avoid the least thing that can displease him; and nothing more plainly proves the weakness of one's regard and affection for one's friend than to show indifference about pleasing him, even in little matters. What kind of love, then, must those have for God, who, if they can but escape His avenging justice, care not how much they displease Him?

(3.) They not only show the weakness of our love for God, but the oftener they are repeated the more they cool and diminish it; for our love of God is always in proportion to the grace of God in our souls: the more the grace of God abounds in our souls, the more we love Him; and the greater our love of Him, the more His grace abounds in us. Now as every deliberate venial sin weakens the grace of God in the soul, of course it also cools the fervour of our love for Him. And as a little dust or smoke, though it does not blind, yet prejudices the sight of the eye, so the least deliberate venial sin obscures the spiritual vision of the soul, and abates the fervour of heavenly desires. Besides, the more we gratify our affection for those creatures which are the objects of our venial sins, the more our love for them must increase; and the more our love increases towards any creature, the more it must be diminished towards God; for "no man can serve two masters."

(4.) In consequence of this weakening and cooling of our love for God, His love diminishes and cools towards us; our indifference about pleasing Him makes Him the more indifferent towards us; the oftener we deliberately offend Him, the more He is displeased with us; and to show how dangerous this is for a soul that, by venial sins, falls away from her first fervour, hear what Jesus Christ says to one in this state: "I know thy works, and thy labour, and thy patience, . . . and thou hast endured for My name, and hast not fainted. But I have somewhat against thee, because thou hast left thy first charity. Be mindful, therefore, from whence thou art fallen, and do penance, and do the first works. Or else I come to thee, and will move thy candlestick out of its place, unless thou do penance," Rev. ii. 2 , etc.

(5.) The more a person goes on repeating such sins, the more indisposed does he become for receiving new graces from God; and God, being the more displeased with him, withdraws His more abundant graces in just punishment of his repeated infidelity, as He Himself declares: "Thus saith the Faithful and True Witness, Who is the beginning of the creation of God: I know thy works, that thou art neither cold nor hot; I would thou wert cold or hot; but because thou art lukewarm, and neither cold nor hot, I will begin to vomit thee out of My mouth. Because thou sayest, I am rich and made wealthy, and I have need of nothing; and thou knowest not that thou art wretched, and miserable, and poor, and blind, and naked," Rev. iii. 14 . Such souls are nauseous and loathsome to God; and though He does not throw them oft" all at once, yet He begins to cast them out of His mouth, by withdrawing from them His graces, of which they have rendered themselves unworthy; and thus leaving them more and more to themselves, at last, if they do not alter their conduct. He rejects them entirely. Because they are not guilty of any gross mortal sin, and perform some outward duties of devotion, they fancy themselves in a safe way; but Almighty God forms a very different judgment of them.

(6.) The great evil of venial sin also appears from the severe punishments the Divine justice has often inflicted in this life upon sins which appear to us to be of a venial nature. Witness Lot's wife turned into a pillar of salt for indulging a natural curiosity; Moses deprived of going into the Holy Land for a small diffidence in striking the rock; Oza struck dead for touching the ark to support it when in danger of falling; David losing seventy thousand of his people by the plague for his vain curiosity in numbering them;

Agrippa consumed alive by worms for taking pleasure in hearing himself praised. Now if a God of infinite justice punished such sins so severely, they must certainly have deserved such punishment, and, therefore, are far from being small evils.

(7.) This is further shown from the way those are punished after death who die guilty of such sins; for so displeasing in the sight of God is the guilt of the least venial sin, that no soul stained with it can ever be admitted to His presence till its guilt be purged away. God is a being of infinite purity Himself, and none but the pure, "the clean of heart, shall see Him," Mat. v. 8 , and therefore into the heavenly Jerusalem "there shall not enter anything defiled," Rev. xxi. 27 : when, therefore, a soul leaves this world stained with the guilt of only venial sins, she is condemned to the sufferings of purgatory till she be perfectly cleansed by them from all spot or blemish, and rendered fit to be admitted to the Divine presence; and how dreadful this cleansing will be, appears from the words of the prophet: "Every one that shall be left in Sion, and shall remain in Jerusalem, shall be called holy, every one that is written in life in Jerusalem • the Lord shall wash away the filth of the daughter of Zion ... by the spirit of judgment, and by the spirit of burning," Isa. iv. 3 . How dreadful that purgation by the very "spirit of judgment and of burning "! How great an evil that stain which requires such a purgation!

(8.) The great and fatal evil of venial sin consists in this, that it disposes and leads on the poor soul to the gulf of mortal sin, according to the express declaration of the Word of God, "He that contemneth small things, shall fall by little and little," Ecclus. xix. 1 , and "he that is faithful in that which is least, is faithful also in that which is greater; and he that is unjust in that which is little, is unjust also in that which is great," Luke, xvi. 10 . And for this several reasons are assigned: (1.) Experience teaches that the greatest things, both in the order of nature and in the order of grace, commonly take their rise from small beginnings; rivers from springs, trees from small seeds. "Behold how great a fire a small spark kindleth!" James, iii. 5 . Our bodies begin from a point; a drop of water neglected, causes the fall of a house; a slight illness disregarded brings on disease and death; the most learned man commences by the alphabet; the greatest saints were not born such, but arrived at sanctity by degrees; so also the greatest sinners begin by small sins, which neglected lead on to greater. A slight motion of anger indulged led Cain to murder his own brother; an impure glance of the eye encouraged, dragged on a David to adultery and murder; and an inordinate attachment to riches, uncorrected, brought Judas to betray his Master. (.?.)

All the foregoing reasons show the same thing; for, by venial sins indulged, we become more disagreeable to God, our love of Him is diminished, and His to us; we are rendered more unfit for receiving His graces, and they are given more sparingly; our passions become stronger, and we grow weaker; and then what is to be the consequence when the time of temptation comes, but that we fall into mortal sin? (3.) Venial sins lead us on step by step towards mortal sin, and take off by degrees our horror of it. It would be impossible for any one to step from the ground to the top of a high stair all at once; but by taking one step after another, he goes up with the greatest ease. A modest person would be shocked at the proposal of any of the greatest crimes of impurity; but, if she gives ear to words of a double meaning, and takes pleasure in them, this will easily prepare the way for bad thoughts; from this there is but a step to desires; and, these encouraged, will lead on to undue liberties in action, and so step by step she will be carried on to every excess. (4.) By committing small sins without remorse, or with affection, we contract a habit of transgressing the law, which, the more it is indulged, the stronger it becomes. (5.) It is certain that our nature, if left to itself, would lead us into all crimes; and we have no other way to prevent this but by checking its desires. Now experience teaches us that the more we yield to these desires, the stronger they become; the more liberty we give to nature, the more unruly does she grow. (6.) Many venial sins are of such a nature, that they become mortal if frequently repeated: such are all sins of injustice, working upon forbidden days, and the like. (7.) It is often very difficult to distinguish the limits between mortal and venial sin; therefore a person who indulges himself in the latter, exposes himself to the continual danger of falling into the former. Now "he that loveth the danger shall perish in it," Ecclus. iii. 27 . (8.) A thing that is in itself only venial, very often, from the circumstances, becomes mortal.

Q. 24. How can a thing, in itself venial, become mortal from the circumstances?

A. From different causes: (1.) If his affection who commits it be so great towards the object of a sin in itself venial that he would be ready to offend God mortally rather than not do it, his doing it with such a disposition is a mortal sin. (2.) If a person commit a venial sin for an end mortally sinful; for example, if he should steal a small quantity of poison of trifling value in order to poison his neighbour, this intention makes the stealing the poison itself a mortal sin, though he should be prevented from using it as he intended. (3.) If he commit a sin in itself venial, but which, by mistake, he believes to be mortal, to him it becomes a mortal sin. (4.) If a sin, in itself venial, be the occasion of great scandal, it becomes mortal to the person who commits it on that account. (5.) If a venial sin be committed from a contempt of the Divine law, this contempt makes it mortal.

Q. 25. What are the proper remedies of sin?

A. There are two principal remedies for the great evil of sin - one on the part of man, which is a sincere repentance; the other on the part of God, which is the grace of Jesus Christ. These two remedies are both of absolute necessity, for it is impossible that we should be delivered from the guilt of our actual sins without a sincere repentance; and it is impossible for us to repent as we ought without the assistance of Divine grace; and though we have a sincere repentance, that alone cannot deliver us from our sins without the infusion of sanctifying grace into our souls. So that the grace of our Saviour is the great remedy which alone can heal the wounds which the soul receives from sin, and wash away its guilt; and repentance on our part is a condition absolutely required, to dispose the soul for receiving that grace, and without which it is impossible that this grace should be bestowed upon us.

CHAPTER XVII.

Of Repentance

Q. What is repentance?

A. Repentance, which is also called penance, is the sincere conversion of the heart from sin to God. To understand this we must observe that in sin there are two great evils, which Almighty God Himself describes in these words, "Be astonished, O ye heavens! at this, ... for My people have done two evils; they have forsaken Me, the fountain of living water, and have digged to themselves cisterns, broken cisterns, that can hold no water," Jer. ii. 12 . In every mortal sin, then, there are these two enormous evils - to wit, the turning away from God, Who is infinitely good, and the very fountain of goodness and life, and the embracing in His stead the monster sin, by the allurements of some deceitful appearance of an imaginary happiness, justly compared to a broken cistern that can hold no water, but only filth and mud. Wherefore repentance, which is the opposite of sin and its destroyer, must likewise have these two conditions - the turning away from sin with horror, detestation, and sorrow for having offended so great a God, and the returning back to God to embrace Him by love, and faithfully to obey His Holy law.

Q. 2. What are the principal parts of which true repentance is composed?

A. The principal parts of true repentance are these three: (1.) A sincere regret and sorrow of heart for our having offended so good a God by sin. (2.) A firm and determined resolution of never offending Him again, followed by an effectual change of life and manners. (3.) A voluntary punishing of ourselves for the sins we have committed, in order to repair the injury done to God by sin, and to satisfy, in some measure, His offended justice.

Section I: Of The Sorrow Of Repentance

Q. 3. What is meant by sorrow for having offended God by sin?

A. Sorrow is a painful feeling of the mind when any evil comes upon ourselves or on those we love; and if we ourselves have been the occasion of bringing evil upon those we love, our displeasure and pain at their suffering are all the greater. When, therefore, we have a sincere love of God, and consider our sins as a grievous outrage and injury by which we have offended Him, and on that account feel a regret in our heart, a pain and displeasure in our mind, that pain, that regret, that displeasure is the sorrow which constitutes true repentance.

Q. 4. What are the qualities which this true sorrow of repentance ought to have?

A. Chiefly these following: (1.) It ought to be internal - that is, seated in the heart and mind; not consisting of mere words or other external signs, nor even a more sensible sorrow, which some tender, affectionate people frequently have, and which shows itself in sobs and tears, but without any real change of heart; but it ought to be in the mind and heart - in the mind, by a full conviction of the evil of sin, and the injury it is to so good a God; and m the heart, which, having a sincere love of God, feels a real pain and regret for having ever displeased Him. Where this is there is true sorrow, though there be neither sighs nor tears; but where this is not, sighs and tears will be of no avail. (2.) It ought to be supernatural - that is, a rising from supernatural motives through the grace of God. A person may be sorry for his sins, because by them he has brought suffering, loss, or disgrace upon himself. A sorrow of this kind will never find mercy with God. This is a mere sorrow of the world, not a sorrow according to God. Now the Scripture tells us that it is only "the sorrow that is according to God which worketh penance steadfast unto salvation; but the sorrow of the world worketh death," 2 Cor. vii. 10. The sorrow of true repentance must arise from our having offended so good a God, from our ingratitude to Jesus Christ, from the danger to which our sins expose us of being for ever separated from God Whom we love, of being eternally condemned among His enemies to hell fire, from the fear of God's judgments, and from the horror of sin on account of its opposition to God. These are supernatural motives which our faith teaches us, and which, by the help of God's grace, excite the true sorrow of repentance in our souls. (3.) It ought to be exceeding great - that is, our sorrow for having lost our God and His grace by sin ought to be greater than if we had lost all that we love in this world; because, as our sorrow for the loss of any good is always in proportion to the love and esteem we bear towards it, so our sorrow and regret for having lost God by sin ought to be greater than if we had lost all things else, seeing we are obliged to love Him above all things. (4.)

It ought to be universal - that is, we ought to have this sorrow for all and every one of our sins without exception; for if we love any one mortal sin, though we should perfectly hate all others, we can never be said to have true repentance. (5.) It ought to be accompanied with a firm resolution of sinning no more, and a willingness to satisfy for past sins; of which afterwards. (6.) It ought also to be accompanied with a firm hope of obtaining pardon through the mercy of God.

Q. 5. Is this sorrow absolutely necessary for true repentance?

A. It is the very essence of true repentance, as appears from innumerable testimonies of Scripture. Thus David says to God, "If Thou hadst desired sacrifice, I would indeed have given it; with burnt-offerings Thou wilt not be delighted; a sacrifice to God is an afflicted spirit; a contrite and humbled heart, O God, Thou wilt not despise," Ps. 1. 18; where we see that no outward means of appeasing the wrath of God, even by sacrifices appointed by Himself for this purpose, will find acceptance with Him unless they be accompanied with a true and sincere sorrow of the heart, which humbles it, and breaks it, as it were, to pieces, and with affliction of the spirit, or regret of the mind, for having offended so good a God, but that an afflicted spirit and contrite heart will never be despised by Him. So also the Scripture says, "When thou shalt seek the Lord thy God, thou shalt find Him; yet so, if thou seek Him with all thy heart, and with all the affliction of thy soul," Deut. iv. 29. Again, the prophet Moses says to his people, "Now, when thou shalt be touched with the repentance of thy heart - and return to Him - the Lord thy God will have mercy on thee," Deut. xxx. 1 , 2, 3. So likewise Jeremiah exhorts sinners in these words to true repentance: "Gird thee with sackcloth, O daughter of my people, and sprinkle thee with ashes; make thee mourning as for an only son, a bitter lamentation," Jer. vi. 26. And God Himself, by His prophet Joel: "Now, therefore," saith the Lord, "be converted to me with all your heart in fasting, and in weeping, and in mourning, and rend your hearts and not your garments, and turn to the Lord your God, for He is gracious and merciful, patient, and rich in mercy," Joel, ii. 12. Such was the true sorrow of David, which he describes in these words: "There is no health in my flesh, because
of Thy wrath; there is no peace for my bones, because of my sins; for my iniquities are gone over my head, and as a heavy burden are become heavy upon me.... I am become miserable, and am bowed down even to the end; I walked sorrowful all the day long," Ps. xxxvii. 4. Such was the repentance of King Ezekias, when he said to God, "I will recount to Thee all my years in the bitterness of my soul," Is. xxxviii. 15. Such, in fine, was the repentance of all true penitents who found mercy with God - the Ninivites, the humble publican, St Mary Magdalene, St Peter, etc.

Q. 6. How many kinds of this sorrow are there?

A. It is considered as divided into two kinds, which agree in all the above-mentioned qualities, and differ only in the motives from which they arise, and in the effects they produce. Of the supernatural motives mentioned above, some are most perfect and excellent, because founded on charity, or the pure love of God for Himself alone - as when we are sorry for our sins, purely because by them we have offended so good a God, Whom we love above all things, without any attention to the evils sin brings upon ourselves. Such was the sorrow of St Mary Magdalene, of whom our Saviour says, "Many sins are forgiven her, because she has loved much." A sorrow that arises from this motive is a perfect sorrow, and is called perfect contrition. Others of the supernatural motives above mentioned are less perfect, because they include an attention to our own interest, accompanied with an initial and less perfect love of God, considering Him more as being good to us than as infinitely good in Himself. Of this kind are our fear of losing heaven, or of being condemned to hell; our fear of the judgments of God, and the like. A sorrow for sin which arises from these motives is therefore called imperfect contrition, and attrition.

Q. 7. How do contrition and attrition differ in their effects?

A. Perfect contrition, as it arises from a perfect love of God for Himself alone, is so pleasing in His sight that the moment a person has it, God is reconciled to him, and forgives his sins; for, as the Scripture says, "Charity," or the perfect love of God, "covereth a multitude of sins," i Pet. iv. 8 ; and such was the effect it had in St Mary Magdalene. It is to be understood, however, that such contrition does not free a person from the obligation of having recourse to the sacrament of penance, where it can be had - the command of receiving that sacrament being laid upon all without exception. Attrition of itself, on the other hand, in no case obtains the remission of sin, but only disposes the soul for receiving that grace by means of the sacrament of penance.

Q. 8. Is this sorrow for sin, which arises from the fear of hell, or of God's judgments, or of losing heaven, a virtuous and laudable sorrow?

A. Most certainly; it is a gift of God, and therefore David prays for it: "Pierce Thou my flesh," says he, "with Thy fear: for I am afraid of Thy judgment," Ps. cxviii. 120 ; and Christ Himself commands us to have this fear of God: "Be not afraid of them that kill the body, and after that have no more that they can do; but I will show whom ye shall fear; fear ye Him Who, after He hath killed, hath power to cast into hell; yea, I say to you, fear Him," Luke, xii. 4.

Section II: Of The Purpose Of Not Sinning Again

Q. 9. What is meant by a purpose of not sinning again?

A. It is a firm and resolute determination of the will carefully to avoid all sin for the time to come, and all the dangerous occasions of sin, arising from the same supernatural motives on which our sorrow for sin is grounded. In fact, this purpose and resolution is a necessary consequence of true sorrow, and an essential part of sincere repentance; for it is impossible sincerely to hate sin, as the greatest of evils, and to be heartily sorry for having offended God, by being guilty of it, without also firmly resolving to fly from that monster for the future, and to use every necessary means for avoiding it.

Q. 10. What are the effects of this sincere purpose of amendment?

A. A total change of our whole behaviour; "a putting off, according to our former conversation, the old man; and a being renewed," not only "in the spirit of our mind," but also "putting on the new man, who, according to God, is created in justice, and holiness, and truth," Ephes. iv. 22 ; or, as the same apostle expresses it more particularly, "Now put you also away all anger, indignation, malice, blasphemy, filthy speech out of your mouth; lie not one to another, stripping yourselves of the old man, with his deeds.... Put ye on, therefore, as the elect of God, holy and beloved, the bowels of mercy and benignity, humility, modesty, patience, but, above all things, have charity, which is the bond of perfection," Col. iii. 8. So that true repentance changes the whole man, his sentiments, his affections, his behaviour; makes him love what he did not love before, God and His Holy law; and makes him hate what he loved before, his sinful pleasures and employments. And this is the great favour which Almighty God promises to bestow upon His people by the prophet Ezekiel, saying, "I will give them one heart, and will put a new spirit in their bowels; and I will take away the stony heart out of their flesh, and will give them a heart of flesh, that they may walk in My commandments, and keep My judgments, and do them; and that they may be My people, and I may be their God," Ezek. xi. 19.

Q. II. Is this conversion and change of life strictly required of true penitents?

A. Nothing is more strongly inculcated throughout the whole Scripture, as a necessary condition of being reconciled with God. Thus, "As I live, saith the Lord God, I desire not the death of the wicked, but that the wicked turn from his way and live. Turn ye, turn ye from your evil ways; and why will you die, O house of Israel?" Ezek. xxxiii. 11. And to show wherein this turning consists. He says, "Cast away from you all transgressions, by which you have transgressed, and make to yourself a new heart and a new spirit, and why will you die. Chouse of Israel?" Ezek. xviii. 31. "When you stretch forth your hands, I will turn away My eyes from you," says God to sinners, "and when you multiply prayer I will not hear, for your hands are full of blood;" that is, you are hateful to Me by reason of your sins. But what must be done to find favour?. He immediately adds, "Wash yourselves, be clean, take away the evil of your devices from My eyes; cease to do perversely, learn to do well, seek judgment, relieve the oppressed, judge for the fatherless, defend the widow, and then come and accuse Me, saith the Lord. If your sins be as scarlet, they shall be made white as snow; and if they be red as crimson, they shall be white as wool," Isa. i. 15. "Seek the Lord," says the same holy prophet, "while He may be found; call upon Him while He is near. Let the wicked man forsake his way, and the unjust man his thoughts, and let him return to the Lord, and He will have mercy upon him; and to our God, for He is bountiful to forgive," Isa. lv. 6. And no wonder that this conversion should be so strictly enjoined; for how can we expect that God should be reconciled with us, if we still continue to offend Him? This is what we ourselves would not do to one that injures us. Hence we find that all true penitents were remarkable for their great change of life- David, St Paul, St Mary Magdalene, Zachaeus, and others.

Q. 12. But considering the weakness of human nature, the strength of evil habits, and the violence of temptation, how is it possible for one to be thus thoroughly changed all at once? Such a perfect change is the work of years?

A. This perfect conversion to God is no doubt the effect of His grace more than the work of man; and Almighty God has not failed to give the world examples of the power of His grace by working all at once a perfect conversion of the whole man, as in the case of the penitents last mentioned. But this is not the ordinary course of His Divine Providence. A change of heart, a firm and determined resolution of the will never more to offend God, is absolutely and essentially required in true repentance. This resolution, though it greatly fortifies the superior will against all passions, evil habits, and temptations, does not entirely and at once destroy them, and therefore does not give the sinner an absolute security against all relapses into sin, which indeed he can never have in this life; but this resolution of amendment, if it be sincere, must work an effectual change, at least in the following particulars: (1.) In avoiding with the utmost care all dangerous occasions of sin; for if he expose himself to the danger, this clearly shows he has no sincere resolution to avoid the sin, seeing the Word of God assures us that "He that loves the danger shall perish in it." (2.) In being most attentive to resist all temptations, especially at the beginning; for if he willingly entertain and dally with the temptation, it is evident that his horror for the sin is not what it ought to be. (3.) In using the proper remedies, especially such as are prescribed by his spiritual director, for subduing his passions and destroying his evil habits; because if he be sincere in desiring the end, he must be assiduous in using the means. (4.) In being most fervent in the duties of prayer, spiritual reading, assisting at Mass, frequenting worthily the sacraments, and the like, as these are the most assured helps to avoid sin, and fortify the soul against it. When a penitent sinner is assiduous in these particulars, his conversion is real, and if he persevere in his efforts, he will avoid falling back into his sins, and in time obtain a perfect victory over them; but if he be negligent in these things, and take little or no more care to avoid sin than he did before, his conversion is unreal, and by no means such as will find favour with God.

Section III: Of Doing Penance For Sin

Q. 13. What is meant by doing penance for sin?

A. The voluntary punishing of ourselves in order to satisfy the justice of God for the offences committed against Him.

Q. 14. Does sin of its own nature require to be punished, or is punishment inflicted only as a warning to others, and for the correction of the guilty themselves?

A. Some people of free-thinking principles in these modern times seem to suppose that sin in itself requires little or no punishment, and that the principal, if not the only, design of punishing is to correct the guilty, and to act as a warning to others. But the whole conduct of the Divine Providence, as well as the feelings of our own heart, manifestly show that sin, of its own nature, essentially requires to be punished, and that wherever the guilt of sin is found, the justice of God acquires a full and perfect right to punish the offender. For (i.) When great numbers of the angels fell into sin, the justice of God pursued them with immediate punishment, and condemned them to hell-fire, which was prepared for that purpose. This surely was not for their correction, but for their eternal destruction; neither was it as a warning to others, for there were no others to be warned by it, the good angels by their allegiance being then confirmed in eternal happiness. So severe a punishment, from a God of infinite goodness, clearly shows that the guilt of their crime most justly and necessarily required it. (2.) The punishment inflicted on all mankind for the sin of our first parents, in being deprived of original justice, shows the same truth beyond reply. This punishment was not for the correction, but for the destruction of the whole race of Adam, which would have effectually followed had not the goodness of God provided a remedy; neither was it for warning, for there were no others to be warned by it, all were already involved. (3.) The eternal torments of hell, inflicted upon all impenitent sinners, no less clearly show the same thing. (4.) The Holy Scripture everywhere speaks of the punishment inflicted by God on sinners as being what their sins necessarily deserve from God's justice, without the smallest hint of its being sent for correction or warning, though this, no doubt, is also commonly intended in the punishments of this life. Nay, in some places it is said that certain more grievous sins cry to heaven for vengeance, and that justice absolutely demands that they should be punished. Correction and warning, therefore, are accessary causes of punishment; but the essential source of punishment is the malignity and guilt of sin, which necessarily deserve and demand it; and justice absolutely requires this satisfaction by the punishment of the guilty. (5.) As God is a being of infinite justice, it is impossible He should always and on every occasion punish sin even with temporal punishments, much less with eternal torments, if sin of its own nature did not justly require it; because in numberless instances, especially in the eternal punishment, His doing so could neither serve for correction nor warning; and as He is a being of infinite goodness, it is impossible He should take pleasure in the sufferings of His creatures. In the order of justice, then, sin absolutely requires punishment, and we find it frequently declared in Scripture that it is the fixed rule of God's justice to render to every one according to his works - rewards for doing good, and punishment for sin; and sin is every where held forth as the primary cause of all our sufferings, both in this life and in the next.

Q. 15. Is it a rule of God's justice never to let sin go unpunished?

A. It is, as appears from the following declarations of Holy writ: "I feared all my works," says Job, "knowing that Thou didst not spare the offender," Job, ix. 28. And again, "Far from God be wickedness, and iniquity from the Almighty; for He will render to a man his work, and according to the ways of every one He will reward him," Job, xxxiv. 10. "God hath spoken once; these two things have I heard, that power belongeth to God, and mercy to thee, O Lord! for Thou wilt render to every man according to his works," Ps. lxi. 12. "I am the Lord," says the great God Himself, "that search the heart and prove the reins; Who give to every one according to his way, and according to the fruit of his devices," Jer. xvii. 10. "For God is great in counsel, and incomprehensible in thought, Whose eyes are open upon all the ways of the children of Adam, to render unto every one according to his ways, and according to the fruit of his devices," Jer. xxxii. 19. Christ Himself assures us that "the Son of Man shall come in the glory of His Father with His angels, and then He will render to every man according to his work," Mat. xvi. 27. "For we must all appear before the judgment - seat of Christ, that every one may receive the proper things of the body, according as he hath done, whether it be good or evil," 2 Cor. v. 10. And St Paul, addressing himself in particular to sinners on this subject, says, "According to thy hardness and impenitent heart, thou treasurest up to thyself wrath against the day of wrath, and revelation of the just judgments of God, Who will render to every man according to his works. To them, indeed, who according to patience in good works seek glory and honour, and interruption, (He will render) eternal life; but to them that are contentious, and who obey not the truth, but give credit to iniquity, wrath and indignation. Tribulation and anguish upon every soul of man that worketh evil,... but glory, honour, and peace to every one that worketh good," Rom. ii. 5.

Q. 16. How does it appear that the sufferings of this life are in punishment of sin?

A. This also is taught everywhere throughout the Holy Scripture: thus "justice exalteth a nation, but sin maketh nations miserable," Prov. xiv. 34 ; and when our Saviour cured the sick man at the pool of Bethsaida, He said to Him, "Behold thou art made whole; sin no more, lest some worse thing happen to thee," John, v. 14. So also the wise man, speaking of the miseries of this life, says, "Such things happen to all flesh, from man even to beast, and upon sinners are sevenfold more. Moreover, death and bloodshed, strife and sword, oppressions, famine, and affliction, and scourges, all these things are created for the wicked," Ecclus. xl. 8. Besides, we find that all the striking instances of God's justice, in sending extraordinary sufferings upon men, are declared in Scripture to be the just fruits of their sin - such as the Deluge, the destruction of Sodom, the plague, famine, and war so often sent upon His people, untimely death of individuals, loss of children, and the like; and lastly, that God often threatens sinners with all these and other temporal miseries in punishment of their sins. Not that the punishing of sin is the only reason why God sends these temporal miseries upon His creatures: in this life mercy is always mixed with justice; and, for the most part, He has in view the correction, improvement, and warning of souls; but sin is the radical source from which all miseries flow.

Q. 17. What do we learn from these truths?

A. We learn (1.) That it is a fixed rule of God's justice that every sin must be punished; (2.) That the final punishment of sin will be in the next world; (3.) That the punishments inflicted on sin in this life are always united with designs of mercy, either as a warning to others or to move the sinner himself to repentance.

Q. 18. Whence arises the obligation of punishing ourselves for our sins? and how comes this to be a part of true repentance?

A. By the appointment and express command of God, Who requires our doing penance, or at least our sincere will to do so, as a necessary part of true repentance, and a condition of obtaining pardon.

Q. 19. How does this appear from Holy Scripture?

A. From the following testimonies: (1.) "Gird yourselves with hair-cloth, lament and howl, for the fierce anger of the Lord is not turned away from us;... wash thy heart from wickedness, O Jerusalem! that thou mayest be saved," Jer. iv. 8 , 14. "Gird thyself with sackcloth, O daughter of my people! and sprinkle thee with ashes: make thee mourning as for an only son, a bitter lamentation," Jer. vi. 26. "Be converted, and do penance for all your iniquities, and iniquity shall not be your ruin," Ezek. xviii. 30. "Now therefore, saith the Lord, be converted to Me with all your heart, in fasting, and in weeping, and in mourning," Joel, ii. 12. In which texts we see that performing penitential works is joined with the other conditions of true repentance, as necessary to avert the anger of God, and find mercy with Him. (2.) When the people went out to St John the Baptist to be baptised by him, he said, "Ye offspring of vipers, who hath shown you to flee from the wrath to come? "And immediately teaching them the means to avoid this wrath, he adds, "Bring forth, therefore, fruits worthy of penance," Luke, iii. 7. St

Paul also declares that the great object of his preaching to the Jews was, "that they should do penance, and turn to God, doing works worthy of penance,'" Acts, xxvi. 20. Now by doing works worthy of penance cannot be meant 'not committing sin,' for this is not doing any work at all, but only abstaining from evil work; neither can it mean doing "-works of virtue and piety" as such, for to this we are obliged, whether we have ever sinned or not. By "works or fruits worthy of penance" then, can only be meant works of piety and virtue performed in a penitential spirit, with a view of punishing ourselves for past sins, and good works, especially those most contrary to our self-love, offered up with the same intention. Hence when the people asked the Baptist, "What then shall we do?" he recommended to them one of the principal penitential works, alms-giving, and mercy towards others: "He that hath two coats, let him give to him that hath none; and he that hath meat, let him do in like manner," Luke, iii. 11.

(3.) Our blessed Saviour, when He entered upon His public life, began to "preach and to say, Do penance, for the kingdom of heaven is at hand," Mat. iv. 17. And to show the necessity of doing so, He says in another place, "Except ye do penance, you shall all likewise perish," Luke, xiii. 5. In like manner when the Jews who were converted at St Peter's first sermon asked, "Men and Brethren, what shall we do?" though the Scripture expressly observes that "they had compunction in their hearts," yet St Peter answered, "Do penance, and be baptised for the remission of your sins," Acts, ii. 37 , 38. Which shows that compunction or sorrow of the heart alone is not sufficient, and that doing penance is also required.

St Paul also, in his famous sermon to the great council of Athens, says, "God now declareth to men that all should everywhere do penance," Acts, xvii. 30. It is true that in these texts the Protestant bibles, instead of Do penance, translate it repent, meaning by that the sorrow of the heart alone, without any outward penitential works. But we must observe that the Christian world, in all former ages, understood these passages as commanding the doing penance; so that this translation is a novelty: besides, it is manifest from other parts of Scripture that the repentance which Christ requires is a sorrow of the heart, accompanied with penitential works painful to self-love. Thus Christ Himself condemns the people of Corazaim and Bethsaida for not "doing penance, sitting in sackcloth and ashes," after the works He had done among them, as the people of Tyre and Sidon would have done had they received the like favours , Luke, x. 13. And He lays it down as an essential condition of our belonging to Him that we "deny ourselves, and take up our cross and follow Him," Mat. xvi. 24. Finally, that doing penance is the true sense of the above texts appears beyond all contradiction from the examples of both saints and sinners who are recorded in Scripture to have been most assiduous in performing that duty.

Q. 20. What examples have we of this in Scripture?

A. St Paul, as we have just seen, affirmed in his sermon at Athens that "God now declareth to men that all should everywhere do penance," where, by saying all and everywhere, he shows that none are excepted - the just as well as sinners being obliged to it; sinners, as a necessary part of that repentance by which they move God to mercy, and avert His just anger; and the just, as a satisfaction to God for their former offences, which His mercy has already pardoned; those who have sinned, in punishment of their past sins; and those who have lived in innocence, as the best preservative of that treasure, and the most effectual means to obtain great favours from God. Hence we find the most striking examples of each in Scripture. (i.) Of sinners: of Achab, King of Israel, it is said, "there was not such another as Achab, who was sold to do evil in the sight of the Lord," 3 Kings, xxi. 25 ; therefore God at last sent the prophet Elias to him, to denounce the dreadful punishments which He had decreed to send upon him: "And when Achab had heard these words, he rent his garments, and put hair-cloth upon his flesh, and fasted, and slept in sack-cloth, and walked with his head cast down." See here the penitential life he led, which so moved the compassion and mercy of the Almighty that He said to Elias, with a kind of surprise and pleasure, "Hast thou not seen Achab humbled before Me? therefore because he has humbled himself for My sake, I will not bring the evil in his days," 3 Kings, xxi. 27 -29.

King Manasses, in punishment of his sins, Avas overcome by the Babylonians, and they "took him and carried him bound with fetters and chains to Babylon. And after that he was in distress, he prayed to the Lord his God, and did penance exceedingly before the God of his Fathers; and he entreated Him and besought Him earnestly; and He heard his prayer, and brought him again to Jerusalem into his kingdom," 2 Chron. xxxiii. II. The wickedness of the people of Ninive was so great that God was resolved to destroy it, and He sent His prophet Jonas to preach, "Yet forty days, and Ninive shall be destroyed. And the men of Ninive proclaimed a fast, and put on sackcloth, from the greatest to the least;... and the king cast away his robe from him, and was clothed in sackcloth, and sat in ashes;... and God saw their works, that they were turned from their evil way; and God had mercy with regard to the evil which He had said that He would do to them, and He did it not,"Jonas, iii. 4. From this example of the Ninivites our Saviour takes occasion to inculcate the necessity of doing penance in the strongest terms: "The men of Ninive," says He, "shall rise in judgment with this generation, and shall condemn it; because they did penance at the preaching of Jonas; and, behold, a greater than Jonas is here," Mat. xii. 41. (2.) Of saints and holy people who had been sinners. David, after his repentance for his unhappy fall, even though he knew his sin was pardoned, led a most penitential life, which he thus describes: "I am poor and needy, and my heart is troubled within me. I am taken away like the shadow when it declineth; and I am shaken off as locusts: my knees are weakened through fasting," Ps. cviii. 22. "My bones are grown dry like fuel for the fire; I am smitten as grass, and my heart is withered, because I forgot to eat my bread; through the voice of my groaning my bone hath cleaved to my flesh.... I have watched, and am become as a sparrow, all alone on the house-top,... for I did eat ashes like bread, and mingled my drink with weeping; because of His anger and indignation," Ps. ci. 4. St Paul had been a persecutor of the Church of Christ; but when he was perfectly reconciled to Christ, and made an apostle, his constant preaching to the Jews was the necessity of doing penance. Now to understand that the penance he preached was not a mere sorrow of the heart alone, but such a sorrow as manifested itself by doing works worthy of penance, see his own example: though he was a chosen vessel, an apostle, a friend of Christ, that had been taken up to the third heaven, yet he says, "I chastise my body, and bring it into subjection; lest perhaps, when I have preached to others, I myself should become a castaway," i Cor. ix. 27. St Paul! the chosen vessel! is afraid of losing his soul! and, as a necessary means to prevent that, "chastises his body, and brings it into subjection!" Can anything more incontestably show the necessity of doing penance? and that a repentance which brought forth such fruits of penance was the repentance so constantly inculcated by this apostle?

(3.) Of those who had preserved their innocence, at least, from mortal sin. Job, an upright man, and one who feared God and avoided evil, yet says of himself, "I have spoken unwisely,... therefore I reprehended myself, and do penance in dust and ashes," Job, xlii. 3 , 6. Judith, a holy woman, who was "greatly renowned among all because she feared the Lord very much, neither was there any one that spoke an ill word of her "(Judith, viii. 8), yet, after her husband's death, led a most penitential life, for she made herself a private chamber in the upper part of her house in which she abode, shut up with her maids; and she wore hair-cloth upon her loins, and fasted all the days of her life, except the Sabbaths and new moons, and the feasts of the house of Israel," ver. 5. Daniel, a most holy youth, and a prophet, thus describes his penitential works: "I set my face to the Lord my God, to pray and make supplication, with fasting and sackcloth and ashes," Dan. ix. 3 ; and again, "In those days, I Daniel mourned the days of three weeks, I ate no pleasant bread, and neither flesh nor wine entered into my mouth, neither was I anointed with ointment till the days of three weeks were accomplished," Dan. X. 2. St John the Baptist, though sanctified in his mother's womb, led a most austere and penitential life in the wilderness. And Anna, the prophetess, is praised in Scripture because she departed not from the temple, by fastings and prayers serving night and day," Luke, ii. 37. Finally, we frequently read in the Acts and Epistles of the apostles of their fastings and watchings. Bestow what could induce so many, both saints and sinners, to employ themselves in works so distasteful to flesh and blood, so opposed to self-love and every natural inclination? What could influence them but the conviction that all sin must be punished, and that God requires of penitents, as a part of true repentance, that they should co-operate with the Divine justice in punishing themselves?

Q. 21. But is it not injurious to the infinite satisfaction paid by Jesus Christ to the Divine justice for our sins to say that we are still obliged to do penance for them? are not His sufferings more than sufficient to satisfy for the whole world?

A. To this it is replied, (1.) That Jesus Christ Himself, and His holy apostle St Paul, did not think it injurious to the satisfaction paid by Him for our sins, when they so strongly inculcated the necessity of our doing penance in their preachings, and when St Paul confirmed it by his example. (2.) Jesus Christ not only suffered in the flesh for our sins, but He was also oppressed in the garden with the most dreadful sorrow that ever entered into the heart of man, on seeing the sins of the whole world laid upon Himself, from the clear knowledge He had of their enormity, and the greatness of the offence done to God by them. He also shed tears on our account, and poured forth most fervent prayers to obtain mercy for us. Now the sorrow, tears, and prayers of Jesus Christ were of no less infinite value than His bodily sufferings, and sufficient to cancel the sins of ten thousand worlds. Shall we say, therefore, that no son-ow, tears, nor prayers are required from us? or that it is injurious to the infinite merits of His sorrow and tears, and of the prayers which He offered up for our sins, to believe that we are still obliged to be sorrowful, to weep, and to pray? (3.) The sorrow, tears, prayers, and sufferings of Christ are doubtless of infinite merit before His Eternal Father, and the most superabundant satisfaction to the Divine justice for the sins of men; but to be available to us, they must be applied to our souls, and this is done only when we perform the conditions Christ demands; for Christ "is become the cause of eternal salvation to all that obey Him," Heb. v. 9 , and to none else; for those "who obey not the Gospel of our Lord Jesus Christ shall suffer eternal punishment in destruction," 2 Thes. i. 8. Now as all agree that, notwithstanding the sufferings of Christ, we are still strictly obliged to be sorrowful, and to pray for our sins, as a condition required for applying His merits to our souls, and that we do so without the least injury to His sorrow and prayers, so the above testimonies and examples of Holy Writ clearly prove that, notwithstanding all His sufferings for our sins, we are still strictly obliged, by His command, to suffer for them, by punishing ourselves, as a condition required for applying the merits of His sufferings to our souls, and that without the least prejudice to the infinite satisfaction paid by Him. But (4.) if we consider the matter properly, we shall see that, instead of injuring the satisfaction of Christ, we highly honour it by doing penance. For suppose a man owing a debt which he is utterly unable to discharge, and another to become his security, would it not be the height of ingratitude if on that account he cast off all responsibility? Or would he not be bound in gratitude and justice to do his utmost to pay at least as far as he was able? This is our case, and the application obvious, especially as we have seen that our Divine Surety expressly requires this of us. And, indeed, if Jesus Christ, the innocent, the Holy Lamb of God, suffered so much for the sins of others, does not every motive of gratitude and justice demand that guilty sinners should themselves suffer something? Hence we find that eternal life is promised only on condition that we suffer with our innocent Surety; we are "heirs, indeed, of God, and joint heirs with Christ; yet so if we suffer with Him, that we may be also glorified with Him," Rom. viii. 17. "A faithful saying; for if we be dead with Him, we shall also live with Him; if we suffer, we shall also reign with Him," 2 Tim. ii. 11. And St Peter assures us that "Christ also suffered for us, leaving us an example that we should follow His steps," i Pet. ii. 21 ; which manifestly shows that, among the many other views Christ had in suffering, one expressly was to encourage us by his example to follow His steps, by voluntary sufferings for our sins. Therefore, by doing penance for our sins, we truly honour the sufferings of Christ, as He requires we should honour them; and hence the Scripture says, "The dead that are in hell, whose spirit is taken away from their bowels, shall not give glory and justice to the Lord; but the soul which is sorrowful for the greatness of the evil she hath done, and goeth bowed down and feeble, and the eyes that fail, and the hungry soul, giveth glory and justice to Thee, O Lord," Baruch, ii. 17.

Q. 22. If it be so absolutely necessary to do penance for our sins, and to imitate the sufferings of Jesus Christ, who shall be saved? for do we not see wickedness and vice everywhere reign, and penitential works in a manner banished from among us? Does not self-love universally prevail, and every one study only his own interest, ease, pleasure, and convenience? Nay, have not the generality of mankind a settled aversion to penance? And do not even those who acknowledge and believe the obligation of it in theory commonly seek to avoid it in practice?

A. In answer to all this, it can only be said that these too true observations are the most convincing proof of that dreadful sentence of Jesus Christ, that "many are called, but few are chosen," and that "many walk in the broad road that leads to destruction, and few in the narrow path that leads to eternal life."

Q. 23. What advantage, then, have we from the infinite satisfaction paid by Jesus Christ for our sins if we be still obliged to do penance for them?

A. Immense and admirable are the advantages we receive from the satisfaction of Christ: for (1.) It is through the merits of His sufferings alone that any penitential works we do can be acceptable to God; for if our penitential works were separated from the merits of Christ, they would be of no value before God, nor of any profit to our souls; but being united to the merits of Christ, they acquire a supernatural value and dignity, which makes them available to our salvation; so that the satisfaction paid by Christ sanctifies our sufferings, gives them a supernatural lustre, and raises them to a great value before God, through which they are accepted by the Divine justice as a satisfaction on our part for our sins; just as the sorrow, tears, and prayers of Christ sanctify these actions in us, and make them agreeable to God; without His sufferings this could never possibly have been the case, nor could we have found any acceptance with God, though we had suffered all the torments of hell for eternity. (2.) It is the satisfaction of Christ alone that delivers us from the eternal punishment due to our sins, changing it into the small temporal punishment which he demands from us; for without Him nothing we ever could do or suffer, could have delivered us from these never-ending torments. (3.) In the sacrament of baptism, Almighty God, with the most unbounded mercy, applies the merits of Christ to our souls without restriction, and accepts of His satisfaction in its full extent, so as to deliver us at once from all our sins, both original and actual, and from the punishment due to them, adopts us as His children, and gives us a full right and title to His eternal kingdom. So that whatever sins a person may have committed before baptism, yet if, after receiving that sacrament worthily, he should immediately die, nothing could hinder him from the immediate possession of eternal bliss. Here the Divine justice gives up all its claim against the offender himself - accepting the satisfaction of Christ, so fully applied for that purpose; here the infinite merits of Christ have their full effect, and the mercy of God appears in all its lustre.

Q. 24. Why does not God treat sinners in the same manner when they repent of the sins committed after baptism?

A. It does not belong to us to inquire into the reasons of the Divine conduct. We should be satisfied with, and adore what He has done; and all the testimonies which we have seen above prove, beyond reply, that it is His will to treat us in a different manner for the sins we Commit after baptism than for those before it. Yet a little reflection will show us that His conduct in this is most reasonable, and that both justice and mercy concur to require it. For, with regard to justice, we must observe that when we are first received into His favour by baptism, for the sake, and in honour of the infinite merits of Jesus Christ, He treats us with unlimited mercy. Justice, with regard to the offender, seems to forego its own rights; all that He requires of us, to entitle us to such amazing mercy, is to believe in Jesus Christ, and be sorry for having offended Him, with a solemn promise to be faithful for the future; and even this faith, repentance, and promise Pie does not actually require when we are baptised in infancy, but receives the promise made in our name. Now, if notwithstanding all this goodness we afterwards return to sin, breaking this solemn vow, this implies such contempt of God, and such unparalleled ingratitude, that in all justice the sinner deserves the most rigorous punishment; and it would be unreasonable, and in some degree unjust, to admit him again into the possession of the same glorious privileges upon the same terms as before; therefore the Divine justice here resumes its rights against the sinner, and absolutely requires he should now suffer in his own person. Even among ourselves this is what common sense dictates. On receiving a first injury, we cheerfully forgive our enemy, are reconciled to him, and do him good offices, without requiring other satisfaction than his asking pardon and promising amendment; yet, if this person should repeat the same or greater injuries, would we again receive him into our friendship on the same terms? Hence the great council of Trent says, "The fruits of the sacrament of penance are different from those of baptism; for by baptism we put on Christ, and become in Him altogether a new creature, receiving the full and entire remission of all our sins; but (if we lose this happy state by sin) we can by no means acquire the same newness and integrity by the sacrament of penance, without great weeping and labours upon our part, the Divine justice so requiring it." - Sess. xiv. cap. 2.

Q. 25. But does not this seem to exclude mercy entirely?

A. By no means • the mercy of_God even here appears in the strongest light. For, considering the dreadful evil of sin when committed after baptism, a sinner, by committing it, forfeits all title to mercy, and God could, without injustice, condemn him to eternal punishment, treating him with the same rigour of justice with which He treated the fallen angels. It is therefore the effect of infinite mercy in God to receive us again into favour on any terms; and it is through the infinite merits of Christ alone that He is moved to do so. In baptism He suspends His justice, and applies to us only the infinite effects of mercy; but when after so much goodness we return to sin, and by so doing render ourselves altogether unworthy of mercy. He alters His conduct towards us; He is still willing, through the merits of Christ, to receive us into favour, but upon condition that we endeavour to satisfy His justice. He treated the fallen angels with the most rigorous justice, without mercy. In baptism He treats us with unbounded mercy, without regard to justice; but in being reconciled to us for sins committed after baptism, He positively requires that justice and mercy should no more be separated, but go together. Through the merits of Christ, on our sincere repentance. He forgives us our sins, and the eternal punishment which they deserve; but He absolutely demands that, by penitential works, we punish ourselves for our ingratitude. So that the effect of mercy here is not to free us entirely from punishment, as in baptism, but to change the eternal into a temporal punishment which we are able to perform, and the performance of which is attended with the greatest advantage to the soul. What still further shows that it is the greatest mercy to require us to do penance is this, that "it is a fearful thing to fall into the hands of the living God," Heb. x. 31 , even in regard to temporal punishments, as appears from the many examples in Scripture of the severity with which His justice punishes sinners in this life, even for sins which to us would seem small. Almighty God, in commanding us to do penance, remits, in a manner, His own right to punish us, accepting small sacrifices on our part, instead of much more severe chastisements which we would have to suffer, if they were inflicted by His Divine justice. What were all the penances done by Achab and the Ninivites compared to what God had decreed to inflict upon them? and yet because they punished themselves by these small afflictions He remitted the greater. Besides, the great design of the Divine mercy in pardoning sinners is doubtless to procure their salvation. Now, mere pardoning past sins would not effectually procure this, if proper care were not taken to prevent the sinner from falling into sin again. Seeing, therefore, that all the unmerited mercies bestowed on him in baptism were not sufficient for this purpose, a more severe method is required to secure his perseverance - that of doing penance, the most powerful means to fortify him against relapse.

Q. 26. What are the advantages that doing penance brings to the soul?

A. (1.) It makes us sensible of the grievousness of our sins. Our great misfortune is, that we have not a just idea of sin; we think too lightly of it; and if we had nothing to suffer for it in this world, we would be apt to lose all horror of it, and consequently would take no care to avoid it; but when we see that Almighty God absolutely requires that we should do penance for sin, this shows us that there is something more dreadful in sin than we had imagined. This reminds us of what we have to expect in the next life, since a good and just God requires sin to be so strictly punished here, and consequently renders us more cautious and careful to avoid it. (2.) The very pain of doing penitential works is a great check to our proneness to sin, and experience teaches that those who diligently punish themselves for their faults find in this a powerful help to amendment. (3.) Many of the penitential works strike directly at the very root of our sins, and extirpate the inordinate affections and vicious inclinations from whence our sins proceed. (4.) Many of them also tend to destroy the bad habits of sin which we have contracted, by obliging us to practise the contrary virtues. (5.) They powerfully appease the wrath of God enkindled by our sins, proving the fervour and sincerity of our repentance; they move Him to be liberal in His graces to us, that we may be enabled effectually to preserve our innocence, and advance in solid virtue.

Q. 27. What is the conclusion to be drawn from all these truths?

A. It is comprehended in these particulars: (1.) That the doing penance for our sins is a necessary part of true repentance. (2.) That by sin we contract a heavy debt of punishment, both temporal and eternal, due to the Divine justice. (3.) That our repentance for sin is not sincere, neither will it obtain the remission of the guilt of sin, nor of the eternal punishment due to it, unless it be accompanied with a sincere will and resolution to discharge the debt of temporal punishment by doing penance. (4.) That therefore this debt of temporal punishment remains due, even though the guilt of sin and its eternal punishment be remitted. (5.) That as justice absolutely demands this debt from sinners, it must be paid, either by voluntary penance inflicted on ourselves, or by more severe sufferings sent by God, and received by us in a penitential spirit. (6.) That if a person should die in the grace of God, but before this debt be discharged, he will be thrown into the prison of purgatory, where he shall remain till he has paid the utmost farthing. (7.) That as no man can know the full amount of this debt, and is perhaps daily increasing it by venial sins and imperfections, it is therefore the greatest Christian wisdom to endeavour constantly to discharge some part of it, by leading a penitential life of daily mortification and self-denial, according to what our Saviour Himself enjoins, saying, "Be at agreement with thy adversary quickly, whilst thou art in the way with him, lest, perhaps, the adversary deliver thee to the judge, and the judge deliver thee to the officer, and thou be cast into prison. Amen, I say to thee, thou shalt not go from thence till thou pay the last farthing," Mat. v. 25. The present life is the way, the Divine justice our adversary, God the judge, purgatory the prison. And to the same purpose the Church of Christ, in one of her greatest and most respected general councils, declares, that "The whole life of a Christian ought to be a perpetual penance." - Council of Trent, Sess. xiv. on Extreme-unction, Introduct.

Section IV: On The Spirit Of Penance

Q. 28. What is meant by the spirit of penance?

A. The spirit of penance is that sincere sorrow and contrition for our sins the necessity of which we have seen above; it is that "sorrow, according to God, which worketh penance steadfast unto salvation," 2 Cor. vii. 10. The effects which this sorrow worketh in the soul arise from the various lights which it brings to the soul, in the view of which the sinner is excited to the exercise of those penitential works which contribute most powerfully to secure his eternal salvation. For (1.) The true spirit of penance shows the sinner the multitude and grievousness of his sins in their true colours, excites a horror and detestation of them, and a proper sense of his own demerits for being guilty of them, and renders him willing to undergo any sufferings as a just punishment. In this view the spirit of penance is a spirit of justice, condemning the criminal to condign punishment. (2.) It shows the sinner the greatness of the injury done to the God of heaven by sin, fills him with grief and sorrow for having so often and so grievously offended and dishonoured so good a God, excites in him a sincere desire of repairing the Divine honour to the best of his power, and for this purpose makes him cheerfully condemn himself to works of humiliation and penance. In this light the spirit of penance is a spirit of restitution and satisfaction, by which the honour of God, injured by sin, is repaired. (3.) It convinces the sinner that his unmortified passions and affections, besides being the declared enemies of God, are his own greatest enemies, having so often dragged him into sin and exposed him to the danger of eternal damnation; it therefore excites in his soul a just hatred against these his mortal enemies, by which he rigorously chastises his body and brings it into subjection, both as a just punishment for past offences and to prevent its betraying him again, lest he should at last become a castaway. So the spirit of penance is a spirit of hatred and revenge against our self-love in all its branches. (4.) It gives the sinner a just sense of all the sufferings of Jesus Christ, and of the infinite obligations we owe Him; shows him the base ingratitude of renewing these sufferings by sin, and excites in his soul a tender compassion and ardent love of Jesus Christ, a sincere sorrow for having been the guilty cause of so much torment to Him, and an earnest desire of resembling Him, and bearing the Cross along with Him; in consequence of this he cheerfully condemns himself to works of penance, that he may honour the sufferings, and follow the example of his beloved Master. In this view, the spirit of penance is a spirit of compassion and love of Jesus Christ, and of conformity to His holy example.

Q. 29. What are the signs by which we may know if we have the true spirit of penance?

A. "By their fruits ye shall know them." The surest signs that this holy spirit resides in the soul are the effects it produces. These we have in a great measure seen already, but they are minutely enumerated by St Paul in these words: "Behold this self-same thing, that you were made sorrowful according to God, how great carefulness doth it work in you; yea defence, yea indignation, yea fear, yea desire, yea zeal, yea revenge," 2 Cor. vii. II. (1.) Carefulness about the great concerns of salvation, convincing the sinner of the supreme importance of that great work, and of the vanity of all other pursuits, and therefore renders him careful and diligent to secure it. (2.) Defence - this carefulness is not an idle anxiety of mind, but an active principle, which makes us use all necessary means for defending our soul against all its enemies, by prayer, spiritual reading, frequenting the holy sacraments, and other such helps to salvation. (3.) Indignation and hatred against sin, and all the dangerous occasions of sin, which the spirit of penance makes us fly from and avoid, though otherwise as useful or dear to us as a hand or an eye. (4.) Fear of the judgment of God and of hell-fire, and especially the fear of offending again so good a God, which is the beginning of true wisdom, and makes us "work out our salvation with fear and trembling." (5.) Desire of flying as far from sin as possible, and of daily advancing our soul in the union and love of God, giving "us a hunger and thirst after justice." (6.) Zeal for the glory of God, and for destroying all His and our enemies, our own passions, by self-denial and mortification; and for promoting His honour to the utmost of our power, considering our infinite obligations to His goodness. (7.) Revenge vindicating the rights of the Divine justice, by cheerfully punishing ourselves for past sins. Happy those in whom these blessed fruits of the true spirit of penance are found!

Q. 30. What are the means by which we may obtain the spirit of penance?

A. (1.) The spirit of penance is the gift of God, as our holy faith teaches; for when St Peter gave an account to the brethren of the conversion of the Gentiles, in the person of Cornelius and his friends, "they glorified God, saying, God then hath also to the Gentiles given repentance unto life," Acts, xi. 18. And St Paul exhorts Timothy, "with modesty to admonish them that resist the truth, if peradventure God may give them repentance to know the truth," 2 Tim. ii. 25. Nay, it is one of the most necessary gifts we can receive from God, as without it there is no salvation for sinners. Now the Scripture assures us that "our heavenly Father will readily give His Holy Spirit to them that ask it," Luke, xi. 13. Consequently the first and principal means to obtain the holy spirit of penance is humble and fervent prayer. This the holy servants of God well knowing were assiduous in their prayers for this purpose: "Convert, me, O Lord, and I shall be converted," saith Jeremiah, "for Thou art my God," Jer. xxxi. 18 ; and David, "Convert us, O Lord! and we shall be converted; show Thy face, and we shall be saved," Ps. lxxix. 4 , where this prayer is frequently repeated. (2.) We must avoid and fly from all those things which would hinder the spirit of penance from coming to our souls - such as idle company, dissipating diversions, plays, dancing, jesting, profane reading, vain apparel, &:c. All which things dissipate the heart, fill the mind with a world of idle ideas, carry off the thoughts, are destructive of the spirit of penance, and therefore particularly unbecoming, and unworthy to be thought of in penitential times. (3.) We must apply ourselves seriously to the consideration and practice of those things which promote and excite truly penitential dispositions in the soul; such as serious meditation on the four last things, and the great truths of eternity, the practice of self-denial and mortification, with works of char-ity and mercy; for experience shows that as those who live pleasant lives and pamper the body never acquire sentiments of penance, so those who practise the works of penance soon obtain the true spirit of it. (4.) Serious and frequent meditation on the great evils of sin contributes in a particular manner to excite the spirit of penance in the soul, giving us a just sense of the heinous evil of sin, of the greatness of the injury done by it to God, and of its dreadful consequences to ourselves. The want of this knowledge, or the failing to reflect upon it, is one of the principal causes why we fall so easily into the misery of sin.

Section V: Of The Works Of Penance

Q. 31. What is understood by works of penance?

A. Works of penance are any kind of punishment which the sinner willingly undergoes, in order to satisfy for sin; and as the nature of punishment requires that it be painful and afflicting to self-love, so anything whatsoever that is naturally painful and afflicting to us, and which we willingly undergo with the view of satisfying for our sins, is a penitential work.

Q. 32. Why do you say that is naturally painful and afflicting to us?

A. Penance or punishment is what naturally gives pain; if it gave no pain it would be no punishment. Now it may sometimes happen that a penitential work which naturally gives pain, yet in certain circumstances may give none to a person when he uses it; but it does not cease on that account to be a penitential work even to him. Thus some find no difficulty in abstaining from flesh-meat; others experience little or no pain in fasting; yet if these people, when obedience requires it, perform these works out of a penitential spirit, to them they are truly penitential works. In like manner a person may be so far advanced in the love of God, and in the virtue of holy mortification, as to have, in a great measure, conquered the natural inclinations of flesh and blood, and even to find pleasure in those things which are naturally painful; yet this, so far from lessening the value of the penitential works of that person, greatly increases it, and shows the ardour of his love to God, from which they proceed.

Q. 33. Why do you say, with a view of doing penance?

A. Because, though the work be ever so painful, yet, if we undergo it without the intention of doing penance, it will be no penance at all; and, if done with any evil view, will even be displeasing to God: as our Saviour expressly declares of the three great penitential works of fasting, alms-giving, and prayer, if they be done with the view of gaining "praise from men," Mat.

vi. The reason is, because in order to be a penitential work it must proceed from the spirit of penance. This is the root, the principal part of penance, without which the exterior works signify nothing. And God Almighty sets such a value upon this internal disposition, that though the external work be small, yet if it proceed from, and be accompanied with, a truly penitential spirit, it becomes of great value before Him. What can be easier than to give a cup of cold water to a thirsty person? yet Christ Himself declares that, if done for His sake, it shall not lose its reward. In like manner, what can be a smaller penitential work than to deprive one's self of a cup of water? Yet it is recorded in sacred writ as a very great action of David, that when three of his valiant men, at the risk of their lives, brought him water from a cistern, which he had taken a longing for, "he would not drink, but offered it to the Lord," 2 Kings (Sam.) xxiii. 16. This ought to be a comfort to those who are not able to do great things: let them do the little they can, with a truly penitential spirit, and it will be accepted.

Q. 34. Into how many classes are penitential works divided?

A. Into three classes, (1.) Those which we are commanded to undergo, under pain of sin, if we disobey. (2.) Those which are left to our own free choice, according to our particular wants, without any other command than the general one of doing penance for sin; and (3.) Those which we are forced to undergo by the order of Providence, whether we will or not; but where it is left to ourselves to make the proper penitential use of them.

Q. 35. What are the penitential works which we are commanded to undergo, under pain of sin if we disobey?

A. Chiefly these following: - (1.) The confession of our sins in the sacrament of penance. This is a great penance and humiliation to our corrupt nature and to self-love; but it is imposed upon us by Almighty God, in place of that shame and confusion which will overwhelm sinners at the last day, continue for all eternity, and prove one of the greatest punishments of sin in the next life. Now, as the penitential works of this life are laid upon us by the justice and mercy of God, in exchange for those of eternity, therefore He has been pleased to appoint the momentary shame and confusion of confessing our sins here to one man like ourselves, in exchange for that eternal confusion which we must otherwise undergo in the next life. Hence this is a penance laid by God Himself upon all, without exception, who have offended Him by mortal sin; and it is commanded with such strictness, that the guilt of sin will not be washed away from our souls unless it be properly complied with. (2.) All those penitential works which our pastor enjoins us in the sacrament of penitence. This also is a penance which we are obliged to perform by the express command of God; and it is without doubt one of the most profitable for our souls; because, being a part of the sacrament, it is sanctified by the grace annexed, and therefore raised to a much higher value in the sight of God than other penitential works, though perhaps more painful, which we do of our own choice. It has also the merit of obedience, which gives it still a greater merit. Now, the obligation we are under of performing this sacramental penance is shown by the works of our Saviour to the pastors of His Church, in the persons of the apostles, when He said, "Whatsoever you shall bind on earth shall be bound in heaven, and whatsoever you shall loose on earth shall be loosed in heaven," Mat. xvi. 19. For, as by the latter words. He assures us that when our pastor looses us from our sins here on earth, we are loosed from them in heaven; so by the former He equally declares that when we are bound on earth by them to perform penance, this obligation is ratified in heaven; for the general term whatsoever includes all. But we must not imagine that, when we have faithfully performed our sacramental penance, we have thereby discharged all we owe to the Divine justice. Alas! what proportion is there between the penances commonly enjoined in the sacrament and the sins by which we have offended God? In ancient times the penances imposed on sinners were exceedingly severe, and often continued for years; but as the love of God waxed cold, the Church was obliged to moderate this discipline, lest through weakness and tepidity Christians should fail to perform them. At present the penances imposed in the sacrament are small, much being left to the penitent's own devotion; and if he is deficient, it must be exacted by God Himself, either here or hereafter. (3.) The public fasts commanded by the Church. These also we are obliged, by the command of God, faith fully to observe; and if we do so with a truly penitential spirit, they will prove exceedingly useful in discharging the debt we owe to the Divine justice, especially as by them we also partake of what the whole Church is doing at the same time.

Q. 36. What are those works of penance which are left to our own choice?

A, They are divided into three classes, and consist in punishing ourselves either in our external senses, or in the passions and affections of the mind and heart, or in the flesh. The two first are seldom attended with any danger from excess, and in them consists the exercise of that self-denial and mortification of the will so much recommended in the Gospel, and so strictly required by Jesus Christ from His followers; therefore, in practising them, we are sure of doing what is most agreeable to God. The third class contains bodily mortifications, by which, with St Paul, we "chastise the body, and bring it into subjection;" but as the indiscreet use of these may be attended with consequences dangerous to health, proper caution and advice ought to be taken in practising them. The practice of each class is as follows: (1.) As to the external senses of seeing, hearing, tasting, kc, by them we in many ways offend God; and doing penance consists in depriving them of what is agreeable to them, even though the object be innocent, but especially if it be sinful or dangerous. Thus Job "made a covenant with his eyes, that he should not so much as think upon a virgin," Job, xxxi. 1. And David would not hear another speak ill of his neighbour in his presence: "The man that in private detracted his neighbour, him did I persecute," Ps. c. 5. Daniel also says of himself, "Desirable bread I did not eat, and wine and flesh did not enter my mouth." It also consists in forcing the senses to undergo what is disagreeable, but not hurtful, as David did when "he mingled ashes with his bread." To this class also belongs doing penance in the tongue by silence, speaking ill of none, defending the absent, and the like. (2.) As to the passions and affections of the soul, as they are the principal springs of all our sins, the doing penance in them is of a wide extent, and of the greatest necessity for the amendment of our life, as well as for the punishment of past offences. The chief way of doing penance here is to force ourselves to the practice of those virtues which are contrary to our vicious affections; to mortify avarice by alms-deeds; hatred, by speaking well of, doing good to, and praying for our enemies; pride, by acts of humility and obedience; gluttony, by eating things unpleasant to the taste; drunkenness, by a total abstinence from strong drinks, and the like. Under this class comes also the mortifying all idle curiosity of seeing or hearing things which do not belong to nor concern us; all vanity in dress, furniture, and the like. (3.) As to bodily penances, they are included under the three general heads of prayer, fasting, and alms-deeds, which are most profitable to those who properly practise them. Under this head are included some particular kinds of bodily penances taken notice of in Scripture, such as hair-cloth, of which it is recorded that Judith wore a "hair-cloth next her loins all the days of her life," Judith, viii. 6. And David says of himself, "I was clothed with hair-cloth, I humbled my soul with fasting," Ps. xxxiv. 13. "I covered my soul with fasting.... I made hair-cloth my garment," Ps. lxviii. 11 , 12. And when he saw the destroying angel causing the plague among his people, in punishment of his sins, "both he and the ancients, clothed in hair-cloth, fell down flat on the ground," i Chron. xxi. 16. So also, in the famous siege of Samaria, the king "rent his garments, and passed by upon the wall, and all the people saw the hair-cloth which he wore within next his flesh," 4 Kings, vi. 30. In this manner did these holy persons do penance for their sins, and appease the wrath of God. St John the Baptist, also, though most innocent, is a great model of this kind of penance, being clothed with a garment made of hair.

Watching is another work of penance much recommended by examples in Scripture. "Oh God, my God," says David, "to Thee I watch by break of day," Ps. lxii.; and, "' I rose at midnight to give praise to God," Ps. cxviii. Of the truly wise man also it is said, "He will give his heart to resort by day-break to the Lord, and will pray in the sight of the Most High," Ecclus. xxx-ix. 6 ; and the manna, "which could not be destroyed by fire, being warmed with a little sunbeam, presently melted away, that it might be known to all that we must prevent the sun to bless Thee, and adore Thee at the dawning of the light," Wisd. xvi. 27. Our Saviour Himself watched whole nights in prayer, St Paul exhorts us to approve ourselves as servants of Christ, "in fasting, in watching," 2 Cor. vi. 5 ; and tells us that it was his own practice to chastise his body "in labour, in toil, in many watchings," 2 Cor. xi. 27. In all which we see that this holy penitential work of watching consists in moderating the quantity of our sleep, in interrupting it, and getting up early in the morning to praise God and pray to Him.

Hard lying also is another penitential work pointed out to us strongly in the Word of God. When David's child was sick he "fasted and lay upon the ground" seven days, to move God to mercy, and to obtain the life of the child. Among the penitential works by which Achab found mercy with God, one was that he "slept in sackcloth;" and Joel exhorts the people to have recourse to the same means of finding mercy: "Gird yourselves and lament, O ye priests.... Go in and lie in sackcloth, ye servants of my God," Joel, i. 13. Ah, if the saints of God did penance in this manner, what ought we sinners to do!

Q. 37. What are those penitential works which we must undergo whether we will or not?

A. The miseries and troubles to which we are daily exposed in this life, and which we cannot avoid. Were we diligent in performing the penitential works contained in the former classes, we might easily discharge a great part of the debt we owe to the Divine justice, but, alas! our backwardness in that respect is most deplorable, and therefore Almighty God, out of His infinite goodness, sends us many trials and afflictions of different kinds, as it were to force us to our real good. Now the sufferings He sends are surely the most proper for us; and, as we must unavoidably undergo them, it becomes an easy matter to discharge our debt by their means. All that is required is to bear them with a penitential spirit, receiving them with patience and submission from the hand of God, and taking them as a penance sent by Him for our sins. Penitential works of this class are innumerable, (1.) The toils and labours of our state of life, are a penance laid upon us by God from the very fall of Adam, in punishment of which God said to Adam, "Cursed is the earth in thy work; with labour and toil shalt thou eat thereof all the days of thy life, in the sweat of thy brow thou shalt earn thy bread," Gen. iii. What a field of penitential works does this give to servants, husbandmen, tradesmen, etc.? (2.) The inclemencies of the weather, heat, cold, rain, frost, snow, etc., afford to all abundant matter for the same purpose.

(3.) Distractions, aridities, and desolations in time of prayer, are a just punishment for the many times we have been deaf to the calls of God, resisted His graces, and given place to idle, unprofitable, or sinful thoughts; but if borne with a penitential spirit, will be an effectual discharge of the debt we have contracted by these faults. (4.) Your children are obstinate, and a torment to you; remember how you behaved towards your parents, your negligence in bringing up your own children, and take the pain they give you as a penance sent from God for these sins. (5.) Servants, your masters and mistresses are harsh and ill-tempered: Masters, your servants are disobedient and careless; what noble opportunities does this give to each of offering up a daily penance most acceptable to God? Sickness and pain attack you; here also is a large and excellent field for making up your account with God to your great advantage. And so of all the other crosses which God sends upon us in this life, which there is no avoiding, but which may easily be turned to the best account by bearing them in penance for our sins. But, oh! how contrary is our conduct in all these cases to what it ought to be! And how often do we abuse these occasions which God sends us, and turn them into occasions of increasing our guilt and our debt by impatience and murmuring under them! How unreasonable is our conduct in this respect! How great our folly!

Section VI: Of The Effects Of True Repentance In The Remission Of Sin

Q. 38. Does true repentance remit sin, or wash it away from the soul?

A. By no means; the remission of sin is solely the work of God, and nothing but His grace can wash away the stains of sin from the soul.

Q. 39. What part then has repentance in the pardon of sin?

A. It (1.) Disposes the soul for receiving from God the pardon of sin; for without repentance the soul is utterly incapable of being restored to the favour and mercy of God, seeing that, as long as the soul loves sin, God must infallibly hate her. (2.) It efficaciously moves God to grant us pardon, because, as Jesus Christ has merited for us the pardon of our sins, on condition of sincere repentance, and as God has repeatedly promised pardon to the repenting sinner, consequently true repentance can never fail to obtain from God the pardon of sin; He is bound in justice to Jesus Christ, and in fidelity to His own promises, to grant it. Besides, true repentance is a gift of God; it is His holy grace that first moves the sinner to it; it is holy grace which enables the sinner to complete it, insomuch that, without the grace of God, it is impossible truly to repent; consequently, when God gives to a sinner the grace of repentance, undoubtedly He will also give the pardon of his sins, with a view to which the grace of repentance was bestowed.

Q. 40. What is meant by the pardon or remission of sin; - in what does it consist?

A. We have seen above that sin defiles, pollutes, and stains the soul in a most miserable manner, and renders her hateful in the sight of God, hideous, loathsome to Him and His holy angels. Now, as long as these defilements of sin remain in the soul, it is impossible God should be reconciled to her. When, therefore, upon the sinner's sincere repentance, Almighty God, through the merits of Christ, pardons sin, He cleanses the soul by His justifying grace; this renders her beautiful and agreeable to God, and restores her to His friendship and favour. So that the pardon or remission of sin, properly speaking, consists in delivering the soul from the guilt of sin, adorning her with the grace of God, and restoring her to His favour.

Q. 41. How does it appear that Almighty God takes away and destroys all the stains and guilt of sin from the soul when He pardons sin?

A. This is manifestly shown from many clear testimonies of Scripture, (1.) From those which expressly affirm it; thus God promises by His prophet, "I will pour upon you clean water, and you shall be cleansed from all your filthiness," Ezek. xxxvi. 25 . God "will turn again and have mercy on us; He will put away our iniquities, and He will cast all our sins into the bottom of the sea," Micha, vii. 19. Before David fell, he said to God, "Thou hast tried me by fire, and iniquity hath not been found in me," Ps. xvi. 3 . But after his unhappy fall he prayed, "Wash me yet more from my iniquity, and cleanse me from my sins, . . . and blot out all mine iniquities," Ps. l. 4, 11. And afterwards, describing the pardon he had received, he said, "As far as the east is from the west, so hath He removed our iniquities from us," Ps. cii. 12 . The angel also touched Isaiah's lips with a coal, and said, "Behold, this hath touched thy lips, and thy iniquity shall be taken away, and thy sins shall be cleansed," Isa. vi. 7 . St Peter also, in his sermon to the Jews, says, "Repent ye therefore, and be converted, that your sins may be blotted out," Acts, iii. 19 . (2.) From those texts where this is expressly declared to be the benefit obtained for us by Jesus Christ; thus, He is "the Lamb of God that taketh away the sins of the world," John, i. 29 . "The Blood of Jesus Christ His Son cleanseth us from all sin," i John, i. 7 ; for "He hath loved us, and washed us from our sins in His Blood," Rev. i. 5 ; "For if the blood of goats and of oxen, etc., sanctify such as are defiled to the cleansing of the flesh, how much more shall the Blood of Christ cleanse our conscience from dead works?" Heb. ix. 14 . (3.) From those texts which declare this to be done from the sacrament of baptism; thus, "Arise and be baptised, and wash away your sins," Acts, xxii. 16 ; and St Paul, speaking of different grievous sins, says, "And such some of you were, but you are washed, but you are sanctified in the name of our Lord Jesus Christ, and in the Spirit of our God," I Cor. vi. II.

Q. 42. By what means does Almighty God wash our souls from the guilt of our sins, when He grants us pardon for them?

A. By His holy grace, or Divine charity, which He pours into the soul; by His Holy Spirit, which washes away all the stains of sin, and also beautifies the soul, making her just and holy in His sight; "Because the charity of God is poured abroad in our hearts by the Holy Ghost, Who is given to us," Rom. v. 5 .

Chapter XVIII

Of The Grace Of God

Q. What is the grace of God?

A. It is a supernatural gift of God, not at all due to us; a Divine quality communicated by God to the soul, which cleanses her from all the stains of sin, and renders her beautiful and pleasing in the eyes of God: It is also a Divine help, which excites us and enables us to do good and avoid evil.

Q. 2. How many kinds of grace are there?

A. Principally two kinds, actual grace and sanctifying grace,

Q. 3. What good does actual grace do to us?

A. It fortifies and strengthens the soul.

Q. 4. What good does sanctifying grace do to us?

A. It cleanses and beautifies the soul.

Section I: Of Actual Grace

Q. 5. What is actual grace?

A. Actual grace is an internal supernatural help, which God communicates to the soul, to enable us to do good and avoid evil.

Q. 6. How does this actual grace operate on the soul?

A. (1.) By enlightening the understanding, to see what ought to be done or avoided, and inclining the will towards what is good, or averting it from evil; and, on this account, it is called exciting grace and preventing grace. It is called exciting grace, because it excites and invites us, as it were, to do good and avoid evil; and it is called preventing grace, because it is wholly the work of God in our souls, and precedes every deliberate or voluntary act of our own, as experience teaches us; for we feel those holy inspirations arise in our souls, without anything done by us to procure them, or having it in our power to hinder them; though, when they do come, we have it in our power either to comply with or to resist them. (2.) When we freely comply with this first motion of actual grace, it continues to fortify and strengthen us to go on and perfect the good work we have begun; and on this account it is called concomitant grace, because it accompanies us during the whole good action; and strengthening or helping grace, because it assists our weakness, and enables us to perform it.

Q. 7. What does the Scripture say of this actual grace?

A. Our Saviour says Himself, "Behold, I stand at the door and knock." See here the exciting grace; and He immediately adds, "If any man shall hear My voice, and open to Me the door, I will come in to him, and will sup with him, and he with Me," Rev. iii. 20. Behold the helping grace, or the continuation of His actual grace, when we comply with its first motions in our souls. To the same effect St Paul says, "It is God Who worketh in you, both to will and to accomplish, according to His good pleasure," Phil. ii. 13. God worketh in us to will, by His exciting grace, without which we could never of ourselves have a good thought: and to accomplish by His helping grace, without which we can do nothing. David was very sensible of this when he said, "My God, His mercy shall prevent me," Ps. lviii. II. And again, "Thou hast held me by my right hand, and by Thy will Thou hast conducted me," Ps. lxxii. 24 "And Thy mercy shall follow me all the days of my life," Ps. xxii. 6. On this subject St Paul also says, "He Who hath begun the good work in you shall perfect it," Phil. i. 6 ; to show that it is God Who first begins, and then enables us by His help to perfect the good work.

Q. 8. Can we, by our own natural strength, without the help of God's grace, do anything towards salvation?

A. No, we cannot, either in thought, word, or deed, nor so much as have a good movement of our heart towards God unless it be first excited by Him. As this is a point of the greatest importance, the foundation of true Christian humility, and the source of all good to our souls, it is necessary to establish it in the clearest manner; the more so, because our pride - the deepest and most dangerous wound our nature has received from sin - recoils at this truth, and endeavours to conceal it from our eyes. From this unhappy blindness towards ourselves, and towards our own weakness and misery, innumerable evils flow: wherefore we must consider fully what the Word of God teaches us concerning this great Christian truth.

(1.) No man can take a single step towards Jesus Christ unless he be moved and assisted thereto by God. This our Saviour declares in express terms: "No man can come to Me except the Father Who hath sent Me draw him," John, vi. 44 , not by compulsion, nor by laying the free-will of man under any necessity, but by the strong and sweet motions of His heavenly grace; and therefore a little after, repeating the same truth, He says, "No man can come to Me, unless it be given him of My Father," ver. 66; to show that this grace is not a force or constraint put upon us, but a gift of God, an effect of His mercy, enlightening our minds to see and inclining our wills to do what is good, and when we consent to and comply with that inclination, assisting us to complete the good work. St Paul also says, "It is not of him that willeth, nor of him that runneth, but of God that showeth mercy," Rom. ix. 16. Because no natural will nor endeavour of our own can ever lead us towards Christ, unless we be excited thereto by the preventing mercy of God.

(2.) We cannot have true faith in Jesus Christ, nor believe the sacred truths of eternity with Divine faith, without the help of His grace. Thus St Paul declares, "To you it is given for Christ to believe in Him," Phil, i. 29. And again, "By grace you are saved through faith; and that not of yourselves, for it is the gift of God," Eph. ii. 8. Hence the Church of Christ, by her general councils, pronounces anathema upon those who teach that, "without the preventing inspiration and help of the Holy Ghost, a man can believe as he ought,'" Cone. Trid. Sess. 6, can. 3.

(3.) A sinner cannot, by his own strength, repent of his sins as he ought, unless he receives the grace of repentance from the mercy of God. This we have seen above, in the preceding chapter, Jtvii. sec. 4, to which add what St Paul writes to the Ephesians, attributing this favour entirely to the mercy, grace, and love of God. "God," says he, "who is rich in mercy, for His exceeding great charity, wherewith He loves us, even when we were dead by sins, hath quickened us together in Christ, by Whose grace ye are saved," Eph. ii. 4.

(4.) We can neither think a good thought nor speak a good word which can be useful towards our salvation without the assistance of God; for we are not sufficient to think anything of ourselves, as of ourselves, but our sufficiency is from God , 2 Cor. iii. 5. "Wherefore I give you to understand... that no man can say the Lord Jesus but by the Holy Ghost," i Cor. xii. 3. And hence the wise man says, "It is the part of the Lord to govern the tongue," Prov. xvi. 1 , to show that we can never speak what is good and conducive to our salvation unless the Lord guide and assist us in what we say.

(5.) We cannot do a good action, or produce any good fruit conducive to eternal happiness, without the help of God. "I am the vine," says Jesus Christ, "you the branches; he that abideth in Me, and I in Him, the same beareth much fruit, for without Me you can do nothing," John, xv. 5. He does not say, without Me you can do little - because this would suppose we could do something of ourselves; but He says absolutely, "Without Me you can do nothing," to show that, whether little or much, we cannot do it without His assistance.

In a word, whatever we do towards our salvation, whatever progress we make in virtue or Christian perfection, all flows from the mercy and grace of God through Jesus Christ. It is He "Who worketh in us both to will and to accomplish, according to His good pleasure," Phil. ii. 13. "It is He who begins the good-work in us, and Who also perfects it," Phil. i. 6. And hence St Paul acknowledges that all the good that is in him, and all the good works he had wrought, flowed from this Divine grace and mercy; "By the grace of God," says he, "I am what I am, and His grace in me hath not been void; but I have laboured more abundantly than all they; yet not I, but the grace of God with me," i Cor. xv. 10.

Q. 9. Why does the apostle say, the grace of God with me?

A. By these words he shows that, although Almighty God is always the first to begin the good work in us, by His exciting and preventing grace; and although it is God Who carries on the good work in us to perfection, by His assisting grace; yet it is not grace alone that does it, but that we must also co-operate with this grace, freely consenting to its motions in our soul, and willingly performing the good work to which it inclines and assists us. Almighty God will cure your infirmities, says St Augustine; but "you must be willing yourself; He heals all that are infirm, but He heals none but those who are willing to be cured," in Ps. 102, 11. 6. He stands at the door of our heart and knocks, by His preventing grace; but we must yield to His call, and open the door of our heart to Him, if we want Him to come in and sup with us; for, as the same St Augustine says, "He that made you without you" - that is, without any co-operation on your part - "will not justify you without you" - that is, without your will and co-operation.

Q. 10. Is it in our power to resist this grace of God, and not consent to it?

A. Most certainly. The grace of God does not force us, nor take away our free-will: it assists our weakness, and enables us to will and do what we could neither will nor do without it; consequently, whether we consent to the motions of grace or resist them, in either case we act with the full freedom of our will: when we consent, we have it in our power to resist; and when we resist, we are able to consent. Free-will is an essential part of our nature; for "God made man from the beginning, and left him in the hand of his own counsel. He added His commandments and precepts: If thou wilt keep the commandments and perform acceptable fidelity for ever, they shall preserve thee. He hath set water and fire before thee; stretch forth thy hand to which thou wilt. Before man is life and death, good and evil; that which he shall choose shall be given him," Ecclus. xv. 14. This liberty and free-will with which God created man was greatly diminished by original sin, and our power of doing good exceedingly weakened, from the violence of concupiscence strengthened in our souls by sin. Now, the grace of Jesus Christ cures this infirmity, fortifies and perfects our liberty, exciting us to good, and enabling us to perform it; but it by no means forces our will. Nay, sad experience teaches us that we too often resist the motions of grace; which, alas! is the source of all our woe.

Q. 11. Why do you say that, without the help of God's grace, we can do nothing towards our salvation?

A. That is to say, that whatever good action we may do by the mere strength of nature, and without the aid of the grace of Jesus Christ, can never, in any manner, conduce to our eternal salvation; because "there is no other name given to men under heaven, by which we can be saved, but the Name of Jesus only, neither is there salvation in any other," Acts, iv. 12. Consequently, whatever we do independent of Him, however laudable it may be in itself, or in the eyes of men, can in no way contribute, neither mediately nor immediately, towards our salvation. Nothing can conduce, in any degree, towards our salvation, but through the merits of Christ. The merits of Jesus Christ are applied to our souls only by His grace: whatever, then, we do in union with His grace, partakes of His merits; and whatever we do without His grace, and by the mere power of nature, partakes not of His merits, and therefore cannot avail towards salvation; hence He himself says, "Without Me you can do nothing "- namely, nothing conducive to salvation; and St Paul says, "No man can say, Lord Jesus, but by the Holy Spirit "- that is, no man can say it so as to conduce to his salvation.

Q. 12. But can man do anything good at all without the grace of God?

A. Observe, although our nature was greatly vitiated by sin, yet it was not totally corrupted and lost to all good. There still remain in us some sparks of that original rectitude in which we were created; and hence, among the numberless vicious dispositions of the heart of man, there are few or no persons to be found who have not some good natural inclinations - some to one moral virtue, some to another. Thus some are inclined to compassion, some to generosity, others to honesty in their dealings. Now, though these good natural dispositions will not sustain a man when they are opposed by violent passions, yet- in ordinary cases he may act according to them, and when he does he performs a good moral action. This he certainly may do by the mere strength of nature: and though such actions can in no respect conduce to salvation, which is a supernatural reward, yet they do not fail to receive from God some temporal recompense, for the divine justice "will render to every one according to his works."

Q. 13. As we cannot possibly do anything conducive to our eternal salvation without the actual grace of God exciting us, and aiding us thereto, does God bestow this grace upon all men without exception?

A. It would certainly be the height of impiety to suppose that God would lay His commands upon us His creatures, and oblige us to obey them, under pain of eternal damnation, the most dreadful of evils, and at the same time withhold those helps without which it is impossible to observe them. Nothing can be more contrary to every idea we have of the wisdom, goodness, and justice of God, than such a supposition. Seeing then that God commands all men without exception to do good and avoid evil. He certainly gives to all the grace necessary to enable them to do so, and by doing so to save their souls. This truth is laid down to us in the Scripture as follows: "Wisdom preacheth abroad, she uttereth her voice in the streets; at the head of the multitudes she cries out, in the entrance of the gates of the city she uttereth her words, saying, O children, how long will you love childishness, and fools covet those things which are hurtful to themselves, and the unwise hate knowledge? Turn ye at my reproof: behold I will utter my spirit to you, and will shew you my words," Prov. i. 20. So speaks the wisdom of God in all places, and to all men, reproving them for their evil ways, inviting them to good, and promising the Divine Spirit to those that give ear to His invitations. Again, "Thou hast mercy upon all, because Thou canst do all things, and winkest at the sins of men because of repentance. For Thou lovest all things that are, and hatest nothing of the things that Thou hast made - but thou sparest all because they are thine, O Lord, Who lovest souls," Wisd. xi. 24. Here we see that God loves all that He has made, consequently all men without exception; that He spares them, and has mercy upon them; therefore He gives to all, without exception, such helps of His grace as are necessary for enabling them to repent, and do good, and save their souls, if they cooperate with them: otherwise His loving them, having mercy on them, and sparing them, would be nugatory, and to no purpose.

Jesus Christ says, "Behold, I stand at the door and knock: if any man shall hear My voice, and open the door, I will come in to him and sup with him, and he with Me. To him that shall overcome I will give to sit with Me on My throne," Rev. iii. 20. Christ then knocks at the hearts of all - there is no exception; and if any man opens, be he what he will, if he gives Christ entrance, and, co-operating with him, shall overcome, eternal glory shall be his reward. On this account it is said of Christ that He is "the true light, which enlighteneth every man that cometh into this world," John, i. 9 ; consequently, every man without exception is enlightened by Christ; for, "to every one of us is given grace, according to the measure of the giving of Christ," Eph. iv. 7. That is, He gives to some more, to some less, as He thinks proper, but to all sufficient for their wants, if they comply with what He gives. He is master of His own gifts, and may give more abundantly to whom He pleases, as He did to the Jews of old, of whom it is said, "He hath not done in like manner to every nation," Ps. cxlvii. 20 ; and He gives five talents to one, two to another, and only one to a third, but that one was sufficient for him who received it, and therefore he was justly condemned for not improving it. Besides these general proofs which show that God gives to all men the graces absolutely necessary for their salvation, there are also several plain testimonies of Scripture which prove the same in particular of each of the three classes into which mankind are divided - true believers who are in the state of grace, true believers who are in the state of sin, and unbelievers.

Q. 14. How is this shown with regard to those who are in the state of grace?

A. That the just who are in the state of grace, and in friendship with God, are never deprived of such helps of the actual grace of God as enable them, if they themselves be willing to co-operate with them, to keep all the commandments of God, and persevere in the state of grace, is an article of Divine faith which assures us (r.) That "God is able to make all grace abound in you, that ye always having all sufficiency in all things may abound to every good work," 2 Cor. ix. 8 ; "For I can do all things in Him who strengtheneth me," Phil. iv. 13. (2.) That the stronger the temptation is, the greater grace is given to enable the just man to overcome it, for "to envy doth the spirit covet that dwelleth in you; but He giveth greater grace," Jas. iv. 5. (3.) That God hath pledged His sacred promise to give them this grace; for "God is faithful, Who will not suffer you to be tempted above that which you are able, but will make also with temptation issue "(that is, a way to escape), "that you may be able to bear it," i Cor. x. 13 ; and the Church in the great council of Trent defines this: "If any one shall say that the commands of God are impossible to be observed by a just man who is in the state of grace, let him be anathema," Sess. vi., can. 18; and hence assures that "God does not forsake those that are justified by His grace, unless He be first forsaken by them," Sess. vi., ch.,11; for "God does not command impossibilities, but by commanding us "to do anything, "He admonishes us to what we can, to pray for what help we need, and then He helps us to make us able." - Ibid.

Q. 15. Why does the council say, to pray for what help we need?

A. It is to show us that the grace enabling us to pray is never wanting, and this grace, if well used, will never fail to obtain all other necessary helps, according to our Saviour's ample promise, "Ask, and ye shall receive; seek, and ye shall find; knock, and it shall be opened unto you;" and, consequently, that it is always in our own power to keep the commandments of God, and overcome all temptations of breaking them, seeing we always have either the actual assistance of God's grace enabling us to do so, or the grace of prayer, by the proper use of which that actual assistance will certainly be obtained.

Q. 16. How does it appear that Almighty God gives the necessary assistance of His grace to true believers who are in the state of sin?

A. Two things God requires of people in this state: first, to repent of their past sins, and return to His friendship; and, secondly, not to go on in a sinful course, but to keep His commandments. Now, as God expressly requires both these things from them, the proofs of the preceding case evince in this also, that He gives such sinners the necessary helps to enable them to do both; to which the following proofs are added: "As I live, saith the Lord God, I will not the death of the wicked, but that the wicked turn from his evil way and live. Turn ye, turn ye, from your evil ways; and why will you die, O house of Israel?" Ezek. xxxiii. 11. Now, if God so earnestly wills the life of the sinner, and so pressingly invites him to turn and live, He must necessarily give him grace to enable him to do so. The same reason holds from what St Peter says, "The Lord dealeth patiently for your sake,

not willing that any should perish, but that all should return to penance,"
2 Pet. iii. 9 ; and our Saviour warmly invites all such to come to Him, and,
consequently, gives them the necessary graces to enable them to follow His
invitation. "Come to Me," says He, "all you that labour and are heavy load-
en, and I will refresh you," Mat. xi.; besides, all the above general proofs
have particular place here.

Q. 17. But what if the sinner be blinded and hardened in his sin?

A. Nothing is more deplorable than the state of a blinded and hardened
sinner. A blinded sinner is one who has taken up some false and dangerous
opinions, and is so positive and fixed in them, that he shuts his eyes to everything that can undeceive him. A hardened sinner is one whose passions
and affections towards some bad object are so strong, that he contemns and
resists all the admonitions which God sends him, whether by the interior
motions of His grace, or the exterior call from His Holy Word, good books,
exhortations of pastors, or the like. Now, this most unhappy state is in itself
sinful, for it is a sin to have our mind or heart bound to any false or sinful
object; it is also a consequence and punishment of former sins; and, what
is no less deplorable, it is the cause and source of other sins. Yet, notwithstanding this is so great an evil, God Almighty, through the riches of His
mercy, does not entirely abandon such sinners, but visits them from time
to time with His holy calls, both by exterior trials and the internal motions
of His Holy Spirit, with which, if they would concur, they might work out
their conversion. This appears from what St Stephen said to the blind and
obdurate Jews, "You stiff-necked and uncircumcised in heart and in ears,
you always resist the Holy Ghost," Acts, vii. 51 , which shows that the Holy
Ghost did not entirely withdraw the offers of His grace from them, but that
they obstinately resisted and rejected them. St Paul also, speaking to such
sinners, says, "Knowest thou not that the benignity of God leadeth thee
to repentance? but according to thy hardness and impenitent heart, thou
treasurest up to thyself wrath against the day of wrath, and the revelation
of the just judgment of God," Rom. ii. 4 ; where we see that the goodness
of God does not give over entirely moving such sinners to repentance, but
their hard heart, rejecting all His calls, justly increases the measure of their
guilt and punishment.

Q. 18. Why do you say that He does not entirely abandon them?

A. Because though God, out of His infinite goodness, does not wholly
forsake such sinners in this life, yet, in just punishment of their repeated

abuses of mercy, He withdraws His more powerful graces from them, visits them seldomer, and even leaves them for a time entirely. On this account, their blindness towards spiritual things becomes greater, and the hardness of their heart more confirmed. And in this sense it is said in Scripture, that God sometimes hardens sinners, blinds them, leaves them to their own inventions, gives them up to their lusts, or to a reprobate sense, and the like; which is certainly the greatest of all the punishments which He inflicts upon sinners in this life, but what such sinners justly deserve for their repeated abuses of mercy.

Q. 19. How comes this to be so dreadful a punishment?

A. Because, as we can do no good of ourselves without the grace of God, so, left to ourselves, without the aid of this holy grace, there is no manner of crime into which we would not plunge headlong. Hear how the Scriptures show us what we are of ourselves, - "God saw that the wickedness of men was great upon the earth, and that all the thought of their heart was bent upon evil at all times," Gen. vi. 5 ; "And the Lord said, The imagination and thought of men's heart are prone to evil from their youth," Gen. viii. 21. "The heart is perverse above all things, and unsearchable, who can know it?" Jer. xvii. 9. "Out of the heart proceed evil thoughts, murders, adulteries, fornications, thefts, false testimonies, blasphemies," Matth. XV. 19. See also the description which St Paul gives, Rom. i. and iii., of the abominations which the heathens fell into, "in times past, when," as he tells us, "God suffered all nations to walk in their own way," Acts, xiv. 15. Therefore, to be left to ourselves, and deprived of the grace of God, is to be left in the hands of our greatest enemy, so as to be hurried on by him to certain damnation.

Q. 20. How does it appear that God gives to unbelievers such helps of His actual grace as are sufficient to enable them to arrive at salvation?

A. Besides the general proofs brought above, which show that He does this to all men, without exception, there are also these two following: First, "God will have men to be saved and to come to the knowledge of the truth," I Tim. ii. 3. He wills all to be saved, as the great end for which He created them; and to come to the knowledge of the truth, as a necessary condition of salvation, because, "without faith it is impossible to please God," Heb. xi. 6. Now, infidels, or unbelievers of all kinds, have not this knowledge of the truth. Seeing, therefore, that God expressly wills they should obtain it and be saved, consequently He gives them such graces as are sufficient, if they co-operate with them, to bring them to it. Secondly, Jesus Christ "gave Himself a redemption for all," I Tim. ii. 6 ; and "He is the propitiation for our sins; and not for ours only, but also for those of the whole world," i John, ii. 2 ; for "He is the Saviour of all men, especially the faithful," i Tim. iv. 13 consequently all must receive, in some manner or other, the fruits of His redemption, with a view to their salvation by means of His grace; therefore all Infidels, Jews, Turks, and Heathens receive from God, in such measure and manner as He sees proper, graces sufficient, if they co-operate with them, to bring them to the knowledge of the truth, and to salvation.

Q. 21. What is the tendency of all those actual graces which God bestows upon all mankind?

A. The ultimate tendency of them all is to procure the salvation of souls; but their immediate tendency is different, according to the different people who receive them. In unbelievers the immediate end of these graces is to enable them to observe the law of nature, by avoiding evil and doing good; which, if they comply with faithfully, greater and greater graces of the same kind would be given them, till at last the Divine wisdom would bring them, in such manner as he sees proper, to the knowledge of the truth and to the faith of Jesus Christ. In the faithful who are in the state of sin, these graces tend immediately to excite them to repentance, and bring them to the grace of justification. In those who are justified and in the state of grace, the actual graces they receive enable them to persevere in that happy state, by obeying the commands of God, and to secure their salvation.

Q. 22. Whence comes it that these noble effects are so seldom produced in the greatest part of mankind?

A. Not from any deficiency in the graces we receive, which are all fully sufficient for producing these effects in our souls, but from the perverse will of man, which resists these motions of the grace of God, refuses to comply with them, and renders them of no effect.

Q. 23. But cannot Almighty God give us such graces as would effectually overcome the perverseness of our will?

A. No doubt, Almighty God has an absolute power over the heart of man, and in the treasures of His infinite wisdom and mercy has such super-abundant and suitable helps and graces to give him, as would infallibly procure his free and willing consent to whatever God requires from him. This power he exercised in a most miraculous manner in the conversion of St Paul, St Mary Magdalen, and others. Hence the Scripture affirms, "That God works in us both to will and to do, according to His good pleasure;" and God Himself says, "I will give you a new heart and a new spirit,..... and I will put My Spirit in the midst of you, and I will cause you to walk in My commandments," Ezek. xxxvi. 26 ; also the Wise Man says, "The heart of the king is in the hand of the Lord, whithersoever He will He shall turn it," Prov. xxi. 1. Now this supreme dominion which God has over the heart and will of man, as our sovereign Lord, He exercises not by forcing our will or infringing our liberty, but by giving us such abundant and suitable graces as He infallibly knows will procure our ready consent, and effectually enable us to do what He pleases, and cheerfully to walk in His commandments. Thus David says, "I have run in the way of Thy Commandments when Thou didst dilate my heart," Ps. cxviii. 32. And the Holy Ghost pronounces that man "Blessed, that could have transgressed, and hath not transgressed, and could do evil things, and hath not done them; therefore are his goods established in the Lord," Ecclus. xxxi. 10 ; where it is manifest, and expressly affirmed, that when, through the grace of God, we observe His commands, we have it in our power to transgress them, and when we abstain from evil we have it in our power to do it; and therefore, that the grace by which we do good and avoid evil, and by which God causes us to walk in His Commandments, and turns our heart whithersoever He pleases, does by no means force us, or destroy our free-will, but strengthens, rectifies, and perfects it. On this account, those graces of God which man resists, and to which he refuses his consent, are called in the language of divines sufficient graces, because they are always sufficient to enable us to do what God requires we should do when He gives them, though by our resistance we do it not; but those graces to which we consent, and with which we co-operate, are called efficacious graces, because the happy effects for which they are given are actually produced by our consent and co-operation with them.

Q. 24. Is Almighty God obliged to give us these superabundant and efficacious graces?

A. Observe: man of himself has no right, claim, or title to any grace from God; being by nature born in sin, and a child of wrath, he is the object of God's justice, but has nothing in himself which can give him the smallest claim to favour. So that God is under no obligation towards man to bestow any grace whatever. But as God has a sincere will for the salvation of all men, and as Jesus Christ died for the salvation of all, and, through the merits of His death, obtained for them such graces as are necessary for enabling them to procure their salvation; therefore, God Almighty becomes obliged by His own goodness, by which He wills all to be saved, and to Jesus Christ, who has purchased for us the necessary helps to salvation, to bestow on all mankind such graces as are necessary and sufficient to enable them to work out their salvation, if they co-operate with them; and these He gives to all, without exception: so that, whoever is lost, is lost through his own fault, by not using, as he might, the graces he receives. Superabundant graces God is obliged to give to none; they are the effects of His pure mercy, and He bestows them on whom He pleases. He is sole master of His own gifts: and as it is impossible for men to comprehend His unsearchable judgments in the distribution of His graces, so none can find fault with what He does, or say to Him, "Why doest Thou so?" This we know for certain, and this is fully sufficient for us to know, that God gives to all what is necessary; that we have it in our power to be saved, if we ourselves will; that the grace of prayer is never wanting, and that if we make a good use of the graces God bestows, and pray as we ought for more, we shall undoubtedly obtain whatever we stand in need of; that, therefore, if we be lost it is wholly our own fault, and if we be saved we owe this to His infinite goodness only, through the merits of Jesus; according to what He says by His Prophet, "Destruction is thy own, Israel; thy help is only in Me," Hosea, xiii. 9.

Q. 25. On what occasions does God commonly bestow His grace upon men?

A. Times and moments are in the hands of the Almighty, who bestows His gifts when and how He pleases, and is not bound by occasions; but of this we are sure, that the necessary helps of His grace are always ready when our wants require them. "We may also be assured that He will never refuse when we pray for them in a proper manner. Besides this, we know from experience that our merciful God frequently sends us pious thoughts and holy inspirations without any other rule than His own good pleasure; and did we attend as we ought to watch over our interior, and keep our heart free from all inordinate attachments to creatures, unbiassed by depraved affections, and undisturbed by passions, we would receive these holy inspirations oftener, and be much more sensible of them. But God most commonly causes internal favours to accompany His external graces.

Q. 26. What do you mean by external graces?

A. All those external helps to salvation which God has appointed; such as the great mysteries of our redemption, a Christian education, the good examples of others, miracles, the preaching of His Word, the exhortations of our spiritual directors, reading good books, and the like, which are intended as helps to our salvation; and when we either read, see, hear, or meditate upon them, they are generally accompanied by corresponding interior graces, in order to render them profitable to our souls. Thus David was brought to a sense of his sin, and to repentance, on the reproof he received from Nathan, by the internal grace accompanying it. The Ninivites did penance at the preaching of Jonas; the good thief was converted at seeing the wonderful patience of Jesus; and so of others without number.

Q. 27. Can these external helps be of any use without internal graces?

A. No, they cannot. "It is the Holy Ghost," says St Augustine, "that operates internally, in order to make the external help of service," Civ. Dei. 1. 15, c. 6. And we read of a sermon of St Paul's at which only one woman was converted, of whom it was said, "whose heart the Lord opened to attend to those things that were said by Paul," Acts, xvi. 14.

Q. 28. What consequences flow from this?

A. Two very important consequences, (1.) That as these external graces are the most ordinary occasions on which Almighty God speaks to the heart, we ought to be extremely assiduous in the daily use of them, meditating often on the great truths of religion, reading pious books, hearing the Word of God, and the like. (2.) That as none of these helps can profit ourselves nor benefit others, when used by us for them, unless God be pleased to bestow His internal grace, we ought, therefore, to be extremely careful to pray earnestly for God's blessing; for "Paul may plant, and Apollo may water, but it is God alone that gives the increase," i Cor. iii. 6.

Section II: Of Sanctifying Grace

Q. 29. What is sanctifying grace?

A. St Peter calls it a "participation of the Divine nature," 2 Pet. i. 4. And St Paul calls it in one place "the charity of God which is poured abroad in our hearts by the Holy Ghost," Rom. v. 5 ; and in another, "the justice of God by faith of Jesus Christ upon all them that believe in Him," Rom. iii. 22. The wise man calls it "a vapour of the power of God, and a certain pure emanation of the glory of the Almighty; and that no undefiled thing can come near it," Wis. vii. 25. From all this it appears that the sanctifying grace of God is a communication which God makes of Himself to our souls; and it is called grace, because it is a free gift of His mercy through the merits of Christ; it is called Justice, because by it our sins are washed away, the disorders of our souls are rectified, and our souls rendered just and holy in His sight; and it is called charity, because it enables us to love God above all things, and our neighbour as ourselves.

Q. 30. Can this be explained by any examples?

A. The two following examples are used for this purpose. First, that of iron and fire: Iron of its own nature is black, cold, and hard; but when heated in a strong fire it loses all its former appearance, and becomes bright and shining like the fire itself. It also becomes hot, soft, and ductile, so as easily to be formed into any shape the workman pleases. In like manner a soul in the state of sin is hateful in the sight of God, cold and tepid towards all that is good, and of itself hard and obdurate in its evil ways; but when the great God communicates Himself to such a soul, by His justifying grace all her defilements are washed away, and she becomes just and beautiful before Him. She is also warmed with His holy love and with true devotion, and becomes pliable to His blessed will in obedience to His commandments. And this explains what St Paul means when he says, "As many of you as have been baptised in Christ, have put on Christ," Gal. iii. 27 ; because by the grace of justification received in baptism the justice and sanctity of Christ are poured forth into our souls, which makes us resemble Him, as the iron heated by the fire resembles the fire itself The other example is that of the soul and the body of man: A dead body without the soul is a loathsome spectacle, incapable of any vital action, and tending of itself to nothing but corruption; but when the soul is united to the body, it becomes alive, and has all the beauty of the human form, performs all the actions of life, and is preserved from corruption. In like manner a soul in the state of sin is dead, and loathsome in the eyes of God and His holy angels. She is incapable, by her own strength, of performing any action of the spiritual life conducive to her eternal salvation, and tends only to run deeper and deeper into the corruption of sin; but when the grace of God is poured into such a soul, she becomes alive, and beautiful in his sight, can easily per-form the duties of the spiritual life, meritorious of eternal salvation, and is strongly fortified against all the corruption of sin. Hence this grace of God is called habitual grace, because it remains constantly in the soul, unless it be destroyed by mortal sin; "because His Spirit dwelleth in you," Rom. viii.

ii. It is also called sanctifying grace, because it sanctifies the soul - that is, makes it holy and pure before God; and it is called justifying grace, because it justifies - that is, cures the disorders of the soul, and renders us just and upright in the eyes of God.

Q. 31. What is meant by justification?

A. It is when the soul passes from the state of sin to the state of grace.

Q. 32. What is meant by being in a state of sin?

A. To be in the state of sin is to be polluted by the guilt of mortal sin, deprived of the grace of God, and at enmity with God.

Q. 33. What is it to be in the state of grace?

A. It is to be cleansed from the guilt of sin, adorned with the grace of God, and in friendship with God.

Q. 34. What are the effects which sanctifying grace produces in the soul?

A. They are many and most excellent: (1.) It washes away all the stains and guilt of sin from the soul, through the merit of the blood of Christ, which it applies to the soul, according to that, "the blood of Jesus Christ His Son cleanseth us from all sin," i John, i. 7. See above, Chap. xvii. Q. 41.

(2.) It cures all the deadly infirmities of the soul, as the prophet declares in these words: "Bless the Lord, O my soul, and never forget all He has done for thee; Who forgiveth all thy iniquities, Who healeth all thy diseases," Ps. cii. 2. And hence our Saviour calls Himself the physician of souls when He says, "They that are in health need not a physician; but they that are ill;... for I am not come to call the just, but sinners," Mat. ix. 12. Not that grace takes away all the effects of sin from the soul; for concupiscence, or that proclivity to sin which followed upon the loss of original justice, still remains; neither does it destroy those evil habits which we have contracted by actual sin; but it strengthens the soul against both, and enables us to fight against and overcome them: for these effects of sin are not sins in themselves, except in as far as we consent to them; when we faithfully resist them they cannot hurt us, but are the field of our victory, and the increase of our crown.

(3.) It beautifies the soul, and renders us agreeable and delightful in the eyes of our Creator, resembling Jesus Christ by the union we have with Him through grace, just as the fire, when it thoroughly penetrates a mass of iron, not only takes away all its natural blackness, but makes it bright and glowing like the fire itself. Hence the Scripture says, "He hath chosen us in Him before the foundation of the world, that we should be holy and unspotted in His sight in charity," Eph. i. 4. And on this account "the Lord loveth the just," Ps. cxlv. 8. "For His soul pleased God," Wis. iv. 14 ; and why? "How beautiful is the chaste generation with glory!" Wis. iv. 1.

(4.) It makes us temples of the Holy Ghost, Who dwells in a particular manner in the soul of the just. "Know you not," says the apostle, "that you are the temple of God, and that the Spirit of God dwelleth in you?... for the temple of God is holy, which you are," I Cor. iii. 16. "Know you not that your members are the temple of the Holy Ghost, Who is in you, Whom you have from God I "i Cor. vi. 19.

(5.) It makes us the adopted children of God: "for whosoever are led by the Spirit of God, they are the sons of God;... you have received the spirit of adoption of sons, whereby we cry (Abba) Father; for the Spirit Himself giveth testimony to our spirit that we are the sons of God," Rom. viii. 14 ; because by the inward motions of Divine love, and the peace of conscience which the children of God experience, they have a kind of testimony of God's favour, which strengthens their hope of salvation, and their con-fidence in God as their loving Father. St John speaks of this dignity with amazement: "Behold," says he, "what manner of charity the Father hath be-stowed upon us, that we should be called, and should be the sons of God! "i John, iii. 1.

(6.) It makes us heirs of the kingdom of heaven, giving us a right and title as sons to that eternal inheritance: for "if sons, heirs also; heirs indeed of God, and joint heirs with Christ," Rom. viii. 17. "And because you are sons, God hath sent the Spirit of His Son into your hearts, crying, Abba, Father. Wherefore he is now no more a servant, but a son; and if a son, an heir also, through God," Gal. iv. 6.

(7.) It adorns the soul with the habits of all Christian virtues, according to the riches of His grace, "which hath superabounded in us in all wisdom and prudence," Eph. i. 8 ; and particularly in these Divine virtues of faith, hope, and charity; for thus the Word of God describes the admirable vir-tues which accompany the spirit of wisdom, and which He communicates to the soul in which He dwells by sanctifying grace: "I called upon God, and the spirit of wisdom came upon me.... Now all good things came to me together with her, and innumerable riches through her hands.... For she is an infinite treasure to men, which they that use become friends of God;... for in her is the spirit of understanding;... for she is a vapour of the power of God, and a certain pure emanation of the glory of the Almighty God; and therefore no defiled thing cometh near her.... She conveyeth herself into holy souls, and maketh friends of God and prophets; for God loveth none but him that dwelleth with wisdom. For she is more beautiful than the sun, and above all the order of the stars; being compared with light, she is found before it.... It is she that teacheth the knowledge of God.... And if a man love justice, her labours have great virtues; for she teacheth temperance, and prudence, and justice, and fortitude, which are such things as men can have nothing more profitable in life.... Her conversation hath no bitterness, nor her company any tediousness, but joy and gladness; and there is a great delight in her friendship, and inexhaustible riches in the works of her hands," Wis. vii., viii., through the whole. Behold what an amiable description of the admirable benefits which the Divine wisdom communicates to the soul in which she dwells by sanctifying grace, and which she never fails effectually to produce in those who faithfully co-operate with her holy inspirations, and study in all their doings to act by her light and direction.

(8.) It gives a dignity, value, and merit to all our good works, which makes them most acceptable in the sight of God, and worthy of an ample reward from Him, both of an increase of grace in this life and of eternal glory in the life to come. For when a soul is united with Jesus Christ by His grace, the good works which that soul performs, in obedience to His holy will, and from a pure intention of pleasing Him, are now no longer the works of corrupt, sinful man, but the works of the friends of God, fruits produced from the branch united to the vine, which is Christ, receiving all their nourishment from the vine, and dignified by His merits communicated to them by grace. Thus He Himself says, "I am the vine, you the branches; he that abideth in Me, and I in him, the same beareth much fruit," John, xv. 5. And to show that these good works obtain an increase of grace, here He says, "Every branch in Me that beareth fruit, He," my Father, "will purge it, that it may bring forth more fruit," John, xv. 2 ; and that they procure both an increase of our sanctification here, and at last eternal life, St Paul assures us in these words, "But now being made free from sin, and become servants to God, you have your fruit unto sanctification, and the end everlasting life; for the wages of sin is death; but the grace of God everlasting life, in Christ Jesus our Lord," Rom. vi. 22. Hence the Holy Scripture every-where proposes the kingdom of heaven as a reward and recompense given by a just God to the good works done in the state of grace. Thus God said to Abraham, when he was ready to sacrifice his son, "By my own self have I sworn, because thou hast done this thing - I will bless thee," Gen. xxii. 16. "I Myself will be your reward," said He upon another occasion, "exceeding great," Gen. xv. 1. "Be glad," says Jesus Christ, "and rejoice, for your reward is great in heaven," Mat. v. 12. So He promises an open reward from our heavenly Father to "prayer, fasting, and alms," Mat. vi. And at the last day He will say to the good, "Come, ye blessed of My Father, possess the king-dom prepared for you; for I was hungry, and ye gave Me meat," etc.. Mat. xxv. 34. "A cup of water given in His name shall not lose its reward," Mat. x. 42. "Our present tribulation worketh for us above measure exceedingly an eternal weight of glory," 2 Cor. iv. 17. Hence St Paul says, "I have fought a good fight, I have finished my course, I have kept the faith; for the rest there is laid up for me a crown of justice, which the Lord, the just Judge, will render to me at that day," 2 Tim. iv. 7. Now all this is the effect of the sanctifying grace of God, Who crowns His own gifts in us; and therefore,

(9.) It brings us at last to eternal happiness, if we persevere in the state of grace to the end; for "being now justified by His blood, we shall be saved from wrath through Him," Rom. v. 9. And "they who receive abundance of grace, and of the gift, and of justice, shall reign in life through one, Jesus Christ," lb. ver. 17. For "according to His mercy He saved us by the laver of regeneration, and renovation of the Holy Ghost, Whom He poured forth upon us abundantly through Jesus Christ our Saviour; that being justified by His grace, we may be heirs according to hope of everlasting life," Tit. iii. 5 From this we see what an immense treasure of spiritual riches the grace of God brings to the soul, and consequently what a great value we ought to put upon it, how diligent we should be to preserve and increase it, and how careful not to lose it. In a word, the grace of God is the great instrument of our salvation; because by it we are delivered from our past sins, and preserved from sin for the time to come. With great reason, then, the wise man sets so great a value upon the Divine wisdom, by whom this sanctifying grace is poured upon our souls, when he said, "I preferred her before kingdoms and thrones, and esteemed riches as nothing, in compar-ison of her; neither did I compare unto her any precious stone; for all gold, in comparison of her, is as a little sand; and silver, in respect to her, shall be accounted as clay. I loved her above health and beauty, and chose to have her instead of light, for her light cannot be put out," "Wis. vii. 8. Such is the esteem every Christian ought to have of the grace of God, as to be ready to part with everything this world can afford rather than lose this heavenly treasure and be separated from the charity of God, which is in Christ Jesus, by consenting to mortal sin. Such was the high esteem that St Paul and all the saints of God had of it, who could all say with that holy apostle, "Who shall separate us from the love of Christ? shall tribulation? shall distress? or famine? or nakedness? or danger? or persecution? or the sword?... for I am sure that neither death nor life, nor angels, nor principalities, nor powers, nor things present, nor things to come, nor height, nor depth, nor any creature, shall be able to separate us from the love of God which is in Christ Jesus," Rom. viii, 35. And why so? because he esteemed the happiness of being united to Jesus Christ by justifying grace before everything else, and utterly despised everything in this world in comparison of that heavenly treasure: "I count all things to be but loss," says he, "for the excellent knowledge of Jesus Christ my Lord, for whom I have suffered the loss of all things, and count them but as- dung, that I may gain Christ and be found in Him, not having my justice, which is of the law, but that which is of the faith of Christ Jesus, which is of God, justice in faith," Phil. iii. 8.

Q. 35. Can the sanctifying grace of God be augmented in our souls?

A. Yes it can; and the more it is increased in a soul, the more pure, the more holy, the more beautiful the soul is, the more inflamed also, and the more fervent her love to God becomes, which is explained by the example of iron and fire above mentioned. Thus the Scripture says, "The path of the just, as a shining light, goeth forwards, and increaseth even to perfect day," Prov, iv. 18.

Hence the frequent exhortations to "be strong in the grace which is in Christ Jesus," 2 Tim. ii. 1 , and "to grow in grace and in the knowledge of our Lord and Saviour Jesus Christ," 2 Pet. iii. 18. Hence the angel in the Revelations cried out, "He that is just, let him be justified still; and he that is holy, let him be sanctified still," Rev. xxii. 11. Which shows how careful we ought to be, not only to preserve, but also to increase this precious treasure in our souls by fervent prayer and frequent good works, which obtain from God an increase of grace, and by worthily frequenting the holy sacraments, the sacred channels by which He communicates it to our souls.

Q. 36. Can justifying grace be diminished and lost from the soul?

A. No doubt the fervour of our charity may be weakened, the brightness of the soul may be obscured, and her beauty diminished; and this is the fatal effect of venial sin and tepidity in the service of God, which, though it does not of itself destroy charity, yet, diminishing its fervour, it disposes and leads on the soul by little and little to mortal sin, by which the grace of justification is entirely banished from the soul. Thus we see that a piece of iron, though heated to the highest point by the force of fire, and glowing and shining with brightness, when taken out of the fire and exposed to the air, gradually loses its splendour, becomes less and less clear and glowing, and at last loses the appearance of fire entirely, and returns to the dull colour which it had before.

Q. 37. How does it appear that a person once justified, and in the grace of God, can lose that justification?

A. This is evident from numberless texts of Scripture. Thus God said to Moses, "He that hath sinned against Me, him will I strike out of My book," Exod. xxxii. 2 ,?> He must have been in His books before he sinned, and therefore justified, yet he loses his grace by his sin. "If any one abide not in Me," says our blessed Saviour, "he shall be cast forth as a branch, and shall wither, and they shall gather him up, and cast him into the fire, and he burneth," John, xv. 6. "When the just shall depart from His justice, and commit iniquities. He shall die in them," Ezek. xxxiii. 18. Hence the frequent exhortations in Scripture to "Serve the Lord in fear," Ps. ii. 11. "Let him that thinketh himself to stand, take heed lest he fall," I Cor. X. 12. "With fear and trembling work out your salvation," Phil. ii. 12. "Take heed, lest being laid aside by the en-or of the unwise, you fall from from your own steadfastness," 2 Pet. iii. 17. And St Paul, though a chosen vessel, "yet chastised his body and brought it into subjection, lest perhaps he should become a castaway," I Cor. ix. 27.

Q. 38. By what means can we recover the grace of justification when we have lost it by sin?

A. The grace of justification is a free gift of the mercy of God through the merits of Christ; and therefore no good works whatsoever which a sinner performs before justification can ever merit or deserve that grace from God. Before justification we are in the state of sin, separated from Jesus Christ; branches cut off from the vine, decayed members of His body, and therefore incapable of bearing fruit, as He Himself assures us: for "as the branch cannot bear fruit of itself," says He, "unless it abide in the vine; so neither can you, unless you abide in Me," John, xv. 4. Hence the Scripture assures us that we are justified freely by His grace, through the redemption that is in Christ Jesus , Rom. iii. 24 , to show that justification is by no means due to any preceding good works of ours: for "if by grace, it is now by works, otherwise grace is no more grace," Rom. xi. 6. But though no good works done in the state of sin can of themselves merit or deserve the grace of justification, yet Almighty God expressly requires certain good works to be done by the sinner, as necessary dispositions for receiving that grace, and without which it will never be granted. These dispositions, however, are His own gifts, produced in the soul of the sinner by the help of actual grace, which God freely bestows upon him for the sake of Christ, and with which the sinner cooperating, disposes his soul for the grace of justification; and when these dispositions are in the soul, the grace of justification is never refused - not as due to the sinner, but as due to Jesus Christ and to God's own fidelity, who has promised that when the sinner is so disposed, He will receive him into His favour, and pardon his sins. So that the justification of a sinner is wholly the gift of God, both because the dispositions necessary to prepare the sinner for receiving it are His gifts, and justification itself is given to these dispositions, not as in justice due to them, but as the gift of God"s mercy, through the merits of Jesus, and for His sake.

Q. 39. What are the dispositions required for the justification of a sinner?

A. The Holy Scripture clearly points out to us these following virtues, as necessary for this end: (1.) Faith in Jesus Christ; for "without faith it is impossible to please God,'" Heb. xi. 6 ; and therefore "the justice of God, by faith of Jesus Christ, unto all and upon all that believe in Him,'" Rom. iii. 22. (2.) The fear of God; for •' the fear of the Lord driveth out sin; for he that is without fear cannot be justified," Ecclus. i. 27. (3.) Hope and confidence in the mercy of God; for "he that trusteth in the Lord shall be healed," Prov. xxviii. 25 ; and therefore "we are saved by hope," Rom. viii. 24. (4.) A sincere love of God; for "he that loveth not, knoweth not God; for God is charity," i John, iv. 8 ; and "he that loveth not, abideth in death," i John, iii. 14. Hence "many sins are forgiven her, because she hath loved much," Luke, vii. 47. (5.) A sincere repentance for our sins; for "except you repent, you shall all likewise perish," Luke, xiii. 3. And therefore "repent and be converted that your sins may be blotted out," Acts, iii. 19. These are the dispositions pre-required by Almighty God as necessary for preparing the soul, and making her capable of receiving the grace of justification; and when we are thus prepared, we must (8.) have recourse to the sacra-ment of baptism if we have not as yet been baptised, or to the sacrament of penitence if we have lost the grace received already in baptism. Not indeed, properly speaking, as if these sacraments were another disposition to prepare us for our justification, but as the sacred instruments ordained by Jesus Christ, by which the grace of justification is poured into the soul when disposed by the above-mentioned virtues.

Q. 40. Will not faith alone serve to dispose a soul for justification?

A. By no means; for we see, from the texts mentioned above, that all these other conditions are required to drive away sin, to heal us, and to deliver us from death as well as faith; besides, St Paul expressly says, although "I should have all faith, so that I could remove mountains, and have not charity, I am nothing," i Cor. xiii. 2. And St James decides this point in express terms, saying, after a long reasoning, to prove what he says, "Do you see that by works a man is justified, and not by faith only? "James, ii. 24. And St Paul further declares that "in Christ Jesus, neither circumcision availeth anything, nor uncircumcision; but faith that worketh by charity," Gal. v. 6.

Q. 41. What kind of works do these apostles speak of?

A. Not any works done by the mere light of nature, nor even the works of the law of Moses; for all these were incapable of bringing us to the grace of justification; for "the law brought nothing to perfection," Heb. vii. 19. And "the gifts and sacrifices of the law cannot, as to the conscience, make him perfect that serveth," Heb. ix. 9 ; "for it is impossible, that with the blood of oxen and goats, sins should be taken away," Heb. x. 4. Therefore the works spoken of by these apostles are faith in Jesus Christ, which is the root and foundation of all Christian works, and those other virtues of fear, hope, love, and repentance, which naturally flow from that faith, as the branches of a tree from the root; and therefore St Paul, after showing the inability of the law and all its sacrifices to purify our consciences, concludes, "Let us draw near with a true heart, in fulness of faith;.... let us hold fast the confession of our hope without wavering;... let us consider one another to provoke unto charity and good works," Heb. x. 22. And writing to the Romans on this subject, he gives this reason: "For we account a man to be justified by faith, without the works of the law" (Rom. iii. 28) - namely, by that faith which, as he told us above, "worketh by charity," Gal. v. 6 ; but not by the works of the law of Moses.

Q. 42. In what manner do these other virtues above mentioned flow from faith as from their root?

A. As the beginning of all good must come from God to our souls, for "no man can come to me," says Jesus Christ, "except the Father, who sent Me, draw him," John, ii. 44 ; so when God of His infinite goodness touches the sinner's heart, and moves him to return to Him by repentance, the first step which the sinner takes in this great work is to believe with a firm faith all those sacred truths which Christ has revealed and His holy Church teaches. This faith, informing him of the severity of God's justice against sin, fills his heart with that wholesome "fear of the Lord, which is the beginning of wisdom," Prov. i. 7 ; and the same faith teaching him the infinite goodness and mercy of God, and His readiness to forgive repenting sinners, raises him up to a great confidence in God, through the merits of Jesus Christ. Then learning, from the same faith, how infinitely good God is in Himself, and how infinitely good to him in the numberless favours He has conferred on him, especially in the great work of our redemption, conceives in his heart a sincere love and affection towards so amiable a benefactor. Then reflecting on his manifold sins, the enormity of which his faith also discovers to him, he is filled with a hearty sorrow for having so ungratefully offended so good a God; he hates and detests his sins, which are displeasing and offensive to God, and firmly purposes to amend his life, and keep the law of God; and thus he turns to the Lord his God by a sincere repentance, and applies to the holy sacraments as the happy and effectual means of being restored to His friendship and favour.

Q. 43. But why did St Peter say only to the Jews, "Repent and be converted, that your sins may be blotted out," Acts, iii. 19 , without saying a word of these other virtues?

A. Because repentance is the last in order, and, when sincere, includes all the others in it. For it is impossible to repent as we ought without believing in God, fearing Him, hoping for pardon, and loving God; all which, though not always positively expressed, are virtually included in true repentance.

Q. 44. How can children be justified by baptism, since they are incapable of these dispositions?

A. If children in their infancy are incapable of having these dispositions, they are also incapable of committing any actual sin which may stand in need of repentance; they never turned away from God by any positive act of their own will, and therefore He does not require from them any positive act of their will to return to Him again - out of His infinite mercy He admits them to the grace of justification by the sacrament of baptism, without

any further disposition on their part; and in the same way He is pleased
to deal with those who, though grown up, have never had the use of reason. But in all others who are capable of committing sin themselves, and
of having the above dispositions. He absolutely requires they should have
these dispositions, without which the grace of justification will not be given
them, neither in the sacrament of baptism for sins committed before baptism, nor in the sacrament of penance for those committed after baptism.

Q. 45. Will not a perfect repentance serve to justify a sinner alone without
any sacrament?

A. A perfect repentance, founded on a perfect love of God, is very seldom
to be met with in sinners, much less can a sinner be certain that he possesses so great a happiness; yet, if so great a grace should be granted by God
to any sinner, there is no doubt but that God will at the same time grant
him the grace of justification; for our Saviour says, "If any man love Me, he
will keep My word, and My Father will love him, and we will come to him,
and will make Our abode with him," John, xiv. 23 ; but as the proof which
Christ here requires of the sincerity of his love is to obey His commands,
he will keep My words; and as the express command of Christ is that we
receive His sacraments, for the sanctification of our souls, therefore such
a one will not be justified, even by his perfect repentance; nor, indeed, will
his repentance be perfect unless it includes an efficacious will and resolution of applying to the sacraments, from which nothing can exempt him
but the impossibility of receiving them. And the reason is, because the sacraments are expressly ordained by Jesus Christ as the only ordinary means
by which the grace of justification is communicated to our souls.

Chapter XIX

Of The Sacraments In General

Q. I. What is a Sacrament?

A. sacrament is an outward sensible action, or sacred sign, ordained by Jesus Christ as a sure and certain means to bring grace to our souls.

Q. 2. How many things are required to make a true sacrament?

A. Three things: first, that there be some outward sensible action performed; secondly, that this be a certain means to bring grace to the soul; and thirdly, that Jesus Christ be the author of it.

Q. 3. What does this outward action consist in?

A. In something said and something done; the thing done is called the matter of the sacrament, and the words spoken the form of it.

Q. 4. To whom does it belong to perform the outward sensible action?

A. The outward action which is properly meant by the word sacrament is the work of men, and it belongs to those to perform it who are authorised and commissioned by Jesus Christ to do so.

Q. 5. To whom does it belong to bestow the inward grace?

A. The pouring down grace to the soul, which, properly speaking, is the effect of the sacrament, is the work of God, as none but God Himself can communicate His grace to the soul.

Q. 6. At what time does God bestow His grace upon the soul?

A. The very same instant that the outward action of any sacrament is completely performed.

Q. 7. Does God ever fail on His part to bestow the grace when the outward action is duly performed?

A. On His part He never fails in this; the connection between the outward sign performed and the inward grace received, is, on the part of God, infallible, being founded upon His fidelity and immutability. For having been pleased to ordain these outward forms to be the instruments, channels, or means by which His grace should be brought to our souls, and having instituted them as an essential part of the Christian religion for this purpose, by so doing He has evidently engaged Himself always to produce the effect whenever the sacrament is performed according to His appointment; therefore, as He is unchangeable and faithful to His engagements, He never will fail on His part to do so.

Q. 8. Is grace always bestowed when the sacrament is duly performed?

A. Alas! it too often happens that the grace of the sacrament is not bestowed, owing to the indisposition of the person who receives it. For though Almighty God is always ready upon His part to bestow the grace, yet if the receiver be indisposed, and His soul incapable of receiving it, the grace will not be given to him, though the outward form be duly administered - not from any failure on the part of God, but from the indisposition of the receiver.

Q. 9. Can you explain this by any example?

A. The familiar process of writing upon paper does so exactly. In writing, when a skilful hand applies the pen and ink, the intended characters never fail to be produced if in the paper there be no impediment. But should it be saturated with oil, not a single letter will be formed. Here the failure arises not from the instruments - the ink, the pen, or the hand that guides it - but from the state of the paper upon which the characters are attempted to be traced. This is a homely but apt illustration of the manner in which the sacraments are prevented from producing their effect on a soul indisposed and incapable of receiving grace.

Q. 10. Is it necessary to be well disposed when one approaches to a sacrament?

A. Most certainly; for if a person presume to receive any sacrament when ill disposed, he not only deprives his soul of the grace of that sacrament, but also commits a grievous sin of sacrilege by profaning those sacred instruments of our salvation. On the other hand, the more perfectly he is disposed by frequent and fervent acts of faith, hope, and charity, and other holy virtues, the more abundant grace he will receive, both because these more perfect dispositions move Almighty God to be more liberal of His graces to him, and they also enlarge the capacity of the soul to receive a more abundant communication of grace.

Q. 11. Can this be explained by any example?

A. As the sacraments are ordained by Jesus Christ to be the never-failing means of communicating His grace to our souls, they therefore contain in themselves an inexhaustible treasure of heavenly grace, from which the soul of every one that approaches them worthily receives as much as it is capable of containing. Now the capacity of the soul depends upon its dispositions - the more perfect they are, the more the capacity of the soul is enlarged, and therefore the greater portion of grace it receives from these heavenly fountains. So that the sacraments may be compared to a fountain, and the soul to a vessel which one carries to it. The fountain, abounding with water, fills every vessel that is applied to it, so far as it can contain; the larger the vessel is, the greater quantity of water it will carry away.

Q. 12. Has this comparison any foundation in Scripture?

A. It is entirely taken from the Scripture, for there the grace of God is compared to water, and the sacraments to the fountain of Jesus Christ, from which that heavenly water flows: thus, "I will pour clean water upon you," says Almighty God, "and you shall be cleansed from all your tilthiness," Ezek. xxxvi. 25 ; and our Saviour, speaking to the woman of Samaria, says, "He that shall drink of the water that I shall give him, shall not thirst for ever; but the water that I shall give him, shall become in him a fountain of water springing up unto everlasting life," John, iv. 13. Isaiah, foreseeing the inexhaustible sources of this heavenly water which were to be ordained by Christ in His holy sacraments, cries out with rapture, "You shall draw water with joy out of the Saviour's fountains! "Is. xii. 3. And the prophet Zacharias, on the same subject, says: "In those days there shall be a fountain open to the house of David, and to the inhabitants of Jerusalem, for the washing of the sinner and the unclean woman,"Zach. xiii. 1.

Q. 13. Why do you say that a sacrament is a sacred sign?

A. Because the outward action which is used in the sacrament is not only the instrument or means by which the grace of God is actually communicated to our souls, but it also represents to us the nature of that grace which we receive, as the principal thing of which it is the sign; it also reminds us of the passion and death of Jesus Christ, through the merits of which His grace is bestowed upon us, and the eternal salvation of our souls, which is the great end for which He bestows it. Thus St Paul says of baptism, "We who are baptised in Christ Jesus, are baptised in His death." See here how baptism is a sign of the death of Christ; and to put us more effectually in mind of this, the Church makes frequent use of the sign of the cross in administering the sacraments, especially in the most essential part of their administration, which teaches us that the whole virtue of the sacraments flows from the death of Christ upon the cross. The apostle goes on: "For we are buried together with Him by baptism unto death; that as Christ is risen from the dead by the glory of the Father, so we also may walk in newness of life," which shows that the sacrament of baptism is a sign of the grace we receive in it, by which we die to sin, and rise to a newness of life, after the example of the resurrection of Jesus. The apostle adds, "But if we have been planted together in the likeness of His death, we shall be also in the likeness of His resurrection," Rom. vi. 3 , to put us in mind that this holy sacrament is also a sign of our rising again at the last day by a glorious resurrection, as the end for obtaining which it was instituted. In like manner, of the holy communion it is said, "As often as you shall eat this bread and drink this chalice, you shall show the death of the Lord until He come," i Cor. xi. 26. See how it is a memorial of the death of Christ. Also, "He that eateth My flesh and drinketh My blood, abideth in Me and I in him," John, vi. 57 ; and '" He that eateth Me, the same shall live by Me," ver. 58. See how the action of receiving under the form of bread and wine is a sign of the inward grace. Lastly, "He that eateth My flesh and drinketh My blood, hath life everlasting, and I will raise him up in the last day," ver. 55. See how it is a pledge of eternal happiness.

Q. 14. Why did God ordain these external signs as the means of communicating His grace to our souls?

A. For several very important reasons: (1.) Li condescension to our weakness. For had man been a being purely spiritual, without any body. Almighty God would doubtless have bestowed His gifts upon him in a manner suitable to such a being, and therefore in a manner purely spiritual. But with us the case is very different. We are composed of a body and a soul; and in our present state of weakness and corruption, the latter is in such subjection to the former that things purely spiritual seldom make a proper impression upon us; nay, by far the greater part of mankind are so enslaved to their senses, that they seem incapable of comprehending anything but what falls under the notice of these organs; so that even the great truths of religion, which they are bound to know, must be suited to their capacity, and made easy and familiar to them by similitudes taken from sensible objects. On this account Almighty God, out of condescension to our weakness, has been pleased to ordain the sensible signs, which we call sacraments, as the instruments of bestowing His grace upon us, that we might the more easily understand the wonderful things He works in our souls by them.

(2.) To confirm our faith in His promises, and be a comfort to our souls. The grace of God, by which we are restored to His friendship and cleansed from our sins, and at the same time strengthened to persevere in His service, is doubtless the most important benefit we can receive from Him in this life; and when we are so unhappy as to have lost His friendship by sin, nothing can be a greater comfort to us than a well-grounded confidence that we are reconciled to Him again. Now, as He has instituted the sacraments with this express promise, that when they are received by a person properly disposed He will never fail on His part to communicate His grace to the soul, this renders the sacraments a great source of consolation • for though we have not an absolute certainty of receiving the grace, because we can never have a certainty of our dispositions being what they ought, yet, as we are absolutely certain of the effects of the sacraments on the part of God, and can have a very high probability of our own dispositions, this is fully sufficient for a well-grounded hope and confidence in God, through the merits of our blessed Redeemer. This degree of certainty - the highest which God allows us in this life - serves, on the one hand, to keep us humble, and to make us "work out our salvation with fear and trembling; "and on the other, gives us a sufficient ground of hope for mercy, and fills us with consolation.

(3.) To unite all the members of His Church in one body; for no society of men can be united unless they be joined by some sensible tie or bond which keeps them together. Now in the Church of Christ the sacraments are bonds which unite all her members, distinguish them from others who do not belong to her, and serve, at the same time, as an open profession of their faith in Jesus Christ, by whom they were ordained: "We are all baptised," says St Paul, "into one body," i Cor. xii. 13 ; and "we being many, are one body, who partake of that one bread," i Cor. x. 17.

(4.) To humble our pride, and teach us our own misery and unworthiness, when we see that all the dispositions we can have, and all the means we can use, are unworthy of the great and inestimable benefit of the grace of justification, and that we are forced after all to submit ourselves to the use of sensible elements for obtaining this favour, and thereby constrained to acknowledge that it is the effect of the pure mercy and goodness of God alone, through the merits of Jesus Christ, and not given as due to any merit in us.

Q. 15. Why do you say that the sacraments are sacred signs, ordained by Jesus Christ.

A. Because the sacraments do not, of their own nature, signify the grace they contain, neither do they do so from the institution of men, much less can any outward action of itself confer the grace of God on our souls. This is wholly owing to the good will and pleasure of Almighty God; for He alone can bestow His grace upon us, and He alone can ordain by what means He pleases to do so; and seeing He has ordained these determined actions which we call sacraments, and no other, as the means of bestowing His grace on man, by these alone, and no other, can we obtain it. Hence it follows that no power upon earth can change what was ordained by Jesus Christ in the outward forms of the sacraments without destroying them entirely; for if any change be made in what He ordained to be done, it is no more the same form to which His grace was annexed, and consequently ceases to be a sacrament at all.

Q. 16. Who are those whom Jesus Christ has authorised and commissioned to administer His sacraments?

A. The administration of the sacraments is one of the sacred powers of the priesthood, which Jesus Christ gave to His apostles, and their successors the bishops and priests of the Church, who are therefore called the "Ministers of Christ, and the dispensers of the mysteries of God," I Cor. iv. 1 , because they are authorised by Christ, as His substitutes, to perform in His name the outward actions, or sacred signs, in which the sacraments consist. So that in the administration of any sacrament two persons always concur, the minister of the sacrament, who, as the organ of Christ, performs the outward part in a visible manner; and Christ Himself, who, as the principal but invisible agent, imparts the inward grace to the soul of the worthy receiver at the very moment that the outward action is performed by His minister.

Q. 17. What things are required in the minister of the sacraments to administer it validly?

A. These three things: (1.) That he be. authorised by Jesus Christ to perform it. Thus the bishops or first pastors of the Church, to whom the plenitude of the priestly powers belong, are authorised by Christ to administer all the sacraments. The priests, who are called the pastors of the second order, are authorised by their office to administer all the sacraments except confirmation and holy orders. The deacons receive power by their ordination to administer baptism with all its solemnities, by commission from the two former; and the inferior orders and all lay persons, both men and women, are authorised, in case of necessity, to administer baptism privately. (2.) That he have the intention at least of doing what the Church does. (3.) That he perform the sacred sign exactly.

Q. 18. Is it not necessary that the person who administers any sacrament be in the state of grace?

A. A person who knows himself to be in the state of sin, and in disgrace with God, and who in. that state should presume to administer any sacrament, would be guilty of a very great sin by so doing; but this would make no difference as to the fruit of the sacrament in the worthy receiver; for the effects of the sacraments are not annexed to the sanctity of the person who administers I them, but to the exact performance of the external rite by a person properly authorised. In this we see the infinite goodness of God, Who, for our greater comfort, would not let the efficacy of His sacraments depend on the sanctity of the minister; because this being a circumstance of which we can have no certain knowledge, nor even probable assurance, had it been required, we should have been deprived of all solid ground of hope, and been left in a state of perpetual doubt and fear whether we had received the grace of the sacrament or not.

Q. 19. What kind of grace do the sacraments communicate to the worthy receiver?

A. Two kinds, justifying grace and sacramental grace.

Q. 20. How do they confer justifying grace?

A. If the receiver be in the state of sin, by the sacraments of baptism and penance he receives the first grace of justification, by which he is cleansed from the guilt of his sins, and restored to the friendship of God. These two sacraments are instituted for this very end; baptism to cleanse us from original sin, and also from all actual sins which an adult person may have committed before baptism; and penance, to cleanse us from all the sins we have committed after baptism; and on this account baptism and penance are called the sacraments of the dead, because they raise the soul from the death of sin to the life of grace. On the other hand, if the person be already in the state of grace, and receive any of the other sacraments, he receives by them an increase of justifying grace, by which his soul is rendered more pure and holy, and more beautiful in the sight of God; and therefore these other sacraments are called the sacraments of the living, because they cannot be received worthily unless the soul of the receiver be alive to God by being in the state of grace. The sacrament of penance, also, is sometimes of this number - namely, when the penitent is already in the state of grace, and has only venial sins upon his conscience; for then, with the pardon of these venial sins by the sacrament of penance, he receives an increase of justifying grace also.

Q. 21. What is meant by sacramental grace?

A. Sacramental grace is that particular actual grace which is peculiar to each sacrament, and which strengthens the worthy receiver and enables him to perform the duties and accomplish the ends for which each particular sacrament was intended. Thus in baptism we receive strengthening grace to enable us to lead a Christian life; in confirmation, to profess our faith in the midst of all dangers, and resist all the enemies of our souls in the holy communion, to preserve and augment the life of the soul, and the love of God; in penance, to preserve us from falling back into sin; in extreme unction, to overcome our spiritual enemies in the hour of death; and in holy orders and matrimony, to discharge properly all the duties of these two states of life.

Q. 22. Have the sacraments any other effect besides bringing these graces to the soul?

A. Three of them - baptism, confirmation, and holy orders - produce also another effect, which is to imprint a character or seal in the soul by the operation of the Holy Ghost; of which the Scripture says, in Christ "also believe you were sealed with the Holy Spirit of promise," Eph. i. 13. And again, "Grieve not the Holy Spirit of God, whereby you are sealed unto the day of redemption," Eph. iv. 30. And of confirmation in particular it is said, "Now He that confirmeth us with you in Christ and He that hath anointed us in God, who hath also sealed us," 2 Cor. i. 21.

Q. 23. What is understood by a character?

A. It is a spiritual mark or sign imprinted in the soul, similar to the impression of a seal upon soft wax, which denotes that the person who receives it is thereby consecrated and dedicated to the service of God, according to the intention for which the sacramant was instituted. Thus the character of baptism denotes that the person who has it is consecrated to God as a Christian, is a member of the Church of Christ, and entitled to all the other sacraments of the Church, as helps to enable him to serve God in that quality. The character of confirmation denotes that the person who has it was dedicated to the service of God as His soldier, and engaged for ever to serve Him in that quality, which the grace of that sacrament enables him to do. The character of priesthood denotes that the person who has it is consecrated to God, to serve at His altar, and that he has received all the sacred powers annexed to that high office.

Q. 24. Does this character remain for ever in the soul?

A. Yes; and on that account the three sacraments which give it can never be received more than once by the same person; for if a person be once a baptised or a confirmed Christian, or a priest, he remains so for ever: and in the next life these sacred characters will be a great increase of glory to those who go to heaven, and of misery to those who go to hell.

Q. 25. How many sacraments are there in the Church of Christ?

A. There are seven - baptism, confinnation, holy eucharist, penance, extreme unction, holy orders, and matrimony.

Q. 26. How can it be proved that there are seven sacraments? Is there any text of Scripture that says so?

A. There is not one text of Scripture which explicitly declares the nature of the sacraments, or determines their precise number. And in this we see the inconsistency of those who pretend to follow no rule but Scripture, and to believe nothing but what is to be found in plain Scripture; while yet they admit two sacraments, and reject the others, though they cannot bring one text of Scripture to authorise their doing so. But that there are seven true and real sacraments instituted by Jesus Christ, and left by Him in His Church for the benefit of His followers, is proved by two unanswerable arguments. First, Because we find in Scripture that there are seven outward actions laid down there, as certain means appointed by God to bring grace to our souls, as will be shown when explaining each sacrament in particular. And, Secondly, Because the Church of Christ in all ages, from the very beginning, has believed and acknowledged the seven sacraments above mentioned, and has administered them as means of grace to her children.

Q. 27. Are all obliged to receive the sacraments according to the need we may have of them?

A. Some of the sacraments are only intended for particular purposes and states of life, and those only are obliged to receive them who embrace those states, such as holy orders and matrimony; but the others are intended for the benefit of all Christians, and therefore all are obliged to receive them, otherwise the grace to remedy their wants will not be granted. For as they are ordained by Jesus Christ as the means by which He bestows His grace upon our souls, and as the ultimate condition for this purpose, presupposing all the other conditions required as dispositions on our side, and as He is free master of His own gifts, and may require what condition He pleases from His creatures, in order to receive them, it is not enough that we perform some of these conditions - we must perform them all; and the sacraments being the last required, and which serve as the very instruments for bestowing upon us the grace intended by them, it is plain that the other conditions without this will not be sufficient, and therefore that it is absolutely necessary to receive the sacraments where they can be had, in order to receive the grace annexed to them.

Q. 28. Why are so many ceremonies used in the administration of the sacraments?

A. To understand this it will be necessary to explain the nature of ceremonies more particularly.

Appendix To The Sacraments In General: Of Sacred Ceremonies

Q. 29. What is properly meant by a rite or ceremony?

A. A rite or ceremony, taken in its most general sense, is an outward action or sign, used by men either for promoting a becoming decorum in the necessary intercourse of society, or for recalling to our mind the remembrance of some truth which does not fall under the notice of our senses, or for exciting certain affections in the mind of those who are present, or for testifying to others the affections of our souls. Thus in all courts of justice there are certain outward forms or ceremonies appointed to be observed as necessary for carrying on the business done there with regularity and order. The ensigns of royalty in the king, robes and badges of office used by magistrates, are so many ceremonies which remind us of the dignity of their station, the authority with which they are invested, and excite the sentiments of respect due to their character. In common life itself the outward actions of bowing or uncovering the head are ceremonies by which we testify our mutual regard and esteem; and the very rules of good breeding in company are but so many rites or ceremonies by which we express our respect for one another, excite and improve our mutual benevolence, and carry on the intercourse of life with becoming decorum and propriety.

Q. 30. Is the use of ceremonies necessary in human life?

A. According to the present providence under which we live, and the frame and disposition of human nature, the use of external rites or ceremonies is so absolutely necessary that it is impossible to discharge the ordinary duties of society, whether civil or religious, without them.

Q. 31. What is meant by a sacred rite or ceremony?

A. A sacred ceremony is an outward action or sign, ordained by the Church of Christ, to be used in the external exercise of religion, and chiefly for three reasons:

(1.) For greater decorum the necessary uniformity in performing the exterior duties of religion. It is impossible to perform the outward acts of religion, such as administering the sacrifice, offering up sacrifice, or the like, without using some external action in doing so - that is, without using ceremonies. Now, in the choice of these, two things ought chiefly to be had in view: First, that the most proper and orderly be used; and, secondly, that all the members of the Church use the same. The majesty of God and the sanctity of religion require the first, in order to excite in the minds of men proper sentiments of reverence and devotion; and experience itself shows how much the sacred ceremonies of religion conduce to this end. The uniformity in religion, so necessary for preserving union among Christians, demands the second, which has also this good effect, that no one is ever at a loss to join with those of his own religion in all its duties, in whatever part of the world he may find himself And this shows how necessary it is that these ceremonies should be enjoined by the public authority of the

Church; because, if it were left to every one to use such ceremonies in religion as he pleases, neither of these two ends could be procured; all would be disorder and confusion.

(2.) That by these outward ceremonies we may give to Almighty God the external worship of our bodies, expressing by their means the internal dispositions of our souls. Thus by using the sign of the cross we profess our faith in a crucified Saviour, and that all our hopes are founded on the merits of His death upon the cross; by kneeling or bowing our bodies, which are postures of humility and supplication, we show our interior dependence on Almighty God, and the respect and reverence we give Him, like the humble publican in the Gospel; and so of others. Now this external worship is an honour offered to God, as it manifests to others our piety towards Him, and by our example excites them to the same; when it proceeds from the heart, is highly agreeable to Him, and what He requires from us; besides, experience teaches that the internal respect and reverence of our souls are not a little influenced by the reverential posture of our bodies.

(3.) That by these outward ceremonies the great truths and instructions of religion may be represented in a sensible and striking manner to the eyes of the people.

There are numbers of people, especially of the lower class, of dull and heavy understandings, who never learn to read, having received no proper education, and who, consequently, are incapable of improving their minds by the necessary knowledge of religion, through their own study. This is the case with great multitudes in all nations at present, but was much more so before the invention of printing, when perhaps not one in many thousands knew to read. For all these it is most necessary to use proper ceremonies, by which the truths of religion may be set before them, that by seeing these daily performed, the truths represented by them may be more deeply imprinted in their minds, and become familiar to them. Thus the sacred ceremonies used in the administration of the sacraments represent either the dispositions with which we ought to receive them, the effects which they produce in our souls, or the obligations we contract by receiving them, as we shall see more particularly under each sacrament.

Q. 32. By whom are religious ceremonies instituted?

A. They were first instituted by God Himself from the very earliest ages of the world; for we find Cain and Abel, the sons of Adam, employed in offering up sacrifices and gifts to God; Noah did the same after the Flood, as also the patriarchs after him. Now they must have been induced to this (as an act of external worship due to God, and which necessarily required some external action, indicating the dispositions of their souls) either by the express command of God Himself, or by the light of reason; for we find that their doing so was pleasing to God, and received His approbation. Besides, God Almighty, in express terms, instituted the sacred ceremony of circumcision with Abraham, as a sign of the covenant made with him, and commanded it to be used by all his posterity, under pain of death, as a distinctive mark of his true religion. Of Jacob, we read that, after his mysterious dream, "arising in the morning he took the stone which he had laid under his head, and set it up for a title, pouring oil upon the top of it,... and he made a vow," Gen. xxviii. i8. And God highly approved of this religious ceremony used by him, saying, "I am the God of Bethel, where thou didst anoint the stone, and made a vow to me," Gen. xxxi. 13. And when afterwards He was pleased to reveal to Moses the whole form of religion with which He required to be worshipped by His people, what a number of august and mysterious ceremonies did He not appoint to be used in all the parts of it, both as memorials of the favours conferred on that people, and as types and figures of the more perfect religion to be afterwards revealed by Jesus Christ! and these ceremonies He commanded to be observed with the strictest attention, so as to threaten the severest punishment upon those who should profane them. In the second place, sacred ceremonies were instituted by Jesus Christ, and the use of them is highly approved and authorised by His example. In curing the man who had been born blind, "He spat on the ground, and made clay of the spittle, and spread the clay upon his eyes; and said to him, Go, wash in the pool of Siloe;.. and he went, and washed, and he came seeing," John, ix. 6. Again, in curing the deaf and dumb man, "Taking him aside from the multitude, He put His fingers into his ears, and spitting. He touched his tongue; and looking up to heaven. He groaned and said, Ephpheta, that is, Be thou opened; and immediately his ears were opened, and the string of his tongue was loosed, and he spoke right," Mark, vii. 11. What a number of ceremonies were used by Jesus Christ upon these two occasions! and for what end? They surely were by no means necessary for curing these two men. A word from Him was fully sufficient for that purpose; but as His actions are recorded for our example, we have in these two cases His sacred authority in approbation of holy ceremonies. Add to His example His express command and institutions; for at the Last Supper, when He instituted the holy sacrament, "Jesus took bread, and blessed, and broke, and gave to His disciples," Mat. xxvi. 26. And after He had done so, with all these ceremonies He gave them express orders to do what He had done, which is literally observed throughout the whole Church to this day. Also, on the day of His resurrection "He breathed on His apostles," and said, "receive ye the Holy Ghost," to show, by that ceremony of breathing upon them, the communication of His Divine Spirit which He thereby gave them , John, xx. 22. Thus Jesus Christ instituted sacred ceremonies by His command, and authorised them by His example; and the Church, on that account, has retained and uses several of those very rites, here related as done by Him, upon different occasions, as we shall afterwards see.

In the third place, sacred ceremonies were instituted by the apostles and their successors; for though our blessed Saviour Himself ordained some, and authorised the use of them in general by His example, yet He left the determination of particular ceremonies to His apostles and their successors in office, the pastors of the Church, whom He appointed, with full authority, to ordain whatever might be proper, according to circumstances, "for the edification of the body of Christ," Eph. iv. And we find that many of the ceremonies used at!Mass, and in administering the sacraments, were instituted by the apostles themselves, as they were used universally through out the whole Church from the very earliest ages, and are attested by the earliest Christian writers to have been received from them. Of this kind are the sign of the cross, holy water, and the greater part of the ceremonies of baptism. The Church also, at different times, has instituted such sacred ceremonies as she judged proper, and circumstances required, according to the power left with her by Jesus Christ for that end.

Q. 33. But are not the religious ceremonies used in the Catholic Church contrary to the simplicity and humility of the Gospel?

A. This is, indeed, a popular outcry against the Church, under an appearance of piety; but on examination it will be discovered to be without reason and devoid of truth: for (1.) Whatever conduces to preserve order and decorum in the worship of God cannot be contrary to the humility and simplicity of religion; for right reason teaches us that order and decorum ought to be observed in all things, but especially in what regards the service of the Almighty; and St Paul expressly commands that "all things be done decently and according to order," i Cor. xiv. 40. And after having laid down some general rules down, he concludes, "The rest I will set in order when I come," i Cor. xi. 34. Now all the public ceremonies of the Church are ordained for this end, and to preserve uniformity in the externals of religion. (2.) Whatever has a connection with virtue, conduces to our improvement in any virtue, and is used for no other view but to render us more virtuous and better disposed towards the service of God, cannot possibly be against the humility and simplicity of religion; for this can never forbid any external action which is performed with an humble and sincere heart in order to honour God. Now all the ceremonies of religion are intended to excite in our minds a high idea of the magnificence and grandeur of Almighty God, and a just sense of our own misery and wretchedness; and they are intended to give public homage to God as our sovereign Lord, and to acknowledge our dependence upon Him. (3.) The humility and simplicity of the Gospel consist in a deep sense of the infinite majesty of God, and of our own unworthiness, and in a total submission to Him, seeking His honour and glory, and the accomplishment of His holy will in all things. Now experience itself teaches that nothing contributes more effectually to excite in our souls a reverential awe and fear of the Divine Majesty, with a sense of our own nothingness in His presence, than those solemn and august ceremonies which the Church uses upon public occasions. (4.) Sacred ceremonies, so far from being contrary to the humility and simplicity of the Gospel, are grounded on the very constitution of our nature, which must be instructed in spiritual things by such helps as fall under our senses; for the same reason that Almighty God, by means of outward things in the holy sacraments, confers His grace, which is spiritual and invisible, on our souls. By not paying due attention to this, many, on pretence of refining religion, and rendering it more spiritual, have begun by retrenching ceremonies which they called superfluous, and from this have proceeded to cut off some of the very essentials of religion: witness the sacrament of baptism, which many nowadays are not ashamed to teach, is nowise necessary to salvation - nay, that it is superstition to believe it to be so.

Q. 34. Do not many of these ceremonies savour too much of worldly pomp, which nourishes pride instead of humility- such as the ornaments of churches, the magnificence of priestly vestments, and the like?

A. It is surprising to see how ingenious people are to deceive themselves when they wish to be deceived. This also is a common reproach of the enemies of the Catholic Church, but shows with how little consideration they speak when they speak against her. Let us suppose the greatest splendour and magnificence to be used in the cases mentioned, in whose heart can they be imagined to nourish pride or vanity? not in the people who see them, more than the ornaments of a royal palace, or the robes which the king uses, could nourish pride in the minds of any of his subjects who were seeing them. On the contrary, experience in both cases teaches that they produce the very opposite effect, and inspire the beholders with sentiments of respect and reverence - not in the priests who use them, for these sacred vestments, however rich and magnificent they may be, serve only to place before their eyes the passion of Jesus Christ, which they represent, and the sacred virtues of humility, purity, mortification, and love of Jesus Christ, with which His priests ought to be adorned. These are humbling lessons for every priest, which the sacred vestments he uses continually preach to him - very opposite, indeed, to worldly pride and vanity. And what shows, beyond reply, how far the magnificence and splendour of churches and sacred ornaments are from inspiring sentiments of pride, is, that we learn, from the history of all ages, that those holy saints who were most remark-able for their profound humility and solid virtue were, at the same time, the most zealous for the splendour and magnificence of everything relating to the service of God. On the other hand, those who cry out most against those things are generally persons devoid of all sense of piety and rever-ence for God, full of themselves and their own opinions, and whose hearts are ulcerated with a malignant envy at seeing that employed for the honour of the Almighty which they would rather see used for themselves. Finally, Can anything be conceived more splendid and magnificent than what God Himself commanded to be done both in the sacred vestments used by His priests in the old law, and the profusion of riches in everything regard-ing His temple? and shall we accuse Him on this account of encouraging worldly pride and vanity in His people? This example of God Himself gives the most ample sanction to all the magnificence that can be used in His holy service.

Q. 35. Ought we, then, to pay a great respect to sacred ceremonies?

A. Most undoubtedly; they deserve that great respect and veneration should be paid them, on account of the ends for which they are used, the sacred truths and holy instructions which they represent, and also the authority by which they are instituted; and therefore the Church, in the General Council of Trent, condemns and pronounces an anathema on all those who shall presume to say that it is lawful to despise or ridicule, or by private authority to alter or change, any of the received and approved ceremonies of the Church. - Sess. vii. can. 13. God Himself approves the respect we pay them, both by the commendations given in Scripture to those who used them, as the humble Publican and St Mary Magdalen, and also by the miraculous victory given to the people of God over the Ama-lekites, which in a manner wholly depended upon the sacred ceremony used by Moses of lifting up his hands in prayer during the engagement; for "when Moses lifted up his hands, Israel overcame, but if he let them down a little, Amalek overcame," Exod. xvii. 11. But as Moses' hands were heavy, "Aaron and Hur stayed up his hands on both sides," till a complete victory was gained. And, indeed, those who speak against the sacred ceremonies which the Church uses manifestly discover either the pride of their own heart, in presuming to be better judges of these matters than the Church of Christ, which He has authorised to appoint them, or their contempt for her sacred authority, or at least a gross ignorance of the subject of which they speak, and of the sacred and important truths which these holy ceremonies represent and convey to the mind.

Q. 36. Why does the Church make use of the Latin language in administering the sacraments, and in her other public offices of religion?

A. When the Christian religion was first published to the world, Latin was the common language of all the western parts of Europe, throughout the Roman empire, and all the public offices of the Church were performed in that language. In process of time, when many barbarous nations broke in upon and dismembered that empire, they soon altered the Latin language, and, by mixing it with their own, produced the various languages now commonly in use in the different European nations. Amidst these changes of languages, the Church wisely judged it necessary to preserve the use of the Latin in all her public offices, chiefly for two reasons: First, to preserve greater uniformity in the externals of religion among all her members, from which this great good also arises, that all her members, wherever they go, at whatever distance from their own country, always find themselves, as it were, at home in all the exercises of religion, as they everywhere find both the selfsame things done, and the same language used, to which they have been accustomed from their infancy. Secondly, all living languages are subject to daily changes, both in the way of speaking and in the meaning of words; this must have occasioned frequent translations of the public Church offices had they followed the changes in the common language of every country; and this could not have been done without introducing much obscurity and many equivocal expressions, which, of course, would have given occasion to introduce new, and consequently false, opinions in the sacred truths of revelation itself: whereas the Latin, being a dead language, fixed in its signification, and incapable of change, the constant use of it in all religious offices contributes, in no small degree, to preserve the purity of religion itself, and shuts the door against all dangerous novelties.

Q. 37. But is not this a loss to the people who do not understand Latin?

A. By no means; for in the first place, the part which the priest has to perform, both in the administration of the sacraments, and in celebrating the
holy sacrifice of the Mass, is not to pray with the people, but to pray to God
for them in their name, as their deputy and representative, and the greater
part of what he says, and everything he does, is suited to the public character he bears so that, though he were to use the vulgar language, the people
could not join in saying the same prayers, much less could they do what he
does. But in the second place, as they are instructed from their childhood
in the nature of what he does, and accustomed to it by daily practice, they
have prayers in their manuals and books of devotion, which are adapted
to them, and by which they accompany him through every part of his
functions in manner proper for their state. Neither are they ignorant of the
nature of the prayers he offers up for them, as they have been explained in
their books of instruction, and therefore can find no difficulty in uniting
their prayers and intentions for the same end.

Q. 38. Is this practice authorised by the Scripture?

A. It is; for during the Babylonish captivity the people lost the knowledge
of the old Hebrew language, in which the Scriptures were written, insomuch that, upon their return to Jerusalem after the captivity, when Nehemias and Esdras the priest read the law to the people, they were obliged
"to interpret to them the words of the law,"Nehem. viii. 13; and from, that
period the vulgar language they spoke was the Syriac, into which the Scriptures were not translated from the Hebrew till after our Saviour's time, and
yet all their public offices were taken from the law, psalms, and prophets in
the old Hebrew. Besides, we find this command given by God Himself: "Let
no man be in the tabernacle when the high priest goeth into the sanctuary
to pray for himself and his house, and for the whole congregation of Israel,
until he come out," Lev. xvi. 17. In consequence of this, it is recorded of
Zacharias, St John Baptist's father, that when, "according to the custom of
the priestly office, it was his lot to offer incense, going into the temple of
the Lord, all the multitude of the people was praying without, at the hour
of incense," Luke, i. 9 ; where we see, by God's express command, public
prayers made by the priest expressly for the people, and the sacrifice of
incense offered for them, and yet not one of them permitted so much as to
be present, much less to hear and understand what the priest was saying to
God for them; yet they assisted without at this function, joined in prayer,
and doubtless were no less partakers of its benefits than if they had both

heard and seen the whole. Finally, Any apparent inconvenience that might seem to arise from having the public offices of the Church in the Latin language, because not understood by the unlearned, is certainly a mere nothing if compared to the greater advantages of using that language, as we have seen above, and to the unavoidable detriment that would follow were these public offices subject to all the variety of vulgar languages, and to the changes which they are continually undergoing.

Q. 39. Why is the sign of the cross so frequently made use of in the administration of the sacraments?

A. The sign of the cross is a sacred ceremony which is used by Catholics more frequently, both in the administration of the sacraments, and in offering up the holy sacrifice, and upon many other occasions, than any other ceremony whatsoever, and there are several strong and important reasons for doing so, which are as follows: -

(1.) This sacred sign of the cross is a means of reminding us of the two great and most important truths of our holy religion, the Unity and Trinity of God, and the incarnation and death of Jesus Christ, which two mysteries are the sum of all Christian knowledge; for there are two things in this life which it is chiefly important to know - our last end, for which we were created, to which all our desires ought to tend, and in which our true and perfect happiness is only to be found; and the way or means by which we can arrive at it. Now God alone is our last end, in Him alone we can find our perfect and essential happiness; and Jesus Christ is the only way by which we can attain to the possession of this happiness, for "He is the way, the truth, and the life; the way by His example, the truth by His doctrine, and the life of our souls by His grace; and "no man," says He, "Cometh to the Father but by Me," John, xiv. 6. So that it is only by imitating His example, believing and obeying His doctrine, and assisted by His grace, that we can be saved; and therefore, to know God and Jesus Christ as we ought, is to know all that is necessary to make us eternally happy; this Jesus Christ Himself declares, saying to His Father, "This is life eternal, that they may know Thee, the only true God, and Jesus Christ Whom Thou hast sent," John, xvii. 3. Now the sign of the cross is a memorial of this wholesome knowledge, and serves to keep us in mind of it, as being the most important thing we have to think upon, or take an interest in, in the whole world; for the words we pronounce when making this sacred sign contain an invocation of the blessed Trinity, one God and three Persons, and the very sign itself recalls to our mind the incarnation and death of Jesus Christ,

God made man.

(2.) The sign of the cross is an external profession of our faith, a distinguishing mark of the members of the Church of Christ; it is the livery of Jesus Christ, by which His followers are known and distinguished from Turks, Jews, heretics, and unbelievers. In making this sign we openly profess that we believe in one God and three Persons; that God the Son was made man, and died on the cross for us, and that we are Catholics, and members of the Church of Christ - that is, of that sacred body of which Christ is the head.

(3.) It is also, on many occasions, an external protestation of our hope and confidence in God, through the merits of Christ, "by Whom we have access in one Spirit to the Father," Eph. ii. 18 ; for when we begin our prayers by making the sign of the cross, we by this profess that our only hope of being heard is through the merits of the cross of Jesus; when we offer up anything to God Almighty, and dedicate it to His service, we sign it with the sign of the cross, to signify that we have no hope of its being acceptable to Him but only through the merits of the death of Jesus; when we bless ourselves or other creatures, we make the sign of the cross, to declare that we expect no blessing from God but through the passion and cross of Jesus; when we administer any sacrament, we make use of the same sacred sign, to show that all the benefit we expect from the sacrament flows only from the same Divine source, the merits of Jesus.

(4.) It is also a memorial of the infinite love of God toward us, who out of pure love for us gave His only begotten Son to die on the cross for our salvation; and as nothing contributes more effectually to inflame our hearts with love towards our friends than the memory of their love to us, hence this sacred sign is an incentive to our love of God and of Jesus Christ; because it is a memorial of His love to us, and of all the great benefits He obtained for us by its means; of His victory over Satan, sin, and hell, His blotting out the handwriting that was against us, His reconciling us with God, and opening to us the kingdom of heaven.

(5.) It is a great defence against all the assaults of the devil. St Paul tells us that Jesus Christ, by His death on the cross, "spoiled principalities and powers, and made a show of them confidently, triumphing openly over them in Himself," Col. ii. 15. It was by the cross that the devil was crucified invisibly by Jesus Christ, his hands bound, his power taken from him, and his kingdom destroyed; for this reason he abhors the cross of Christ, and the very sign of it is hateful to him; and on this account all the holy Fathers, those ancient and venerable champions of the Christian religion, have left in their writings the warmest commendations of this holy sign, as a most powerful defence and protection against our infernal enemies; and many examples are recorded in the history of the Church, in all ages, of its wonderful efficacy in this respect, and of numberless miracles being wrought by the holy servants of God by its means.

(6.) It is the sacred mark ordered by God Himself to be put upon all those that belong to Him, as a means to defend them against the destroying angels in the day of His wrath, which is thus declared in Scripture: "The Lord called to the man that was clothed with linen, and had a writer's inkhorn at his loins, and said to him, Go through the midst of the city, through the midst of Jerusalem, and mark Thau upon the foreheads of the men that sigh and mourn for all the abominations that are committed in the midst thereof. And to the others, (the six angels that had each one his weapon of destruction in his hand, ver. 2) He said in my hearing, Go ye after him through the city, and strike; let not your eye spare, nor be ye moved with pity; utterly destroy old and young maidens, children, and women; but on whomsoever ye shall see Thau, kill him not," Ezek. ix. 4. Thau is the last letter of the Hebrew alphabet, and in the old Hebrew characters was the form of a cross, as our T is to this day, as is attested by St Jerome and other interpreters. The same vision was repeated to St John in the Revelations, who says: "I saw another angel descending from the rising sun, having the seal of the living God: and he cried with a loud voice to the four angels to whom it was given to hurt the earth, and the sea, saying. Hurt not the earth, nor the sea, nor the trees, till we seal the servants of our God in their foreheads," Rev. vii. 2. All which was prefigured by the blood of the paschal lamb, which God ordered His people in Egypt to "put upon the side-posts and upper door-post of their houses "(Exod. xii. 7) as their defence when He sent His angel to destroy all the first-born of Egypt: "For when I shall see the blood," says He, "I shall pass over you, and the plague shall not be upon you to destroy you," ver. 13. The paschal lamb was a type of Jesus Christ upon the cross, and the sign of His cross upon our foreheads is a sign of His precious blood shed upon the cross for us, which, like the blood of the paschal lamb, preserves us from the destroying angel.

Q. 40. In what manner must we use this holy sign in order to be partakers of these benefits?

A. St Paul, speaking of the ceremony of circumcision, says: "Circumcision profiteth, indeed, if thou keep the law; but if thou be a transgressor of the law, thy circumcision is made uncircumcision.... The circumcision is that of the heart in the spirit, not in the letter," Rom. ii. 25 , 29. As circumcision was the mark of the people of God under the law, so the sign of the cross is the mark of the followers of Christ under the Gospel; consequently, "The sign of the cross profiteth, indeed, if we obey the Gospel, if it be planted in the heart and spirit as well as in the body;" but without this it will only be an empty sign, or rather will turn out to our greater condemnation. The sign of the cross is the sign of humility, of patience, of meekness, of charity, the darling virtues of Jesus Christ, which in the most admirable manner He practised upon the cross. What will it profit, then, to make the sign of the cross upon the body, if these virtues, which it represents, are not seated in the heart and spirit?

Q. 41. Is the use of the sign of the cross very ancient in the Church?

A. It is as ancient as Christianity itself; and the practice of the primitive Christians in using it is thus described by Tertullian, a learned Christian writer of the second century: "At ever)- step, at our coming in and going out, when we put on our clothes or shoes, when we wash, when we sit down to table, when we light a candle, when we go to bed - whatever con-versation employs us, we imprint on our foreheads the sign of the cross."
- De Coron.Milit, c. 3.

For all the above reasons, then, this sacred sign is frequently made use of by the members of the Catholic Church, both in their private devotions and in the public exercises of religion, and in a particular manner in the administration of all the sacraments, that it may serve to keep us perpetu-ally in mind that all the graces and benefits we receive from them flow only from the merits of the passion and death of Jesus Christ upon the cross, as will appear in explaining the ceremonies of each sacrament in particular.

Chapter XX

Of The Sacrament Of Baptism

Q. 1. "What is the design or end for which the sacrament of baptism was instituted?

A. The design of this sacrament is to make us Christians, to deliver us from the slavery of Satan under which we are born, to unite us to Jesus Christ, as members of His body, and to give us a right and title to receive all the other sacraments and helps of religion in this life, and eternal happiness in the life to come.

Q. 2. How is all this done?

A. By the new birth which we receive in baptism, by which we become the children of God, being spiritually born again by the grace which is here bestowed upon us. In our natural birth from our earthly parents, we are born carnal-minded, sullied with sin, subject to eternal death, and aliens from God. In this new birth, which is the work of the Holy Ghost by the sacrament of baptism, our souls are formed anew, we become spiritual partakers of the Divine nature, heavenly-minded, and fit for the kingdom of God, as His children and heirs of His kingdom. Thus Jesus Christ explains this when He says, "That which is born of the flesh is flesh, and that which is born of the Spirit is spirit," John, iii. 6 .

Q. 3. Is baptism a true sacrament?

A. It is; because it has all the things requisite in a sacrament.

Q. 4. What is the outward sensible sign used in baptism?

A. Pouring water upon the person to be baptized, and saying, at the same time, these words, "I baptize thee in the name of the Father, and of the Son, and of the Holy Ghost."

Q. 5. How is this action performed?

A. By pouring water on the person to be baptized, or dipping him into it; and it is the order and custom in the Catholic Church to pour or dip three times at the names of the three Divine Persons, though the three times are not necessary for the validity of baptism.

Q. 6. What think you of those who administer baptism so slightly that it is doubtful whether it can in any sense be called an ablution or washing: for instance, those who administer it with a fillip of a wet finger?

A. Such as these run a great risk of not baptizing at all.

Q. 7. What is the inward grace which baptism brings to the soul?

A. The sanctifying grace of God, by which the soul is regenerated, cleansed from all the stains of original sin, and of actual sin if there be any, and is made a child of God, a member of His Church, and an heir of heaven.

Q. 8. Where do we find that Jesus Christ is the instituting of this sacrament?

A. From the commission which He gave to the pastors of the Church, in the persons of the apostles, when He said, "Go ye and teach all nations, baptizing them in the name of the Father, and of the Son, and of the Holy Ghost," Mat. xxviii. 19 .

Q. 9. How is this outward action a sign of the inward grace received?

A. The word baptize is a Greek word, which signifies to wash with water; when, therefore, water is poured upon the body outwardly, and these words pronounced, "I baptize thee "- that is, I wash thee with water - "in the name of the Father, and of the Son, and of the Holy Ghost," this represents the inward washing of the soul, by the sanctifying grace of God which is poured down upon it.

Q. 10. "What kind of water must be used in baptism?

A. Natural elementary water only, such as is produced by nature, and not by the art of man; and it is immaterial whether it be taken from the sea, a spring, a river, or a well, or be rain-water, or the like. And in this we see the infinite goodness of God, Who was pleased to ordain, for the matter of this sacrament, a thing so common in every place, that none might be in danger of being deprived of it.

Q. 11. When are the words to be pronounced?

A. At the very same time that the water is poured on the one to be baptized, and by the same person.

Q. 12. And must all the words be pronounced?

A. If the words "I baptize," or "thee," or "in the name," or any of the Divine Persons were omitted, it would be no baptism.

Q. 13. Who are authorised to give the sacrament of baptism?

A. The bishops and priests of the Church are authorised, in virtue of the priesthood, to administer baptism, and deacons, by commission from them, can do the same, with all its solemnities; but in cases of necessity, where these cannot be had, any lay person, man or woman, is authorised to do it, which also shows the infinite goodness of Jesus Christ, lest any one should be deprived of a sacrament so absolutely necessary for salvation, if the administration of it had been wholly confined to the ministers of the Church only.

Section I: Of The Effects Of Baptism

Q. 14. What are the effects of baptism?

A. The effects of baptism are these: (1.) It cleanses the soul from the guilt of all preceding sins, whether original or actual. (2.) It frees us from the eternal punishment due to sin, and from all the temporal punishment also which the justice of God could command for the sins one may have committed before baptism. (3.) It adorns the soul with the grace of justification, and with all those other graces and virtues which accompany it; which we have seen above, Chap, xviii. Q. 33. (4.) It makes us Christians, imprinting the sacred character of a Christian on the soul; and as a consequence of all this, (5.) It regenerates us by a new spiritual birth, making us children of God, members of His Church, heirs of heaven, and capable of receiving all the other sacraments and spiritual benefits which Christ has left in His Church, and gives us a right and title to receive them as our wants may require, as also to receive the necessary helps of actual grace to enable us to live a good Christian life, and preserve the sanctity we have received in baptism. (6.) It gives us a right and title to the kingdom of heaven.

Q. 15. How can it be shown that baptism washes away our sins, and justifies us in the sight of God?

A. From several strong and plain testimonies of Scripture, (1.) St Paul, writing to Titus on this subject, speaks thus: "We ourselves, also, were some time unwise, incredulous, erring slaves to divers desires and pleasures, living in malice and envy, hateful and hating one another. But when the goodness and kindness of God our Saviour appeared, not by the works of justice which we have done, but according to His mercy, He saved us by the laver of regeneration and renovation of the Holy Ghost, Whom He hath poured forth upon us abundantly through Jesus Christ our Saviour, that being justified by His grace, we may be heirs, according to hope, of life everlasting," Tit. iii. 3 . In this beautiful passage the apostle first acknowledges his former sins, then declares that the kindness he had received from God, in delivering him from them, was not owing to his own merits, but to the free mercy of God; that the means by which he was saved from them was the "laver or washing of regeneration," the sacrament of baptism, by which he was renewed, by the operation of the Holy Ghost, through the merits of Christ, and that by the grace received in this laver of regeneration he was "justified," and made an heir of life everlasting. (2.) "Christ loved His Church," says the same apostle, "and delivered Himself for it, that He might sanctify it, cleansing it by the laver of water in the word of life," Eph. V. 25 . See here we are assured that Christ died for His Church, on purpose that He might cleanse and sanctify her by means of the sacrament of baptism, which consists in the washing of water, accompanied with the word of life, the invocation of the adorable Trinity. (3.) At St Peter's first sermon, when the Jews asked him what they must do, he made answer, "Do penance, and be baptized every one of you in the name of Jesus Christ, for the remission of your sins," Acts, ii. 38 . (4.) When Ananias came to St Paul after his conversion, he said to him, "Rise up and be baptized, and wash away thy sins," Acts, xxii. 16 . (5.) St Peter compares baptism to the ark of Noah, and observes that, as the ark saved all those who were in it from the water of the Deluge, so "baptism being of the like form, saveth you also; not the putting away the filth of the flesh, but the examination of a good conscience towards God, by the resurrection of Jesus Christ,"I Pet. iii. 21, where it is expressly declared that we are saved by baptism, through the merits of Christ, by washing our conscience towards God.

Q. 16. In what manner does baptism free us from the punishment of sin?

A. As baptism is the door by which we enter into the fold of Jesus Christ, the first means by which we receive the grace of reconciliation with God, therefore the merits of His death are by baptism applied to our souls in so superabundant a manner as fully to satisfy the Divine justice for all demands against us, whether for original or actual sin; and therefore God grants in it a full and perfect remission of our past sins, and of all the punishment due to them. So that though a person had been guilty of the most enormous sins, yet if upon his sincere repentance he receives the grace of baptism, and should die in that happy state, his soul would go at once to heaven, having nothing to hinder its entrance into that seat of bliss and happiness. And this is the reason why, when grown-up persons are baptized, no penitential works are imposed upon them, which is one great difference between this sacrament and that of penance, in which latter, though the guilt and eternal punishment be remitted, yet a debt of temporal punishment still remains to be paid.

Q. 17. Does baptism free us from the infirmities and wounds of our nature occasioned by original sin - namely, concupiscence, ignorance, and the like?

A. No. These are more the necessary effects of original sin than a punishment inflicted for it; and God is pleased not to take them away by the grace of baptism, but leaves them, (1.) To humble our pride, by the daily experience of our own weakness. (2.) To detach our hearts from this world, and make us consider it as a place of punishment in which we are exposed to so many afflictions from these infirmities of nature. (3.) To make us long after heaven, where alone we shall be delivered from all our miseries. (4.) To try our fidelity, and exercise our virtue in fighting against these internal enemies, that by gaining the victory we may increase our crown. But baptism is of great advantage to us in this battle; because, by the sacramental grace peculiar to baptism, the violence of these enemies is greatly restrained, the ardour of our passions is moderated, and copious help is given us to enable us to overcome them.

Section II: Of The Necessity Of Baptism

Q. 18. Is baptism necessary for our salvation?

A. It is doubtless the most necessary of all the sacraments, because without it we are incapable of receiving any other sacrament, and because it is ordained by Jesus Christ as the only means of receiving the first grace of justification, by which alone we can be delivered from original sin, and partake of the merits of Christ's sufferings, so as to become members of His body.

Q. 19. How does this appear from Scripture?

A. From the following testimonies: (1.) Our Saviour, in His conversation with Nicodemus, declares, that "except a man be born again, he cannot see the kingdom of God; "and a little after He shows how this new birth is bestowed upon us; "Verily, verily, I say to thee. Except a man be born again of water and the Holy Ghost, he cannot enter into the kingdom of God," John, iii. 3 , 5. Here we see that this new birth, absolutely necessary for salvation, is bestowed upon us by water; that by the use of this outward rite the Spirit of God comes to our souls to operate in us that spiritual birth; and that these two, the outward rite and the inward regeneration, are, by the appointment of God, so connected, that if the rite be not used, the new birth will not be bestowed, and that, therefore, without that sacred rite of baptism, we can never see the kingdom of God, (2.) When our Saviour gave His apostles their commission to teach and baptize all nations. He immediately adds: "He that believeth and is baptized shall be saved, and he that believeth not shall be condemned," Mark, xvi. 16 ; in which words we observe that our Saviour here, in the same breath, commands the apostles to teach and to baptize all nations; consequently He requires that all nations should believe the truths taught by the apostles and be baptized. And in fact He promises salvation not to faith alone, but to faith and baptism together, which evidently shows the necessity of the one as well as of the other. It is true in what He adds, "He that believeth not shall be condemned," He mentions faith alone; but the reason is. He is here speaking only of adults, or those who are of an age capable of being instructed, in whom actual faith, or the positive belief of the truths taught by the apostles, is pre-required as a disposition absolutely necessary for baptism. The want of baptism, then, is necessarily included in their not believing; and these words in their full sense run thus: He that believeth not, and of consequence is not baptised, shall be condemned. (3.) The Jews who were converted at St Peter's first sermon believed what he had delivered to them concerning Jesus Christ, and consequently had true faith; they had also compunction in their hearts - that is, at least a beginning of repentance; but when they asked, "Men and brethren, what must we do? "St Peter answered, "Do penance and be baptized every one of you, for the remission of your sins," Acts, ii. 38 . He saw they believed in Jesus Christ, therefore he made no mention of faith, but he declares they must give proof of the sincerity of their repentance by doing penance for their sins, and then apply to baptism as the means ordained by God for giving us the grace of justification for the remission of our sins, insomuch that where it can be had, neither faith nor repentance will suffice without it. St Paul, on his conversion, had true faith in Jesus Christ, was thoroughly converted, and gave himself up wholly to Jesus Christ, saying, "Lord, what wilt Thou have me to do? "continued three days doing penance in praying and fasting; and yet, after all this, when Ananias came to him, he said, "Arise and be baptized, and wash away thy sins," Acts, xxii. 16 . In which words is evidently shown the absolute necessity of baptism for our justification, and also that neither faith nor repentance, nor prayer nor fasting, will suffice without it, where it can be had.

Q. 20. Why do you say where it can he had? Is it possible in any case to be justified without baptism?

A. Properly speaking, it is impossible to be justified without baptism, as all the above texts clearly proved for where it cannot actually be had, it must at least be in desire. Now there are two cases in which a man may be justified and saved without actually receiving the sacrament of baptism; first, if an infidel should become acquainted with the true faith of Christ, and embrace it, but in such circumstances that it was not in his power to be baptized, notwithstanding his earnest desire of that sacrament, if this desire be accompanied with a perfect repentance for his sins, founded in the love of God above all things, this would supply the want of actual baptism, and a person dying in such dispositions would certainly be saved. Secondly, If any person shall suffer martyrdom for the faith of Christ, before he has been able to receive baptism, this will also supply the want of the sacrament. In this case the person is baptized in his own blood; in the other case, he is said to be baptized in desire.

Q. 21. What becomes of young children who die without baptism?

A. If a young child were put to death for the sake of Christ, this would be to it the baptism of blood, and carry it to heaven; but, except in this case, as such infants are incapable of having the desire of baptism, with the other necessary dispositions, if they are not actually baptized with water, they cannot go to heaven, our Saviour's words being perfectly clear and express, - "Except a man be born again of water and the Holy Ghost, he cannot enter into the kingdom of God," John, iii. 5 . As to what becomes of such unbaptized children, divines are divided in their opinions - some say one thing, some another; but as God Almighty has not been pleased to reveal it to His Church, we know nothing with certainty about it.

Q. 22. As baptism is of such absolute necessity for salvation, can a person receive it more than once?

A. By no means; and it would be a sacrilege to attempt it; for the great end of baptism is to free us from original sin, and make us Christians, imprinting the sacred character of a Christian on our souls. Now, when we are freed from original sin we are freed from it for ever; when that sacred character of a Christian is imprinted on the soul, it remains there for ever, and can never be effaced. Therefore the effects of the sacrament of baptism can never be produced in our soul a second time.

Q. 23. What dispositions are required for receiving this sacrament?

A. In young children no dispositions are required, because they are incapable of any; but in adults, the dispositions required for receiving the graces of baptism are: (1.) That the person be willing to receive it; (2.) That he have faith in Jesus Christ; and (3.) That he have true repentance of his sins.

Section III: Of The Ceremonies Of Baptism

Q. 24. What are we to observe in general of the ceremonies used in administering the sacrament of baptism?

A. Chiefly these three things: (1.) That they are all taken from the Holy Scriptures, or from some of the great truths of our religion; (2.) That they represent to us either the dispositions necessary for receiving baptism worthily, the great benefits which this sacrament confers, or the obligations we contract by receiving it; and, (3.) That the prayers used along with these ceremonies all tend to obtain for the person baptized an abundant share of the graces of the sacrament, and strength to enable him to discharge his obligations.

Q. 25. How are these ceremonies divided?

A. Some go before baptism, some accompany the sacramental action, and some follow after it.

Q. 26. What are the ceremonies that go before baptism? and what is their origin and signification?

A. Before we explain the ceremonies themselves, we must observe that, in places where the Catholic religion is established, the water kept in the baptismal font, to be used in this sacrament throughout the year, is solemnly blessed on the eve of Easter and Pentecost. It is blessed on the eve of Easter, because "all we who are baptized in Christ Jesus, are baptized in His death; for we are buried together with Him by baptism unto death, that, as Christ is risen from the dead by the glory of the Father, so we also may walk in newness of life," Rom. vi. 3 . It is blessed on the eve of Pentecost, because it is the Holy Ghost who gives to the waters of baptism the power and efficacy of sanctifying our souls, and because the baptism of Christ is "with the Holy Ghost and with fire," Mat. iii. 11 . In blessing these waters a lighted torch is put into the font, to represent the fire of Divine love which is communicated to the soul by baptism, and the light of good example, which all who are baptized ought to give; and holy oil and chrism are mixed with the water, to represent the spiritual union of the soul with God, by the grace received in baptism, - and all this is done by order of the Church, for the greater respect, though not necessary for the validity of the sacrament. When, then, a person is presented for baptism, the priest meets him at the door of the Church, to denote that as he is not as yet of the number of the faithful, he has no right to enter into that sacred place; and there, after asking what he asks from the Church, and telling him the conditions on which the request will be granted, he proceeds as follows to prepare him for receiving it: -

(1.) He breathes upon him and says, "Depart from him, thou unclean spirit, and give place to the Holy Ghost the Comforter. This ceremony is taken from the example of God Himself, Who, "having formed man of the slime of the earth, breathed into his face the breath of life, and man became a living soul," Gen. ii. 7 ; and from the example of Jesus Christ, Who, being to communicate to His apostles the Holy Ghost, breathed on them and said, "Receive ye the Holy Ghost," John, xx. 22 . And it signifies that by baptism we receive a new and spiritual life by grace through the operation of the Holy Ghost, Who is given to us, and makes us His temples.

(2.) He makes the sign of the cross upon his forehead and on his breast, because God ordered all those that belonged to Him to have "the mark Than set upon their foreheads," Ezek. ix. 4 , which is "the sign of the living God," Rev. vii. 2 , and denotes that the person who receives it begins now to be one of the flock of Jesus Christ, and will, by the sacrament of baptism, soon be admitted to His fold, according to that of our Saviour, "Other sheep I have who are not of this fold, them also must I bring, and they shall hear My voice, and there shall be one fold and one shepherd," John, x. 16 .

Now this sacred sign is placed on the forehead to show that, after baptism, we should never be ashamed of the cross of Christ, nor afraid to profess His doctrine; and it is placed on the breast, near the heart, to show that we ought to love the cross of Christ, and cheerfully submit to bear whatever portion of it He shall afterwards be pleased to lay upon us; being assured that "if we suffer with Him, we shall also reign with Him," 2 Tim. ii. 12 .

(3.) He puts a particle of blessed salt into the person's mouth, saying, Receive the salt of wisdom; may it be with thee a propitiation unto life everlasting. This ceremony is taken from a command of God in the old law, which says, "Whatsoever sacrifice thou offerest, thou shalt season it with salt," Levit. ii. 13 ; because salt is an emblem of wisdom or discretion, without which none of our performances are agreeable to God; and Christ Himself says, "Have salt in you," Mark, ix. 49 - meaning that heavenly wisdom, of which He says, "Be ye therefore wise as serpents, and simple as doves," Mat. x. 16 . This ceremony therefore denotes that by baptism we are solemnly dedicated and consecrated to God as a sacrifice and oblation to His holy will, and that we ought ever after to preserve our souls from the corruption of sin by the salt of heavenly wisdom, by which alone we ought to regulate our whole life and conversation. Now our Saviour proposes the wisdom of the serpent as an emblem of the wisdom of a Christian; because, as that animal (according to St Chrysostom), when pursued by its enemies, uses all care to preserve its head, whatever becomes of its body, so the wisdom of the Gospel teaches us to be only solicitous for the salvation of our souls, and ready to part with everything rather than lose our souls, according to that of our Saviour, "What will it profit a man to gain the whole world, and lose his soul?" Mark, viii. 36

(4.) The priest proceeds to the exorcisms, by which, in the name of Jesus Christ, and through the merits of His death upon the cross (the sign of which is here frequently made upon the person to be baptized), he commands the devil to depart from this soul, whom God has chosen to be admitted to the grace of baptism, and orders him to give place to the Holy Ghost, who comes to take possession of him and make him His temple. This he does in consequence of that power over unclean spirits which Jesus Christ left to the pastors of His Church, to whom "He gave power over unclean spirits, to cast them out," Mat. x. 1 ; or, as St Mark expresses it, "He gave them power to cast out devils," Mark, iii. 15 ; and St Luke, "He gave them power and authority over all devils," Luke, ix. 1 . By this means, the person being prepared to be admitted into the Church, as one delivered in a great measure from the power of Satan, and belonging to Jesus Christ, the priest introduces him into that part of the church where the baptismal font is, saying, Enter into the Church of God, that thou mayest have part with Christ unto everlasting life. And while they are proceeding to the font, the priest, together with the person to be baptized (or his godfather and god-mother, if he be a child), recite, in an audible voice, the Apostle's Creed and the Lord's Prayer, to show that it is only by true faith in Jesus Christ that we are entitled to enter into His Church and become members of His body.

(5.) Then the priest recites another exorcism, and at the end of it touches the ears and nostrils of the person to be baptized with a little saliva, saying, Ephphcta, that is, Be thou opened into an odour of sweetness; but be thou put to flight, O devil, for the Jiidgjnent of God is at hand. This ceremony is taken from the example of Jesus Christ, Who, when they had brought to Him one that was deaf and dumb, . . . taking him aside from the multitude, put His fingers into his ears, and spitting, touched his tongue, and . . . said to him, Ephpheta, that is. Be thou opened; and immediately his ears were opened, and the string of his tongue was loosed, and he spoke right," Mark, vii. 32 ; and by it is signified that, as Jesus Christ by this ceremony cured the deaf and dumb man, so by the grace of baptism the ears of our soul are opened to hear the word of God and the inspirations of His Holy Spirit; and that obeying His holy will, manifested to us by this means, we become "an odour of sweetness, an acceptable sacrifice, well-pleasing to God," Phil. iv. i8; and likewise, by our good example, "A good odour of Christ in them that are saved, and in them that perish," 2 Cor. ii. 15 . These are the ceremonies which go before baptism, and are, as it were, a preparation for it.

Q. 27. What are the ceremonies that accompany the sacramental action?

A. As baptism is a covenant between God and the soul, there are two essential conditions required on our part to prepare us for receiving it - to renounce for ever the devil and the world, and to adhere to Jesus Christ by faith; wherefore, being now arrived at the sacred font, (1.) The person to be baptized (or his godfather and godmother in his name) makes a solemn renunciation of the devil, and of all his works and pomps, declaring that he renounces for ever the service of the devil, and that he detests all the maxims and vanities of the world, which are the pomps of the devil, and that he abhors all sins, which are his works; that he embraces the service of Jesus Christ, and vows and promises to adhere constantly to the maxims and rules of His Gospel, and to continue His faithful disciple. This is the sacred obligation in which we engage at baptism, this is the solemn promise we make, upon the keeping of which our eternal destiny so much depends.

(2.) Then the priests anoint him with holy oil on the breast and between the shoulders, making the sign of the cross, and saying, I anoint thee with the oil of salvation, in Christ Jesus our Lord, that thou may est have life everlasting. This ceremony is taken from the example of what God did in the old law, where He commanded that all those things which immediately belonged to His service, and were to be sanctified and consecrated for that end, should be anointed with holy oil; as is declared in the thirtieth and fortieth chapters of Exodus, "And thou shalt consecrate all with the oil of unction, that they may be most holy," Exod. xl. 11 . Now, the outward unction with oil is an emblem of the inward grace of the Holy Ghost, which sanctifies the soul; for, as oil gives light and heat, heals wounds, and strengthens weak parts, so the grace of the Holy Ghost enlightens the understanding, inflames the heart, heals the wounds of the soul, and strengthens its weakness. Hence of our Saviour it is said, "that God anointed Him with the Holy Ghost," Acts, x. 38 . And St John says to his disciples, "You have an unction from the Holy One, and know all things," i John, ii. 20 . This ceremony, therefore, signifies that the person who is to be baptized, having renounced the devil, and undertaken to fight manfully against him, will receive abundant grace from the Holy Ghost in baptism, to direct him in this warfare, to assist and strengthen him against all his spiritual enemies; and, at the same time, is consecrated to God by this holy unction. He is anointed, therefore, on the breast, to show that this grace will fortify his breast with courage and resolution; and between the shoulders, to show that the grace of baptism will sweeten the yoke of Christ, and make the burden of His commands light, easy, and agreeable.

(3.) The priest interrogates the person to be baptized concerning his faith in the blessed Trinity, the incarnation and death of our Saviour; because our Saviour says, "he that believes and is baptized shall be saved," Mark, xvi. i6; to show that faith is a necessary disposition before baptism; and as children cannot actually have it themselves, their godfathers and godmothers answer for them, with the obligation of seeing them instructed in religion when they come to an age capable of it. Lastly, The priest inquires if the person be willing to be baptized, because none can receive baptism against their will; and receiving his consent, he immediately baptizes him by performing the sacramental action.

Q. 28. What are the ceremonies which are used after baptism?

A. (1.) The new Christian is immediately anointed on the crown of the head with holy chrism, in imitation of the anointing of kings and priests, by God's command in the old law; and signifies that royal priesthood, to which we are raised by baptism, according to that of St Peter, "You are a chosen generation, a kingly priesthood, a holy nation," i Pet. ii. 9 .

(2.) He is clothed with a white garment, as an emblem of the spotless innocence with which his soul is adorned; and the priest prays that he may carry it unstained before the judgment-seat of Christ.

(3.) A lighted candle is put into his hand, as an emblem of the light of good example, which he is obliged to give by obeying the commands of God, according to what our Saviour says, "So let your light shine before men, that they may see your good works, and glorify your Father who is in heaven," Mat. v. 16 . While the priest gives him this candle, he exhorts him to keep his baptism without reproof, and obey the commands of God, that he may be ready when the bridegroom comes to enter with him into the marriage chamber.

(4.) The priest then bids him depart in peace.

Section IV: Of The Godfathers And Godmothers

Q. 29. What is the meaning of having godfathers and godmothers in baptism?

A. It is, (1.) That they may present to the Church the person that is to be baptized, and be the witnesses of his baptism. (2.) That they may answer in his name when the person to be baptized is a child. (3.) That they may be sureties to the Church for his performance of the promises they make for him; and, (4.) That they may be his instructors in all the duties of a Christian. (5.) To give the child's name to the priest.

Q. 30. How many godfathers and godmothers should there be?

A. One godfather for a boy, and one godmother for a girl is sufficient; or, at most, one godfather and one godmother for one person to be baptized.

Q. 31. What qualifications are required in those who are chosen for this office?

A. That a person be proper for this office, it is necessary, (1.) That he be a member of the Church, otherwise he cannot be fit for bringing up the child in the true faith. (2.) That he be sufficiently instructed in his religion and in Christian doctrine, otherwise he cannot be able to teach it to another. (3.) That he lead a Christian life, free from any public scandal, otherwise his example will destroy, instead of edifying, the child to whom he is godfather.

Q. 32. What are the obligations of the godfathers and godmothers?

A. Chiefly these: (1.) To see that their child be instructed in Christian doctrine, and to supply any defect in this respect, on the part of his natural parents, caused either by death or negligence. (2.) To watch over his morals when he begins to grow up, and encourage him by their good advices and admonitions, to live a pious Christian life, and to fulfil the sacred promises they made in his name in baptism.

Q. 33. What kindred do they contract by being godfathers and godmothers?

A. They contract a spiritual kindred, both with the child and its natural parents, which is an impediment to marriage with them; and the same is contracted in the sacrament of confirmation.

Chapter XXI

Of The Sacrament Of Confirmation

Q. I. What is the end or design for which confirmation was ordained?

A. The design of the sacrament of confirmation is to perfect and complete the sanctification received in baptism, by bringing down the Holy Ghost in a more particular manner to dwell in our souls, to fortify and confirm us in our faith, and enable us more effectually to resist all the enemies of our souls.

Q. 2. Can this be explained by any example?

A. It is most fitly explained by the example of the holy apostles; for though they had been for three years in the school of Jesus Christ, had enjoyed His blessed company, seen His holy example, and been witnesses of His miracles; and although, during all that time. He had instructed them, both in public and private, in the truths of His Gospel; yet it is surprising to see how imperfect they still were, how little they understood the great truths He had revealed to them, and how much less they practised the lessons He had given them. Insomuch that, even at the Last Supper, "there was a strife amongst them, which of them should seem to be greater," Luke, xxii. 24 , notwithstanding all the lessons of humility He had given them; and so far were they from profiting by His instructions about suffering for His sake, that when He was taken in the garden, "they all forsook Him and fled away," Mat. xxvi. 56. And a little after St Peter himself denied Him, and cursed and swore he knew Him not. All this shows how imperfect they still were; and the reason is, that the Holy Ghost had not yet come down upon them. But as soon as they received this Divine Spirit on Pentecost, they immediately became new men; their minds were enlightened to understand all that their blessed Master had taught them; their hearts were inflamed with a most ardent love for Him, and a zeal for His honour and glory; the grace of this Holy Spirit "endowed them with a power from on high," Luke, xxiv. 49 , which confirmed them in all good, and enabled them, in a most wonderful manner, cheerfully to undergo all dangers, to overcome all difficulties, and to suffer all torments, for the sake of their Lord and Master, so as even to "rejoice that they were accounted worthy to suffer reproach for the name of Jesus," Acts, V. 41. By which we see that the sanctification of our souls is, in a special manner, the work of the Holy Ghost. Now, as we are called, by our very vocation as Christians, to be saints, and to be perfect, according to that of our Saviour, "Be you perfect, as also your heavenly Father is perfect," Mat. v. 48 , therefore our blessed Redeemer was pleased of His infinite goodness to institute the holy sacrament of confirmation, as the never-failing means in His Church of communicating His Divine Spirit to His followers, to confirm them in His service, and enable them to attain the sanctity and perfection required of them.

Q. 3. Is confirmation a true sacrament?

A. It is; because it has all the three things necessary to constitute a sacrament.

Q. 4. What is the outward sensible sign used in confirmation?

A. Taking the whole of it, as laid down in the Holy Scriptures, it consists of three things: (1.) The bishop, to whom alone it belongs to give confirmation, stretching out his hands over those that are to be confirmed, prays for them all in general, that the Holy Ghost may come down upon them with his sevenfold graces. (2.) Coming to each one in particular, he lays his hand upon him; and, (3.) at the same time anoints his forehead with holy chrism in the form of the cross, saying these words, "I sign thee with the sign of the cross, I confirm thee with the chrism of salvation, in the name of the Father, and of the Son, and of the Holy Ghost.

Q. 5. Where do we find in Scripture that this outward action is instituted by Jesus Christ, to be the means of bringing the Holy Ghost to our souls?

A. In the Acts of the Apostles, we are told that when St Philip the deacon had, by his preachings and miracles, converted the Samaritans, "they were baptized, both men and women," Acts, viii. 12 , which, when the apostles who were at Jerusalem had heard, "they sent to them Peter and John; who, when they were come, they (1.) prayed for them that they might receive the Holy Ghost... then, (2.) They laid their hands upon them, and they received the Holy Ghost," ver. 14. In which passage we see that prayer and the laying on of hands were the outward means used by these apostles for communicating the Holy Ghost; prayer as a preparation, and the laying on of hands as the immediate means appointed for that purpose.

Q. 6. Where do we find the anointing and confirming?

A. The Scripture speaking upon any subject does not always mention every circumstance relating to it in one place, but sometimes one circumstance, sometimes another; and it is by collecting these different passages together that we possess the whole. St Paul, speaking of this sacrament in his Epistle to the Corinthians, describes it thus: "Now He that confirmeth us with you in Christ, and He that hath anointed us is God, Who hath also sealed us, and given the pledge of the Spirit in our hearts," 2 Cor. i. 21. In which words he mentions both the confirming and the anointing us, and also the sealing us, or the sacred character which this sacrament imprints in our souls; and at the same time he declares that all this is the work of God - that is, that God is the author of it. From these two passages we have the whole of this sacrament explained to us, both as to the outward action as above described, and the inward grace, or the sacred effects which it produces in the soul.

Q. 7. What are the effects of the sacrament of confirmation?

A. (1.) It brings down the Holy Ghost in a particular manner to our souls with all His gifts and graces, increasing the justification of our souls, and making us more pure and holy in the eyes of God; see above, Chap, viii., Q. 34, 35. (2.) It confirms and strengthens us in our holy faith, and enables us to profess it before tyrants and persecutors, and to fight manfully against all the enemies of our souls, so as to bear all the crosses and trials of this life with Christian meekness and humility, after the example of Jesus. (3.) It imprints a sacred character or seal on the soul, which shows that we have been confirmed, and, as it were, enlisted in the service of Jesus Christ, to fight under His banner against all His and our enemies; and therefore, as is the case in baptism, this sacrament can never be received more than once, because this character once received can never be effaced.

Q. 8. As confirmation brings down the Holy Ghost to sanctify our souls, do all that receive confirmation become saints?

A. Happy would it be, indeed, for the world if this were the case; but, alas! this happens but too seldom: and the reason is that, in order to become a saint, two things are required - the assistance of the Holy Ghost, and our co-operation. Both these are absolutely necessary. Without the Divine assistance we can do nothing towards our salvation; and though Almighty God should bestow His chosen graces upon us, if we resist them, or do not co-operate with them, we shall never advance a single step towards Christian perfection. Hence St Paul says, "Not I, but the grace of God with me," I Cor. XV. 10 ; not I alone, nor the grace of God alone, but "the grace of God with me," the grace of God assisting, and I co-operating. Now, in the sacrament of confirmation God Almighty does His part; He gives us His Holy Spirit, with all the graces necessary to enable us to become saints if we co-operate with them; and if few become saints, even after receiving these graces, the fault is entirely our own, because we do not profit by them as we might. And, alas! how few make the proper use of them I

Q. 9. How is the outward action of confirmation a sign of the grace received?

A. The imposition of hands represents the communication of the Holy Ghost to the soul, and the anointing the forehead with holy chrism represents the nature and plenitude of the grace received by the internal unction of the Holy Ghost.

Q. 10. How so?

A. The chrism is a sacred ointment, composed of oil of olives, and balm of Gilead, solemnly blessed by the bishop on holy Thursday. The oil represents the fulness of the grace received; both because, as oil, when dropped upon anything, spreads itself upon it, and insinuates itself into all its parts, so the grace of this holy sacrament penetrates into the soul, and diffuses itself throughout all her powers; and also, because oil, being a mild substance, represents that spirit of meekness and patience under the cross, which is one of the principal effects of confirmation. At the same time, as balm has the peculiar property of preserving bodies after death from putrefaction, it fitly represents the fortifying grace received in confirmation, by which our souls are preserved from the corruption of sin, after our sins have been destroyed by the sacrament of baptism.

Q. II. Do all receive an equal grace in the sacrament of confirmation?

A. The sacred character imprinted on the soul by confirmation is the same in all; but the other graces are given in proportion to the designs which God has in view for the person who receives this sacrament, and to the dispositions with which he comes to receive it.

Q. 12. What are the dispositions necessary for receiving confirmation worthily?

A. These three: (1.) That the receiver be sufficiently instructed, according to his age and capacity, in the necessary knowledge of Christian doctrine; (2.) That he be in the state of grace; and, (3.) That beforehand he spend some time in prayer.

Q. 13. Why must he be instructed in his Christian doctrine?

A. Because without this he cannot have a proper sense of what he is doing, nor conceive those devout affections towards God which dispose the soul for receiving the grace of the sacrament. Besides, all are bound to acquire a knowledge of the essential and necessary truths of religion according to their age and capacity.

Q. 14. Why must he be in the state of grace?

A. Because the Scripture assures us that "the Holy Spirit of Wisdom will not enter into a malicious soul, nor dwell in a body subject to sins," Wis. i. 4 ; and therefore it would be a grievous sacrilege were a person, knowing himself to be in a state of sin, to presume to receive this sacrament without taking the necessary measures to put his soul into the state of grace, and be reconciled with God.

Q. 15. Why should he spend some time beforehand in prayer?

A. For two reasons: (1.) From the example of the apostles, who, during the ten days between the ascension of our Lord and the coming of the Holy Ghost on Pentecost, "continued with one accord in prayer with the women, and Mary the mother of Jesus, and with His brethren," Acts, i. 14. Now, if the apostles, by the particular inspiration of God, employed themselves in prayer to prepare themselves for the coming of the Holy Ghost, how much more ought we? (2.) Because our Saviour has assured us that our "Father from heaven will give His good Spirit to them that ask it," Luke, xi. 13. See also above. Chap, viii., Q. t,6.

Q. 16. What are the best prayers for this purpose?

A. The hymns and prayers appointed by the Church for invoking the Holy Ghost, and for begging His grace, contained in manuals and other books of devotion.

Q. 17. Is confirmation necessary for salvation?

A. It is not absolutely necessary, yet it would certainly be a sin to neglect to receive it when one can have it, especially if, by neglecting a present occasion, a person exposes himself to the danger of being deprived of the sacrament; and still more if he be exposed to temptations and persecutions on account of his holy religion; and it would be a very grievous sin if one should neglect it out of disregard or contempt.

Q. 18. What are the ceremonies used in confirmation?

A. Besides those used in the sacramental action, there are these following: -

(1.) The anointing of the forehead is made by the sign of the cross, to show that, being now confirmed in the service of Jesus Christ, and enlisted as His soldiers, we ought never to be ashamed of our Master's livery, but boldly profess ourselves disciples of a crucified Saviour, and members of His Church, in spite of all that the world can do against us, either by ridicule or persecution; being mindful of His words, "Whosoever shall be ashamed of Me and of My words, in this adulterous and sinful generation, the Son of Man shall be ashamed of him when He shall come in the glory of His Father with the holy angels," Mark, viii. 38.

(2.) Immediately after confirmation the bishop gives the person confirmed a little blow on the cheek, to teach him that, being now a soldier of Jesus Christ, he must manfully fight against all His enemies, and bear with meekness and patience all crosses, persecutions, and trials, for the sake and glory of his Lord and Master.

(3.) In giving him this little blow, the bishop says. Peace be with you, to teach him that the only way to true peace in this world, as well as in the next, is to suffer patiently for Christ's sake, and also to encourage him to do so from the hopes of the reward, according to our Lord's promise, "Learn of Me, for I am meek and humble of heart, and you shall find rest to your souls," Mat. xi. 29.

(4.) The person confirmed takes a new name, which ought to be the name of some saint, whom he chooses for his particular patron, and whose virtuous example he ought to strive to imitate.

(5.) The person confirmed has one godfather, if a boy, and one godmother, if a girl, of whom the same things are to be observed as of those in baptism.

To Be Continued in The Sincere Christian
Volume II

313

THE END